# LANDMARK CASES IN MEDICAL LAW

This new addition to Hart Publishing's Landmark Cases series brings together leading figures in the field to discuss a selection of the most significant cases in medical law. These are cases which either signpost a new development for medical law, illustrate an important development of the law, or signpost likely future developments of the law. The cases are explored in their social and historical context to understand better what has influenced the development of the law. This collection provides a fascinating insight into the interaction of medical law and broader social changes to our bodies, illness and medical professionals.

# Landmark Cases in Medical Law

Edited by
Jonathan Herring
and
Jesse Wall

·HART·
PUBLISHING
OXFORD AND PORTLAND, OREGON
2017

**Hart Publishing**
An imprint of Bloomsbury Publishing Plc

Hart Publishing Ltd
Kemp House
Chawley Park
Cumnor Hill
Oxford OX2 9PH
UK

Bloomsbury Publishing Plc
50 Bedford Square
London
WC1B 3DP
UK

www.hartpub.co.uk
www.bloomsbury.com

Published in North America (US and Canada) by
Hart Publishing
c/o International Specialized Book Services
920 NE 58th Avenue, Suite 300
Portland, OR 97213-3786
USA

www.isbs.com

HART PUBLISHING, the Hart/Stag logo, BLOOMSBURY and the
Diana logo are trademarks of Bloomsbury Publishing Plc

First published in hardback, 2015
Paperback edition, 2017

**British Library Cataloguing-in-Publication Data**
A catalogue record for this book is available from the British Library.

ISBN: PB: 978-1-50991-772-3
HB: 978-1-84946-564-9

Typeset by Compuscript Ltd, Shannon
Printed and bound in Great Britain by
Lightning Source UK Ltd

To find out more about our authors and books visit www.hartpublishing.co.uk. Here you will
find extracts, author information, details of forthcoming events and the option to sign up for our
newsletters.

Dedicated to Professor Peter Skegg

# Contents

# List of Contributors

**Charles Foster** is a Fellow of Green Templeton College, University of Oxford.

**Marie Fox** is a Professor of Socio-legal Studies at the University of Birmingham.

**Imogen Goold** is a Fellow in Law at St Anne's College, University of Oxford.

**Kate Greasley** is a Junior Research Fellow at University College, University of Oxford.

**Sarah Green** is a Fellow in Law at St Hilda's College, University of Oxford.

**Jonathan Herring** is a Professor of Law at the University of Oxford.

**Laura Hoyano** is a Fellow in Law at Wadham College, University of Oxford.

**Kirsty Keywood** is a Senior Lecturer at the University of Manchester.

**José Miola** is a Professor of Medical Law at the University of Leicester.

**Kirsty Moreton** is a PhD candidate and Postgraduate Teaching Assistant at Birmingham University.

**Shaun D Pattinson** is Professor of Medical Law and Ethics at Durham University.

**Genevra Richardson** is a Professor of Law at King's College London.

**Loane Skene** is Professor of Law at the University of Melbourne.

**Mark Taylor** is a Senior Lecturer at the University of Sheffield.

**Jesse Wall** is a Lecturer at the University of Otago.

# Table of Cases

**European Court of Human Rights**

**France**

**Ireland (Republic of)**

# Table of Legislation

## Australia

## European Union

## Ireland (Republic of)

## United States of America

# Table of International Conventions

# Introduction

JONATHAN HERRING AND JESSE WALL

M EDICAL LAW IS a relatively recent arrival on the academic scene. As two leading medical lawyers have noted: 'Perusal of the Law Reports before 1980 will reveal no more than a handful of reported cases which address either the civil liability of doctors or how the law should respond to controversial problems of medical ethics'.[1]

How different it is now. No respectable university law course would be seen without a medical or health law course. The subject is enormously popular among students, reflected in the fact the subject now has an extensive array of textbooks, monographs, and journals. LLMs on medical law and ethics abound. The journey from being a baby legal enterprise to a fully grown adult member of the legal academy has been rapid. Now is a good time to look back at some of the key milestones in the development of the case law of the subject. That is what is undertaken in this book.

It is perhaps a sign of its maturity that there has been serious debate about the remit of medical law. This is most apparent in the debates over whether we should be discussing 'medical law' or 'health law'. The precise contours and focus of the subject continue to be the subject of lively debate. There are complaints that the subject has for too long omitted a consideration of public health law;[2] or the role played by informal carers.[3] Others complain of the focus on issues that face doctors, with less attention to the matters of concern to other healthcare professionals.[4] Of course, the academic boxes into which we like to place cases and areas of study are artificial creations. A case on the mental capacity to consent to sexual relations, for example, may well claim to be a criminal law case, a family law case or a medical law case, depending on one's preference. Further there are extensive debates over how the issues are to be presented. The issues discussed by medical lawyers regularly appear in the media and are some of the most profound facing our societies today: whether it be how to ration medical treatment given tightening resources; or the moral status of fetus; or the right to life.

---

[1] M Brazier and N Glover, 'Does medical law have a future?' in D Hayton (ed), *Law's Futures* (Oxford, Hart Publishing, 2000).

[2] J Coggon, *What Makes Health Public?* (Cambridge, Cambridge University Press, 2013).

[3] J Herring, *Caring and the Law* (Oxford, Hart Publishing, 2013).

[4] V Harpwood, 'The manipulation of medical practice' in M Freeman (ed), *Law and Medicine* (Oxford, Oxford University Press, 2000).

Politics, sociology, queer studies, philosophy, medical ethics, feminism, can all be used to illuminate the issues raised. And many other perspectives could be added to that list.

We do not seek to resolve these debates in this book. Instead we have focused on what, in the relatively short history of medical law, have emerged to be key cases for some medical lawyers. No doubt some readers will balk at some selections and be astonished at the omission of others. Time may tell whether the selections reflect more the issues of our day or the prejudices of the editors, than cases which genuinely form the bedrock of the subject.

## I. THE LANDSCAPE, THE SUB-TERRAIN AND THE HORIZON

The chapters that follow discuss the cases providing the seminal and authoritative judgments that have determined the general contours of medical law. They are landmarks insofar as these cases guide us in surveying the medico-legal landscape. Whilst these cases are illustrative of how the law governs the provision of healthcare, none of the cases attracts unqualified praise from the authors in this book. Rather, three general and critical themes run throughout this collection: some authors caution that landmark cases need to be interpreted against the remaining legal landscape, other authors question whether the landmark case aligns with the underlying ethical sub-terrain, whilst others use the landmark case as a marker between the settled law and the unresolved legal issues that remain on the horizon. In this introduction, we will provide an overview of the chapters along these three themes.

## A.  Landmark Cases and the Remaining Legal Landscape

A common theme throughout this collection is a plea by authors to view each landmark case carefully in the context of the remaining legal landscape. For some cases, this calls for a careful interpretation of what the landmark case represents; for others it requires the landmark case to be revised (or even reversed) in order to fit with more recent case law or conventional legal principles.

Mark Taylor asks us to resist the temptation to view *Source Informatics*[5] as permitting those holding personal information to disclose it to third parties provided that the information is anonymised. Taylor's concern is that such an approach 'underplays the impact that the anonymisation and subsequent use of abstracted or transformed data might have upon individuals'. Moreover, on a closer reading of the common law duty of confidence, Taylor explains how the common law requirement of conscionable

---

[5]  *R v Department of Health ex parte Source Informatics Ltd* [2000] 1 All ER 786.

use ought to be applied to protect both informational autonomy and the relationships of confidence that the common law duty serves to protect. Although the decision 'helped to establish the scope and nature of the common law duty of confidence in personal information', Taylor's contribution suggests that *Source Informatics* 'may provide a means to proscribe unconscionable use' of personal records, and is therefore a landmark case that we ought to approach with caution.

José Miola's account of *Bolam*[6] provides a cautionary tale of viewing landmark or seminal cases without a sense of context. Miola explains that the subsequent 'descriptive' interpretation of the requirement in negligence that medical professionals exercise 'the standard of the ordinary skilled man exercising and professing to have that special skill' denied the courts 'the power of oversight over medical conduct', and expanded *Bolam* 'a long way beyond its intended boundaries to a point where it had become ubiquitous within medical law'. A change in 'judicial attitude' provided for a 'normative' interpretation of the standard of care set out in *Bolam*, restoring—to some extent—*Bolam* to its 'proper limits'. As Miola explains, a number of medical law doctrines have been shaped by this process of *Bolam*-isation and de-*Bolam*isation. Hence, *Bolam* is not a static decision that sets the law in place, but has become used to expand or contract the role of the judiciary in determining what conducts amounts to negligence.

Shaun Pattinson suggests that the 'true significance' of the *Burke*[7] litigation is 'not so much what it did, but rather what it did not do'. Whereas Munby J at first instance 'sought to recognise circumstances in which a patient had a legal right to be provided with life-prolonging treatment', the Court of Appeal 'missed the opportunity to give proper recognition to the rights of potentially vulnerable patients'. Although *Burke* remains the 'seminal and only' authority that addresses a patient's request for continued artificial nutrition and hydration, Pattinson contends that the judgment ought to be read in the context of subsequent case law that 'displays a willingness to grant greater weight to the previously autonomous wishes of an incapacitated patient'. The unwillingness in the *Burke* litigation to recognise the right to receive the medical treatment is a landmark that ought to be viewed in the context of how the law gives effect to the previously expressed wishes of the patient receiving treatment. On Pattinson's analysis, *Burke* may cease to be significant if it is viewed in the context of more recent cases.

Sarah Green's analysis of *Chester v Afshar*[8] illustrates how this landmark case fails to fit with the remainder of the legal landscape. According to Green, *Chester* 'is neither consonant with orthodox causal principles, nor justified by reference to any established exception to those principles'. The majority

---

[6] *Bolam v Friern Hospital Management Committee* [1957] 1 WLR 582.
[7] *R (on the application of Burke) v General Medical Council* [2005] EWCA Civ 1003.
[8] *Chester v Afshar* [2004] UKHL 41.

of the House of Lords departed from the conventional principles of causation on the basis of the scope of the surgeon's duty of care and concern for a 'meaningful' duty to warn patients of the risks associated with a procedure. As Green explains, 'neither of these claims adequately supports the radical departure from established principles of causation'. Rather, in circumstances such as those in *Chester*, 'since the content of the chance in question is completely independent of [the defendant's] actions', the defendant 'should not be held liable for the way the chance turned out'. *Chester*, Green argues, made 'bad law', and 'the fact that it did means that it is a landmark indeed. It can only be hoped that it attracts few visitors'.

## B. Landmark Cases and the Ethical Sub-terrain

Some chapters are more concerned with how the law aligns with the underlying ethical issues. For some landmark cases, there is a chasm between the legal landscape and the ethical sub-terrain, whilst for other cases there are important connections between the law and the underlying ethical assumptions.

Jonathan Herring's account of *Re B*[9] challenges the view that the case represents 'an emblem of progress'. Although the court arrived at the correct outcome in rejecting the view of the parents that it was best to let a disabled child die, Herring demonstrates that the reasoning in the decision 'reveals many disablist attitudes'. Moreover, Herring argues that subsequent case law, statutory provisions and commentary 'still emphasises a sharp divide between the able bodied and the disabled' and proceeds upon the 'unspoken assumption that the world would be a better place without "disability"'. In opposition to this assumption, Herring contends that 'disability is inherent to humanity, and not an anathema to it'. Hence, despite agreeing with the outcome in *Re B*, Herring's chapter argues that the underlying assumptions about disabled people are misguided and still influence the medico-legal landscape.

Marie Fox's and Kirsty Moreton's commentary on *Re MB*[10] and *St George's Healthcare NHS Trust*[11] queries whether the value of these judgments, 'lies at the level of rhetoric rather than practice'. Although 'their pivotal contribution lies in affirming the core values of self-determination and respect for bodily integrity by upholding a competent adult pregnant woman's right to refuse to consent to any medical treatment', the reasoning in both cases acknowledges that the pregnant woman bears some kind of increased 'personal responsibilities'. From the 'vantage point of an embodied ethic of care', Fox and Moreton

---

[9] *Re B (a minor) (wardship: medical treatment)* [1990] 3 All ER 927.
[10] *Re MB (an adult: medical treatment)* [1997] EWCA Civ 1361.
[11] *St George's Healthcare NHS Trust v S* [1998] EWCA Civ 1349.

highlight the need for 'multiple narratives of the female body' that 'complicate ideologies rooted in notions of material altruism and sacrifice'. It is their
suggestion that although 'a pregnant woman does owe moral obligations of
care to the fetus she has chosen to gestate and give birth to', 'it is imperative
that the law should refrain from enforcing these obligations by requiring the
pregnant woman to submit to unwanted medical intervention'. The landmark cases provide a 'seemingly clear stance on women's autonomy', yet the
way in which the underlying ethical issues have so far been understood and
constructed require revision.

Charles Foster's analysis of *Bland*[12] takes us on a search for the ratio of
the decision to allow Anthony Bland to die. After a careful interpretation
of each judgment, Foster identifies eight (ethical, meta-physical and legal)
ingredients that featured, to different degrees, in each judgment. The decision, for Foster, was 'right on its facts, and it has not led to the dilution of
the notion of the sanctity of life, as some feared'. The judgments left 'the
criminal law of murder more or less undistorted' and the case can be praised
for 'the seriousness of its moral deliberations'. By engaging in the various
ethical, meta-physical and legal dimensions of the decision, Foster demonstrates how *Bland* can be read as a landmark case that 'attempts to map the
boundary between medical law and medical ethics'. While Foster praises the
depth of ethical analysis in *Bland*, in the next cases to be discussed in this
section its absence has created difficulties.

The oldest case in the book is *Doodeward v Spence*.[13] In her analysis of this
case Loane Skene explains how aspects of that decision have retained force
and been developed to respond to contemporary issues, while others have
been set aside. Hence she argues that the principle that human bodily material cannot amount to property unless work or skill has been undertaken on
it, has largely been set aside. However, the 'work or skill exception' has been
developed as a means by which to generate property rights for those who
exercised their talents, especially in Australian law. It is notable that the subsequent case law has largely concerned reproductive material which parties
wish to use in assisted reproduction. Such a use of this material would have
been unimaginable to the judges considering the *Doodeward* decision. The
fact that that decision is still relied upon today in dealing with disputes over
bodily material in vastly different circumstances to those obtaining in 1908
reflects the reluctance of Parliament to legislate in this highly controversial
and troublesome area. Indeed it is notable that in England the legislation
largely delegates the licensing function to a non-governmental organisation,
the Human Fertilisation and Embryology Authority, enabling it to respond
to technological advances and changing social practices, without repeatedly
embroiling the legislature in controversial issues.

---

[12] *Airedale NHS Trust v Bland* [1993] AC 783.
[13] *Doodeward v Spence* (1908) 6 CLR 406.

In her companion chapter Loane Skene considers one particular case which seeks to tackle the legacy of *Doodeward*, namely, *Yearworth and others v North Bristol NHS Trust*.[14] As Skene notes, while few people would disagree with the conclusion that the men (whose stored sperm was negligently destroyed by a hospital) were entitled to damages, the reasoning used to get there was 'essentially pragmatic'. The major problem revealed by *Yearworth* is the lack of moral basis for the reasoning in *Doodeward*. These two cases can, therefore, be seen as a showcase for the importance of exploring the complex interaction between medical law and ethics. Had *Doodeward* contained a careful explanation of the no property rule, it would have made the task of the court in *Yearworth* much easier. It could have explained why that principle had no application on the facts of this case or even that social and technological changes justified a re-examination of the principle. However, the no property rule was presented in *Doodeward* as simply a black-letter rule that required no justification, and so the court in *Yearworth* was left with having to relying on technical legal tools (the law of bailment) to reach the conclusion that seemed correct.

Jesse Wall's analysis of *ex parte B*[15] explains why medical law exercises a significant degree of deference towards the judgement of public authorities as to how healthcare resources are allocated. It was because the decision to fund the treatment in *ex part B* involved a high degree of polycentricity, that it required an evaluation between competing healthcare outcomes, and was made pursuant to a general statutory duty, that the decision not to fund the treatment was subject only to the 'loose constraints of reasonableness'. Wall suggests that this legal approach to resourcing decisions 'is premised upon the ethical assumption that the allocation of healthcare resources ought to be towards the aim of maximising the longevity and quality of life of all patients'. For Wall, there is an important connection to be made between the legal landscape of reviewing healthcare resourcing decisions and the subterrain of ethical questions on how we ought to allocate healthcare resources.

*R (on the application of Purdy) v Director of Public Prosecutions*[16] can be seen as a case which has helped recast the assisted dying debate. Kate Greasley opines that following the decision, 'the shape of legal argument about assisted dying will always be informed by the starting premise that prohibiting assisted suicide breaches a fundamental right'. One of the significant features of that case was the role played by human rights in the analysis and the reasoning. As demonstrated by her concluding words, just quoted, the rights in this case are seen by many as providing a starting point in the debate. If the right to choose to die is now the starting point then those opposing euthanasia must provide a justification for departing from

---

[14] *Yearworth and others v North Bristol NHS Trust* [2009] EWCA Civ 37.
[15] *R v Cambridge Health Authority, ex parte B (a minor)* (1995) 23 BMLR 1.
[16] *R (on the application of Purdy) v Director of Public Prosecutions* [2009] UKHL 45.

it. This is in marked contrast to what might have been the approach absent a rights-based analysis by the court, namely that killing or assisting in the suicide of another is a criminal offence and requires justification if it is to be decriminalised.

Greasley's analysis reveals that at the heart of the debate over assisted dying are disputes between grand principles, over-simplistically sometimes presented as: the right of autonomy vs the sanctity of life; but in the case law, and particularly *Purdy*, these are placed alongside personal stories of tragedy and resilience. Indeed Greasley suggests that it was an appreciation of the position of Debbie Purdy that pressurised the courts into finding a way of providing a solution that might meet her claims and those of similarly situated people. The legal creativity in finding some kind of solution reflects an acceptance of the horrific position of these individuals. Indeed once the case is treated as falling within Article 8 of the ECHR the court is required to justify each and every restriction on that right. The Crown Prosecution Service guidance became the focus of the litigation, not because it was solution that Debbie Purdy particularly wanted, but because it was most susceptible to legal challenge. It was most vulnerable to challenge as failing to produce a sufficiently tailored exception to the Article 8 right. Interestingly, following her success in the litigation Debbie Purdy is reported to have put any plans for assisted suicide on hold.[17] As Greasley concludes, the legal structure of the arguments following Purdy, is reflected in the public arguments on assisted dying. In those subsequent arguments increasingly less weight is placed on notions of the sanctity of life and rather, in Greasley's terms, 'a debate about how the interests some might have in a controlled death are to be balanced with the possible negative effects of relaxing the prohibition on assisted dying'. The legal and ethical terrains in the area of assisted dying have, at least to some extent, merged.

## C. Landmark Cases and Horizons

Some landmark cases serve as important markers between how far the law has come and what else remains to be addressed by the law. As a number of authors have identified in their chapters, despite the developments in the landmark case, there remain pressing legal issues on the horizon.

Genevra Richardson's account of *Bournewood*[18] highlights 'a significant problem affecting a large and highly vulnerable patient group' that is 'yet to be fully resolved fifteen years later'. As Richardson explains, the *Bournewood* decision 'drew close attention to a significant gap in the law's

---

[17] BBC News, 'Campaigner Debbie Purdy "stopped suicide plans"', at: www.bbc.co.uk/news/uk-england-leeds-13104708.

[18] *R v Bournewood Community and Mental Health NHS Trust, ex parte L* [1999] 1 AC 458.

provision for people with mental disabilities'. The gap is created by the distinction between the statutory powers under the Mental Health Act 1983 (MHA) for 'the imposition of hospital detention and treatment in the absence of consent' and the informal care and treatment for mental disorders that is provided 'for the vast majority of mental health patients'. The gap reflects the important distinction between mental incapacity and mental disability. Richardson explains that the Deprivation of Liberty Safeguards (DoLS) in the Mental Capacity Act 2005 were implemented as a response to the '*Bournewood* gap'. Yet, according to Richardson, there remains on the horizon an 'underlying tension' between the legal principles that govern mental disorder and the legal principles that govern mental incapacity as well as questions over the implications of the UN Convention of the Rights of Persons with Disabilities for the DoLS and the MHA.

Imogen Goold suggests that *A, B and C v Ireland*[19] is, in some ways, 'an anti-landmark'. Goold explains that the 'indisputable impact' of the decision of the European Court on Human Rights is that 'it makes clear that where abortion is permitted ... the relevant legislature must lay down explicit directions on when abortion will, and will not, be lawful'. The upshot is that 'clear laws should make it easier for women to obtain abortions when their lives are in danger'. Yet, Goold also carefully explains why the decision in *A, B and C* 'was conservative in two senses': 'it left the Irish position on abortion essentially unchanged' and 'made no great changes to European jurisprudence'. It is because the European Court afforded Ireland 'a wide margin of appreciation' that it was 'less inclined to intervene to prevent interferences with qualified rights', Goold's account of *A, B and C* illustrates how there are a series the substantive legal issues on the horizon that remain unresolved in European law.

In her chapter on *Re B (a minor) (wardship: sterilisation)*[20] Kirsty Keywood explores the attitudes towards those lacking capacity and the notion of 'best interests', which tend to dominate the legal response to those who are unable to make decisions for themselves. She notes that the decision in this case, that it was in the best interests of a young woman with limited intellectual capacities to be sterilised, was not regarded as particularly controversial at the time it was heard. Indeed, she notes that most attention was paid by academic commentators to the correctness of the legal procedures used and jurisdictional issues, rather than the actual outcome.

Keywood argues that the sterilisation of those with learning disabilities has become more controversial. There are underexplored gendered aspects to the case law: nearly all involve women. In her revisiting of the decision she explores how attitudes towards the sexuality of people with learning disabilities at that time are revealed in the judgment. She sees the case occurring at

[19] *A, B and C v Ireland* [2010] ECHR 2032.
[20] *Re B (a minor) (wardship: sterilisation)* [1988] AC 199.

a time when there was an 'important rupture with the traditional discourses and paradigms that had framed policy responses to disability—particularly learning disability'. An analysis that was previously dominated by paternalistic concerns about the well-being of the woman concerned and any children born; fears over the monstrousness of disabled sexuality; and even eugenics; was being replaced with a focus on 'human rights, justice and empowerment'. As Keywood indicates, in no small part this move in analysis has been motivated by a greater willingness to listen to those with learning disabilities and a fuller understanding of the social construction of impairment. However, as she notes, the journey on these issues is not over, with concepts of dependency, care and vulnerability also playing a major role in responses to disability today. How these different responses will shape the law to develop in the future is uncertain. What we can be sure of is that the 'best interest' analysis in *Re B* will be seen as unduly narrow as the courts continue to develop their approach.

*McFarlane v Tayside Health Board*[21] and *Cattanach v Melchior*[22] both concern cases of 'wrongful conception', where improperly performed sterilisations led to unwanted pregnancies. Laura Hoyano in her sophisticated analyses of these judgments demonstrates the paucity of legal principle that emerges from the judicial speeches. As she points out, 'The majority speeches are characterised more by anxiety to avoid perceived pitfalls than by clarity in mapping their pathways across what they saw as a treacherous bog'. Perhaps her observation that both decisions contained all-male sets of judiciary provides one explanation for why the issue of compensation for unwanted pregnancy was seen as such a tricky issue to deal with.

Hoyano reveals that competing notions of justice have been used in the case law. Corrective justice, distributive justice and retributive justice can all be identified in the various opinions. She demonstrates how the failure to clearly establish the theoretical basis for the law on negligence is laid bare in these cases. She quotes Justice Kirby who described judgments in this area as 'overwhelming legal analysis with emotion';[23] although one might wonder whether a greater emotional insight into the predicament of unwanted birth and pregnancy could have illuminated a different path for the courts.

Hoyano notes that '*Cattanach v Melchior* was decided in a fevered political climate of anxiety about large and sudden increases in medical indemnity and public liability insurance premiums'. As this comment notes, underpinning much of clinical negligence may be the suspicion that payment of huge sums of money from public health budgets to a few individuals who are lucky enough to succeed in litigation, is not the best way of spending public money, which could otherwise meet the healthcare needs of many people.

---

[21] *McFarlane v Tayside Health Board* [2000] 2 AC 59 (SC (HL)).
[22] *Cattanach v Melchior* [2003] HCA 38, (2003) 215 CLR 1.
[23] ibid [151].

This suspicion becomes particularly acute when questions are raised about the true nature of the loss. As Hoyano indicates, that difficult ethical issue is rarely openly addressed by the courts.

## II. CONCLUSION

The cases discussed in this book have consumed considerable time and space not only in the lecture halls and the libraries of our universities, but also at the kitchen tables and newspaper stands of the land. Readers of the book will hopefully be fascinated by the troubled adolescence of medical law and ethics. As these cases reveal, some decisions which appear to be perfectly sensible at the time, within a surprisingly short time can appear shot through with prejudice; marked more by the standards of the time than firm legal principles. Yet in other decisions we see the honing of principles which can provide real insight for dealing with some of the complex issues facing the courts. The legal landscape shifts, as the ethical principles seen to underpin society shift, and as technological advances open up new vistas. No doubt some of the cases we have identified will slip away and become mere molehills. Others will be built upon by ever-developing case law and legal analysis to become foundational landmarks. The problem is that at this stage it is hard to tell what will be the fate of the cases discussed in the chapters that follow.

# 1

# *Doodeward v Spence* (1908)

LOANE SKENE

## I. INTRODUCTION

D
OODEWARD V SPENCE[1] was decided by the High Court of Australia in 1908, more than a century ago. However, to the present day, the principles it established have remained central in the Australian law on the acquisition of proprietary interests in human bodily material. The High Court held that a person from whom bodily material has been removed ('the originator') does not have proprietary rights in that material after it has been removed—a principle commonly stated in the terms 'there is no property in bodily material' or 'you don't own your own body'. However, another person may gain a proprietary right in an originator's removed bodily material by undertaking 'work or skill' on it;[2] or changing it so that it has 'different attributes'.

One reason why this case has been so influential in Australian law is that there have been no cases in the High Court of Australia on these issues since *Doodeward* was decided. There have been a number of cases in *State* courts that have raised similar issues (in particular the recent cases discussed later in this chapter involving the posthumous use of semen by widows in reproductive treatment). However, under the principles of legal precedent in Australia, State courts are bound by decisions of the High Court and there has been no opportunity for the High Court to re-examine the fundamental principles of law stated in *Doodeward*. Until Parliament intervenes, State judges are bound by the 'no property' principle that was established in *Doodeward* and they must adapt it so that it can be applied fairly in modern situations that could not have been envisaged when *Doodeward* was decided.

In the UK on the other hand, these issues have been considered much more recently at appellate level. In 2009, in *Yearworth and others v North*

---

[1] *Doodeward v Spence* (1908) 6 CLR 406; [1908] HCA 45 (31 July 1908) (*Doodeward*).
[2] This principle presumably also applies to the person from whom the tissue was removed, if he or she has undertaken work and skill on it; but there is no direct authority on this point.

*Bristol NHS Trust*,[3] the Court of Appeal for England and Wales roundly criticised the 'no property' principle stated in *Doodeward* and based its decision on other grounds. However, it did not reject *Doodeward* entirely. In particular, it accepted the view of Griffiths CJ in *Doodeward* (quoted below) that proprietary rights can be acquired by undertaking 'work or skill', or by changing the bodily material so that it acquires 'different attributes'. That principle also underlies section 39(2)(c) of the Human Tissue Act 2004, which applies in England, Wales and Northern Ireland and refers to the 'application of skill'.[4]

However, in *Yearworth*, the Court of Appeal said that proprietary rights may also arise in other ways and there may be rights in favour of the originator. This means that the law in Australia and the UK has diverged because Australian courts have not accepted the latter proposition, namely that the originator may gain proprietary rights without undertaking 'work or skill', or the material acquiring 'different attributes'. Since *Yearworth*, different analysis and principles have therefore been applied to cases in the two countries with quite similar facts.

## II. *DOODEWARD v SPENCE*: THE FACTS

The facts of *Doodeward* are set out in the judgments of Griffiths CJ and Higgins J. The appellant brought an action for conversion and detinue for the recovery of the preserved body of what was called in the case 'a two-headed baby' (a malformed fetus), delivered still-born to a New Zealand woman 40 years earlier. The mother's medical attendant had taken away the fetus, 'preserved it with spirits in a bottle, and kept it in his surgery as a curiosity, that at his death ... was sold by auction with his other personal effects'.[5] The appellant's father purchased the bottle and contents at the auction for about £36 and exhibited them for gain. The respondent, a Sub-Inspector of Police, seized them under warrant. He later returned the bottle and the spirits but retained the fetus at the University museum.

In the Supreme Court, the cases cited related to corpses awaiting burial and established that human bodies after death do not vest in anyone, though certain persons have a duty to bury the body and may bring an action for mandamus to have the body delivered to them for that purpose: *R v Fox*.[6]

---

[3] *Jonathan Yearworth and others v North Bristol NHS Trust* [2009] EWCA Civ 37 (*Yearworth*); available at: www.bailii.org/ew/cases/EWCA/Civ/2009/37.html. This case is discussed in chapter 14 in this volume.

[4] Semen is not governed by that Act, but by the Human Fertilisation and Embryology Act 1990.

[5] Quoted statements in this paragraph and later in the chapter are from the judgment, unless otherwise stated.

[6] *R v Fox* (1841) 2 QB 246. See also cases listed in n 8 below on this point.

However, a body could not be the subject of larceny if it was wrongfully taken, as no one 'owned' it.

On the basis of these principles, the Supreme Court held that there could be no right of property in a dead body and therefore the body could not be the subject of an action in detinue; and (according to Pring J), the same principle applied to body parts removed from the body. The High Court agreed but there were some differences in the judicial reasoning.

III. THE JUDGMENTS

## Griffiths CJ

Griffiths CJ said that there were two main issues in the case. First, is an unburied human corpse (or removed human bodily material, in a wider context) property? And secondly, can a person gain property rights in relation to such a corpse or material, so that [he or she] can sue for its recovery if it is unlawfully removed?

Regarding the 'no property' argument, Griffiths J did not accept that a thing that could not be subject to larceny could therefore not be the subject of detinue if it were taken. For example, 'the dead body of an animal *feræ naturæ* is not at death the property of any one, but it may be appropriated by the finder'. He believed that there was no general rule on these matters, and even if there were, there must be exceptions. He would not 'accept the dogma of the verbal inerrancy of ancient text writers'. As he pointed out, 'equally respectable authority, and of equal antiquity, may be cited for establishing as a matter of law the reality of witchcraft'. The court was 'free to regard [this case] as a case of first instance arising in the 20th century, and to decide it in accordance with general principles of law, which are usually in accord with reason and common sense'.

Adopting this approach, he focused on the appellant's right to possession of the preserved fetus. There was no reason for the possession to be unlawful, either *in re ipsá* or on the grounds of 'religion or public health or public decency'. And if the appellant was in lawful possession of the fetus, 'the law will by appropriate remedies redress any ... disturbance [with that lawful possession]'. Moreover, '[t]he very term "lawful possession" connotes a right to invoke the law for its protection'.[7] The same is true of parts of a human body. Otherwise, 'the many valuable collections of anatomical and pathological

---

[7] Compare this statement with the view of Higgins J in *Doodeward*, casting doubt on the appellant's right to lawful possession: 'The medical man in this case got possession of the corpse, and there is no evidence that the parents consented. But even the parents could not give him any right to the corpse'. In his view, if the law supported an action to recover a corpse that had been taken from that person, 'The Court is to be used as a catspaw by a body snatcher'.

specimens or preparations formed and maintained by scientific bodies, were formed and are maintained in violation of the law'. Thus, he concluded, 'a human body, or a portion of a human body, is capable by law of becoming the subject of property', which a person may lawfully possess. Moreover, a person who lawfully possesses it may transfer the possession to another person and any person who has lawful possession has a right to have the material returned if it is unlawfully removed.

Griffiths CJ's statement regarding the circumstances in which a person has a legal right to retain possession of bodily material has been widely quoted in cases up to the present day:

> [W]hen a person has by the lawful exercise of work or skill so dealt with a human body or part of a human body in his lawful possession that it has acquired some attributes differentiating it from a mere corpse awaiting burial, he acquires a right to retain possession of it, at least as against any person not entitled to have it delivered to him for the purpose of burial, but subject, of course, to any positive law which forbids its retention under the particular circumstances.

In the present case, the doctor initially acquired the malformed fetus lawfully and he bestowed 'some—perhaps not much—work and skill ... [and] it had acquired an actual pecuniary value' as it was later sold after his death. An action would therefore lie for an interference with the appellant's right of possession.

## Barton J

Barton J focused on whether there was a duty to bury the fetus so that retaining it without burial would be a misdemeanour; and *semble*, thus make the doctor's initial possession or retention of the fetus unlawful. He concluded that there was no duty to provide a Christian burial for 'a dead-born fœtal monster' that 'was never alive in the ordinary sense of human life ... has never drawn the breath of life' and has been 'preserved in spirits as a curiosity during four decades'. This was a 'well-preserved specimen of nature's freaks' and it 'could not fall within 'the meaning conveyed by the term "unburied corpse"', to which the cases and textbooks have referred in stating that there is a duty to bury a human corpse. Through the period of its preservation, it had acquired a material value not because it was a human body, but rather because it was not. He 'entirely agree[d]' with the reasons of the Chief Justice and, without saying so directly, the conclusion that the doctor's initial possession and retention of the fetus was lawful. First, there was no duty to bury such a thing; and secondly, it had acquired different attributes by its preservation. Barton J added that he did not mean to 'cast the slightest doubt upon the general rule that an unburied corpse is not the subject of property'.

Thus, taking these two judgments together, Griffiths CJ and Barton J agreed that the doctor was entitled to lawful possession of the fetus and that the law would enforce that right by ordering that the fetus should be returned to the doctor (or his successor). However, they differed regarding the grounds on which the right to possession first arose. Griffiths CJ said it arose because the doctor had undertaken work or skill in preserving the fetus. Barton J said that the appellant was entitled to retain possession because neither he nor anyone else had a duty to bury the fetus. In effect, the person in possession could lawfully retain possession unless someone else could prove a better right to possession. Griffiths CJ stated the 'no property principle'. Barton J said nothing on this point.

## Higgins J

Higgins J did consider the 'work or skill' argument and appeared to accept it. He gave the example of a mummy that may be property because 'the mummy has been turned into something very different by the skill of the embalmer'. However, he said that, in the present case, 'No skill or labour has been exercised on [the fetus]; and there has been no change in its character'. He was satisfied that the fetus was not property but he said that

> if this corpse can be the property of any one, it is the property of the plaintiff as against the defendant. It is enough that the plaintiff was in possession of the corpse, and that the defendant took it having no better title to it than the plaintiff.

This approach seems similar to that of Barton J as summarised above. A claim to possession may be based on being in possession without more, because, in the words of Higgins J, 'a mere possessor is treated by the law as having the property in goods as against one who takes them from him wrongfully'.

Although Higgins J determined that the fetus was not property because 'work or skill' had not been undertaken on it, he also said that it *could not* be property. It was 'a thing which is incapable of being property' so an action in detinue or trover could not succeed. Even if a person claimed as a possessor instead of an owner in such a case, it would be the same, as property is vital in both cases. An action in trover could not be brought for a hawk or a deer, 'Property involves a right of exclusive and permanent possession'; and 'no one ever heard of an action of trover or detinue for a human being whether alive or dead unless in the case of a slave [where the slave is merchandise—property—and not a person]'. He then cited a number of cases stating that there cannot be property in a dead body.[8] He said

---

[8] Eg *Handyside's Case* (1749) 2 East PC 652; *Haynes's Case* (1614) 12 Co Rep 113; Coke, *Institutes of the Lawes of England* 3 Co Inst 110, 203; *R v Sharpe* (1857) 169 ER 959, Dears & B 160 at 163. After reviewing American cases, he concluded that 'even in the United States Courts, the great preponderance of authority is in favour of the old English principle [that there is no property in a corpse]'.

that a still-born birth where the baby has not lived independently of the mother is in the same category. After reviewing the authorities, all clearly stating that there is no property in a corpse, he was 'unable to see how we can ignore such definite decisions and pronouncements as to the law'. He did not explain how his statement regarding the mummy could fit in with this categorical rejection of the 'no property' principle.

Finally Higgins J questioned the basis on which the appellant sought possession of the fetus. 'We are not told why the plaintiff wants the corpse ... He has been exhibiting it for gain, and may possibly want it for gain in the future—if he can evade the police'. He also said: 'if the body is to remain unburied, I do not see why the University Museum is not as much entitled to it as the plaintiff'.

In summary, therefore, it can be seen that Griffiths CJ accepted and based his judgment on the principle that a human corpse is not property but a property right could arise by a person undertaking 'work or skill' on it. Barton J based his judgment on a right to possession existing where no one has a better right to possession, and did not discuss the legal basis of the right to possession. He mentioned that the fetus had acquired different attributes from being preserved but said he didn't intend to cast doubt on the 'no property' rule. Similarly, Higgins J, despite his comment about a mummy becoming property, appeared to reject the principle that a property right could arise in a body because it is 'a thing which is incapable of being property'. He rejected the notion that a right to possession could arise simply from the fact of possession, saying that a later possessor would seem to have as much right to possession as an earlier one.

It might be thought from this examination of the three judgments, that although the 'no property' principle was accepted in broad terms by the three judges, the idea that property rights could be established by 'work or skill' or conferring 'different attributes' on bodily material had varied support. Only Griffiths CJ based his judgment on that principle and the other two judges barely mentioned it. Yet that principle has since become the one that has been most widely cited in the case law.

## IV. LATER CASES

Since *Doodeward* was decided, the general principle that bodily material cannot be property has been rejected in many cases in different areas of the law, often on pragmatic rather than reasoned grounds.[9] For example, in

---

[9] L Skene, 'The current approach of the courts [regarding proprietary interests in human bodily material]' (2013) 40 *Journal of Medical Ethics* 1008–24. In addition to the cases mentioned in this paragraph, see *Dobson v North Tyneside Health Authority* [1996] EWCA Civ 1301; [1997] 1 WLR 596; *Hecht v Superior Court of Los Angeles County (Kane)* (1993) 20 Cal Rptr 2d 275.

1974, an English court held that urine was property so that taking it without authority was theft;[10] in 1976, a similar ruling was made regarding blood;[11] in 1992, an Australian court held that blood products are goods covered by consumer protection legislation;[12] in 1998, a court held that an artist who removed body parts from the Royal College of Surgeons to draw them had stolen them;[13] and in 2000, a Master of the Supreme Court of Western Australia held that stored tissue was property, and granted access for forensic tests.[14] In the last case, the Master observed that '*Doodeward* was decided ... some 50 years before Watson and Crick described the DNA double helix' and that '[I]t defies reason to not regard tissue samples as property'.

Doubt has been cast upon another principle stated in *Doodeward*—the requirement that a person must be *lawfully* in possession to obtain a proprietary right by undertaking 'work or skill'. In *Moore v Regents of the University of California*,[15] the court held that a researcher who developed a new cell line without consent from the originator whose cells were used in the research (so arguably acting unlawfully) was still entitled to the profits, and the originator had no right to share in the profits. The issue of the 'lawfulness' of the researcher's initial possession of the cells did not affect the decision, no doubt influenced by the public interest in protecting the vitally important developing biotechnology industry.

However, the main principle for which *Doodeward* has been cited—that property rights can be obtained by undertaking 'work or skill' or conferring 'different attributes' on removed bodily material—has continued to be influential in cases in the UK, the US and Australia. Once it was accepted that removed bodily material could become property in such a way, the more difficult question was *who* had the property rights in it. It was on this issue that *Doodeward* has been most often cited. For example, the body parts stolen by the artist in the case above were said to have become property by acquiring 'different attributes' after being dissected and preserved for exhibition or teaching purposes.[16] Similarly, the researcher in the cell line case above had clearly undertaken 'work or skill' or conferred 'different attributes' on the originator's cells.[17] However, the 'work and skill'/'different attributes' argument sits less easily with urine and blood that has simply been removed from the body for forensic tests.

---

[10] *R v Welsh* [1974] RTR 478.
[11] *R v Rothery* [1976] RTR 550.
[12] *PQ v Australian Red Cross Society* [1992] 1 VR 19.
[13] *R v Kelly; R v Lindsay* [1998] EWCA Crim 1578; [1999] QB 621.
[14] *Roche v Douglas* [2000] WASC 146.
[15] *Moore v Regents of the University of California*, 51 Cal 3d 120, 271 Cal Rptr 146, 793 P 2d 479, cert denied 499 US 936 (1991).
[16] *R v Kelly; R v Lindsay* [1998] EWCA Crim 1578; [1999] QB 621.
[17] *Moore v Regents of the University of California*, 51 Cal 3d 120, 271 Cal Rptr 146, 793 P 2d 479, cert denied 499 US 936 (1991).

More recently, the argument that property rights can arise in bodily material only by 'work or skill' or conferring 'different attributes' has been the subject of judicial criticism, especially in England, but also in Australia. In *Yearworth*,[18] the Court of Appeal for England and Wales held that men who had deposited their semen for freezing before undergoing cancer treatment were entitled to be compensated when it was later negligently destroyed. These rights did not depend on anyone undertaking 'work or skill' on the semen. The court held that, 'for the purposes of a claim in negligence' the men had 'ownership of the sperm which they had ejaculated' because when the sperm was deposited 'the sole object ... was that, in certain events, it might later be used for their benefit', and that there was therefore a bailment. The court called for a 're-analysis of the common law's treatment of and approach to the issue of ownership of parts or products of a living human body, whether for present purposes (viz an action in negligence) or otherwise'.

Australian courts have also been critical of *Doodeward*. In one case, the judge, White J, noted 'the "quirky" *Doodeward* exception' to the 'no property' rule.[19] However, like other State judges, she was bound by the High Court and had to follow *Doodeward*. But despite the constraints imposed by the weight of *Doodeward* as a precedent, the State courts have adopted an interesting line of reasoning in cases concerning, like *Yearworth*, proprietary rights in semen that is proposed to be used posthumously in reproductive treatment.

In *Yearworth*, the issue was the rights of the men who had stored the semen for their later use. In the Australian cases, the issue has been the rights of the widows of the deceased men. In the first of these cases, *Bazley v Wesley Monash IVF Pty Ltd*,[20] a justice of the Supreme Court of Queensland accepted, out of sympathy for a widow's loss of reproductive chances, her argument that she was entitled to possession of her husband's stored semen because she was the personal representative and principal beneficiary of his estate. Similarly, in another case, *Jocelyn Edwards; Re the estate of the late Mark Edwards*,[21] a widow was also held to be entitled to possession of her deceased husband's semen but, in that case, the semen had been removed after his death under a court order, so it could not be part of his estate. A similar approach was adopted in *Re H*,[22] in which a widow was ultimately awarded her husband's stored semen on the basis of the 'work or skill principle' established in *Doodeward*. The semen had been lawfully collected under a court order and 'work or skill' had been expended in

---

[18] *Yearworth* (n 3 above).
[19] *Kate Jane Bazley v Wesley Monash IVF Pty Ltd* [2010] QSC 118, [31] (*Bazley*).
[20] ibid.
[21] *Jocelyn Edwards; Re the estate of the late Mark Edwards* [2011] NSWSC 478.
[22] *Re H, AE (No 3)* [2013] SASC 196,

collecting it (an open testicular biopsy). It was therefore property. In deciding whose property it was, Gray JA, like Hulme J in *Edwards*, held that the person for whom the semen was extracted (the widow) was entitled to possession.

Because the judges in these cases were bound by *Doodeward*, the stored semen could not be regarded as property unless 'work or skill' had been undertaken on it, or it had acquired 'different attributes' as a result of its preservation. However, even if that was the case, it was not the widows who had undertaken the 'work or skill' in preserving the semen, so a proprietary right could not be established on that basis in their favour. The response to that objection might be that the 'work or skill' had been undertaken on their behalf; that is, the doctors who obtained and preserved the husbands' semen were acting as the widows' *agents*. The concept of agency was suggested by Hulme J in *Edwards*. Instead of regarding the doctors and technicians who preserved and stored Mr Edwards' sperm as acting for their own purposes, he said, 'the better view' was to regard them as acting 'on behalf of Ms Edwards ... [i]n effect ... as her agents'.[23] This was also the approach in *Re H*.

Agency was not mentioned in *Yearworth* or *Bazley* though it could have applied in the circumstances of those cases. However, in *Yearworth*, as noted earlier, the Court of Appeal expressly chose not to apply the *Doodeward* test, so the issue of agency did not arise. The Court decided the case on other grounds, namely that the men had proprietary rights arising from the bailment of their semen for their later use. They were therefore entitled to be compensated when it was negligently destroyed.

## V. CONCLUSION

Some aspects of the *Doodeward* judgments have been largely rejected in the years since the case was decided, for example, that human bodily material cannot become property unless 'work or skill' has been undertaken on it; or it has acquired 'different attributes'. However, the so-called '*Doodeward* exception' to the 'no property' rule, whereby undertaking 'work or skill' or conferring 'different attributes', on bodily material, may give rise to proprietary rights in favour of the person who did those things, has continued to be influential, especially in Australian case law; and recently it has been extended by the agency principle to confer rights on people who did not undertake the 'work or skill' themselves. Although the '*Doodeward* exception' was soundly criticised and virtually rejected in *Yearworth*, and Australian judges have also acknowledged its lack of logic, Australian courts are constrained by the status of *Doodeward* as a decision of the High Court

---

[23] [2011] NSWSC 478, [88].

of Australia, whose decisions are binding on State courts. In recent cases involving access by widows to the stored semen of their deceased husbands (*Bazley*, *Edwards* and *Re H*), Australian courts have accepted that stored semen can be property and that widows may gain access to it for reproductive treatment. The reason given in two of these cases was that work or skill was undertaken on the stored semen on behalf of the men who stored their semen and, in turn, for their widows. This notion of 'agency' in the application of the '*Doodeward* exception' appears to be essentially an Australian innovation, though a similar argument could have been made in *Yearworth*. If this principle in *Doodeward* is to be rejected, at least in a wider context, that will require legislation.

# 2

# *Bolam v Friern Hospital Management Committee* [1957]: Medical Law's Accordion

## JOSÉ MIOLA

### I. INTRODUCTION

*B*OLAM—A FIRST instance direction to a jury from 1957 by McNair J—at first sight appears to be an unlikely contender for the status of landmark case in medical law.[1] Yet, at least in what might be considered its heyday in the 1980s and early 1990s, that is exactly what it became. Not only was the decision interpreted in such a way that made the chances of plaintiffs winning cases in negligence close to non-existent and denied the courts the power of oversight over medical conduct, but it also expanded a long way beyond its intended boundaries to the point where it became virtually ubiquitous within medical law. Thus, ethical questions relating to how much information a doctor must give her patient before her consent can be considered valid, whether to sterilise adults with learning disabilities and even whether to remove artificial nutrition and hydration from patients in a persistent vegetative state became '*Bolam*-ised'.

This expansion of *Bolam*'s remit way beyond that intended by McNair J would always be controversial. Thus, in the 1990s there began an attempt both to narrow the influence of the case—particularly in the more ethical areas mentioned above—so as to return *Bolam* to its original sphere of influence of negligence and to reinterpret the test itself to allow the courts to be more than a mere rubber stamp. Indeed, one notable aspect is that the problems caused by *Bolam*-isation were not due to the judgment itself. Rather, they were a consequence of the way in which it was interpreted *by subsequent courts*. These later judgments expanded *Bolam*'s sphere of influence, and the courts have been at least partially responsible for correcting this mistake themselves. To this author, the way that *Bolam* is interpreted

---

[1] *Bolam v Friern Hospital Management Committee* [1957] 1 WLR 582.

today is much closer (though not completely true) to what was intended by McNair J—but for nigh on 40 years *Bolam* became out of control and, as we shall see, reigned supreme in medical law.

## II. *BOLAM*—THE FACTS AND THE DECISION

The facts of the case are relatively simple. John Bolam was a voluntary patient at a psychiatric hospital, being treated for depression. He was offered electro convulsive therapy (ECT) as a treatment, and consented to this. Unfortunately, when the procedure was performed he suffered serious fractures. He sued on three grounds. First, that he should have been warned of the risk of fracture so that he could make his own mind up about whether to consent to the treatment. Secondly, that he should have been given relaxant drugs and, finally, that there should have been more effective manual restraints, the latter two of which might have lessened the risk of fracture. What we can see, then, are two issues relating to the technique used (orthodox negligence) and another relating to informed consent. McNair J held that all should be decided with reference to reasonable medical practice, and noted that the doctor who had performed the procedure had merely followed the practices that he had been taught and that were in operation at Friern Hospital at the time. The key question was whether this practice was one that the reasonable doctor would adopt, and how that should come to be determined. The judge first addressed this by defining what negligence was:

> [I]n an ordinary case which does not involve any special skill, negligence in law means a failure to do some act which a *reasonable man* in the circumstances would do, or doing some act which in the circumstances a reasonable man would not do ... But where you get a situation which involves the use of some special skill or competence, then the test whether there has been negligence or not ... is the standard of the *ordinary skilled man* exercising and professing to have that special skill ... A man need not possess the highest skill at the risk of being found negligent ... [I]t is sufficient if he exercises the *ordinary skill* of an *ordinary competent man* exercising that particular art.[2] (emphasis added)

Thus in order to act in a 'reasonable' fashion the doctor must perform with 'ordinary skill'. But what might this mean? In a passage that was to become infamous as the embodiment of the *Bolam* test as initially interpreted, McNair J clarified that in order to find against the defendant doctor it was not enough to simply produce evidence that some others might have done other than the doctor did:

> A doctor is not guilty of negligence if he has acted in accordance with a practice accepted as proper by a *responsible* body of medical men skilled in that particular

---

[2] ibid 586.

art ... Putting it the other way round, a doctor is not negligent, if he is acting in accordance with such a practice, merely because there is a body of opinion that takes the contrary view.[3] (emphasis added)

There must therefore be more than *merely* a body that would not have done what the doctor did for her conduct to be negligent—and where the difficulties in interpreting *Bolam* have arisen is in relation to the status of this expert evidence. The italicised adjectives in the two quotes above— 'reasonable', 'responsible' and 'ordinary' provide the crux of the disagreement. McNair J uses all three words—plus a fourth, 'respectable'—to describe the body of evidence that the defendant doctor must adduce, but the adjectives can be divided into two distinct categories.[4] The first, which relates to the word 'ordinary', is descriptive in nature. If the doctor has to act with 'ordinary care', then she has to act in a way that other doctors might. There is, in this test, no room for evaluation—the court is merely a rubber stamp once it has ascertained that other doctors may have acted in the same way. Conversely, the adjectives 'reasonable', 'responsible' and 'respectable' are normative in nature and require more than simply ascertaining what doctors *do*. Rather, they ask that the court assess the quality of that evidence. Even if the whole of the medical community acts in a certain way, such conduct would certainly be 'ordinary', but might still be classed as 'unreasonable', 'irresponsible' or 'not respectable' because the latter three relate to the quality of the conduct rather than its mere existence. As Norrie noted, normativity 'necessarily carries with it a connotation which allows the court to say what *ought to have been done* in the circumstances'.[5]

The difference between the descriptive and normative approaches has grave consequences for the role of the courts. If the descriptive approach is adopted, then the only task available to the judge or jury lies in asking *whether* there is a body of evidence that might have done as the defendant doctor did. If there is, then the doctor was obviously acting with 'ordinary care' and thus will not have breached her duty. The court's role is passive, and the evidence itself (in the form of the content of the conduct) is almost immaterial. A normative interpretation of *Bolam*, however, asks the court instead to actually engage with the evidence, asking what doctors *should* do. Thus, the interaction is with the evidence itself rather than who has provided it or whether it is provided at all.

Before considering the approach taken by courts interpreting *Bolam*, we should ascertain what McNair J might have meant—indeed, given that in medical law many cases seem to claim to apply *Bolam*, we should at least be certain that it was not being misapplied. To this author, it is clear that

---

[3] ibid 587.
[4] K Norrie, 'Common Practice and the Standard of Care in Medical Negligence' [1985] *Juridical Review* 145.
[5] ibid 152.

McNair J meant for the jury to apply his test in a normative manner. As evidence for this I would argue that the mere fact that he left the question of the doctor's liability to the jury at all should be sufficient for us to conclude that it *was* open to them to evaluate the evidence rather than simply check that it existed. This right to evaluate is evident in the following passage in his address to the jury:

> [I]t is not essential for you to decide which of two practices is the better practice, as long as you accept that what … [the doctor] did was in accordance with a practice accepted by responsible persons; but if the result of the evidence is that you are satisfied that this practice is better than the practice spoken of on the other side, then it is a stronger case.[6]

I would go further and say that we can specifically see in that quote McNair J providing the jury with the freedom to choose the evidence whichever experts—be they for the plaintiff or defendant—they preferred, a matter to which we shall return later. However, the courts were initially to apply the case using the descriptive interpretation.

## III. 'OLD' *BOLAM* AND ITS EXPANDING INFLUENCE

To say that *Bolam* in its descriptive incarnation was keenly taken to by the courts would be an understatement. Particularly in the 1980s there seemed nothing in medical law that was safe from the clutches of *Bolam*—as Davies put it, the judicial attitude became 'when in doubt, *Bolam*ise'.[7] Bolam thus became significant in two ways. First, the descriptive interpretation of McNair J's judgment was extremely restrictive to patients. All that the doctor had to do was to provide evidence from others that they *might* have done the same as the defendant did in the circumstances. Secondly, *Bolam* expanded outwards—like the accordion of this chapter's title. The *Bolam* test was originally created to be a test that related to matters of technical medical skill (although the case itself did contain an informed consent element). However, one of the features of *Bolam*-isation is the fact that the court considered almost all aspects of medical practice to involve the exercise of technical medical skill and thus be subject to *Bolam*. The case thus widened its scope to cover these areas, and issues such as informed consent, whether to provide contraceptive advice and treatment to minors and whether to sterilise adults with learning difficulties were *Bolam*-ised.[8] Notably, the issues listed in the previous sentence do not involve the application of technical medical skill,

---

[6] *Bolam* (n 1 above) 587.

[7] M Davies, 'The 'New *Bolam*': Another False Dawn for Medical Negligence?' (1996) 12 *Professional Negligence* 120, 120.

[8] The first and last of these were openly *Bolam*-ised while the second was, as I argued with Margot Brazier, 'covert' *Bolam*isation—see M Brazier and J Miola, 'Bye-Bye *Bolam*: A Medical Litigation Revolution?' (2000) 8 *Medical Law Review* 85.

but instead are more ethical in nature. Yet all fell under *Bolam*'s jurisdiction, at least for a time, thus increasing its sphere of influence so significantly that this interpretation was to essentially shape medical law for some decades. In the rest of this section, the restrictive interpretation and burgeoning influence are discussed. This period, before the courts and legislature reined in its influence, can be described as being 'old' *Bolam*.[9]

The approach of the courts in relation to the interpretation of *Bolam* is best exemplified by the decision of the House of Lords in the case of *Maynard*.[10] In that case, concerning whether to conduct a test for Hodgkin's disease without waiting for the results of a test for tuberculosis (which, if positive, would have removed the need for the invasive Hodgkin's test), the trial judge had been impressed by the evidence of the plaintiff's expert, and found for him. This of course meant that the evidence for the defence was rejected. The question for the House of Lords was simple: was the trial judge entitled to reject the evidence for the defendant and prefer that of the plaintiff? In a judgment that demonstrates the low bar that doctors had to clear, Lord Scarman found that the judge was *not* entitled to do so:

> [A] judge's 'preference' for one body of distinguished professional opinion to another also professionally distinguished is not sufficient to establish negligence in a practitioner whose actions have received the seal of approval of those whose opinions, honestly expressed, honestly held, were not preferred. If this was the real reason for the judge's finding, he erred in law ... For in the realm of diagnosis and treatment, negligence is not established by preferring one respectable body of professional opinion to another. Failure to exercise the ordinary skill of a doctor (in the appropriate specialty, if he be a specialist) is necessary.[11]

Of note is not just that the test is openly descriptive ('ordinary skill'), but also that all that seems to be required is that all that the evidence needs to be is 'honest' and the judge has no right to reject it. This is not the only example of this interpretation, and it is easy to see why it was so difficult for plaintiffs to win cases. As I argued with Margot Brazier,

> a series of judgments ... have given rise to a perception that all *Bolam* requires is that the defendant fields experts from his or her medical specialty prepared to testify that they would have followed the same form of management of the patient-plaintiff that the defendant did ... The judge will play no role in evaluating that evidence.[12]

The law had thus become little more than a rubber stamp, and as mentioned above adopted the most restrictive interpretation of *Bolam* possible in relation to plaintiffs. It was easy to see why such a judicial approach would cause dissatisfaction, and this was exacerbated by the fact that 'old' *Bolam* expanded

---

[9] More precisely, the change from it addressed below was described by some, such as Davies, as being the 'new' *Bolam*.

[10] *Maynard v West Midlands Regional Health Authority* [1984] 1 WLR 634.

[11] ibid 639.

[12] Brazier and Miola (n 8 above) 88.

into other areas of law where there was less justification for even using *Bolam* at all. The first of these is informed consent. In 1985 the House of Lords case of *Sidaway* confirmed that doctors must disclose to patients all material risks inherent in any procedure, but they disagreed regarding how the materiality of risk should be defined and determined.[13] The two opposites—although there was a third, compromise approach—involved a consideration of the place of *Bolam*.[14] For Lord Scarman, autonomy was a fundamental human right and thus the amount of information to be presented to the patient should be determined by the patient rather than the doctor. In such circumstances, he said, *Bolam* would be inappropriate:

> It would be a strange conclusion if the courts should be led to conclude that our law, which undoubtedly recognises a right in the patient to decide whether he will accept or reject the treatment proposed, should permit the doctors to determine whether and in what circumstances a duty arises requiring the doctor to warn his patient of the risks inherent in the treatment which he proposes.[15]

Lord Diplock, conversely, used *Bolam* to determine the materiality or otherwise of a risk, and his approach was far more paternalistic in nature:

> The only effect that mention of risks can have on the patient's mind, if it has any at all, can be in the direction of deterring the patient from undergoing the treatment which in the expert opinion of the doctor it is in the patient's interest to undergo.[16]

Lord Diplock's judgment is not quite as insensitive to patient autonomy as it is sometimes assumed to be—but the patient's rights are clearly more the focus of Lord Scarman's judgment than that of Lord Diplock.[17] Nevertheless, the temptation for the use of *Bolam* to end in paternalism was demonstrated in the two Court of Appeal cases that followed *Sidaway*, in which the Court faced the unenviable task of teasing out which of the competing judgments in the House of Lords should be followed. In *Gold* and *Blyth*, both decided in 1987, the Court of Appeal twice concluded that the judgment of Lord Diplock should be taken as constituting that of the majority in *Sidaway*.[18] In both cases the court came to a paternalistic decision. In *Gold*, a case involving the question of whether there should be a distinction between

---

[13] *Sidaway v Board of Governors of Bethlem Royal Hospital* [1985] 1 All ER 643. For an account of the different judgments and approaches see J Miola, 'On the Materiality of Risk: Paper Tigers and Panaceas' (2009) 17 *Medical Law Review* 76.

[14] The third did also, most lucidly expressed by Lord Bridge. We return to his judgment later in this chapter.

[15] *Sidaway* (n 13 above) 649.

[16] ibid 659.

[17] See Miola, 'On the Materiality of Risk' (n 13 above).

[18] *Gold v Haringey Health Authority* [1987] 2 All ER 888; *Blyth v Bloomsbury Health Authority* [1993] 4 Med LR 151. It should be noted that Lord Scarman himself felt precisely the opposite, as he made clear in a speech at the Royal Society of Medicine. See Lord Scarman, 'Consent, Communication and Responsibility' (1986) 79 *Journal of the Royal Society of Medicine* 697.

therapeutic and non-therapeutic treatment in relation to how much information the patient should be provided with, the court held that there should be
no distinction and that *Bolam* should apply as normal. In *Blyth*, concerning
whether when questions were asked full answers should be given, the court
was even clearer, and Neill LJ held that even then there is no obligation to
answer comprehensively—but only to do what *Bolam* required:

> [There is no] rule of law to the effect that where questions are asked by the patient,
> or doubts are expressed, a doctor is under an obligation to put the patient in pos-
> session of all the information ... The amount of information to be given must
> depend on the circumstances, and as a general proposition it is governed by what
> is called the *Bolam* test.[19]

In neither judgment is there a one single mention of the patient's right to
autonomy. The use of *Bolam*—and in this case its expansion into a non-
technically medical field—can therefore be seen to lead to paternalism and
a consequent lack of autonomy. This is also evident in another of the issues
into which *Bolam* expanded—the concept of best interests. While many of
the cases in this area of law relate to the potential sterilisation of adults
with learning disabilities, it is important to note that this test applies to *all*
incapable patients. Thus, medical treatment (or its withdrawal) is lawful if
it is in the patient's best interests whatever the circumstances. This applies
to decisions regarding sterilisation; whether to resuscitate an elderly patient
with dementia and even whether to remove artificial nutrition and hydration or ventilation from a patient in a coma. Needless to say, again these
decisions are not technically medical in nature.

Yet they were openly *Bolam*-ised. In the 1989 case of *F v West Berkshire
Health Authority*, the House of Lords was asked to decide whether it would
be lawful to sterilise an adult with a learning disability.[20] After confirming
that a patient incapable of making decisions for herself can only receive
treatment that is in her best interests, Lord Brandon continued by seeking
to define how they may be ascertained. Despite the Court of Appeal being
unanimously of the opinion that *Bolam* was 'insufficiently stringent' to
determine a patient's best interests, Lord Brandon was undeterred.[21] Thus:

> [I]f doctors were to be required, in deciding whether an operation or other treat-
> ment was in the best interests of adults incompetent to give consent, to apply
> some test more stringent than the *Bolam* test, the result would be that such adults
> would, in some circumstances at least, be deprived of the benefit of medical treat-
> ment which adults competent to give consent would enjoy.[22]

---

[19] *Blyth* (n 18 above) 160.
[20] *F v West Berkshire Health Authority* [1990] 2 AC 1.
[21] ibid 67.
[22] ibid 68.

As with informed consent, there is a paternalistic notion that what is best is merely what is *medically* best for patients, and that this is best determined by the medical professionals. *Bolam* can again be seen to have expanded its influence—on this occasion considerably so—and yet again in a way that is as restrictive to patients as seems possible. But *Bolam*'s reach was not just limited to issues where it was openly used—this is despite the fact that the reach of the two topics described above is so wide that few elements of medical law were untouched by them. Rather, there are other examples of *Bolam* being invoked implicitly. Sometimes, troublingly, this is as a metaphor for 'medical ethics', thus tacitly using the fact that the issue is ethical in nature to *justify Bolam*-isation. An example of this is consent by minors, which Margot Brazier and I described as 'covert' *Bolam*-isation.[23] As we noted, *Bolam* is never mentioned in the case of *Gillick*—relating to consent by children under 16 years of age—but it is clear that it is relevant.[24] The House of Lords noted that if the child had the capacity to make a decision about her medical treatment, and the doctor believed it to be in her interests, it would be lawful to provide contraceptive advice and treatment.[25]

In both stages of this test any challenge would have to be based on *Bolam*. It should also be noted that the definition and scope of these two concepts—maturity and interests—are not obviously intrinsically medical in the sense that medical practitioners are uniquely qualified to decide them. In relation to the latter, Lord Fraser in *Gillick* came to the conclusion that even so medicalisation was appropriate:

> [T]he medical profession have in modern times become entrusted with very wide discretionary powers going beyond the strict limits of clinical judgments and, in my opinion, there is nothing strange about entrusting them with this further responsibility *which they alone are in a position to discharge satisfactorily.*[26] (emphasis added)

Subsequent cases regarding consent relating to minors went even further and explicitly trusted medical ethics to ensure medical good behaviour.[27] In this way it can be seen that *Bolam*, even when not explicitly used, would become the mechanism for challenging decisions abrogated to the medical profession even where courts had identified that those decisions were not really medical in nature. This was done unashamedly and openly. *Bolam* had thus become both virtually ubiquitous within medical law and applied in the most restrictive way possible to patients. This led

---

[23] See Brazier and Miola (n 8 above) 93–95.
[24] *Gillick v West Norfolk and Wisbech Health Authority* [1985] 3 All ER 402.
[25] Brazier and Miola (n 8 above) 93–95.
[26] *Gillick* (n 23 above) 413.
[27] See *Re R (A Minor) (Wardship: Medical Treatment)* [1991] 4 All ER 177; *Re W (A Minor) (Wardship: Medical Treatment)* [1992] 4 All ER 627 and J Miola, *Medical Ethics and Medical Law: A Symbiotic Relationship* (Oxford, Hart Publishing, 2007) ch 5.

Sheila McLean to argue that *Bolam*-isation was infringing upon patients' human rights:

> the buffer which might be expected to stand between medicalisation and human rights—namely the law—has proved unwilling, unable or inefficient when asked to adjudicate on or control issues which are at best tangentially medical.[28]

This was clearly a state of affairs that could not be sustained, and the only surprise was the amount of time that it took for there to be pressure for *Bolam*'s iron grip on medical law to be loosened. The contraction of its empire, as we shall see below, might already be said to have begun, but the single biggest single came in 1997 when the interpretation of *Bolam* was to change from the oppressive descriptive version of the test to a more normative approach.

### IV. *BOLITHO*—'NEW' *BOLAM* ARRIVES

The facts of *Bolitho*—the case where the House of Lords were to reinterpret *Bolam*—are easier to relay than the legal issues.[29] Patrick Bolitho was taken to hospital with breathing difficulties and, while there, suffered three episodes where his breathing was obstructed. On each occasion medical help was called but did not arrive. On two occasions his breathing normalised. However it did not do so in the third episode, and the lack of oxygen left him with brain damage. The medical evidence indicated that the only thing that would have prevented this was intubation. The legal question for the court actually relates to causation as well as how to interpret *Bolam*.[30] However, what concerns us here is the latter.

In terms of the interpretation of *Bolam*, Lord Browne-Wilkinson held that it was after all open to the courts to examine and, if appropriate, reject medical evidence on behalf of the defendant.[31] Therefore, courts would not simply have to accept the evidence just because it existed. In defining when it might be appropriate for a court to reject such evidence, Lord Browne-Wilkinson set the bar high:

> the court has to be satisfied that the exponents of the body of opinion relied upon can demonstrate that such opinion has a logical basis ... If, *in a rare case*, it can be demonstrated that *the professional opinion is not capable of withstanding logical analysis*, the judge is entitled to hold that the body of opinion is not reasonable or responsible.[32] (emphasis added)

---

[28] S MacLean, *Old Law, New Medicine: Medical Ethics and Human Rights* (London, Pandora Publishing, 1999) 2.

[29] *Bolitho v City and Hackney Health Authority* [1998] AC 232.

[30] For an excellent account and analysis of the case see A Grubb, 'Negligence: Causation and *Bolam*' (1998) 6 *Medical Law Review* 378.

[31] *Bolitho* (n 29 above) 241.

[32] ibid 233.

The italicised words are critical. Indeed, the *Bolitho* version of the *Bolam* test does not allow for a judge to simply prefer the evidence of the plaintiff to that of the defendant. Rather, it only allows the judge or jury to reject the medical evidence if it lacks logic. In other words, it must be so lacking in sense that nobody could defend it.[33] It is not intended that the test should make judges arbiters of medical conduct in the sense that they will simply choose which expert they think that they like the best—it is explicitly intended as a power that should seldom be used.[34] This can be seen through the authorities cited by Lord Browne-Wilkinson in support of his approach: *Bolam* itself and, more surprisingly, *Maynard*. With respect to the former, Lord Browne-Wilkinson correctly identified the normative words used by McNair J:

> In the *Bolam* case itself, McNair J stated ... that the defendant had to have acted in accordance with a practice accepted as proper by a 'responsible body of medical men'. Later ... he referred to 'a standard of practice accepted as proper by a competent reasonable body of opinion'.[35]

More controversial is the use of *Maynard* to support the normative reinterpretation. Having identified the normative words in *Bolam*, Lord Browne-Wilkinson noted that in *Maynard*

> Lord Scarman refers to a 'respectable' body of professional opinion. The use of these adjectives—responsible, reasonable and respectable—all show that the court has to be satisfied that the exponents of the body of opinion relied upon can demonstrate that such opinion has a logical basis.[36]

Lord Browne-Wilkinson is correct in the sense that Lord Scarman *does* refer to a 'respectable' body of opinion, so technically speaking *Maynard* does not preclude the judge from rejecting the evidence of a body that is *not* respectable. Nevertheless a reading of the judgment and, in particular, the passage quoted earlier in this chapter, cannot leave the reader with any conclusion other than the fact that it was not Lord Scarman's intention that the test be akin to that in *Bolitho*. Lord Browne-Wilkinson thus seized upon what is essentially a lacuna in Lord Scarman's judgment in order to change the interpretation of *Bolam* without admitting to doing so.

Some, including Margot Brazier and I, argued that *Bolitho* restored *Bolam* to its 'proper limits'.[37] I would now revise this opinion. I was convinced during a PhD viva that *Bolitho* does not go as far as intended in *Bolam*.[38]

---

[33] ibid.
[34] Hence the use of the word 'rare'.
[35] *Bolitho* (n 29 above) 241.
[36] ibid 242.
[37] Brazier and Miola (n 8 above) 107. See also Grubb (n 30 above) 378, who declared of the *Bolitho* judgment: 'Eureka! The courts have got it at last'.
[38] The viva was for Dr Joanne Beswick at the University of Manchester in 2013. The idea is hers.

Bolitho does not allow the judge to 'prefer' one expert over another. Rather, it provides that she may *reject* evidence from an expert if it fails to withstand logical analysis. *Bolam*, however, *does* allow for simple preference. Indeed, as one of the quotes above in this chapter makes clear, McNair J himself offered the jury the opportunity to *choose* which side's experts it liked better.

So while *Bolitho* moves the interpretation of *Bolam* from a descriptive one to a normative one—and at least restores the law's ability to assess the evidence, it does not go as far as the original judge intended. Therefore, there was scope for *Bolitho* to have gone further than it did had the House of Lords wished to do so. Yet what the case does do is demonstrate that at the very least a blind adherence to medical practice would no longer be the approach of the courts—a notion supported by Lord Woolf, who in 2001 wrote an article accepting that the courts had been overly deferential to the medical profession in the past but would not continue to be so in the future, and providing reasons for this.[39] It should also be noted that, as argued below, *Bolitho* was not a sudden, unforeseen shift in judicial approach, but a part of what can be seen as a logical process of de-*Bolam*isation that had already begun in other areas of medical law. After the expansion, the contraction was already in progress.

## V. CONTRACTING AGAIN—(SOME OF) THE WALLS CLOSE IN

### A. Before *Bolitho*—Laying the Ground

Even before *Bolitho*, there had been signs within medical law that 'old' *Bolam* would have to be discarded. The initial areas to feel this change were the outlying issues upon which *Bolam*-isation had infringed as its influence had grown. In other words, before *Bolam* was reconsidered in its own context of medical negligence, it had already been questioned in areas into which *Bolam* had expanded. The three examples given earlier in this chapter as evidence of *Bolam*'s widening provide an instructive demonstration of this process in reverse. The first example used was that of informed consent, and in this area of medical law there have been big changes, and they certainly began before *Bolitho*. However, the genesis of the change was in Australia.

In the landmark case of *Rogers v Whitaker*, the Australian Supreme Court was to entirely reject the *Bolam* test in relation to informed consent

---

[39] Lord Woolf, 'Are the Courts Excessively Deferential to the Medical Profession?' (2001) 9 *Medical Law Review* 1.

and the materiality of risk, as the purpose of the law was to protect patient autonomy.[40] Therefore,

> Because the choice to be made calls for *a decision by the patient* on information known to the medical practitioner but not to the patient, *it would be illogical to hold that the amount of information to be provided by the medical practitioner can be determined from the perspective of the medical practitioner alone* or, for that matter, of the medical profession.[41] (emphasis added)

While the reasoning is similar to that of Lord Scarman in *Sidaway*, the Supreme Court of Australia went even further and not only demanded that the patient be informed of what the reasonable patient would wish to be informed of, but also introduced a subjective element stating that in some circumstances she should be informed of what *she as an individual* would want to know:

> a risk is material if, in the circumstances of the particular case, a reasonable person in the patient's position, if warned of the risk, would be likely to attach significance to it or if the medical practitioner is or should be reasonably aware that the particular patient, if warned of the risk, would be likely to attach significance to it.[42]

English courts picked up on this, and almost immediately started shying away from Lord Diplock's *Bolam*-ite judgment in *Sidaway*. Thus, in two pre-*Bolitho* cases from 1994 the courts not only spoke of the compromise judgment of Lord Bridge being the leading one in *Sidaway*, they actually rejected medical evidence in support of the defendant and found for the plaintiffs.[43] In one of them, *Smith*, the court actually referred to the decision in *Rogers*.[44] What is noticeable in these cases is that as the courts sought to distance themselves from *Bolam* the emphasis on the patient's right to autonomy increased. Thus, it would appear that in informed consent cases the courts had identified the fact that 'old' *Bolam* was a limit to autonomy and so rejected it. As we shall see, this change in approach was to accelerate after *Bolitho*, but in informed consent *Bolam*'s card was marked well before it.

Similarly, law-makers applying the law's conception of best interests began to try to move away from *Bolam* before *Bolitho*. Indeed the decision of *F v West Berkshire Health Authority*, in which the House of Lords *Bolam*-ised best interests, caused such consternation that the Law Commission decided not long after to examine the law relating to incapable adults.[45] The beginning of the report lists one of the reasons for reviewing the law to be the decision of the House of Lords and the fact that it 'could not provide

---

[40] *Rogers v Whitaker* [1992] HCA 58, (1992) 175 CLR 479.
[41] ibid 489.
[42] ibid 490.
[43] *McAllister v Lewisham and North Southwark Health Authority* [1994] 5 Med LR 343; *Smith v Tunbridge Wells Health Authority* [1994] 5 Med LR 334. See J Miola, 'On the Materiality of Risk' (n 13 above) Section V.
[44] The judge declared that he could not follow it, but the intention is clear: he would have liked to do so. See the comment at the bottom of the law report by Margaret Puxon QC for support for this view.
[45] Law Commission, *Mental Incapacity* (Law Com 231, 1995).

a comprehensive solution'—a polite way of expressing dissatisfaction.[46] Indeed, the Commission was to make its lack of support for the decision quite clear later in the report, noting that not even the medical profession was in favour of retaining the test in *F*:

> The apparent conflation of the criterion for assessing complaints about professional negligence with the criterion for treating persons unable to consent has been the butt of vehement criticism. No medical professional or body responding ... [to the consultation] argued in favour of retaining such a definition of 'best interests' ... The British Medical Association ... supported our provisional proposals for statutory guidance 'without reservation'.[47]

Again, it was felt that the use of *Bolam* would be insufficiently sensitive to the self-determination of patients to be able to determine best interests from anything other than a purely medical perspective. Something else was needed to balance it out. The suggestion was an amalgamation of the patient's medical interests and a 'substituted judgement' aspect asking what the patient would have wanted if they had capacity. *Bolam* became relevant but not determinative—an approach akin to that which *Bolitho* was to take—and it survived into what became the Mental Capacity Act (MCA) in 2005, to which we return later.

In contrast, the issue of consent for minors has gone the other way. In two Court of Appeal judgments in 1991 and 1992, Lord Donaldson MR held that while *Gillick* gave competent minors the right to consent to treatment, this did not extend to allowing them to refuse it.[48] Thus a doctor would be permitted to treat the patient, even in the face of her refusal of consent, if either of the parents consented on her behalf (even if the other also refused). However, the Master of the Rolls also noted that in such circumstances it would not be compulsory for the doctor to treat, but the decision would present the doctor with 'a professional and ethical, but not with a legal, problem'.[49] He went even further in *Re W*, acknowledging that he had left a legal lacuna but confident in the medical profession's ability to make the correct decision:

> Hair-raising possibilities were canvassed of abortions being carried out by doctors in reliance upon the consent of parents and despite the refusal of consent by 16- and 17-year-olds. Whilst this may be possible as a matter of law, *I do not see any likelihood taking account of medical ethics*, unless the abortion was truly in the best interests of the child. This is not to say that it could not happen.[50] (emphasis added)

Here the approach is different—and it would seem that *Bolam* remained alive and well. The medical profession was still trusted to make decisions, and challenges would have to be through *Bolam*. Moreover, the courts

---

[46] ibid [1.4].
[47] ibid [3.26].
[48] *Re R* and *Re W* (n 27 above).
[49] *Re R* (n 27 above) 184.
[50] *Re W* (n 27 above) 635.

seemed not just happy with that but actively encouraging it. It is possible to draw a distinction, however, between this issue and the previous two, and that is that it is more likely that the courts were simply trying to protect children. In other words, their medical interests were prioritised because judges still felt that this was the most appropriate thing to do—they could benefit from more autonomy and less *Bolam* later in their lives.

Although *Bolam* was not treated in the same way in all three examples above, it is plain to see that its influence was at least waning in two of them, and perhaps only the specific nature of the third example prevented the same there. Given this, what we can see is examples of judicial attitudes that suggest that *Bolitho* was the culmination of a process rather than a shocking single event. In short, 'old' *Bolam* had outlived its time and *Bolitho* simply administered the coup de grace. But if 'old' *Bolam* was defined by the way in which it was interpreted, then surely the same would be the case for the 'new' version. Again, the approaches from our examples differ.

### B. Post-*Bolitho*—Achieving Equilibrium?

If anything, *Bolitho* provided the green light for the pace of legal change in informed consent to accelerate. Slightly more than a year after the decision of the House of Lords, the Court of Appeal had the opportunity to again consider the issue of the materiality of risk, and the then Master of the Rolls—Lord Woolf, in the case of *Pearce*—took the opportunity to progress the law even further.[51] The facts are unimportant, but in the case Lord Woolf conflated the reasonable doctor (*Bolam*) and reasonable patient (Lord Scarman in *Sidaway*) tests by stating that 'if there is a significant risk which would affect the judgment of a reasonable patient' then the reasonable doctor would be under a duty to inform the patient of that risk.[52] Thus although the test for the materiality of risk technically remained that of the reasonable doctor, Lord Woolf demanded that the reasonable doctor would disclose all the information that the reasonable patient would want to be informed of—a neat sidestep that allowed him to effectively introduce Lord Scarman's test by stealth.[53] Again, the reason was the prioritisation of patient autonomy. Moreover, in the 2003 case of *Wyatt v Curtis* a subsequent Court of Appeal held that where the reasonable doctor and reasonable patient disagree about the amount of information to be disclosed then the duty of the doctor is to disclose what the latter would wish to be informed of.[54] Thus the law of informed consent—in less than

---

[51] *Pearce v United Bristol Healthcare NHS Trust* [1999] PIQR 53.
[52] ibid 59.
[53] See R Heywood, 'Subjectivity in Risk Disclosure: Considering the Position of the Particular Patient' (2009) 25 *Professional Negligence* 3.
[54] *Wyatt v Curtis* [2003] EWCA Civ 1779.

20 years—went from a committed disciple of *Bolam* to essentially accepting Lord Scarman's reasonable patient approach from *Sidaway*. The courts have gone further again in relation to causation, and even changed established law, as it did not sufficiently respect autonomy, but this is not within the ambit of this article to discuss.[55] Moreover, having used another Australian case as justification for this, it would be unsurprising to see *Rogers* adopted in future.[56] In conclusion, informed consent can be said to have been almost completely de-*Bolam*-ised, and the general direction of the law suggests that the process will be complete sooner rather than later.

The situation is slightly different in relation to best interests. The MCA 2005 finally came into force in 2007, and the approach to best interests—a combination of medical best interests and substituted judgement—remained in what became section 4 of the Act.[57] But even before the Act came into force, the courts had already themselves undertaken the process of separating *Bolam* from best interests. In the Court of Appeal case of *Re SL*, for example, Butler-Sloss LJ made it clear that while *Bolam* could only narrow down options—there might be more than one respectable body of opinion after all—best interests required a *single* answer.[58] This meant that the court, after using *Bolam*, would look at wider considerations to ascertain which single option was in the patient's best interests. Again, *Bolam* was seen as insufficiently stringent (an echo of the view of the Court of Appeal in *F*) to determine the patient's welfare, and it is noteworthy that the courts by now trusted themselves to fill in the gaps rather than simply deferring to the medical profession.

As for the MCA, the courts have interpreted that in the same way. Indeed, as Dunn and Foster have noted, their best interests calculation is now a balance between autonomy and welfare.[59] Under the Act, there is a specific requirement to consider the patient's ascertainable past and present wishes, and to take advice from relatives regarding what the patient would have wanted. Again, the principle of autonomy has been invoked to, at the very least, clip *Bolam*'s wings. Best interests are now far from a solely medical construct but this is not to say that *Bolam* is irrelevant or even that welfare considerations always come second to autonomy. This can be seen in the recent case of *E*, which concerned an adult anorexic who wished to die.[60] She had on several occasions expressed this wish, and even made an advance directive to this effect (although the judge found that she lacked capacity

---

[55] *Chester v Afshar* [2004] 4 All ER 587. See S Devaney, 'Autonomy Rules OK' (2005) 13 *Medical Law Review* 102.

[56] The Australian case applied was *Chapel v Hart* (1998) 195 CLR 232.

[57] M Donnelly, 'Best Interests, Patient Participation and the Mental Capacity Act 2005' (2009) 17 *Medical Law Review* 1.

[58] *Re SL (Adult Patient: Sterilisation)* [2000] Lloyds Rep Med 339.

[59] M Dunn and C Foster, 'Autonomy and Welfare as *Amici Curiae*' (2010) 18 *Medical Law Review* 86.

[60] *A Health Authority v E* [2012] EWHC 1639 (Fam).

when she did so).[61] Even her parents had come to the reluctant, agonising conclusion that it would be best to accede to her wishes. The court, in balancing her interests, listed factors in favour of allowing her to die, and those in favour of force-feeding her. The former consisted of the fact that it was what she demonstrably wanted (even when competent), and the latter that it was against her medical interests.[62] On that occasion, they prioritised her medical interests and authorised the force-feeding. The case is perhaps extreme, but it shows that while *Bolam* is not the *sole* consideration, it is not being marginalised in the way that it has been in informed consent. Quite properly, the incapable patient's medical interests remain relevant to any decision made.

In contrast, the law relating to decision-making by minors remains solidly medicalised, and thus the covert *Bolam*-isation persists. The decisions in *Re R* and *Re W* are still good law, and thus children can consent to but not refuse treatment determinatively. Where they refuse, and their parents agree with them, the courts have not hesitated to overrule the family's wishes and authorise treatment on the basis that it is in the child's best (medical) interests. In one case the child's refusal was even overruled on the basis that they were not in possession of information that was deliberately withheld from them.[63] Thus, while there are disagreements regarding the fairness of the legal rules, their existence is not in question.[64] So, in relation to child consent, medical interests continue to prevail. As mentioned earlier, this is neither surprising nor indefensible. This is one area where *Bolam* has survived unscathed—an exception to the general trend.

If the significance of *Bolam* lay not so much in the judgment itself, but how it was interpreted, then surely the same would be important with respect to *Bolitho*. So how has it fared in its natural habitat: negligence? Initially, one study found that the courts were reluctant to use *Bolitho*.[65] Since then, they have warmed to their task and *Bolitho* is now uncontroversial.[66] Moreover, it has been interpreted in the way that Lord Browne-Wilkinson intended, and the courts appear to be asking two questions of medical evidence: is there a body of opinion that would do as the doctor did? If so, can the evidence from that body withstand logical analysis? As mentioned above,

---

[61] See J Coggon, 'Anorexia Nervosa, Best Interests and the Patient's Human Right to "A Wholesale Overwhelming of Her Autonomy" A Health Authority v. E [2012] EWHC 1639 (COP) [2012] HRLR 29' (2014) 22 *Medical Law Review* 119, available on advance access at: medlaw.oxfordjournals.org/content/early/2013/11/05/medlaw.fwt031.

[62] ibid [115]–[116].

[63] *Re L (Medical Treatment: Gillick Competency)* [1998] 2 FLR 810.

[64] See S Gilmore and J Herring, '"No" is the Hardest Word' (2011) 23 *Child & Family Law Quarterly* 3 and E Cave and J Wallbank, 'Minors' Capacity to Refuse Treatment: A Reply to Gilmore and Herring' (2012) 20 *Medical Law Review* 423.

[65] A Maclean, 'Beyond *Bolam* and *Bolitho*' (2002) 5 *Medical Law International* 205.

[66] R Mulheron, 'Trumping *Bolam*: A Critical Analysis of *Bolitho*'s "Gloss"' (2010) 69 *Cambridge Law Journal* 609.

this does not go as far as McNair J intended, though it is far closer to what *Bolam* was intended to be than the way in which it was applied before 1997.

## VI. THE PLACE OF *BOLAM* TODAY—AND WHAT ABOUT THE FUTURE?

We appear to be close to where we started. *Bolam* has not quite been restored to its 'proper limits' in two senses. First, *Bolitho* does not do what McNair J intended as the court still cannot simply *prefer* evidence from one side or another. Secondly, *Bolam*'s expansion beyond negligence has not quite been reversed. Indeed, we have seen in our three issues a variety of approaches: informed consent has almost fully de-*Bolam*ised. The law relating to best interests has placed far more emphasis on autonomy than was the case before, and this has led to a lessening of *Bolam*'s influence, although it still has a voice. Interestingly, in both cases *Bolam* was identified as an enemy of autonomy and treated accordingly—the increased welfare considerations relating to adults lacking capacity can explain the remnants of *Bolam* that remain. The balance between autonomy and welfare, and the prioritisation of the latter, also explains the lack of de-*Bolam*isation in relation to the right of minors to make decisions about their medical treatment. *Bolitho* was, I have argued, the culmination of a process rather than an unexpected event. Essentially, there was a change in judicial attitude and *Bolam* had to change, both in terms of reversing its expansion and interpreting it normatively. Thus it now follows medical law's prevailing wind, which emphasises autonomy more than it did. This again marks a difference; for once it set the trend instead.

# 3

# Re B (A Minor) (Wardship: Sterilisation) [1988]: 'People Like Us Don't Have Babies'[1]

## Learning Disability, Prospective Parenthood and Legal Transformations

KIRSTY KEYWOOD

### I. INTRODUCTION

IN 1987, JUST three weeks shy of her eighteenth birthday, Jeanette, a young woman with learning disabilities was the subject of a ruling from the House of Lords.[2] Their Lordships had to determine whether the Court of Appeal had acted correctly in confirming that Jeanette be subjected to a sterilisation procedure. The case marked the first opportunity for the appeal courts in England and Wales to consider the legality of sterilising, for contraceptive purposes, people with learning disabilities who could not give a legally valid consent to the procedure. There was no apparent medical need for this procedure and Jeanette had not consented to it; nor was she suffering from a particular disease or illness required this intervention. The reasons for sterilising Jeanette were explicitly 'social'.[3] The concern for her, expressed by many who were responsible for her care, lay in the fact that she was a maturing young woman with a developing interest in her own body and the possibility of sexual pleasure, but for whom the risks of pregnancy resulting from sexual contact were considered to be disastrous. At the time,

---

[1] D Atkinson and F Williams (eds), *Know Me As I Am: An Anthology of Prose, Poetry and Art by People with Learning Difficulties* (Oxford, Oxford University Press, 1990) 175.

[2] *Re B (a minor) (wardship: sterilisation)* [1988] AC 199, [1987] 2 All ER 206.

[3] Although what counts as a social rather than a therapeutic sterilisation is a rather contested evaluation. See especially the Court's response to proposed sterilisation for menstrual management: *Re GF (a patient)* [1991] FCR 786, sub nom *Re GF (medical treatment)* [1992] 1 FLR 293.

the outcome of the ruling for Jeanette received very little academic criticism,[4] with the majority of commentators reflecting on the correctness of the legal processes employed to reach a judgment and the relevance of particular factors to determine the question.[5] This was perhaps somewhat surprising, given that a number of other jurisdictions had prohibited such sterilisations, mindful of the associations with eugenic-informed health and social policy which had initiated mass sterilisation programmes in many countries.[6]

Almost 30 years on, the courts continue to receive applications concerning the proposed sterilisation of adults and young people with learning disabilities. Notably, and with only two exceptions, the reported cases have concerned the performance of the procedure upon women. This chapter revisits Jeanette's case, situating the court proceedings in the context of welfare policy at the time, in order to make sense of the law's response to the emerging sexuality of people with learning disabilities. I suggest that the professional, familial and legal responses to Jeanette's situation occur at a point in history which, in retrospect, marks a shift in the traditional discourses and paradigms that had framed policy responses to disability—particularly learning disability—since the Enlightenment. In addition, I suggest that other important shifts were underway at this time, as the case enters the legal arena when traditional assumptions about law's deferential relation to medical power were beginning to be questioned and intellectual conceptualisations of sexuality and adolescent autonomy were undergoing critical interrogation. This chapter explores what impact, if any, these emerging conceptual and policy shifts had in Jeanette's case.

Moving forward in time, I explore more recent judicial response to sterilising people with learning disabilities in a world where policy, academia and 'bottom up' perspectives from users, carers and advocates have responded differently to the issue of sterilisation, focusing instead on notions of choice, inclusion and empowerment. Changing intellectual paradigms which have led to a shift from essentialising notions of disability to social constructions of impairment have, in recent times, prompted the courts to ask a different set of questions to those asked by the Court in Jeanette's case. A more recent focus in the academic literature on issues such as vulnerability have been identified as having the potential foster further shifts in the judicial narrative. This chapter concludes with some reflection as to how law might respond in future to these emerging paradigms.

---

[4] See the notable exception of: R Lee and D Morgan, 'Sterilisation and Mental Handicap: Sapping the Strength of the State?' (1988) 15 *Journal of Law & Society* 229.

[5] See, eg A Grubb and D Pearl, 'Sterilisation and the Courts' (1987) 46 *Cambridge Law Journal* 439; J Fortin, 'Sterilisation, the Mentally Ill and Consent to Treatment' (1988) 51 *Modern Law Review* 634; J Shaw, 'Sterilisation of Mentally Handicapped People: Judges Rule Ok?' (1990) 53 *Modern Law Review* 91.

[6] *In re Eve* (1986) 31 DLR (4th) 1.

## II. THE EMERGENCE OF LEARNING DISABILITY: MEDICAL KNOWLEDGE AND SOCIAL POLICY

In order to make sense of how the courts respond to Jeanette, we must first come to understand how learning disability is understood in legal and social domains. An examination of the historical, socio-political terrain will enable the reader to identify the processes through which Jeanette is understood both within and without the courtroom at this point in history. To this end, it is useful to begin with Borsay's examination of social policy responses to disability. Here, she identifies the hallmarks of modernity which have framed disability policy since the Enlightenment and which were deeply embedded in the policy fabric of Britain during the 1980s. The grounding of rational thought and knowledge as the principal basis upon which social engineering and welfare developments were built; a developed capitalist economy, which in turn generated social stratification according to very different hierarchies associated with income and wealth; and a code of individual rights, have provided the bedrock upon which the foundations of social policy on learning disability have been built.[7] Critical to the framing of social policy on learning disability was the emergence of medical discourse as a dominant episteme in the eighteenth century. Made possible by changes in economic and cultural practices brought about by industrialisation[8] and an expectation that social contribution was an important component of citizenship,[9] medical knowledge gained dominance through formulation of the norms of medical science; the development of technologies for diagnosis, treatment and management; together with the establishment of classifications and typologies of disease and disorder.[10] This privileging of medical discourse serves not only to generate and consolidate professional hierarchies, but also to delimit the boundaries of its own sphere of knowledge, thereby restricting encroachment of other perspectives and narratives that seek to offer a different account.[11] Whilst many individuals with learning disabilities had remained supported at home, engaging in economically productive cottage industries, the advent of the industrial revolution heralded the move of many people with learning disabilities to institutional settings (whether in workhouses, asylums, long stay hospitals, or residential homes) or subject

---

[7] A Borsay, *Disability and Social Policy in Britain since 1750: A History of Exclusion* (Basingstoke, Palgrave, 2004) 1–8.

[8] BS Turner, *Medical Power and Social Knowledge*, 3rd edn (London, Sage, 1995) pt III; M Oliver and C Barnes, *The New Politics of Disablement* (Basingstoke, Palgrave Macmillan, 2012) ch 3.

[9] SL Snyder and DT Mitchell, *Cultural Locations of Disability* (Chicago IL, University of Chicago Press, 2010); MH Rioux, 'Disability: the place of judgement in a world of fact' (1997) 41 *Journal of Intellectual Disability Research* 102.

[10] See, eg D Armstrong, 'The Rise of Surveillance Medicine' (1995) 17 *Sociology of Health & Illness* 393.

[11] See, eg M Foucault, *The Birth of the Clinic* (London, Routledge, 2003).

to professional involvement by those tasked with 'managing' the perceived challenges and limitations posed by their impairment whilst continuing to live in the community.[12]

The role that medicine played in these times of economic and social transition was not incidental. Joanna Ryan, in exploring the development of institutions to accommodate people with learning disabilities notes that 'it is not just that hospitals have had to cope with people whom society has rejected ... it is also that the medical professional has sanctioned this rejection by producing a whole way of thinking that justifies it'.[13] This ongoing medical, institutional management of learning disability remains active today, as people with learning disabilities are supported in residential services, subject to the Mental Health Act 1983,[14] placed in assessment and treatment units,[15] or subject to community-based assessment and intervention by general and specialist service providers.[16] Whilst a focus on the placement of people with learning disabilities in community rather than hospital settings became a government priority in the 1960s and 70s,[17] the understanding of disability that underpinned many of the policy responses to people like Jeanette was unchanged. The processes of identification, management and supervision of learning disability contributed to a framework for understanding learning disability that was premised on the differentiation of people with learning disabilities from bodily and psychological norms, which in turn generated a series of policy responses that resulted in social exclusion.[18] Jayne Clapton,

---

[12] On the history of learning disability see, eg D Atkinson, M Jacobs and J Walmsley, *Forgotten Lives: Exploring the History of Learning Disability* (Kidderminster, BILD, 1997); L Brigham, D Atkinson, M Jackson, S Rolph and J Walmsley (eds), *Crossing Boundaries: Change and Continuity in the History of Learning Disability* (Kidderminster, BILD, 2000); D Wright and A Digby (eds), *From Idiocy to Mental Deficiency: Historical Perspectives on People with Learning Disabilities* (Abingdon, Routledge, 1996).

[13] J Ryan and F Thomas, *The Politics of Mental Handicap* (London, Free Association Books, 1987) 15.

[14] Mental Health Act 1983, s 1(2)(a).

[15] On the recent controversy concerning the long-term use of these facilities for people with learning disabilities, see 'People with Learning Disabilities "Stuck in Institutions", New Statistics Reveal' (*Learning Disability Today*, 2014): www.learningdisabilitytoday.co.uk/people_with_learning_disabilities_stuck_in_institutions_new_statistics_reveal_25769814687. aspx; Department of Health, *DH Winterbourne View Review Concordat: Programme of Action* (Department of Health, 2012).

[16] Note that some NHS funding allocations are connected to the measure of service responses to learning disability through, eg, primary care providers having a register of people with learning disabilities: NHS, *Quality and Outcomes Framework Guidance for GMS Contract 2013* (NHS Employers, 2013). For the outcome of a review of commissioning arrangements for community-based learning disability services see: *Transforming Care and Commissioning Steering Group, Winterbourne View—Time for Change: Transforming the Commissioning of Services for People with Learning Disabilities and/or Autism* (NHS England, 2014).

[17] See, eg Ministry of Health, *A Hospital Plan for England and Wales* (Cmnd 1604, 1962); DHSS, *Better Services for the Mentally Handicapped* (Cmn 4683, 1971).

[18] The implementation of techniques such as IQ testing to ascertain intellectual subnormality was used, for example, to identify and restrict access to those who were considered

writing of her experiences as a houseparent of a number of young people with learning disabilities in the early 1980s, captures powerfully the sense of dislocation from the ordinary narratives and rituals of people's lives; narratives that are often absent for people with learning disabilities. She observes that:

> It is not unusual that, when writing about such people [with learning disabilities], their defining deficits are noted. Their incapacities and inadequacies in relation to their intellectual incompetence traditionally dominate descriptions of their personhood ... Their lives had been determined by the lack of personal histories—stories and photos; the lack of familial relationships; the lack of life's everyday choices; these were the deficits inflicted by a stigmatising society which took little responsibility for such actions.[19]

Such an approach to learning disability resonates with the perspectives of many who supported people with learning disabilities at that time and has some lineage with the policy discourses surrounding the care and management of people with learning disabilities in the 1970s. These are heavily infused with a narrative of the person with a learning disability, who, by virtue of their inherent deficiency, warrants specific regulation. Although the ethos around supporting people with learning disabilities was couched in discourses of equality of opportunity, there remained at heart, a deeply medicalised conception of disability. Examples are numerous, but two are offered here. The 1971 Report, *Better Services for the Mentally Handicapped*,[20] advocated the removal of people with learning disabilities from long-stay hospitals and into community-based residential placements. At first glance, de-institutionalisation clearly has enormous potential to herald increased social inclusion, but it does not necessarily follow.[21] Nor did it seem to do so in the 1970s. The 1971 report is suffused with the discourse of disability as defect and tragedy. The introduction to the report identifies the 'great strain' on family members,[22] the isolation and loneliness experienced by parents[23] and the 'suffering' experienced by other siblings.[24] Despite advocating that 'each handicapped person should live with his own family as long as this

---

unsuitable beneficiaries of education. Jeanette, given the complexity of her needs, would have been one of the early beneficiaries of the removal of the restriction of people with a 'disability of mind' having access to school education, on the basis that they were 'unsuitable for education at school': Education (Handicapped Children) Act 1970 and The Education of Handicapped Children (Transfer of Staff and Property) Order 1971 (SI 1971/341).

[19] J Clapton, 'The Quilter's Journal' in S Rolph, D Atkinson, M Nind and J Welshman, *Witness to Change: Families, Learning Difficulties and History* (Kidderminster, BILD, 2005) 267.

[20] DHSS, *Better Services* (1971).

[21] See, eg NA Malin and DG Race, 'The Impact of Social Policy on Changes in Professional Practice Within Learning Disability Services: Different Standards for Children and Adults? A Two-Part Examination' (2010) 14 *Journal of Intellectual Disabilities* 315, 319.

[22] DHSS (n 17 above) [14].

[23] ibid [16].

[24] ibid [17].

does not impose an undue burden on them or him, and he and his family should receive full advice and support', it is difficult to imagine how the framing of a person with a learning disability might be experienced as anything other than an undue burden at that time. Indeed, this may explain why, more than a decade after this initiative, many people already living in long-stay hospitals did not experience the discharge into the community that the 1971 report had anticipated.[25] The quest for granting people equality of opportunity, advocated in this and other policy documents,[26] is tempered by the explicit recognition that people with disabilities, because of their individual limitations, will only be able to do so much. Mary Warnock's report, *Special Educational Needs: Report of the Committee of Enquiry into the Education of Handicapped Children and Young People*,[27] provided the basis for the Education Act 1981 and had the positive impact of distancing children previously from long-term health service management.[28] Even here, the discourse of disability as defect survives. Warnock's reflections on the achievements of the Committee note that

> whatever our intentions, we had not wholly avoided the old medical model of mental handicap. We still thought that children who had special educational needs were children with something the matter with them, at least from the standpoint of their teachers.[29]

Their social exclusion and experienced impediments to leading a meaningful life were attributed to their intellectual functioning rather than the structural arrangements which made such limitations meaningful in modern Britain. Internationally, too, there is recognition that rights are to be fostered and recognised, but only to the extent that the person's disability allows.[30]

Policy responses to learning disability were characterised by Wolfensberger as broadly falling within four categories: destruction of their perceived difference; segregation; reversal of the impairing condition; or prevention.[31] In the context of *Re B*, we see the legal response to Jeanette

---

[25] Ryan and Thomas, *The Politics* (1987) n 13 above, 156.

[26] M Warnock, 'The Work of the Warnock Committee' in P Mittler and V Sinason (eds), *Changing Policy and Practice for People with Learning Disabilities* (Cassell Education) (New York, Continuum Publishing Co, 1996) ch 5, 56.

[27] M Warnock, *Special Educational Needs: Report of the Committee of Enquiry into the Education of Handicapped Children and Young People* (Cmnd 7212, 1981).

[28] Malin and Race, 'The Impact of Social Policy' (2010) n 21 above, 317.

[29] Warnock, 'The Work' (1996) n 26 above, 56.

[30] United Nations, *Declaration on the Rights of Mentally Retarded Persons* (General Assembly Resolution 2856 (XXVI) of 20 December 1971) art 1: The mentally retarded person has, *to the maximum degree of feasibility*, the same rights as other human beings (emphasis added). See, too, the criticism of the World Health Organisation's (now lapsed) International Classification of Impairments, Disabilities and Handicaps (WHO 1980), in C Barnes and G Mercer, *Disability* (Polity, 2003) 13–15.

[31] W Wolfensberger, *Normalization: The Principle of Normalization in Human Services* (National Institute of Mental Retardation, 1972) 24.

as hinging on prevention by way of curtailing her reproductive choices. In so doing, their Lordships draw on the key discursive theme of disability as deficiency, thereby replicating the medical 'model' of disability which has endured through the modern age. Three discursive themes are deployed by the House of Lords to underscore Jeanette's disability and to justify the proposed surgical solution. These are focused on a replication of the medical 'model' of learning disability; a framing of Jeanette's needs as essentially 'medical'; and a rejection of rights discourse.

## III. LEARNING DISABILITY IN THE HOUSE OF LORDS

Jeanette's life story is told by the courts in terms of deficiency and abnormality. Although she has ongoing contact with her mother, Jeanette has lived in a residential placement since the age of four and is a ward of court. Lord Hailsham's observations about Jeanette set the tone for their Lordships' ruling as to whether sterilisation would be in Jeanette's best interests and therefore a legitimate exercise of its wardship jurisdiction:

> The ward in the present case is of the mental age of five or six. She speaks only in sentences limited to one or two words. Although her condition is controlled by a drug, she is epileptic. She does not understand and cannot learn the causal connection between intercourse and pregnancy and the birth of children. She would be incapable of giving a valid consent to contracting a marriage. She would not understand, or be capable of easily supporting, the inconveniences and pains of pregnancy. As she menstruates irregularly, pregnancy would be difficult to detect or diagnose in time to terminate it easily. Were she to carry a child to full term she would not understand what was happening to her, she would be likely to panic, and would probably have to be delivered by caesarean section, but, owing to her emotional state, and the fact that she has a high pain threshold she would be quite likely to pick at the operational wound and tear it open. In any event, she would be 'terrified, distressed and extremely violent' during normal labour. She has no maternal instincts and is not likely to develop any. She does not desire children, and, if she bore a child, would be unable to care for it.[32]

Every element of this description is cast in terms either that highlight her limitations and inabilities, or that stress her difference from expected intellectual or bodily norms. We learn little subsequently about her that is not cased in terms of her deficiencies of 'normal' attainment, eg what she wants; what she enjoys; whether she wants to have a sexual relationship; whether she wants children; what she might wish for herself in the future. If such matters were not ascertainable, there is no discussion as to what interventions might be appropriate to elicit this information. These matters are simply not within the frame of reference for their Lordships in determining what is in

---

[32] *Re B* (n 2 above) 202.

Jeanette's best interests. Similarly, we see the courts making reference to her vulnerability as if this is an inescapable feature of her impairment, rather than the result of the impact of her environment. Lord Hailsham reports that she is at risk of sexual exploitation, having previously been found 'in a compromising situation in a bathroom',[33] while Lord Oliver notes that she has made sexual approaches to the staff and has been touching her genitals. There is no alternative response to Jeanette's sexual vulnerability that hinges on support and intervention to safeguard Jeanette's wellbeing.

This narrative of the disability as being inherent in the person, rather than a product of social, political and economic organisation drives the construction of learning disability presented by the courts here. It resonates with traditional narratives of people with learning disabilities as the embodiment of defect, present in a range of forms from the medieval period.[34] That narrative underwent further refinement and assumed particular prominence in the early twentieth century, whereby the association of learning disability with social contagion was actively produced through the perpetuation and acceptance of eugenic ideology. People with learning disabilities, along with other minority groups, were regarded as responsible for social decline through their procreation. The development and orientation of medical knowledge to investigate the supposed organic causes of social degeneracy and to improve racial and genetic purity, served not only to consolidate the primacy of medical practitioners as possessing superior expertise in the field of learning disability (in contrast to the care and support provided by voluntary organisation and lay people) but also to frame the person with learning disabilities as inherently risky. While the United States Supreme Court in *Buck v Bell* had confirmed the constitutional propriety of sterilisation, noting that 'three generations of imbeciles are enough',[35] the management of the social risks supposedly posed by people with learning disabilities was secured in the United Kingdom primarily by way of sexual segregation within institutions. The ideology was present, its means of implementation differed. Indeed, it was noted by the *Departmental Committee on Sterilisation* in 1933, that the voluntary (meaning non-objecting rather than consensual) sterilisation of 'defectives' would not obviate the need for institutional confinement, noting that 'the impossibility of procreation will not save them from being a social menace'.[36] By the time of Jeanette's case before the House of Lords, the damaging impact of eugenic ideology was continuing

---

[33] ibid 203.
[34] See, eg the range of conceptualisations of the person with learning disabilities as change-ling, as a product of a mother's sexual intercourse with the devil; as punishment for the wrongs of mankind in general, or of the parents in particular. Ryan and Thomas (n 13 above) ch 5.
[35] *Buck v Bell* 274 US 200 (1927) 207 (Oliver Wendell Holmes Jr).
[36] *Report of the Departmental Committee on Sterilisation* (Cmd 4485, 1933) [53]. Note that although the Report unanimously supported 'voluntary' sterilisation for eugenic purposes, its recommendations were never implemented.

to be exposed.[37] Whether the judiciary would be willing to defer to clinical expertise over the appropriateness of a practice which had historically been complicit in the execution of eugenic policies, was of particular interest. There is no doubt that the shadow of eugenic ideology, which had supported the mass sterilisation of hundreds of thousands of socially undesirable individuals in order to guarantee a genetically superior population,[38] hung conspicuously over their Lordships' deliberations.

Their Lordships were forceful in their disavowal of any association between their decision making and eugenic ideology.[39] Despite that, there are disquieting references to Jeanette which resonate with some of the ideas surrounding, in particular, the sexuality of people with learning disabilities during that era. The association between learning disability and animality, widely reported in legal other domains, finds expression in the courtroom. Jeanette's vulnerability to sexual exploitation is significantly considered not only to be a risk to her own wellbeing, but also to present 'a danger to others', for example.[40] Quite what 'danger' their lordships had in mind is not articulated here. We are also told that when Jeanette is first placed in residential care, she is 'like a wild animal'.[41] These associations echo the animalistic imagery reportedly used by care workers supporting adults with learning disabilities in a long stay hospital in the late 1970s, and the framing of consent as defence to sexual offences as being satisfied if the woman with learning disabilities gave in to her 'animal instinct'.[42] This association of her animal-like nature, serves to underscore Jeanette's difference and legitimises a range of interventions that may not otherwise be considered

---

[37] By the late 1970s, many jurisdictions had abolished eugenic sterilisation laws. See, eg BM Dickens, 'Sterilization and Retardation' (1982) 5 *International Journal of Law & Psychiatry* 295, 304.

[38] See, eg G Broberg and N Roll-Hansen (eds), *Eugenics and the Welfare State: Sterilization Policy in Norway, Sweden, Denmark, and Finland* (Michigan State University Press, 2005); PA Lombardo (ed), *A Century of Eugenics in America: From the Indiana Experiment to the Human Genome Era* (Indiana University Press, 2011); E Dyck, *Facing Eugenics: Reproduction, Sterilization, and the Politics of Choice* (University of Toronto Press, 2013); A Bashford and P Levine (eds), *The Oxford Handbook of the History of Eugenics* (OUP, 2010).

[39] *Re B* (n 2 above) 202 (Lord Hailsham); 204 (Lord Bridge); 207 (Lord Oliver).

[40] ibid 202.

[41] ibid 204.

[42] 'They're like cattle, aren't they? ... They look like a bunch of fucking monkeys, don't they', Ryan and Thomas (n 13 above) 62. The notion of a woman with learning disabilities having animal instincts which would provide a defence to a charge of unlawful sexual intercourse was first reported in 1866 in the case of *R v Fletcher* (1866) LR 1 CCR 39, 'a consent produced by mere animal instinct would be sufficient to prevent the act from constituting a rape'. See also, the case of *R v Jenkins* (2000), unreported, concerning the prosecution of a care worker for having unlawful sexual intercourse with a 'defective' in contravention of Sexual Offences Act 1956, s 7. In that case, the trial judge directed that the defence of consent was held to have been established when the woman relied upon her 'animal instincts'. For a summary of the case, see Law Commission, *Consent in Sex Offences: A Report to the Home Office Sex Offences Review* (Law Comm, 2000).

acceptable and to foreclose other ways of thinking about her that might open a different range of possibilities for supporting Jeanette. An exploration of the precise nature of Jeanette's sexual wants and desires is entirely absent from this assessment, possibly because there is an assumption here that this aspect of her is unknowable, immeasurable. The incommensurability of her sexuality can be read as requiring containment through surgical intervention.

## IV.  LAW'S DEFERENCE TO MEDICINE

The privileging of medical discourse in the sterilisation is secured through a predominantly medical determination of Jeanette's best interests. The prior question of Jeanette's capacity to consent is largely unattended by their Lordships. The decision to sterilise in Jeanette's case is premised on a framing of her best interests as indicating, medically, only one credible solution. Whilst other professionals and lay people have been involved in supporting Jeanette, it is the medical narrative about risk which determines Jeanette's best interests in this case, demonstrating the strength of Beck's observation that 'the "third force" of jurisprudence has to take recourse to medically produced and controlled norms and circumstances, which according to the social construction of rationality can ultimately be decided only by medical people and by no one else'.[43] It is particularly striking to note, for example, that in assessing the relative risks and benefits of performing a sterilisation as opposed to resorting to other methods of contraceptive management, there is a very different approach taken to risk assessment. There is a very careful and detailed assessment of the risk of contraceptive failure by the court, which can be contrasted with the highly speculative discussion of the risk of pregnancy occurring. We are told that Jeanette is 'showing signs of sexual awareness and sexual drive'[44] and from this alone, the risk of pregnancy is anticipated.

Whilst the best interests principle provides the legal basis for the House's authorisation of the sterilisation procedure, it is significant that the court consults a consultant in obstetrics and gynaecology, a consultant paediatrician and a consultant in adolescent psychiatry to determine where Jeanette's best interests lie. Unsurprisingly, the focus of discussion turns on a detailed evaluation of the risks involved in alternative contraceptive options and the implications for Jeanette in giving birth, rather than a consideration of broader welfare factors pertinent to Jeanette's emotional wellbeing and future development. Eradicating the 'unacceptable risk of pregnancy',[45]

---

[43] U Beck, *Risk Society: Towards a New Modernity* (New Delhi, Sage, 1992) 210.
[44] *Re B* (n 2 above) 208.
[45] *Re B* (n 2 above) 206 (Lord Templeman).

medically determined, is sanctioned by their Lordships as the only effective solution, notwithstanding the absence of any appraisal of the psychological and emotional impact of subjecting Jeanette to a form of surgery to address an, as yet, speculative risk of pregnancy. The social care perspective sits at the margins in Jeanette's case and is significant only insofar as it can shed light on whether Jeanette would reliably accept contraceptive medication.[46] Whilst not mandated by legal doctrine to adopt a grossly medicalised analysis, the approach by the judiciary to such best interests determinations has been characterised as a form of 'covert *Bolam*-isation', in which the judiciary consider themselves effectively constrained from expressing preference for one body of responsible medical opinion over another, or from rejecting responsible medical opinion entirely.[47] In framing Jeanette's needs as medical, the court's approach to Jeanette's situation is firmly anchored in the traditional framing of the individual as the source of their difference; their bodies constituting the resource upon which the solution must be performed. In this way, the question for the House of Lords here was not 'what can we do for Jeanette?' but rather 'what can we do *to* her?'

This elevation of medical knowledge as the dominant source of knowledge to determine what should happen to Jeanette is exemplified in two further aspects of the House of Lords' ruling. Their Lordships rejected any such distinction between sterilisations that were termed in other jurisdictions as 'therapeutic'—targeted essentially at the treatment of disease or illness, or 'non-therapeutic', which was denoted to indicate a sterilisation for contraceptive purposes. This distinction had been accepted in other jurisdictions in order to determine whether a sterilisation might lawfully be performed at all,[48] or alternatively, whether its lawful performance would require prior judicial approval.[49] The distinction had no credible value, according to their Lordships and was irrelevant to the approach to decision making that characterised the welfare approach.[50] Moreover, with the exception of Lord Templeman, their Lordships identified nothing distinct about sterilisation that mandated judicial authorisation of sterilisation procedures.[51] The medical assessment of welfare, upon which healthcare decision making is predicated, is not recognised as providing only a partial, not to mention simplistic, framing of Jeanette's support needs. The assessment is understood as a private matter, to be resolved between doctors and the

---

[46] ibid 209.
[47] M Brazier and J Miola, 'Bye Bye Bolam: A Medical Litigation Revolution?' (2000) 8 *Medical Law Review* 85.
[48] *In re Eve* (n 6 above) 1, the Canadian Supreme Court indicated that only 'therapeutic' sterilisations could be authorised under the court's parens patriae jurisdiction.
[49] See, eg *Marion's Case* (1992) 175 CLR 218.
[50] See, eg *Re B* (n 2 above) 203 (Lord Hailsham).
[51] ibid 205–6.

patient's parents (or those who exercise parental responsibility) without the public scrutiny of the courtroom. This location of the family within the private sphere resonates with a range of legal interventions that have served to obscure deeply problematic practices from critical gaze.[52] It further rein-scribes the 'naturalness' of family (or, in the Jeanette's case, formal caring) relationships in which contraceptive decision making, recommended by medical professionals, becomes seen as part and parcel of family life into which the law need not and should not tread.

## V. THE PROBLEM OF RIGHTS

A potential counterpoint to the dominant medical framing of disability that may have assisted the judges in reaching their decision was to be found in the discourse of human rights. In the case of *Re D*, a case concerning the proposed sterilisation in 1976 of an 11-year-old girl with Sotos Syndrome, Heilbron J rejected the evidence of the consultant gynaecologist that the determination of D's best interests was an entirely medical exercise.[53] For Heilbron J, the determination of best interests must also have regard also to the social impacts on D in the short and long term, and recognise the impact of such a procedure on D's right to reproduce. Could the rhetoric of human rights displace the weight of medical privilege in the courtroom? Two such rights are thrown into sharp relief by the ruling in *Re B*: the right to liberty and the right to reproduce. Jeanette's case is emblematic of some of the concerns and preoccupations surrounding the move away from closely monitored childhood and making the transition to adulthood. They were not unique to people with learning disabilities and had attracted consider-able attention and reflection in legal and policy circles here and abroad dur-ing this period.[54] What sets Jeanette apart from most other children of her generation, however, is the presence of her disability and its accommodation within an institutional setting.

For people with learning disabilities in England and Wales, the com-menced closure of long-stay hospitals in the 1970s and 1980s was prompted in significant part by economic considerations (eg maintenance and repair costs, staffing costs, overcrowding in institutional care, coupled with a

---

[52] See, eg S Boyd (ed), *Challenging the Public/private Divide: Feminism, Law, and Public Policy* (Toronto ONT, University of Toronto Press, 1997).

[53] *Re D (a minor) (wardship: sterilisation)* [1976] Fam 185, 198.

[54] See, eg, the adoption of the *UN Convention on the Rights of the Child* 1989, General Assembly resolution 44/25 of 20 November 1989; BC Hafen and JO Hafen, 'Abandoning Chil-dren to Their Autonomy: The United Nations Convention on the Rights of the Child' (1996) 37 *Harvard International Law Journal* 449; The Children Act 1989, which confers the right of a child subject to an interim care order (s 38(6)), or a supervision order (sch 3, para 4(4)) who has made an 'informed decision' to refuse a medical or psychological examination.

growing population of people with learning disabilities)[55] rather than the success of the disability activists' mandate for social justice. During this period, people with learning disabilities were seen as objects of professional beneficence rather than bearers of rights. Whilst this period may be thought to have heralded a new transition of people into the community, into which people with learning disabilities were to enjoy 'patterns of life and conditions of everyday living which are as close as possible to the regular circumstances and ways of life of society',[56] individual liberty, however, was seen as a transactional commodity, whereby physical freedom would be secured at the expense of reproductive capacity. Certainly, narrative accounts by mental welfare officers and medical superintendants under the Mental Deficiency Act 1913, which remained in force until 1959, bear testimony to the practice of placing people with learning disabilities, currently living in the community, into institutional care, or subjecting them to increasing levels of community supervision and control if there were indications that they were forming a romantic attachment or making plans for marriage.[57] At that time, professional intervention resulted in a loss of physical liberty but retention of procreative freedom. In the 1980s, the trade-off is reversed.[58] It is noted in the Court of Appeal in Jeanette's case that other ways of seeking to protect her from pregnancy will have a detrimental impact on the extent to which she may enjoy her freedom. Dillon LJ notes that 'the greater freedom she is allowed, the greater obviously the risk of sexual intercourse and pregnancy'.[59] Jeanette's increased liberty is therefore necessarily secured, according to the Court, by limiting her reproductive choices.

Moreover, Jeanette's procreative rights are seen as contingent not only upon the extent of Jeanette's liberty, but also on her capacity to exercise them. Justice Heilbron, giving judgment in a case concerning the proposed sterilisation of an 11-year-old girl with learning disabilities 12 years previously, had explicitly acknowledged the impact of a proposed sterilisation on the girl's right to reproduce.[60] In Jeanette's case, their Lordships did not consider this argument to have merit. Lord Oliver noted that 'the right to reproduce is of value only if accompanied by the ability to make a choice and in the instant case there is no question of the minor ever being able to

---

[55] DHSS (n 17 above) [118].

[56] B Nirje, 'The Normalization Principle and its Human Management Implications' in RB Kugel and W Wolfensberger (eds), *Changing Patterns for Residential Services for the Mentally Retarded* (Washington DC, President's Committee for the Mentally Retarded, 1969).

[57] S Rolph, D Atkinson, M Nind and J Welshman, *Witness to Change: Families, Learning Difficulties and History* (Kidderminster, BILD, 2005) 117.

[58] See, eg parental and professional support for sterilisation at this time: E Brantlinger, 'Attitudes toward the Sterilization of People with Learning Disabilities' (1992) 17 *Journal of the Association of Persons with Severe Handicaps* 4; L Patterson-Keels, E Quint, D Brown, 'Family Views on Sterilization for their Mentally Retarded Children' (1994) 39 *Journal of Reproductive Medicine* 701.

[59] *Re B (a minor) (wardship: sterilisation)* [1987] 2 All ER 206, 209 h.

[60] *Re D* (n 53 above) 193.

make such a choice or indeed to appreciate the need to make one'.[61] The contingent nature of the right to reproduce articulated by their Lordships demonstrates that not all human rights are to be enjoyed equally.

Their Lordships discussion about the capacities necessary to exercise rights is particularly surprising, for the question of adolescent decision making had become critically important in legal contexts at the time of Jeanette's case. Only two years prior to this case, their Lordships had been called upon to determine the lawfulness of a DHSS circular which anticipated the provision of contraceptive advice and treatment to girls under the age of 16.[62] In determining that a young person under the age of 16 did not, by sole virtue of age, lack legal capacity to make decisions about medical treatment, Lord Fraser indicated that

> [p]rovided the patient, whether a boy or a girl, is capable of understanding what is proposed, and of expressing his or her own wishes, I see no good reason for holding that he or she lacks the capacity to express them validly and effectively and to authorise the medical man to make the examination or give the treatment which he advises.[63]

The significance of a child's intellectual abilities to make a decision about medical treatment was critical to their Lordships' ruling in *Gillick*. In so ruling, they outlined, at considerable length, and in terms which have subsequently been criticised for being overly-prescriptive,[64] the range of information that must be understood and appraised in order for a child's consent to contraceptive advice and treatment to be valid. At first sight, the *Gillick* ruling appeared to herald a new dawn for children's autonomy, offering the potential for increased engagement with young people to empower them in their healthcare choices, even in the face of parental opposition. This conceptualisation of the adolescent as a potential autonomous rights-bearer was reinforced in 1989 by the UK's ratification of the UN Convention on the Rights of the Child, which imposes an obligation on the state to

> assure to the child who is capable of forming his or her own views the right to express those views freely in all matters affecting the child, the views of the child being given due weight in accordance with the age and maturity of the child.[65]

---

[61] *Re B* (n 2 above) 211 (Lord Oliver).
[62] *Gillick v West Norfolk and Wisbech Area Health Authority and another* [1985] 3 All ER 402.
[63] ibid 409.
[64] *Gillick* (n 62 above) 423 (Lord Scarman): 'It is not enough that she should understand the nature of the advice which is being given: she must also have a sufficient maturity to understand what is involved. There are moral and family questions, especially her relationship with her parents; long-term problems associated with the emotional impact of pregnancy and its termination; and there are the risks to health of sexual intercourse at her age, risks which contraception may diminish but cannot eliminate. It follows that a doctor will have to satisfy himself that she is able to appraise these factors before he can safely proceed on the basis that she has at law capacity to consent to contraceptive treatment'.
[65] *UN Convention on the Rights of the Child* 1989 (n 54 above) Art 12.

Despite the commencement of what seemed, at least in 1985,[66] to mark significant shift in the courts conceptualisation of adolescent autonomy, which in turn heralded a thoroughgoing critique of the law's framing of the limits of parental authority, young women like Jeanette seemed conspicuously absent from such analyses. To some extent readers may not be surprised by this, given the extent of Jeanette's limitations that were acknowledged by the House of Lords. But the notion of adolescence as stage of transition common to all young people, during which an evolution of individual capacities takes place and which in turn warrants dwindling intervention by parents and other decision-making proxies, is foreclosed. Yet again, Jeanette's rights and opportunities for decision making are regarded as qualitatively and normatively distinct from those of non-disabled young people like Miss Gillick. Jeanette's disability is read by the courts as requiring a rather different legal mode of analysis and response.

Despite considerable changes to the institutional frameworks that accommodated and supported learning disabled people during this time, the narratives and discourses around disability which were established during the modern period continued to set the scene for Jeanette's case. Looking back at this point in time, however, it is apparent that a series of new ways of thinking about disability, human rights and the sexuality of people with learning disabilities were gaining momentum. Here, I examine what impact these competing narratives might have had on Jeanette's case and the young and adult women like her who were facing sterilisation. Such reflections are not intended to illustrate why the courts were wrong in their treatment of Jeanette, but to highlight that the ruling in *Re B* was unresponsive to these claims. These reasons for this failure of response are explored at the end of the chapter.

## VI. DISPUTING THE NATURAL—SEXUALITY AND DISABILITY AS SOCIALLY CONSTRUCTED

The framing of Jeanette's sexuality by their Lordships took place at a time when a new narrative around the sexuality of disabled people was becoming widely published in academic research literature. Drawing heavily on the sociological method of social constructionism, which gained momentum in the 1970s and 80s,[67] this body of work sought to break with the conceptualisation of sexuality as inherent and immutable, focusing instead

---

[66] The retreat from the second strand of their Lordships' ruling in *Gillick*, which focused on the limits of parental authority in the face of adolescent consent to treatment, is discussed at p 59 of this volume.

[67] The genesis of this analytical method is attributed in large part to PL Berger and T Luckmann, *The Social Construction of Reality: A Treatise in the Sociology of Knowledge* (New York, Anchor Books, 1966).

on the methods by which sexuality is socially situated and produced. Foucault's work in 1976 on the history of sexuality further charted the different historical shifts and 'surfaces of emergence' which made possible very different social and political responses to sexuality over time.[68] His work, particularly surrounding the role of medical science in normalising particular sexual practices and sexual partners, had the potential to challenge the medico-centric framing of sterilisation as an appropriate medical response. It is noteworthy, for example, that the recommendation that Jeanette be sterilised is framed almost entirely by reference to medical risks, and the social, emotional and developmental perspectives that ought to feed into such an analysis (examining for example whether Jeanette would like to have a sexual relationship or to have babies; whether she is able to make a decision about sexual contact or might be able to do so in the future; how, if she does not want to have sexual contact, she might be protected from abuse) are entirely absent. The constructionist approach, which characterised sexuality as a social rather than a natural phenomenon, not only identified and interrogated the two main stereotypes around which the sexuality of people with learning disabilities had been framed (the animalistic and the innocent) but opened up new ways of thinking about sexuality. This work was influential in interrogating the attitudes of various stakeholders to the sexuality of people with learning disabilities, but also explored how sexuality could be supported and accommodated at the level of policy,[69] operational planning,[70] skills training for staff and family members,[71] and support for individuals with learning disabilities.[72]

Similarly, this constructivist approach was forcing a radical rethink of the nature of disability and appropriate social responses to it. In 1975 the Union of the Physically Impaired Against Segregation conceptualised disability not as individual defect but saw responsibility for disabling practices as residing with our social structures and arrangements: 'In our view, it is society which disables physically impaired people. Disability is something imposed on top of our impairments, by the way we are unnecessarily isolated and excluded from full participation in society'.[73] This framing of disability had three critically significant impacts for policy and research in the 1970s

[68] M Foucault, *The History of Sexuality Volume 1: An Introduction* (New York, Vintage, 1990).

[69] A Craft (ed), *Mental Handicap and Sexuality: Issues and Perspective* (Tunbridge Wells, Costello, 1987).

[70] A Craft and M Craft, *Sex Education and Counselling for Mentally Handicapped People* (Tunbridge Wells, Costello, 1983).

[71] A Craft and M Craft (eds), *Sex and the Mentally Handicapped: Guide for Parents and Carers* (Routledge & Kegan Paul, 1978).

[72] H Dixon, *Sexuality and Mental Handicap: An Educator's Resource Book* (Wisbech, LDA, 1988).

[73] The Union of the Physically Impaired Against Segregation and the Disability Alliance, *Fundamental Principles of Disability* (London, UPIAS, 1975) 3.

and 1980s. First, it paved the way for an acknowledgment that the social environment is the genesis of disability and the cause of people's social exclusion; secondly, it cast the impact of disability is a matter of public concern, rather than an individual tragedy to be managed privately; finally it demanded that responses to tackle the inequalities arising from disability operate at a structural, rather than an individual level.[74] Whilst the social model advocated by activists and academics took some time to embed into policy frameworks at national and international level, it has been suggested that there are certainly traces of the social model of disability to be found in some social policy and parliamentary reports during this time. The 1979 *Report into Mental Handicap Nursing and Care*, examined the appropriate forms of professional support that should be provided to people with learning disabilities.[75] Although the recommendations of the report were not adopted, the Report is credited with devising 'a set of principles to guide all services, in terms very close to the sort of language that had appeared in the Normalization text and various publications and teachings in the UK and elsewhere'.[76] Certainly, the normalisation ethos—that individuals are supported to live socially valued roles—is one of the key principles around which the model of care advocated by the Report is constructed.[77] The Report identifies three key principles that are in tune with many of the values that underpin the social model of disability: the right to enjoy normal patterns of life; to be treated as individuals; and to receive appropriate support in order to benefit from social goods and develop their potential.[78] Moreover, the White Paper, *Caring for People: Community Care in the Next Decade and Beyond*,[79] which led to the National Health Service and Community Care Act 1990, has been recognised as offering, at least in terms of its underlying values if not its implementation, a systemic, person-centred framework for the provision of care which has been regarded as remaining faithful to the values of choice, inclusion,[80] rights and independence[81] that continue to underpin contemporary social policy on learning disability.[82]

---

[74] See, eg M Oliver and C Barnes, *The New Politics of Disablement* (2012) ch 1: 'The social model breaks the causal link between impairment and disability. The reality of impairment is not denied but is not the cause of disabled people's economic and social disadvantage. Instead, the emphasis shifts to how far, and in what ways, society restricts their opportunities to participate in mainstream economic and social activities, rendering them more or less dependent ... the social model therefore shifts attention to disabled people's common experiences of oppression and exclusion and those areas that might be changed by collective political action and social change'.

[75] *Report into Mental Handicap Nursing and Care* (Cmnd 7468, 1979).

[76] Malin and Race (n 21 above) 316.

[77] *Report into Mental Handicap* (1979) n 75 above, ch 3.

[78] ibid [89].

[79] *Caring for People: Community Care in the Next Decade and Beyond* (Cm 849, 1989).

[80] Malin and Race (n 21 above) 323.

[81] K Bunning and S Horton, '"Border Crossing" as a Route to Inclusion: A Shared Cause with People with a Learning Disability' (2007) 21 *Aphasiology* 9, 14.

[82] Department of Health, *Valuing People: A New Strategy for Learning Disability for the 21st Century* (Cm 5082, 2001).

## VII. REPOSITIONING THE 'MEDICAL'

Despite their Lordships' adherence to medical knowledge in order to pronounce upon Jeanette's best interests, a challenge to the dominance of medical knowledge and proxy decision making in relation to children in the courtroom was taking root at home and abroad. Judicial engagement with the ethical doctrine of informed consent had invited an appraisal of the role of the judiciary in determining what information a patient needed to receive in order to make a healthcare decision. In short, the question to be determined was whether the judiciary should defer to medical expertise as to what information concerning risks, side-effects and possible alternatives to the proposed treatment the patient ought to be given. By the time of the ruling in Jeanette's case, many jurisdictions had rejected the claim that information disclosure is simply part and parcel of the clinician's expertise and ought, therefore, be determined according to conventional clinical negligence principles. Preferring instead to determine liability according to what a reasonable person in the patient's position would want to know, rather than what a reasonable doctor considered it appropriate to disclose, was seen as a means through which effective respect to patient autonomy could be paid and the role of clinicians circumscribed.[83] Whilst the House of Lords had rejected such an approach in 1985,[84] there was recognition by the majority of their Lordships in *Sidaway* that there would be some medical risks that it was incumbent upon medical practitioners to disclose, irrespective of the bounds of clinical judgement.[85] Although the limits on clinical discretion here are modest indeed, we see here the beginnings of a judicial evolution which increasingly takes seriously the importance of patient autonomy and the necessary judicial oversight that must be deployed to evaluate the legitimate exercise of medical discretion. Amounting to nothing more than 'restoring *Bolam* to its proper limits',[86] the judgment at least signals a willingness to challenge medical power, albeit in its most extreme and exceptional manifestations. Allied to this development is the House of Lords' ruling in *Gillick* that a young person below the age of 16, and therefore outwith the scope of the Family Law Reform Act 1969, acquired decision-making rights in respect of medical treatment and advice that could not be over-ridden or vetoed by her parents. The emergence of a discourse of entitlement in the context of children's medical treatment in *Gillick*, such that 'parental right yields to the child's right to make his own decisions

---

[83] See, eg *Reibl v Hughes* [1980] 2 SCR 880.

[84] *Sidaway v Board of Governors of the Bethlem Royal Hospital and the Maudsley Hospital and Others* [1985] AC 871.

[85] ibid 895 (Lord Keith); 900 (Lord Bridge); 903 (Lord Templeman).

[86] See Brazier and Miola, 'Bye Bye Bolam' (2008) n 47 above.

when he reaches a sufficient understanding and intelligence to be capable of making up his own mind',[87] offered the opportunity for increased decision making by young people in the health domain. It was also understood, by logical implication, to indicate that a minor's capacitous refusal of medical treatment and advice could not be over-ridden, thereby restricting unwanted medical intervention.

These judicial innovations, whilst in both cases acknowledging that clinical judgement would be displaced or limited in 'exceptional' circumstances, at least offered the prospect of a different mode of analysis of the proper role of medical knowledge in cases such as Jeanette's. Allied with the shifting intellectual conceptions of disability and sexuality, we may pause to reflect on what impact, if any, these changes have had subsequently.

## VIII. THE POSSIBILITIES FOR LEGAL TRANSFORMATION

The mode of reasoning adopted by their Lordships in Jeanette's case set the tone for the sterilisation cases that were reported subsequently. All but two cases concerned the sterilisation of women and most concerned the proposed sterilisation of adults rather than minors. Judicial deference to medical knowledge as a determinant of a person's best interests continued to dominate proceedings throughout the 1980s, resulting in conceptions of impairment that remained faithful to individual rather social models of disability.[88] The courts continued to premise their judgments on unsophisticated accounts of learning disability, which remained steeped in narratives of tragedy and dysfunction through the referencing of the person's abilities in terms of mental age,[89] their functional inabilities and a negation of the possibility of social and emotional advancement.[90] Moreover, the dual framing of the sexuality of people with learning disabilities as either animalistic or child-like[91] foreclosed any sophisticated assessment of how services might support an individual with learning disabilities to lead a sexual life,[92] and ignored what had become by the 1990s a well-documented

---

[87] *Gillick* (n 62 above) 422 (Lord Scarman).

[88] See, eg *T v T* [1988] Fam 52.

[89] See, eg *Re P (a minor) (wardship: sterilization)* [1989] 1 FLR 182.

[90] Re M *(a minor) (wardship: sterilization)* [1988] 2 FLR 497.

[91] *Re SL (adult patient) (medical treatment)* [2001] Fam 15; *Re A (medical treatment: male sterilisation)* [2000] 1 FLR 549. For a critical commentary on the framing of sexuality, see K Keywood, '"I'd Rather Keep Him Chaste": Retelling the Story of Sterilisation, Learning Disability and (Non-)Sexed Embodiment' (2001) 9 *Feminist Legal Studies* 185.

[92] In *Re W (mental patient) (sterilisation)* [1993] 1 FLR 381, 383, Hollis J commented that a 20-year-old woman could not be taught to protect herself from unwanted sexual advances and that consequently there was a risk that someone might take advantage of her. It was not recognised, however, that the elimination of the risk of pregnancy would do nothing to eliminate the risk of sexual abuse.

risk of sexual abuse.[93] Indeed, this deference was cemented further in 1989 when the House of Lords ruled that the *Bolam* principle was to provide the legal mechanism upon which the clinical determination of best interests decision making for adults lacking capacity was to rest.[94] Its effects were shocking and resulted in charges that this 'would protect all but the complete maverick whom not one of his colleagues would back in his decision to sterilise',[95] until the Court of Appeal restricted the role of *Bolam* in this domain 10 years later.

## IX.  AN INCREASED SCRUTINY?

In the late 1990s, there is a gradual shift to a more proactive approach by the judiciary. This consisted of the judges scrutinising more closely the stated risks of pregnancy and examining the risks associated with the performance of a sterilisation. In *Re S*, for example, there is explicit acknowledgment from Johnson J that the risks concerning future pregnancy are largely speculative and must be weighed in the balance as against the more certain risks associated with the performance of surgery.[96] And an acknowledgment of the risks of sexual abuse, which are not eclipsed by the performance of a surgical procedure.[97] There remains, however, a reliance on sterilisation as an appropriate response to increased freedom experienced by people with learning disabilities living in the community and there remains little recognition of the impairing impacts of a system of social organisation which is prepared to sacrifice reproductive liberty when support arrangements are wanting.[98]

In the years that followed, further changes in the courts' approach evolved slowly, against a backdrop of further legal and policy developments, which ranged from the extended reach of socially-grounded models of disability to issues of global development,[99] the development of national strategies to

---

[93] The publication in 1989 of early research on sexual abuse and learning disability paved the way for subsequent studies on the incidence of abuse. See A Craft and H Brown (eds), *Thinking the Unthinkable: Papers on Sexual Abuse and People with Learning Difficulties* (London, FPA Education, 1989); V Turk and H Brown, 'The Sexual Abuse of Adults with Learning Disabilities: Results of a Two-Year Incidence Survey' (1993) 6 *Mental Handicap Research* 193.

[94] *Re F (mental patient: sterilisation)* [1990] 2 AC 1.

[95] M Brazier, 'Down the Slippery Slope' (1990) 6 *Professional Negligence* 25, 27.

[96] *Re S (medical treatment: adult sterilisation)* [1998] Fam Law 325.

[97] See, eg *Re LC (medical treatment: sterilisation)* [1997] 2 FLR 258.

[98] Johnson J's remarks are particularly striking here: 'It is ironic that if a young woman is being cared for and supervised by caring and responsible parents, then the wish of the parents is to be overridden; whereas a similar decision will be upheld if made by parents who are careless and irresponsible'. *Re S* (n 96 above) 325.

[99] See, eg M Carpenter, 'The Capabilities Approach and Critical Social Policy: Lessons from the Majority world?' (2009) 29 *Critical Social Policy* 351; T Burchardt, 'Capabilities and Disability: the Capabilities Framework and the Social Model of Disability' (2004) 19 *Disability & Society* 735.

improve inclusion for disadvantaged patients groups,[100] the introduction of disability discrimination legislation,[101] the entry into force of the Human Rights Act 1998 and, more recently, the United Kingdom's ratification of the United Nations Convention on the Rights of Persons with Disabilities in 2007.[102]

The speed of this transformation may seem to some to be lamentably slow. Of course this is in part because conceptual transformations inevitably take a considerable time to bed down into local and national policy and still longer in terms of operational implementation.[103] It is also important to note that a number of legal and policy discourses in this field cut across one another and did not produce a unified set of claims upon which a responsive solution for young people with learning disabilities could be reached. To offer one example here, the legal transformations concerning the repositioning of clinical judgement in the courtroom in the mid-1980s did not remain constant. Despite the optimism that the *Gillick* ruling heralded a new dawn for adolescent autonomy, the courts rapidly retreated from any conferral of adolescent rights in respect of treatment decision making and have made plain the role of medical expertise as a gatekeeper of children's decision-making opportunities. The ruling in *Re R*[104] marked a sharp retreat from *Gillick*, indicating that the competent child has a right to make decisions about treatment that the doctor considers is in her best interests. Where the child refuses treatment, it may nevertheless be provided by a person with parental responsibility or by the Court. In consequence, it is not the right of the *Gillick* competent child to consent to or refuse treatment which determines the lawfulness of medical treatment, but rather the exercise of medical judgement in determining what is in the patient's best interests. This retreat from the potentially empowering ruling in *Gillick* has prompted commentators to revisit the ruling and identify, concealed beneath the surface of an apparently emancipatory ruling, a firm judicial deference to medical expertise to determine when contraceptive advice and treatment should be given.[105] The rhetorical and normative force of rights, whether at domestic or international level, has yielded no significant shift in

---

[100] Department of Health, *Our Health, Our Care, Our Say: A New Direction for Community Services* (Cm 3767, 2006).

[101] Disability Discrimination Act 1995. See also, Equality Act 2010.

[102] A/RES/61/106.

[103] See, eg T Gilbert, A Cochrane and S Greenwell, 'Professional Discourse and Service Cultures: An Organisation Typology Developed From Health and Welfare Services for People with Learning Disabilities' (2003) 40 *Journal of Nursing Studies* 781.

[104] *Re R (a minor) (wardship: consent to treatment)* [1992] Fam 11.

[105] J Miola, *Medical Ethics and Medical Law: A Symbiotic Relationship* (Bloomsbury, 2007) ch 5.

outcome for young people's decision making.[106] Moreover, despite further limitations of judicial deference to medical knowledge in the field of negligent information disclosure and a greater acknowledgment of the primacy of patient autonomy in medical decision making,[107] the extent to which the judiciary may determine that information disclosure is negligent, notwithstanding the exercise of clinical judgement, remained sharply contested until 2015.[108] The dominance of medical knowledge in the courtroom remains alive and well almost 30 years on.

## X.  A SYSTEM RESPONSIVE TO CHANGE?

Efforts have been underway for very many years to bring about legal transformation and yet still the shift to a different way of thinking about learning disability is slow to evolve. A systems-theoretical analysis of this medical dominance would locate the rationale for judicial deference not only as a manifestation of the professionalisation mandate deployed by medicine, but also as one means of ensuring legal coherence and normative integrity.[109] If we regard law as a distinct system, with its own rules of operation and norms of viability, we must accept that there is no unmediated access to non-legal knowledge. Adopting this perspective, John Harrington highlights the circularity of much judicial reasoning, whereby judicial pronouncements are premised on ethical codes which in turn are premised on legal pronouncements in order to demonstrate the paradoxical nature of law; it is different from other forms of knowledge yet it must engage with them without sacrificing its own disciplinary integrity.[110] That integrity is safeguarded by means of a series of programming strategies that include a 'mix of distinctions and displacements'[111] in order to recreate and rationalise non-legal knowledge in legal judgments. One such displacement—the deferral to medical knowledge—has been manifest in the context of best interests decision making in sterilisation cases, to the detriment of other perspectives.

---

[106] S Fovargue and S Ost, 'Does the Theoretical Framework Change the Legal End Result for Mature Minors Refusing Medical Treatment or Creating Self-Generated Pornography?' (2013) 13 *Medical Law International* 6.

[107] See *Pearce and another v United Bristol Healthcare NHS Trust* (1998) 48 BMLR 118; *Chester v Afshar* [2004] UKHL 41.

[108] *NM v Lanarkshire Health Board* [2015] UKSC 11.

[109] For a consideration of this perspective in the context of sterilisation cases, see K Keywood, 'Disabling Sex: Some Legal Thinking about Sterilisation, Learning Disability and Embodiment' in A Morris and S Nott (eds), *Well Women: The Gendered Nature of Healthcare Provision* (Aldershot, Ashgate, 2002).

[110] J Harrington, 'Of Paradox and Plausibility: The Dynamic of Change in Medical Law' (2014) 22 *Medical Law Review* 305, 311.

[111] ibid 311.

When viewed in this way, we may come to see that judicial deference to medicine may be seen as an important, albeit ultimately unhelpful strategy for the effective functioning of law. This is not to suggest, however, that other strategies for change are precluded. Law remains, despite its normative closure, cognitively open and able to respond to the communications from the social system, or from other closed subsystems such as medicine. By way of illustration, it is worth reflecting on an important shift in the way in which the law has responded to the changing conceptions of disability and to the need to incorporate non-medical factors into best interests decision making. This was achieved through a refinement of the role played by the *Bolam* principle under the common law framework for adults lacking capacity and a re-evaluation of the factors relevant to best interests decisions for minors. In 2000, the Court of Appeal identified two stages to the process of best interests decision making, indicating that the role of clinical judgement is to outline, through the exercise of responsible medical practice, the range of medical options that might be offered to the patient.[112] The role of the court, or the decision maker, was then to elect from those options that which is best, taking into account a range of non-medical factors.[113] Thus while what is best may be selected from a range of medical options, it will not necessarily be so. This strategy of distinction places *Bolam* within firm doctrinal parameters, thereby freeing up the court to consider a range of non-clinical factors such as the patient's emotional wellbeing,[114] her wishes,[115] the potential for future changes in her circumstances,[116] the opportunity to provide support to facilitate her decision making,[117] and her happiness.[118] Whilst this broad array of non-medical perspectives did not feed immediately into the courts' deliberations, it is clear that there has been an increased, albeit slowly-evolving and somewhat piecemeal, recognition of the relevance of these factors. It is highly likely that were Jeanette to appear before the courts today, her case would receive a very different form of legal scrutiny.

---

[112] *Re SL* (n 91 above).

[113] *Re SL* (n 91 above) 27.

[114] See Munby J's observations concerning the proposed termination of pregnancy in respect of a 14-year-old girl: 'A child or incapacitated adult may, in strict law, lack autonomy. But the court must surely attach very considerable weight indeed to the albeit qualified autonomy of a mother who in relation to a matter as personal, intimate and sensitive as pregnancy is expressing clear wishes and feelings, whichever way, as to whether or not she wants a termination': *In the Matter of X (a child)* [2014] EWHC 1871 (Fam) [10].

[115] *An NHS Trust v DE* [2013] EWHC 2562 (Fam).

[116] See, eg *A Local Authority v K* [2013] EWHC 242 (COP).

[117] *Mental Health Trust and another v DD (by her litigation friend, the Official Solicitor) and another* [2014] EWCOP 13.

[118] *An NHS Trust* (n 115 above).

The law must, of course, be responsive to the social environment and further challenges in the field of disability politics lie ahead. New paradigms such as vulnerability[119] offer potential for yet further reframing of the legal response to the sexuality of young people with learning disabilities. The dynamic and contingent nature of legal transformation means that the story of sterilisation will never be fully told. The story continues to evolve, new possibilities emerge and, with these shifts, there are new opportunities for change and resistance in the way things come to be understood.

[119] See, eg C MacKenzie, W Rogers and S Dodds (eds), *Vulnerability: New Essays in Ethics and Feminist Philosophy* (Oxford, Oxford University Press, 2014); M Fineman and A Grear (ed), *Vulnerability: Reflections on a New Ethical Foundation for Law and Politics* (Aldershot, Ashgate, 2013).

# 4

# *Re B (A Minor) (Wardship: Medical Treatment)* [1981]

## 'The Child Must Live': Disability, Parents and the Law

### JONATHAN HERRING

### I. INTRODUCTION

SHOULD A SEVERELY disabled baby be allowed to die? Or even be euthanised? To some such questions are offensive, implying that the life of a disabled child[1] is worth less than any other child. It relies on a host of negative assumptions about disabled people. The only good thing about such questions is that they make explicit the unpleasantness of the claim that the lives of disabled people are not worth living, which is otherwise kept under the surface.

The case under discussion in this chapter, *Re B (a minor) (wardship: medical treatment)*[2] can be seen as a victory for disability rights. The court firmly rejected the view of the parents that it was best to let a disabled child die. When I discuss this case with students there is near universal horror at the attitude taken by the doctors and parents, and relief at the court's response. At the time of *Re B* it has been claimed it was common practice to bring about the deaths of children with learning difficulties or physical impairments.[3] It is often suggested when *Re B* is discussed that our attitudes towards disability have progressed; the sad history can be put behind us;

---

[1] There is debate over the correct terminology to use. I use the term disabled child, as it is the most commonly used by disabled people writing within the disabilities studies movement because it captures the notion that a person is disabled (predominantly or solely) by oppressive circumstances and social structures, rather than disability being something inherent in the person.

[2] *Re B (a minor) (wardship: medical treatment)* [1990] 3 All ER 927.

[3] J Read and L Clements, 'Demonstrably Awful: The Right to Life and the Selective Non-Treatment of Disabled Babies and Young Children' (2004) 31 *Journal of Law and Society* 482.

and the case is an emblem of progress.[4] Yet in this chapter I will challenge that view. I will argue that despite its correct outcome the reasoning in the decision reveals many disablist attitudes and I will explore how the attitudes can still be found in the law and academic writing today.

## II. FACTS

There are limited details about the facts of the case because the court imposed reporting restrictions to ensure no news 'leaked out'. This summary of the facts is, therefore, largely taken from the court report. Baby Alexandra was born on 28 July 1981. She had Down's Syndrome (DS). She also had an intestinal blockage, which could be easily removed. Without its removal she would die within a few days. The parents believed it was better for her to die rather than live and suffer disabilities. That, they suggested, would be the kindest thing to do. One newspaper report said that Alexandra was the second child of a married couple from Chester and that the mother was in her thirties.[5] However, in her article discussing the case Dame Elizabeth Butler Sloss described the parents as 'elderly first time parents'.[6] So the exact circumstances of the couple are unknown. The surgeon agreed with the approach of the parents, stating:

> I decided therefore to respect the wishes of the parents and not to perform the operation, a decision which would, I believe (after about 20 years in the medical profession), be taken by the great majority of surgeons faced with a similar situation.[7]

The local authority[8] on learning of the case intervened and made Alexandra a ward of court.

At the first instance hearing, Ewbank J refused to grant the local authority's application, but the Court of Appeal, for reasons which shall be explained shortly, authorised the operation. The surgery was performed and was a success. The local authority indicated in the court proceedings that it intended to arrange for Alexandra to be adopted.[9] However, according to Michael Freeman, following the surgery Alexandra was returned to the care of her parents, who were by then willing to look after her.[10]

---

[4] Eg S Smith, *End of Life Decisions in Medical Care* (Cambridge, Cambridge University Press, 2012) 51.

[5] Anon, 'Down's Syndrome Baby's Mother had Six Tests', *The Times*, 11 August 1981.

[6] Rt Hon Dame Elizabeth Butler Sloss, 'Legal Aspects of Medical Ethics' (2006) 2 *Web Journal of Current Legal Issues* 1.

[7] *Re B (a minor)* (n 2 above), 928 g.

[8] It has never been identified.

[9] Anon, 'Handicap Babies "Drugged and Starved until they Die"', *The Glasgow Herald*, 2 October 1981.

[10] M Freeman, 'Do Children Have the Right not to be Born?' in M Freeman (ed), *The Moral Status of Children* (The Hague, Martinus Nijhoff, 1997) 171.

## III. THE JUDGMENTS

At first instance Ewbank J refused to authorise the procedure. He believed the wishes of parents in such cases had to be respected and that it was not in the best interests of the girl to be given the operation. On the same day the case was taken on appeal. The Court of Appeal overruled that judgment and authorised the procedure. At the heart of their approach was the principle that the court had to determine the best interests of the child. It was wrong to ask whether or not the wishes of the parents should be respected. That would be to create a presumption in favour of following the wishes of the parents. Instead the focus of the court's attention should simply be on what was in the best interests of the child. The following passage in the judgment of Templeman LJ summarises the court's analysis:

> It is a decision which of course must be made in the light of the evidence and views expressed by the parents and the doctors, but at the end of the day it devolves on this court in this particular instance to decide whether the life of this child is demonstrably going to be so awful that in effect the child must be condemned to die, or whether the life of this child is still so imponderable that it would be wrong for her to be condemned to die. There may be cases, I know not, of severe proved damage where the future is so certain and where the life of the child is so bound to be full of pain and suffering that the court might be driven to a different conclusion, but in the present case the choice which lies before the court is this: whether to allow an operation to take place which may result in the child living for 20 or 30 years as a mongoloid or whether (and I think this must be brutally the result) to terminate the life of a mongoloid child because she also has an intestinal complaint. Faced with that choice I have no doubt that it is the duty of this court to decide that the child must live.[11]

The Court of Appeal confirmed that generally it would be assumed that it was in a person's best interests to live. Applying the best interests test to this case it held that it had not been shown that the life of Alexandra would be so awful as not to be worth living. Dunn LJ stated that there was no evidence that this child's 'short life' was likely to be an intolerable one.

A central aspect of the judgment was the separation of the welfare of the child and the views of the parent. Even if the parents did not wish to care for a disabled child, the local authority was clear that adoptive or foster parents could be found to care for Alexandra. The parents were not being forced to care for a child against their wishes and so acting in her interests did not need to infringe their rights.

---

[11] *Re B (a minor)* (n 2 above) 929 e–f.

## IV. THE CONTEXT OF THE DECISION

Janet Reed and Luke Clements argue that the decision 'fundamentally recast the legal landscape'.[12] It is the first reported decision to make it clear that in cases concerning disputes over the medical treatment of children it is for the court, not the parents, to determine whether the operation can proceed. Further, the case makes it clear that the practice of allowing children to die, simply on the basis they were disabled, was not lawful.[13] While today that may seem unremarkable, as Reed and Clements note:

> Templeman in his extraordinary judgment simply came down in favour of life at a time when many respected physicians and large swathes of the public (not to mention Ewbank J and Farquarson J)[14] were not prepared to accord parentally rejected disabled babies this right. The fact that a child would live with disability was not sufficient grounds to justify ending a life ... Disabled babies and children were implicitly placed in a separate category from their non-disabled peers with the consequence that they need not be afforded the same rights or protections.[15]

The 1960s and 1970s had seen rapid improvements in the medical care of children, especially low weight babies. Increasingly, surgeons were faced with questions over the extent to which these treatments should be offered to disabled children. A typical attitude was expressed by John Lorber, a leading clinician, who was concerned that 'advanced techniques' should not be used to keep alive 'those who would have died but who now live with distressing physical or mental handicaps or both, often for years, without hope of ever having an independent existence compatible with human dignity'.[16] He advocated a policy of 'selective non-treatment' with the stated objective of avoiding treating those who would survive with 'severe handicaps', which was defined to include those who were 'retarded', including those with DS. Lorber's approach was described by Reed and Clement as 'influential, widely respected, and enduring'.

Fran Wright explains that this fitted in with broader attitudes towards disability:

> In the early 1980s, the view that a life with Down Syndrome was not a life worth living was not uncommon. Babies and children with Down Syndrome did not receive the same access to medical treatment as other babies and children. Medical conditions that were treated in 'normal' children were less likely to be treated where the baby or child had Down Syndrome. Even where treatment was on offer, when parents refused consent for that treatment, doctors were likely to accept the

---

[12] Read and Clements, 'Demonstrably Awful' (2004) n 3 above, 495–500.
[13] I Kennedy, 'Reflections on the Arthur Trial', *New Society*, 7 January 1982, 13.
[14] A reference to Farquarson J's judgment in the *Arthur* Case.
[15] Read and Clements (n 3 above) 487.
[16] J Lorber, 'Ethical Problems in the Management of Myelomeningocele and Hydrocephalus' (1975) 10 *Journal of the Royal College of Physicians* 47, 47.

parents' decision even if that meant that the child died. The lives of children with Down Syndrome were very different from those of other children. Where parents rejected or could not support a baby or child with Down Syndrome, the result was likely to be institutionalization. Children with Down Syndrome were usually schooled separately from other children and, as adults, were unlikely to have the opportunity to live independently or take paid work.[17]

It is when understood in this context that the decision in *Re B* can be seen as significant, indeed radical. So while the decision is uncontroversial in the current climate at the time it was not.

## V. CRITIQUE OF THE DECISION

As mentioned at the start of this chapter, in one sense the judgment can be seen as a victory for the rights of disabled people. The shocking attitude of the parents, supported by the judge at first instance, was firmly rejected by the Court of Appeal. They did not view DS as something so appalling that it rendered a life valueless. Notably the court sought to assess the life of the disabled child in her own right, not simply as an 'object' over which the parents had the power to decide or as a child defined entirely by the impact of her disability. Particularly welcome is the attempt of the court to focus on the quality of life from the perspective of *this* child, rather than from the viewpoint of some 'norm'.

In *Wyatt v Portsmouth Hospital NHS Trust* a decision of the Court of Appeal in 2005, Ward LJ, discussing *Re B*, indicated that society and the law had moved beyond the attitudes expressed by the parents and doctors in that case:

> What emerges clearly from *Re B*, in our judgment, is the bedrock proposition that the question which the court had to determine was what was in the best interests of B. Was it in her interests to have the operation, and live the life of a Down Syndrome child, or not to have the operation, and die literally within a week? Put in those stark terms, the answer in 2005 may seem much clearer than it was in 1981, given in particular our increased knowledge of the educational and social goals which many Down's Syndrome children are capable of achieving.[18]

With respect, I am less confident that we can proud of how we have move beyond the attitudes revealed in the *Re B* case. To explore why, I turn to two themes emerging from the writings from disability studies.

---

[17] F Wright, 'The More Things Change, the More they Stay the Same: Criminal Law, Down Syndrome, and A Life Worth Living' (2011) 1 *Law, Crime and History* 62.

[18] *Wyatt v Portsmouth Hospital NHS Trust* [2005] EWCA Civ 1881, [67].

## VI. THEORIES OF DISABILITY

As is well known there are two main theories of disability. The standard medicalised model sees disability as a departure from a norm. This is based on an idealised vision of what a body should be able to do and what it looks like. Notable variants from this ideal are treated as disabilities if they are seen to cause disadvantage. The primary response of the medical model to disability is to try and mend the body so that it accords to the norm or to ensure that disabled people are not born in the first place. The ideal for the medical model would the removal of all disability. Most disability activists reject that approach and advocate a social model.

The social model views disability as caused by the social conditions, which can render some things disabilities and others not.[19] It recognises that it is social forces which through their provision or lack of provision mean that certain forms of bodies are disabled: they are disabled by the fact that social spaces, services and provisions are modelled around certain kinds of bodies, to the disadvantage of others.[20] This is not limited to the lack of provision of physical equipment. Social expectations label certain children as having 'learning disabilities' because they lack selected skills[21] or because we do not value the skills they do have.[22] The 1976 Union of Physically Impaired Against Segregation (UPIAS), adopting the social model, defined disability in this way:

> Disability is something imposed on top of our impairments by the way we are unnecessarily isolated and excluded from full participation in society. Disabled people are therefore an oppressed group in society. To understand this it is necessary to grasp the distinction between the physical impairment and the social situation, called 'disability,' of people with such impairment. Thus, we define impairment as lacking part of or all of a limb, or having a defective limb, organ or mechanism of the body; and disability as the disadvantage or restriction of activity caused by a contemporary social organization which takes no or little account of people who have physical impairments and thus excludes them from participation in the mainstream of social activities. Physical disability is therefore a particular form of social oppression.[23]

Some commentators therefore distinguish between impairments, which are biologically caused restrictions on what a body can do, and disabilities

---

[19] For an excellent discussion see T Shakespeare, *Disability Rights and Wrongs* (London, Routledge, 2006).

[20] J Morris, 'Impairment and Disability: Constructing an Ethics of Care that Promotes Human Rights' (2001) 16 *Hypatia* 1.

[21] V Leiter, '"Nobody's Just Normal, You Know": The Social Creation of Developmental Disability' (2007) 65 *Social Science & Medicine* 1630.

[22] C Foster, 'My son's dyslexic and I'm glad': www.charlesfoster.co.uk/?p=590.

[23] Union of Physically Impaired Against Segregation, *Fundamental Principles of Disability* (UPIAS, 1975).

which cause adverse results from those impairments.[24] In his detailed analysis of DS people in the UK, Kahn concludes that the social model explains the most significant disadvantages they face:

> The argument here is that the experience of social discrimination as well as prejudice, stigmatisation, and a general history of segregation have done much to constrict the life opportunities of persons with Down's syndrome. These prevailing negative conditions and social circumstances have been, and continue to be, dominant factors in the various experiences of, and expectations for, disadvantage on the part of persons with Down's syndrome as well as their families.[25]

Rosemarie Garland Thomson, writing from a disability perspective, highlights the consequences of the social approach:

> First, it understands disability as a system of exclusions that stigmatizes human differences. Second, it uncovers communities and identities that the bodies we consider disabled have produced. Third, it reveals discriminatory attitudes and practices directed at those bodies. Fourth, it exposes disability as a social category of analysis. Fifth, it frames disability as an effect of power relations. Feminist disability studies shows that disability—similar to race and gender—is a system of representation that marks bodies as subordinate, rather than an essential property of bodies that supposedly have something wrong with them.[26]

I will not enter here into whether the social or medical model of disability is correct.[27] I largely favour the social model. I accept there are some limitations on bodies which can never be remedied by social provision. However, all our bodies suffer impairments of various kinds. One aspect of the social model is particularly significant and that is it highlights the way in which all bodies suffer restrictions and inabilities. We tend as a society to be proud of the 'accommodations' (such as wheelchair ramps) that we create to help 'disabled people' while ignoring all the many accommodations that are made for 'non-disabled people'.

There are clearly many issues to discuss in relation to these themes. However, I want to bring out two issues highlighted in the disability studies writing which underpin the attitude prevalent among doctors and wider society at the time of *Re B*, which I believe were in fact also reflected in the judgments in *Re B* and are still prevalent today.

---

[24] T Shakespeare, 'Choices and Rights: Eugenics, Genetics and Disability Equality' (1998) 13 *Disability & Society* 665.

[25] T Krahn, 'Regulating Preimplantation Genetic Diagnosis: The Case of Down's Syndrome' (2011) 19 *Medical Law Review* 157.

[26] R Garland-Thomson, 'Feminist Disabilities Studies' (2005) 30 *Signs* 1557.

[27] For a rejection of the social view see J Harris, 'Is there a Coherent Social Conception of Disability?' (2000) 26 *Journal of Medical Ethics* 95.

## A. False Division Between Ability and Disability

First, a sharp line is drawn between the able bodied and the disabled bodied.[28] There is a reaction of discomfort to an interaction with a 'disabled body' and perhaps a lurking fear that 'I might end up like that'.[29] I suspect this is behind the reinforcing of the disabled person as 'other'. A good example can be found in the language used by the Court of Appeal. The child is described as a 'mongol' and 'mongoloid'. The Down's Syndrome Association says the terms mongol or mong are offensive terms to describe children with DS. The objections to the term come from the fact it was developed from a suggestion that those with DS had the appearance of people from Mongolia. This reflects, arguably, an understanding of the disabled as 'strange' from a 'far away unknowable place'. In 1962 Mongolia delegates from the World Health Organization requested that the use of 'mongolism' and 'mongol' be dropped from WHO publications, as it reflected both disablist and racist connotations.[30] The WHO thereafter dropped use of the term. Concerns about this terminology were, therefore, present at the time of *Re B*, but were still used in the court, with an apparent lack of understanding of their potential for offence. Remarkably the term 'mongol' is even found in a court decision as late as 1997.[31]

This presentation of the disabled body as 'other' ignores our universal disability. As Martha Fineman has argued, vulnerability is a 'universal, inevitable, enduring aspect of the human condition'.[32] We are all limited by our bodies in different ways by what we can and cannot do. At different points in our lives, our bodies restrict us in different ways. In one sense at birth, we are all profoundly disabled and dependent on others. Even those in the 'prime of health' are dependent on others for services from public transport, to the supply of energy, to the provision of food.[33] We all have a range of limitations and society is willing to meet some by not all of them. Those which society does not meet are labelled as disabilities.

Rosemarie Garland-Thomson uses the term misfits to capture the way disabled people are side-lined. This is a helpful metaphor. It can be used to explain how at different points in lives and in different situations our bodies fit or fail to fit with the situation surrounding us. Rather than stigmatising the 'disabled' we should recognised our misfittedness that we all experience

---

[28] S Vehmas and N Watson, 'Moral wrongs, disadvantages, and disability: a critique of critical disability studies' (2013) *Disability & Society*, available at: dx.doi.org/10.1080/0968 7599.2013.831751.

[29] E Emens, 'Framing Disability' (2012) 5 *University of Illinois Law Review* 1383.

[30] Down's Syndrome Scotland, *Statement regarding Ricky Gervais' use of 'Mong' on Twitter* (Down's Syndrome Scotland, 2011).

[31] *Re T* [1997] 1 WLR 242, 249 (Butler Sloss LJ).

[32] M Fineman, 'The Vulnerable Subject: Anchoring Equality in the Human Condition' (2008) 20 *Yale Journal of Law and Feminism* 1.

[33] K Lindemann, 'The Ethics of Receiving' (2003) 24 *Theoretical Medicine and Bioethics* 501.

at different ways and in different times.[34] It invites society to think about what it does and does not provide to citizens. It would recognise the adaptability and resourcefulness used by 'misfits' and the way these are undeveloped in the fitting bodies. As Garland-Thompson argues, misfits can provide enormous benefits.

Claude Monet painted more impressionistically as he became blind. The artist Chuck Close evolved a distinctive style of realism in response to paralysis. The philosopher Jürgen Habermas recently wrote that the experience of having a cleft palate and the accompanying multiple surgeries positively shaped his intellectual development.[35]

## B. The Inability of Disability

Discussions of disability typically focus on what the disabled person cannot do. Templeman LJ in *Re B* stated:

> On the one hand, the probability is that she will not be a 'cabbage', as it is called when people's faculties are entirely destroyed. On the other hand, it is certain that she will be very severely mentally and physically handicapped.

Contrast the comments in *Re B* with Cobb J's comment on a recent case regarding an adult with DS: 'K is, by every account, a delightful, warm, engaging and affectionate young woman. She was born with Down's Syndrome and has an associated mild/moderate learning disability'.[36] What is refreshing about this is that K is not defined by her disability. The reference to it comes after a description of more important attributes. The emphasis is on what she is and what she can do, rather than what limits her. Sadly, it is far more common for disabled people to be defined by what they cannot do than what they can or what they are. It is no surprise that, therefore, parents seek to avoid their children being labelled by conditions they have.

There are several points to bring out here. The first is that the inability is defined as against a norm. As Clapton puts it:

> Such a construction, which privileges a particular understanding of personhood, assumes a prototypical disembodied person—that is, typically a male characterized by independence and the presence of rationality and reason; or in other words, that which constitutes, in the philosophical sense, 'normal'.[37]

The construction of this norm can be used as a tool of power. Negative discourses about disability move from an assumption of an 'inferior other'

---

[34] R Garland-Thomson, 'Misfits: A Feminist Materialist Disability Concept' (2011) 26 *Hypatia* 591.

[35] ibid 604.

[36] *A Local Authority v K* [2013] EWHC 242, [2].

[37] J Clapton, 'Tragedy and Catastrophe: Contentious Discourses of Ethics and Disability' (2003) 47 *Journal of Intellectual Disability Research* 540.

based on the fallacious argument that different from the norm means less worthy.[38] We are perhaps so used to these kinds of assessment being made by the court that we forget what we are doing.

The second is that a person is so much more than inabilities. We define ourselves by what we can do, not what we cannot.[39] So when Peter Singer writes:

> To have a child with Down syndrome is to have a very different experience from having a normal child. It can still be a warm and loving experience, but we must have lowered expectations of our child's abilities. We cannot expect a child with Down syndrome to play the guitar, to develop an appreciation of science fiction, to learn a foreign language, to chat with us about the latest Woody Allen movie, or to be a respectable athlete, basketballer or tennis player.[40]

My instinctive reaction is that I (who am in conventional terms abled bodied) cannot play the guitar; have absolutely no appreciation of science fiction; could not keep up a conversation on Woody Allen movies; nor hope to be a respectable performer in any of the sports mentioned. Does that make me 'abnormal'? We have in our lives many opportunities open to us and are able to take up only a few. We define ourselves by what we do, not what we decide not to do.

These attitudes, I have argued, underpin the attitude of the parents, but also the response of the court to disability in *Re B*. I will now argue how they can still be found in legal decisions and academic writing today.

## VII. THE NATURE OF PERSONHOOD

Some philosophers are very sympathetic towards the views of parents in *Re B*. Ethicist Jonathan Fletcher has written that there is

> no reason to feel guilty about putting a Down's Syndrome baby away, whether it's 'put away' in the sense of hidden in a sanitorium or in a more lethal sense. It is sad, yes. Dreadful. But it carries no guilt. True guilt arises only from the offence against a person, and a Down's is not a person.[41]

The reasoning behind such a view is that moral personhood is established through having a certain psychological and cognitive attributes. These may include, for example,

> self-consciousness, awareness of and concern for oneself as a temporally-extended subject; practical rationality, rational agency, or autonomy; moral responsibility;

---

[38] ibid.

[39] A Silvers, 'On the Possibility and Desirability of Constructing a Neutral Conception of Disability' (2003) 242 *Theoretical Medicine* 471, 479.

[40] P Singer, *Rethinking Life and Death* (1993) 256.

[41] A Soloman, *Far from the Tree: Parents, Children and the Search for Identity* (New York NY, Scribner, 2012) 181.

a capacity to recognize other selves and to be motivated to justify one's actions to them; the capacity to be held, and hold others, morally accountable.[42]

So Tooley argues: 'An organism possesses a serious right to life only if it possesses the concept of a self as a continuing subject of experiences and other mental states, and believes that it is itself such a continuing entity'.[43] This means that Tooley and others argue that very young babies and people with profound mental disabilities may lack the mental capacity necessary to give life its value. The lives of the profoundly disabled are worth less than others. There is some ambiguity over how mentally incapacitated a person must be for this to arise. Addressing DS specifically, Peter Singer, a leading philosopher in this camp, argues that parents of a DS child should be permitted to decide that their child should not receive medical treatment. He refers to one case, complaining that the child was kept alive against the wishes of her mother 'despite the fact that she would never be able to live an independent life, or to think and talk as normal humans do'.[44] He adds:

> We do not doubt that it is right to shoot badly injured or sick animals if they are in pain and their chances of recovery are negligible. To 'allow nature to take its course', withholding treatment but refusing to kill, would obviously be wrong. It is only our misplaced respect for the doctrine of the sanctity of human life that prevents us from seeing that what it is obviously wrong to do to a horse, it is equally wrong to do to a disabled infant.[45]

Such views are prominent in current debates. Probably the most cited article in medical ethics in recent years was a highly controversial article in the *Journal of Medical Ethics* by Alberto Giubilini and Francesca Minerva.[46] Here they suggest that new-born babies have not yet acquired sufficient attributes to become a person. 'Post-birth abortion' should therefore be permitted.[47] Giubilini and Minerva support the killing of DS babies because 'to bring up such children [children with DS] might be an unbearable burden on the family and on society as a whole, when the state economically provides for their care'. Their article and the literature that it spawned, both in favour and against, indicates that this issue is very much a live one.

There are a number of possible responses to these kinds of argument.

First, it may simply be that these writers lack an adequate understanding of what a disabled person is like. Several of the quotes above indicate

---

[42] D Wasserman, A Asch, J Blustein and D Putman, *Cognitive Disability and Moral Status*: plato.stanford.edu/entries/cognitive-disability/.
[43] M Tooley, 'Abortion and Infanticide' (1972) 2 *Philosophy and Public Affairs* 37, 44.
[44] P Singer, *Practical Ethics* (Cambridge, Cambridge University Press) 73.
[45] ibid.
[46] A Giubilini and F Minerva, 'After-birth Abortion: Why should the Baby Live?' (2013) 39 *Journal of Medical Ethics* 216.
[47] They accept infanticide might be the more common term but they prefer 'post-term abortion' to tie the practice into abortion.

a highly restrictive view about the quality of life and capabilities of a disabled person. Indeed, it seems implicit within Singer's argument in particular that if he were persuaded that the capabilities of a child with DS were much higher than he thought he would change his view. That may well be possible. Detailed studies of disabled people indicate that the despite the 'catastrophe narrative', there is 'disability paradox', namely that many disabled people have much happier lives than average, and families of disabled children report being better off than children with able bodied children.[48] Looking particularly at Down's syndrome, reports of family break up are much lower than many average families[49] and there are fewer problems raising DS children.[50] In one leading study[51] only 1 in 20 parents of children reported regretted having a child with DS, with the vast majority reporting they loved and were proud of the child.[52] Siblings have particular strong reports in pride and love for their DS sibling.[53] Of course raising a child with DS is not all roses, and parents with children with DS are required to spend more time care-giving than other parents, but that may be no bad thing.[54]

However, I think there is a more fundamental response to the arguments of Singer et al than discussing whether studies show that people with DS do or not suffer in various ways. That is because the abilities of those with DS (and many other conditions) vary enormously.[55] So much depends on social responses, education, parenting and biological development that we cannot say now, any more than we can of any baby, what abilities they will or will nor have in the future.[56] We can no more justify killing a DS baby because it might lack ability X, than we can kill any other baby on the same basis.

Secondly, and more fundamentally, their approach picks on intellectual understanding and abilities as being at the core of personhood. That is a view that I would fundamentally reject. I would locate the source of human value in terms of relationships of mutual recognition and concern, or memberships of a moral community.[57] Under such an approach mental capabilities are not central to relationships. I would argue that it is through

[48] Peter A Ubel et al, 'Whose Quality of Life? A Commentary Exploring Discrepancies Between Health State Evaluations of Patients and the General Public' (2003) 12 *Quality of Life Research* 599, 601, 603–4.

[49] R Urbano and R Hodapp, 'Divorce in Families of Children with Down Syndrome: A Population-Based Study' (2007) 112 *American Journal of Mental Retardation* 261, 261.

[50] B Skotko, S Levine and R Goldstein, 'Having a Son or Daughter with Down Syndrome: Perspectives from Mothers and Fathers' (2011) 155 *American Journal of Medical Genetics* 2335.

[51] ibid.

[52] ibid.

[53] ibid.

[54] A Esbensen, M Mailick Seltzer, 'Accounting for the "Down Syndrome Advantage"' (2011) 116 *American Journal of Intellectual Development and Disability* 3.

[55] Wright, 'The More Things Change' (2011), n 17 above.

[56] Krahn, 'Regulating Preimplantation' (2011), n 25 above.

[57] Wasserman et al (n 42 above).

our relationships that our human selves are made.[58] This is a bold claim I cannot establish here, but I would make the following points.

We define and understand ourselves in terms of our relationships. Whether as supporter of Chelsea Football Club or as a Catholic or as member of the Cumberbatch family, a person understands himself in connection to others. It is our relationships that give our life meaning, and constitute our identity. That is why bereavement and relationship breakdown are two of the greatest sadnesses most people experience. Yet our relationships are not based on intellectual interaction (although they can be). The rush of warmth for the new-born baby is not the recognition of a kindred mind. Relationships are constituted through a vast range of means, which are not restricted to the intellectual. Many people, for example, find sexual relations, in a particularly profound way, to be a very deep connection (although they need not be). There are points at which words fail and only a hug will do. These indicate that intellectual interaction is only part of what makes a relationship and need not be a central part of it.[59] Do many people seek in their friends intellectual capacity rather than humour, joy or kindness?[60] It is understandable that an academic, considering what is valuable in life, will highlight academic and intellectual skills. But there is so much more to life than our minds. The point is well captured by one parent of a DS child who says this:

> Those of us with a Down's Syndrome child (our son, Robert, is almost 24) often wish that all our children had this extraordinary syndrome which defeats anger and malice, replacing them with humor, thoughtfulness and devotion to friends and family.[61]

It is perhaps the response of Eva Feder Kittay to the arguments of Singer et al which is most interesting.[62] She cares for her daughter, Sesha, who is severely disabled. Her powerful essays reveal a struggle to respond intellectually to an argument she finds so disturbing. It cannot be easy to respond to an argument she interprets to mean that her daughter is not 'one of us'. It is not surprising that she seeks comfort in the suggestion that the views of writers such as Singer are based on a 'totally inadequate familiarity with the population that is adversely affected by the arguments they put forward'.

[58] A Jaworska and J Tannenbaum, 'Person-Rearing Relationships as a Key to Higher Moral Status' (2014) 124 *Ethics* 242.

[59] H Reinders, *Receiving The Gift Of Friendship: Profound Disability, Theological Anthropology, And Ethics* (Grand Rapids MI, Eerdmans, 2008).

[60] S Vehmas, 'Discriminative Assumptions of Utilitarian Bioethics Regarding Individuals with Intellectual Disabilities' (1999) 14 *Disability and Society* 37.

[61] Quoted in Ann Bradley, 'Why Shouldn't Women Abort Disabled Fetuses?' (September 1995) *Living Marxism* 82.

[62] E Feder Kittay, 'The Personal is Philosophical is Political: A Philosopher and Mother of a Cognitively Disabled Person Sends Notes From The Battlefield' in Eva Feder Kittay and Licia Carlson (eds), *Cognitive Disability and its Challenge to Moral Philosophy* (Oxford, Wiley-Blackwell, 2010).

She explains that intellectual capacity is not central to relationships because it is

> a place in a matrix of relationships embedded in social practices through which the relations acquire meanings. It is by virtue of the meanings that the relationships acquire in social practices that duties are delineated, ways we enter and exit relationships are determined, emotional responses are deemed appropriate, and so forth. A social relation in this sense need not be dependent on ongoing interpersonal relationships between conscious individuals. A parent who has died and with whom one can no longer have any interchange still stands in the social relation of parent to us, calling forth emotions and moral attitudes that are appropriate or inappropriate.[63]

## VIII.  BEST INTERESTS

A major theme from *Re B* is that where there is an issue brought before the court concerning the medical treatment of a child, the central question is the best interests of the child. The cases following *Re B* have consistently applied this and the courts have been reluctant to expand on it. As Lady Hale stated in *Aintree University Hospitals NHS Foundation Trust v James*: 'Every patient, and every case, is different and must be decided on its own facts'.[64] She quoted Hedley J, who wisely put it at first instance in *Portsmouth Hospitals NHS Trust v Wyatt*,[65] that '[t]he infinite variety of the human condition never ceases to surprise and it is that fact that defeats any attempt to be more precise in a definition of best interests'.[66] The current approach is summarised here *An NHS Foundation Trust v R (Child)*:

> The court must, taking account of all relevant matters and treating the child's welfare in the widest sense as its paramount consideration, decide what is in the child's best interests, looking at it from the child's point of view and applying a strong, though rebuttable, presumption in favour of a course of action that would prolong life.[67]

There is a considerable literature on the nature of the best interests test; the appropriate understanding of the sanctity of life and the correct weight to attach to parents views.[68] Here I will focus on the importance of the relationship between parents and child.

---

[63] ibid.

[64] *Aintree University Hospitals NHS Foundation Trust v James* [2013] UKSC 67, [36].

[65] *Portsmouth Hospitals NHS Trust v Wyatt* [2004] EWHC 2247 (Fam).

[66] *Aintree* (n 64 above) [23].

[67] *An NHS Foundation Trust v R (Child)* [2013] EWHC 2340 (Fam).

[68] R McDougall and L Notini, 'Overriding parents' medical decisions for their children: a systematic review of normative literature' (2013) 40 *Journal of Medical Ethics* 448.

Most of the recent cases on disputes over medical treatment[69] have involved cases where parents have objected to the withdrawal of treatment from children. The cases often have a similar flavour. The expert medical evidence sets out the child's condition and lists their inabilities. Typically their prognosis is of a short, painful life and their conclusion that it is best to let the child die or at least not intervene to keep the child alive. The parents, conversely, rely on their experiences with the child and emphasise their close relationship with the child.

A typical decision is the recent one of *An NHS Foundation Trust v R (Child)*.[70] The issue concerned whether ventilation would be withdrawn leading to death of a young boy called Reyhan. His family wanted him to live at home with long-term ventilation. The doctors believed this would be too burdensome. He had Down's Syndrome and Mitochondrial myopathy. He was described as having a minimal level of awareness. It was accepted that there was a drop in his heart rate when in contact with his family, suggesting a degree of awareness. The views of parents were summarised in this way:

> The parents do not consent to the withdrawal of treatment, due to their firmly held belief that Reyhan shares a loving bond with his family and has a quality of life that enables him to interact. They perceive that he experiences pleasure during their interactions with him and that this is indicated by a small smile, moving his eyes towards the sound of their voices, hand movements and increased activity. Moreover, as practising Muslims they hold conscientious beliefs about the sanctity of life and the duty of the family.[71]

Nevertheless the judge concluded that the removal of ventilation was appropriate. He concluded that there was no dependable evidence that Reyhan could 'interact cognitively or purposefully with his environment'. Despite the presumption in favour of life and the views of the parents, the judge concluded:

> I note the views of the family, who believe that he has greater abilities, and indeed that these will increase over time, but I find that these are not objectively verifiable but are better understood as a projection of their hopes and ambitions for him. Reyhan inspires them, and their great love for him is reflected back ... The family members wish to continue on this journey, believing that they can carry Reyhan on their shoulders and put him down only when the time is right. This in my view overlooks the reality. If Reyhan is to continue on the journey of long-term ventilation, he will have to walk every step of the way himself. Others can surround and

---

[69] *Wyatt v Portsmouth Hospital NHS Trust* [2005] EWCA Civ 1181; *NHS Trust v MB* [2006] EWHC 507(Fam); *Re OT* [2009] EWHC 633 (Fam); *NHS Trust v Baby X* (2011) 127 BMLR 188; *Re M* [2012] 1 WLR 1653.
[70] *An NHS Foundation Trust v R (Child)* [2013] EWHC 2340 (Fam).
[71] ibid, [14].

encourage him, but it is Reyhan, and Reyhan alone, who will have to bear the burdens while experiencing little if any pleasure. And the road that he would be asked to walk is one that would grow steeper with every passing week.[72]

There is no doubt this is a difficult case. There is much to welcome in the judicial recognition of the depth of the relationship between the family and child. However, adopting the approach made earlier in this chapter, the decision, I believe, does not adequately take into account the significance of the family-child relationship. If, as argued earlier, it is our relationships with others that constitute our selves and give value to our lives, the notion of attempting to consider the best interests of an isolated figure is a fiction. We need to consider the individual constituted by and understood within the context of their relationship. The talk here of Reyhan having to take the steps of his journey alone, albeit with encouragement from the family, fails to acknowledge the significance of the interconnected lives in these cases.

I am therefore arguing that we need to make a best interests assessment of this child, within the group of connected individuals, with their mutual responsibilities and love. This is not a matter of giving parents rights over the child but recognising the power of relationships. Jo Bridgeman in her excellent book captures these points well. Relying on the empirical evidence looking the relationship between parents, very sick children and the medical team, she emphasises that 'these babies are very highly valued, loved and grieved for'.[73] She argues:

> For a child to be allowed to die, following the order of a court, in circumstances in which the child's parents do not agree that it is in the best interests of their child must leave the parents with uncertainty about whether they did all they could to protect their child at a time when they most need the support of those who shared with them the journey through their child's life and death.[74]

She is critical of the legal framework which pits the competing views of parents and professionals against each other.[75] Much of the literature suggests that most parents seek a model where the doctors and parents work together for the good of the family, within a 'moral community', where each side listens to the others and has the freedom to talk through issues without condemnation to reach a decision which all can accept as valid and they can live with.[76] No doubt many medical professionals would seek that as well. The problem is that the current approach of the law takes the competing

---

[72] ibid, [47] and [60].
[73] J Bridgeman, *Parental Responsibility: Young Children and Healthcare Law* (Cambridge, Cambridge University Press, 2007) 194.
[74] ibid, 195.
[75] ibid, 195.
[76] L Caeymaex, M Speranza, C Vasilescu, C Danan, M-M Bourrat, M Carel and C Jousselme, 'Living with a Crucial Decision: A Qualitative Study of Parental Narratives Three Years after the Loss of Their Newborn in the NICU' (2011) 6 *PLoS ONE* e28633.

understandings and seeks to 'weigh them up' and to reach an 'objective' assessment of what is in the child's best interests. What in fact we have is different perspectives and it is not a matter of determining who has the best argument or the highest score on the balance sheet. Rather, the approach of courts should reflect a more collaborative approach.[77] We must particularly bear in mind the intense feeling among parents that they must do the best for their child.[78] No doubt a large part of the problem is the legal setting. A formal court hearing, often in haste, is not the appropriate setting for these cases. It should be recognised that the notion of best interests is a rich one and all parties have their own unique and important insights.

## IX. PRENATAL TESTING

Since *Re B* we have not had a case before the courts where parents have objected to treatment for a DS child. From a positive perspective this may reflect changing social attitudes towards disability. However, it may not. There is now extensive pre-natal testing for DS and the availability of abortion following a testing. A House of Commons survey found that 90 per cent of fetuses tested positive for DS were aborted.[79] Of the DS children born, the mothers of around 30 per cent had not been tested.[80] DS is probably the best known reason for pre-natal testing.[81]

Section 1(1)(a) Abortion Act 1967 states that a pregnancy of less than 24 weeks' duration can be terminated where 'the continuation of the pregnancy would involve risk, greater than if the pregnancy were terminated, of injury to the physical or mental health of the pregnant woman or any existing children of her family'. However, if the pregnancy is more than 24 weeks abortions are only allowed under two sets of circumstances. One involves a serious threat to the life of the mother. The other is where there is 'a *substantial risk* that if the child were born it would suffer from such physical or mental abnormalities as to be *seriously handicapped*'.[82]

This provision has been strongly criticised by disability activists. The complaint is commonly put in terms of the 'expressivist objection'. The weaker version of this argument suggests that when a woman decides

---

[77] I Laing, 'Conflict resolution in end-of-life decisions in the neonatal unit' (2013) 18 *Seminars in Neonatal Medicine* 83.

[78] M Goggin, 'Parents Perceptions of Withdrawal of Life Support Treatment to Newborn Infants' (2012) 88 *Early Human Development* 79.

[79] F Bruce, *Parliamentary Inquiry into Abortion on the Grounds of Disability* (House of Commons, 2013).

[80] ibid.

[81] E Prussinga, E Sobob, E Walkerc and P Kurtin, 'Between "Desperation" and Disability Rights: A Narrative Analysis of Complementary/Alternative Medicine Use by Parents for Children with Down Syndrome' (2005) 60 *Social Science & Medicine* 587.

[82] Abortion Act 1967, s 1(1)(d).

to have an abortion on the grounds of disability she is expressing the view that it is better that a child who is born with a disability is not born. As Erik Parens and Adrienne Asch put it: 'to select against disabling traits expresses a hurtful attitude about and sends a hurtful message to people who live with those same traits'.[83]

I do not find this straight forward presentation of the argument convincing. It is unlikely that there is a single reason of this kind in relation to abortion, which is complex. Most abortion decisions involve an agonised decision comparing competing factors and responsibilities.[84] To reduce them to a simple 'she aborted because of the disability' is unfair. Secondly, the decision is likely to be made in a particular context looking at the obligations and responsibilities of the particular individual. It cannot reasonable be taken as a general statement about disabled people.

A more persuasive version of the expressivist argument is as follows. The legislation promotes the view that disability alone is a good enough reason to permit abortion. The legislation (not the women making the decision) is declaring that disability is a sufficiently good reason to allow an abortion, even after 24 weeks. The precise justification for the decision is unclear. If the focus is on the disruption caused to the woman's life then the argument seems implausible. There are many reasons why the birth of a child can cause serious disruption to someone's life. Reasons connected to disability may be one, but there seems no reason to believe that the disruption caused by the child's disability is in a different league to say, an illness of the parents; the end of the parents' relationship; caring responsibilities to other family members. The legislation encourages a view that a single trait defines that person. As already mentioned, the case of DS covers a wide range of outcomes and tells you very little about an individual life. Yet the legislation and practice encourages that assumption.[85] Just to be clear, I am not arguing that abortion over 24 weeks should not be lawful,[86] I am arguing that singling out disability as one of the few grounds on which it is, is unjustifiable.

The provision must also be seen in light of the surrounding medical and cultural circumstances. One woman reports: 'We came under huge pressure to have an abortion and the strongest argument given was that a disabled child "would affect our lifestyle", in other words be a burden on us'.[87]

---

[83] E Parens and A Asch, 'Disability Rights Critique Of Prenatal Genetic Testing: Reflections and Recommendations' (1999) 29 *Hastings Center Report* 1.

[84] J Herring, 'The Loneliness of Status: the Legal and Moral Significance of Birth' in F Ebtehaj, J Herring, M Johnson and M Richards (eds), *Birth Rites and Rights* (Oxford, Hart Publishing, 2011) 97.

[85] Parens and Asch (n 83 above).

[86] I would allow termination of a pregnancy up to birth for reasons indicated in Herring (n 84 above).

[87] Bruce (n 79 above).

The House of Commons report found widespread evidence of assumptions that a positive test would lead to an abortion, and of a failure to properly inform women of what DS conditions are really like.[88] The statutory provision, medical advice and broader social assumptions combine to put considerable pressure on women to abort DS babies.

## X. CONCLUSION

*Re B* in some ways represented a positive step for disabled people. It involved a firm rejection of the view that the lives of disabled people were not worth living, being a tragedy for the individual and a catastrophe for the family. However, the decision and the ensuing case law and debates have continued to present highly negative attitudes towards disability. It has been argued in this chapter that much of the literature still emphasises a sharp divide between the able bodied and the disabled and fails to recognise our own inherent vulnerabilities and disabilities, and our reliance on social support and care. We also see a persistent focus on what disabled people cannot do, rather than a consideration of what they can. In the disability provisions in the Abortion Act and in the discussions of moral personhood a person's disability comes to define them and even challenge their moral status. This chapter has argued in favour of recognising our mutual disability and the importance of relationship in defining what we are. Lying behind *Re B* and much the debate is an unspoken assumption that the world would be a better place without 'disability'. To Sophia Isako Wong the response is clear:

> For me and 350,000 families at home with Down syndrome in the United States alone, the scenario of a world without people like Leo is just as horrifying and unimaginable as a world without women.[89]

I agree. Parents seek 'the perfect baby'.[90] Yet the perfect child would be as interesting as the perfect person. In short, not very interesting. It is in our foibles, our weaknesses and our quirks that make people so much fun and parenting so fascinating. It's our caring relationships that make our lives valuable. Disability is inherent to humanity, not an anathema to it.

---

[88] ibid. See also A Ho, 'The Individualist Model of Autonomy and the Challenge of Disability' (2008) 5 *Bioethical Inquiry* 193.

[89] S Wong, 'At Home with Down Syndrome and Gender' (2002) 17 *Hypatia* 89.

[90] Gail Heidi Landsman, *Reconstructing Motherhood and Disability in an Age of 'Perfect' Babies* (Abingdon, Routledge, 2009).

# 5

# *Airedale NHS Trust v Bland* [1993]

## CHARLES FOSTER

### I. INTRODUCTION

ON 15 APRIL 1989 Anthony Bland, then aged 17, was in the terraces at Hillsborough watching a football match. The crowd surged forward, and he was crushed. He sustained catastrophic damage to his cerebral cortex.

He went into persistent vegetative state (PVS).[1] This meant, assuming the diagnosis was correct, that he had no perception, sensation or cognition, and never again would have. He could breathe unaided, and his eyes sometimes opened reflexively, but he had to receive nutrition and hydration via a naso-gastric tube.

He lay in a hospital bed until 1992. It was then that his clinicians and parents agreed that it was pointless to continue to maintain him. It would be best, they decided, to stop providing him with food and fluids, and so let him die. They sought advice from the coroner, who thought that there might be a problem with the proposed course. Wouldn't they be doing something with the intention of killing, and in fact killing? If so, wouldn't they be guilty of murder?

They sought, and were granted, a declaration in the Family Division that the proposed course was lawful. The Court of Appeal agreed. On 4 February 1993, nearly four years after that fateful match, the House of Lords agreed too.[2]

It is hard to determine the ratio of *Bland*. There were five speeches in the House of Lords. Each suggested a different route to the conclusion that the naso-gastric feeding/hydrating could be stopped. This chapter tries to identify the ratio. It analyses the speeches and examines the way that the case has been treated by subsequent appellate courts.

---

[1] Now commonly known as Permanent Vegetative State. The significance of the distinction is discussed in J Mason and G Laurie, 'The management of the Persistent Vegetative State in the British Isles' (1996) 4 *Juridical Review* 263.
[2] *Airedale NHS Trust v Bland* [1993] AC 789.

Part of the problem in identifying the ratio, it is suggested, is that all of their Lordships were engaged in the business of rationalisation rather than reasoning. They had decided, more intuitively than forensically, that Anthony Bland should be allowed to die, and that it would be wrong to convict the clinicians of murder. Each then devised a more or less legally coherent justification for those conclusions. They were very keen to avoid the suggestion that they were engaged in judicial legislation. While some talked openly about the role of policy, none was prepared to say that the decision itself was a policy decision. Yet it was. Pushing what was plainly a policy decision into the existing structure of the law made the result, to some eyes, intellectually uncomfortable.

This is not necessarily a criticism of the judges. It may be a criticism of the law they had to apply. Or, possibly, no law could be devised which would make the procedure of adjudication less unsatisfactory.

## II. COMMON GROUND

### A. The Issues were Justiciable

Several of the judges (and most notably Lord Browne-Wilkinson[3] and Lord Mustill[4]) expressed misgivings about whether the issues at the heart of the case (being ethical, not legal issues) should properly be considered by the judges. Yet they decided that nonetheless they could and should adjudicate.

One effect of these misgivings is that the language of the speeches in the House of Lords is conspicuously less philosophical and more legal than, for instance, the judgment of Hoffmann LJ in the Court of Appeal, who embarked on an extended analysis of the ethics of withdrawal,[5] on the grounds that 'This is not an area in which any difference can be allowed to exist between what is legal and what is morally right'.[6]

Whether the House really did (or could) exclude moral considerations from their determinations is debatable and debated. Some say that it was disingenuous of the House to say that their decision was merely legal. In any event both Lord Browne-Wilkinson and Lord Mustill called for Parliament to review the issues.[7] Lord Browne-Wilkinson said that

> it seems to me imperative that the moral, social and legal issues raised by this case should be considered by Parliament. The judges' function in this area of the law

---

[3] ibid 877–81.
[4] ibid 887–91.
[5] ibid 825–34.
[6] ibid 825.
[7] Lord Lowry observed, too, at 877: 'It is important, particularly in the area of criminal law which governs conduct, that society's notions of what is the law and what is right should coincide. One role of the legislator is to detect any disparity between these notions and to take appropriate action to close the gap'.

should be to apply the principles which society, through the democratic process, adopts, not to impose their standards on society.[8]

Lord Mustill thought that

[t]he whole matter cries out for exploration in depth by Parliament and then for the establishment by legislation not only of a new set of ethically and intellectually consistent rules, distinct from the general criminal law, but also of a sound procedural framework within which the rules can be applied to individual cases. The rapid advance of medical technology makes this an ever more urgent task, and I venture to hope that Parliament will soon take it in hand.[9]

His hope was vain: Parliament has done nothing.

*Bland* remains an important authority on the location of the constitutional boundary between the legislature and the judiciary, but that aspect is not considered further in this chapter.

## B. Bland was Alive

It was agreed that Anthony Bland was alive. Life did not depend on cortical function or any of its corollaries such as sensation, cognition or the capacity for relationship. The brain stem definition of death was adopted.[10]

## C. The Definition of Murder

In general omitting to do an act which would prevent death cannot constitute the actus reus of murder, but where there is a duty to the deceased to do the omitted act, such an omission can constitute the actus reus of manslaughter (*R v Stone* [1977] QB 354) or murder (*R v Gibbins* (1918) 1 Cr App R 134). Which of these it is will depend on the mens rea.[11]

### III. THE SPEECHES

Many of the speeches have common elements. Yet each common element does not necessarily do the same work. The reasoning is summarised here

---

[8] ibid 880.
[9] ibid 891.
[10] See, for instance, Lord Goff at 863: 'I start with the simple fact that, in law, Anthony is still alive. It is true that his condition is such that it can be described as a living death; but he is nevertheless still alive ... it has come to be accepted that death occurs when the brain, and in particular the brain stem, has been destroyed ... The evidence is that Anthony's brain stem is still alive and functioning and it follows that, in the present state of medical science, he is still alive and should be so regarded as a matter of law'.
[11] See Lord Browne-Wilkinson at 881.

in (generally) the order in which each judge's points emerge, to indicate the place that each step has in the reasoning.

## Lord Keith[12]

He argued:

(a)   Where a person is unconscious, and hence unable to give or withhold consent to medical treatment, 'it is lawful, under the principle of necessity, for medical men to apply such treatment as in their informed opinion is in the best interests of the unconscious patient'.[13]

(b)   The object of medical treatment and care is to benefit the patient.[14]

(c)   'In the case of a permanently insensate being, who if continuing to live would never experience the slightest actual discomfort, it is difficult, if not impossible, to make any relevant comparison between continued existence and the absence of it. It is, however, perhaps permissible to say that to an individual with no cognitive capacity whatever, and no prospect of ever recovering any such capacity in this world, it must be a matter of complete indifference whether he lives or dies'.[15]

(d)   The administration of nourishment by naso-gastric tube involved the 'application of a medical technique', although one should not rest too much on this observation: 'regard should be had to the whole regime, including the artificial feeding, which at present keeps Anthony Bland alive'.[16]

(e)   While, generally, a medical practitioner was under a duty to continue treatment 'where continuance of it would confer some benefit', there was no such duty 'where a large body of informed and responsible medical opinion is to the effect that no benefit at all would be conferred by continuance'.[17] That was the case here. (It is unclear whether, in endorsing the deployment of the *Bolam* test[18] in these circumstances, Lord Keith was saying that responsible clinicians would agree with his own conclusions about the interests of permanently insensate patients, summarised at (c) above.)

(f)   This conclusion did not offend the principle of the sanctity of life. The principle is not an absolute one. It does not, for instance, authorise the compulsory feeding of hunger strikers, or compel clinicians to keep

[12]   ibid 856–59.
[13]   ibid 857.
[14]   ibid 857.
[15]   ibid 858.
[16]   ibid 858.
[17]   ibid 858–59.
[18]   *Bolam v Friern Barnet Hospital Management Committee* [1957] 1 WLR 582.

terminally ill patients temporarily alive where to do so would simply prolong their suffering.[19]


## Lord Goff[20]

(a)  As Lord Keith opined, the doctrine of the sanctity of life, important though it is, is not absolute.[21]

(b)  There is a crucial distinction between active killing (even mercy killing by a compassionate doctor) and causing death by not providing, or by ceasing to continue to provide, life-sustaining treatment. The former is unlawful; the latter is not lawful in the absence of a duty to provide or to continue to provide treatment. While the act/omission distinction is not entirely satisfactory, the law undoubtedly enshrines it.[22] Its use here though was, really, a policy decision.[23]

(c)  Discontinuing naso-gastric feeding is properly characterised as an omission.[24]

(d)  There is no absolute obligation on a clinician to prolong life, regardless of the quality of the patient's life.[25]

(e)  The decision whether or not to take life-prolonging steps must, assuming that the patient is incapacitous, be made in the best interests of the patient.

> '[I]f the justification for treating a patient who lacks the capacity to consent lies in the fact that the treatment is provided in his best interests, it must follow that the treatment may, and indeed ultimately should, be discontinued where it is no longer in his best interests to provide it. The question which lies at the heart of the present case is, as I see it, whether on that principle the doctors responsible for the treatment and care of Anthony Bland can justifiably discontinue the process of artificial feeding upon which the prolongation of his life depends'.[26]

(f)  It follows that life-sustaining treatment may, 'and indeed ultimately should' be discontinued when continuation ceases to be in the patient's best interests.[27] Here, Anthony Bland's best interests did not demand

---

[19] *Airedale* (n 2 above) 859.
[20] ibid 859–75.
[21] ibid 863–65.
[22] ibid 865–67.
[23] ibid 866.
[24] ibid 866.
[25] ibid 867.
[26] ibid 867.
[27] ibid 867.

continuation of the life-sustaining feeding. Life-prolonging intervention was, 'in medical terms, useless'. That futility justified its termination.[28]

(g)   'The question is not whether the doctor should take a course which will kill his patient, or even take a course which has the effect of accelerating his death. The question is whether the doctor should or should not continue to provide his patient with medical treatment or care which, if continued, will prolong his patient's life'.[29]

(h)   An argument that there was a breach of a basic duty to provide food and hydration to a dependent person in the clinicians' care had to fail: there was 'overwhelming evidence that, in the medical profession, artificial feeding is regarded as a form of medical treatment; and even if it is not strictly medical treatment, it must form part of the medical care of the patient'.[30] It was analogous to the provision of air by way of a ventilator.[31]

(i)   The 'medical treatment' label was relevant because the *Bolam* test was relevant. It had been held in *In re F*[32] that, in deciding on the treatment to be given (or not given) to an incapacitous person, the doctor must act in accordance with a responsible body of medical opinion.[33] Here, a responsible body of such opinion would favour withdrawal, and accordingly there was no breach of the relevant duty.

## Lord Lowry[34]

(a)   The administration of nutrition and hydration in these circumstances is part of medical treatment.[35]

(b)   Accordingly the *Bolam* test applies in deciding whether or not continued administration was in the best interests of the patient.[36]

(c)   There was an intention to bring about Anthony Bland's death.[37]

(d)   But there is not the actus reus of murder because

'if it is not in the interests of an insentient patient to continue the life-supporting care and treatment, the doctor would be acting unlawfully if he continued the care and treatment and would perform no guilty act by discontinuing'.[38]

---

[28] ibid 869.
[29] ibid 868.
[30] ibid 870.
[31] ibid 870.
[32] *In re F* [1990] 2 AC 1.
[33] *Airedale* (n 2 above) 870.
[34] ibid 875–77.
[35] ibid 876.
[36] ibid 876.
[37] ibid 876.
[38] ibid 876.

## Lord Browne-Wilkinson[39]

(a)  The mens rea of murder was present: there was an intention to bring about death.[40]

(b)  The failure to continue to feed did not constitute an act: it was an omission.[41]

(c)  If there was no right lawfully to continue to invade the bodily integrity of Anthony Bland without his consent, there could be no breach of any duty to continue to provide feeding.[42]

(d)  The right to administer invasive medical care is wholly dependent on that administration being in the patient's best interests.[43]

(e)  A doctor's decision about best interests is to be assessed by reference to the *Bolam* test.[44]

(f)  '[I]t must follow from this that if there comes a stage where the responsible doctor comes to the reasonable conclusion (which accords with the views of a responsible body of medical opinion) that further continuance of an intrusive life support system is not in the best interests of the patient, he can no longer lawfully continue that life support system: to do so would constitute the crime of battery and the tort of trespass to the person. Therefore he cannot be in breach of any duty to maintain the patient's life. Therefore he is not guilty of murder by omission'.[45]

(g)  '[T]he critical decision to be made is whether it is in the best interests of Anthony Bland to continue the invasive medical care involved in artificial feeding. That question is not the same as, "Is it in Anthony Bland's best interests that he should die?" The latter question assumes that it is lawful to perpetuate the patient's life: but such perpetuation of life can only be achieved if it is lawful to continue to invade the bodily integrity of the patient by invasive medical care. Unless the doctor has reached the affirmative conclusion that it is in the patient's best interest to continue the invasive care, such care must cease'.[46]

(h)  Anthony Bland was not, and would never be, aware of anything. There was plainly a responsible body (indeed an overwhelming body) of medical opinion that could see no benefit in continued feeding.[47]

---

[39] ibid 877–85.
[40] ibid 881.
[41] ibid 881.
[42] ibid 883.
[43] ibid 883.
[44] ibid 883.
[45] ibid 883–84.
[46] ibid 884.
[47] ibid 884–85.

In these circumstances, it is perfectly reasonable for the responsible doctors to conclude that there is no affirmative benefit to Anthony Bland in continuing the invasive medical procedures necessary to sustain his life. Having so concluded, they are neither entitled nor under a duty to continue such medical care. Therefore they will not be guilty of murder if they discontinue such care.[48]

## Lord Mustill[49]

(a)   The general principle is that acts which cause serious injury (and, a fortiori, death) cannot lawfully be done—even with the consent of the victim.[50]

(b)   'How is it that, consistently with the proposition just stated, a doctor can with immunity perform on a consenting patient an act which would be a very serious crime if done by someone else? The answer must be that bodily invasions in the course of proper medical treatment stand completely outside the criminal law. The reason why the consent of the patient is so important is not that it furnishes a defence in itself, but because it is usually essential to the propriety of medical treatment. Thus, if the consent is absent, and is not dispensed with in special circumstances by operation of law, the acts of the doctor lose their immunity'.[51]

(c)   The consent of the patient is normally essential to the lawfulness of a medical intervention, but since consent (eg in a case such as Anthony Bland's) cannot always be obtained, the courts have developed a principle whereby in emergencies, or in the case of permanent incapacity (*In Re F)* intervention is justified if it is the patient's best interests.[52]

(d)   Murder normally requires an act, except in some hard-to-define cases where there is a duty to prevent death.[53]

(e)   The distinction between acts and omissions was undoubtedly embedded in the English criminal law. It had to play a part in the decision here, however uncomfortable it was to rely on it.

> 'The conclusion that the declarations can be upheld depends crucially on [the distinction] ... The acute unease which I feel about adopting this way through the legal and ethical maze is I believe due in an important part to the sensation that however much the terminologies may differ the ethical status

[48] ibid 885.
[49] ibid 885–99.
[50] ibid 891.
[51] ibid 891.
[52] ibid 892.
[53] ibid 893.

of the two courses of action is for all relevant purposes indistinguishable. By dismissing this appeal I fear that your Lordships' House may only emphasise the distortions of a legal structure which is already both morally and intellectually misshapen. Still, the law is there and we must take it as it stands'.[54]

(f)   There was no comfort in the law of causation: It could not be said that the death was caused not by the doctors but by the Hillsborough Disaster.[55,56]

(g)   'The interest of the state in preserving the lives of its citizens is very strong, but it is not absolute. There are contrary interests, and sometimes they prevail'.[57]

(h)   The relevant best interests are those of the patient, not of the wider community (for instance in having the benefit of funds that would otherwise be spent on maintaining the patient).[58]

(i)   It could not be said that Anthony Bland had an interest in avoiding the distress to others (such as his family) caused by seeing him in the condition of PVS.[59]

(j)   Anthony Bland had no interests of any kind:

'Thus, although the termination of his life is not in the best interests of Anthony Bland, his best interests in being kept alive have also disappeared, taking with them the justification for the non-consensual regime and the

---

[54]   ibid 887.

[55]   ibid 895–96.

[56]   Note, though, that where a capacitous patient insists on the discontinuation of life-sustaining treatment, the cause of death is regarded as that which created the need for the treatment: see *B v An NHS Trust* [2002] 2 All ER 449. The reason for the distinction is obvious. *Bland* was essentially a case about the circumstances in which doctors owe a duty to continue life-sustaining treatment. Had it been decided that there was no causal link between the doctors' duty and the death (and thus no possibility of conventional criminal or civil liability), it would seem to follow that there was never any actionable duty on any doctor to do anything—a plainly absurd result. Andrew McGee forcefully advocates a new look at the question of causation—at least as (often neglected) context in which the acts/omissions distinction operates, and in order to make clear the line between euthanasia and the withdrawal of life-sustaining treatment. He says: 'The fact that the issue in these cases is always whether to discontinue treatment which is *artificially prolonging* the life of the patient has received insufficient attention, yet it is the key to what I would describe as the abyssal difference between lawful withholding or withdrawal of treatment and euthanasia. What is proposed in euthanasia is that *we* wrest from nature control of our ultimate fate ... In lawful withdrawal, by contrast, the very opposite is the case: we interfere with nature, not in killing the patient, but *in keeping the patient alive* ... In short, the moral relevance of the distinction [is]: *euthanasia interferes with nature's dominion*, whereas withdrawal of treatment *restores* to nature her dominion after we had taken it away when *artificially* prolonging the patient's life'. A McGee, 'Finding a way through the ethical and legal maze: withdrawal of medical treatment and euthanasia' (2005) 13 *Medical Law Review* 357, 382–83. See the further discussion in A McGee, 'Me and my body: the relevance of the difference for the distinction between withdrawing life support and euthanasia' (2001) *Journal of Law, Medicine and Ethics* 671.

[57]   *Airedale* (n 2 above) 894.

[58]   ibid 896.

[59]   ibid 897.

co-relative duty to keep it in being ... Since there is no longer a duty to provide nourishment and hydration a failure to do so cannot be a criminal offence'.[60]

(k)   Accordingly there was no duty to provide nutrition and hydration, and failure to provide them was not a criminal offence.[61]

## IV. THE INGREDIENTS IN THE MIX

Each judge had his own recipe. Each differs, at least slightly, from all the others. There are at least eight identifiable ingredients. We now examine each of them, asking whether each was essential to the recipe, and how the end result would have been materially different if that ingredient had been omitted, or used in a different way. The ingredients are:

— The sanctity of life is important, but not absolute.
— There was an intention to bring about death.
— Acts and omissions are legally different.
— Stopping feeding is an omission.
— Feeding by way of naso-gastric tube is treatment.
— The *Bolam* test is relevant in the determination of best interests.
— Continued feeding was not in Tony Bland's best interests.
— There was no duty to continue feeding (and indeed, per some, there was a duty not to continue feeding).

## A. The Sanctity of Life

Although this was said by all the judges to be foundational—an unarguable axiom—it was not dissected or defined, even by those (such as Hoffmann LJ in the Court of Appeal)[62] who said most about it. Its demands seem to have been regarded as obvious. Those demands amounted only to an insistence that human life was intrinsically valuable, and that however truncated the ability of a patient to enjoy the characteristics often associated with embodied humanity, one should always hesitate long before concluding that the interest in continued existence was trumped by any other consideration. The principle was, however, not absolute.

This is an amorphous formulation, yet it has been criticised as embodying an incorrect, vitalist understanding of the doctrine. If one starts off by

[60]   ibid 897–98.
[61]   ibid 898.
[62]   ibid 826–27.

seeing the main argument against withdrawal of life sustaining treatment as a vitalist argument (the criticism goes), then, since vitalism is plainly unsustainable, withdrawal won't have any real opposition. This is an accusation that the House of Lords (with the connivance of counsel for the Official Solicitor)[63] set up vitalism as a straw man.[64]

This is John Keown's argument. He says:

> The principle of the sanctity of life is often advocated but much less often understood. In Western thought, the development of the principle has owed much to the Judaeo-Christian tradition. That tradition's doctrine of the sanctity of life holds that human life is created in the image of God and is, therefore, possessed of an intrinsic dignity which entitles it to protection from unjust attack. With or without that theological underpinning, the doctrine grounds the principle that one ought never intentionally to kill an innocent human being. The 'right to life' is essentially a right not to be intentionally killed.[65]

This formulation, he points out,[66] is consistent with Article 2 of the European Convention on Human Rights, which provides: 'Everyone's right to life shall be protected by law. No one shall be deprived of his life intentionally save in the execution of a sentence of a court following his conviction of a crime for which this penalty is provided by law.'

This appeal to Article 2 is rather curious. The appeal is only worthwhile if Article 2's reference to intentional killing is a complete summary of the state's expression of the notion of the sanctity of life. But of course it is not: The first sentence of Article 2 is simply 'Everyone's right to life shall be protected by law'—a right which is, no doubt, an expression of the doctrine of the sanctity of life, and which is itself expressed, inter alia, in all the law, both civil and criminal, which deals with accidental killing.[67]

---

[63] John Finnis, for instance, observes, in response to Lord Mustill's famous comment about the 'morally and intellectually misshapen' foundations of the law, that 'Foundations morally and legally better were in fact available. But they were never, it seems, put forward by counsel or identified for consideration in the judgments, searching and thoughtful though these are': J Finnis, 'Bland: crossing the Rubicon' (1993) 109 *LQR* 329, 329.

[64] John Finnis, John Keown and others are concerned about this alleged misrepresentation because, inter alia, they think that it will lead to a widely and deeply repercussive erosion of the authority of the sanctity of life. Despite some rather crowing attempts by, for instance, Peter Singer, to say that *Bland* has had precisely this effect (see P Singer, *Rethinking Life and Death* (New York, St Martin's Griffin, 1994) 75; P Singer, 'Is the sanctity of life ethic terminally ill?' (1995) 9 *Bioethics* 327), it is hard to see that their fears were well founded.

[65] J Keown, 'Restoring Moral and Intellectual Shape to the Law After *Bland*' (1997) 113 *LQR* 482, 482–83.

[66] ibid 483.

[67] See, eg, *R (Amin) v Secretary of State for the Home Department* [2003] UKHL 51; *R (Middleton) v HM Coroner for the Western District of Somerset* [2004] UKHL 10; *Savage v South Essex Partnership NHS Foundation Trust* [2009] 2 WLR 115; *Rabone v Pennine Care NHS Foundation Trust* [2012] UKSC 2.

For Keown, what follows from his understanding of the sanctity of life is that:

> Conduct which is intended to shorten life—'intention' bearing its ordinary meaning of **purpose**—is always wrong. Conduct which may foreseeably shorten life is not always wrong. Whether it is it will turn largely on whether there is a sufficient justification for taking the risk of shortening life.
>
> A doctor treating a terminally-ill cancer patient suffering pain clearly has a sufficient justification for administering palliative drugs with intent to ease the pain, even though a foreseeable side-effect may or will be the shortening of life. Similarly, a doctor may properly withhold or withdraw a life-prolonging treatment which is futile (that is, cannot secure a significant therapeutic benefit) or which the patient would find too burdensome, even though the doctor foresees that non-treatment may or will result in the patient's life ending sooner than would otherwise be the case. Doctors may not, on the other hand, take unreasonable risks with patients' lives. It is one thing for a doctor to perform neurosurgery to remove a malignant tumour, even though the operation may prove fatal; quite another to perform it merely because the patient has a headache.[68]

For Keown, in the context of the *Bland* decision, this understanding of the doctrine of the sanctity of life gives a good part of the answer to the conundrum. Doctors are under a duty to uphold the doctrine. The doctrine holds that 'there can be no moral obligation to administer ... a treatment which is not worthwhile'.[69] Subject to the question of whether naso-gastric feeding is 'treatment', then, the puzzle is solved.

John Finnis adds another criticism to Keown's denunciation of the House's understanding of the sanctity of life. It is a criticism of its understanding of just what it is that is sacred. He argues that the House was dualist, and that dualism itself, as well as being embarrassingly out of date, doesn't square with what we know about human beings.

> The judgments all suggest a dualistic distinction between Bland himself and his body: eg 'his spirit has left him and all that remains is the shell of his body' (Sir Stephen Brown P); 'his body is alive, but he has no life ... He is alive but has no life at all' (Hoffmann LJ). This sort of dualism, which thinks of the body as if it were some kind of habitation for and instrument of the real person, is defended by few philosophers indeed (religious or otherwise). It renders inexplicable the unity in complexity which one experiences in everything one consciously does. It speaks as if there were two things, other and other: a non-bodily person and a non-personal living body. But neither of these can one recognize as oneself. One's living body is intrinsic, not merely instrumental, to one's personal life. Each of us has a human life (not a vegetable life plus an animal life plus a personal life); when it is flourishing that life includes all of one's vital functions including speech,

---

[68] Keown (n 65 above) 484–85.
[69] ibid 485.

deliberation and choice; when gravely impaired it lacks some of those functions without ceasing to be the life of the person so impaired.[70]

He might have added that this dualism doesn't square either with the policies at work throughout the rest of the law. A prosecutor would not accept, from a defendant charged with raping a patient in PVS, a plea of guilty to sexual violation of a corpse, or of some vague, undirected offence of violating public decency. The violation there is of a mind-body-spirit unity, which is what the law almost invariably means when it talks about persons.

The sanctity of life doctrine, as understood by Keown, makes attempts to judge the worthwhileness of the patient's life wholly illegitimate. It 'merely takes the patient's condition into account in deciding on the worthwhileness of a proposed treatment'.[71] One can ask: 'Worthwhile?' of a treatment, but not of a life. It is this corollary that has been the subject of both apparent endorsement and bitter criticism.

In *Re A (children) (conjoined twins: surgical separation)* Ward LJ, expressly referring to and approving Keown's view, said that he was required to balance the worthwhileness of the treatment to the conjoined twins, but that this was a 'quite different exercise from the proscribed (because it offends the sanctity of life principle) consideration of the worth of one life compared with the other'.[72]

Yet, say others, the distinction between the worthwhileness of treatment and the worthwhileness of a life is unworkable; an exercise in semantics, or, if real at all, insufficiently robust to do the strenuous moral and legal work demanded of it. How, it is asked, can one decide whether life-sustaining treatment is worthwhile without asking what effect it is going to have on the patient, and making a value judgment about whether the life that is prolonged is, overall, a benefit to the patient? Unless one makes this judgment, it is argued (for instance by David Price), one is committed to the vitalist position that Keown and Finnis so emphatically eschew.[73]

To rely on futility, as Keown and Finnis do, is (say Price and others), to beg the very quality of life questions that Keown and Finnis say are illegitimate. Here is Price:

[F]utility is a nebulous concept applied too sweepingly and without sufficient care, including by the judiciary. Keown maintains that a treatment is futile if it offers no

---

[70] Finnis (n 63 above) 334.

[71] Keown (n 65 above) 486; see too J Keown, 'Courting Euthanasia? Tony Bland and the House of Lords' (1993) 9 *Ethics & Medicine* 3, 36.

[72] *Re A (children) (conjoined twins: surgical separation)* [2000] 4 All ER 961, 1010.

[73] D Price, 'Fairly Bland: an alternative view of a supposed new 'Death Ethic' and the BMA Guidelines' (2001) 21 *Legal Studies* 618, 638; D Price, 'What shape to euthanasia after Bland? Historical, contemporary and futuristic paradigms' (2009) 125 *LQR* 142; cp J Keown, 'Beyond Bland: a critique of the BMA guidance on withholding and withdrawing medical treatment' (2000) 20 *Legal Studies* 66; J Keown, 'Restoring the sanctity of life and replacing the caricature: a reply to David Price' (2006) 26 *Legal Studies* 109.

reasonable hope of therapeutic benefit. Indeed, 'futility' in its proper sense attaches to treatment which will not achieve its intended clinical effect, for example where further chemotherapy will not achieve any further remission of a cancer or cardiac resuscitation measures will not restore functioning cardiac rhythm ... [Here] it is clearly not obligatory from either an ethical, legal or medical perspective ... Regrettably, however, the expression is often employed in circumstances where it is intended to imply that relief will only prove temporary or where the patient's life will be enhanced to no, or only a very limited degree by it, i.e. it is of no benefit to the patient. These wholly different usages incorporate an ethical element though *and necessarily allude to the very condition of the patient in the future which the sanctity of life principle is ostensibly attempting to strain out.*[74,75] (emphasis added)

For Price, Keown's invocation of the idea of disproportionate treatment (disproportionate where the treatment is 'excessively burdensome')[76] is similarly problematic. It carries the same freight as futility and, further, seems to be obviously irrelevant in the case of PVS:

Returning to Tony Bland, it is difficult to see how any medical treatment could have been 'excessively burdensome' to him in view of his insensate state, and therefore such a position would appear to commit one to providing all affordable life-sustaining treatments indefinitely; an outcome viewed broadly as being wholly inappropriate.[77]

For me, Price's criticisms are compelling. Spin it how you like, there is no way, short of vitalism (and vitalism is so wrong—ethically and, certainly, legally—that it is hard to know where to start in criticising it), to avoid quality of life judgements in making decisions about the continuation of life-sustaining treatment. *Bland* is, and is rightly, about how to make *those* decisions well in the case of patients in PVS.

Note, though, that although for both Keown and Finnis the doctrine of the sanctity of life is important because of its theological roots, it is, for both of them, *legally* important because of what it says and does not say about the role of intention in the withdrawal of life-sustaining treatment. To reiterate: for them, the sanctity of life means that one must not intentionally kill. They go on to say that there was no legal intention to kill Tony Bland, and that if the House had agreed with them about this absence of intention, the case would have been decided in the way that it was without dangerously distorting the law.

We move on, then, to examine the element of intention.

---

[74] Price, 'Fairly Bland: an alternative view of a supposed new "Death Ethic" and the BMA Guidelines' (n 73 above) 626.

[75] For further discussion of the elusive definition of futility, see R Cranford and L Gostin, 'Futility: A concept in search of a definition' (1992) 20 *Law, Medicine and Healthcare* 307.

[76] J Keown, 'Restoring moral and intellectual shape to the law after Bland' (1997) 113 *LQR* 481, 485.

[77] Price, 'Fairly Bland: an alternative view of a supposed new "Death Ethic" and the BMA Guidelines' (n 73 above) 629.

## B. Intention to Bring about Death

Finnis and Keown see the case of Tony Bland as a classic case of double effect: death was foreseen as a consequence of stopping naso-gastric feeding/hydration, but it was not intended. Accordingly the mens rea of murder was absent, and there was no tectonic legal problem to be addressed.

Finnis writes:

> One intends to bring about X if and only if the bringing about of X is either an end or a means in the proposal which one shapes by deliberation (however rapidly formed or habitually executed) and chooses to adopt. So if one withdraws life-sustaining measures precisely because that has been requested by a competent patient on grounds of their burdensomeness, one need not be purposing, aiming at, or intending the patient's foreseeably certain death. One's purpose and intent is to honour the patient's wish to be relieved of (or free others from) their burden. One does, on the other hand, intend to bring about death (as a means) if one withdraws nutrition because it is the one sure way of ensuring, through death, that benefits will be paid under a term life insurance policy, or that a régime of nursing care which threatens to last for years will be terminated and the costs applied instead to recarpeting, or that parents will be relieved of their grief at the spectacle of their child's hopeless disability. In the absence of findings by the trial judge (and, apparently, of cross-examination designed to elicit—as in a criminal trial—the responsible physician's deliberations and thus intentions), the appellate courts should have proceeded on the basis that there may well have been, but perhaps was not, an intention to terminate Bland's life.[78]

There is a vast, byzantine literature on the distinction between intention and foresight. Surely, as a matter of common sense, it is plain that the distinction is real. Andrew McGee proposes that '[a]n intended consequence, unlike a foreseen one, is a consequence that is deliberately *aimed at* or is the *purpose* of the action',[79] and supports this distinction with several compelling examples: a police officer who breaks bad news to the relatives of a missing person foresees but does not intend their upset; a barrister who has to sit up all night to prepare his brief for the next day will foresee, but not intend, his tiredness; a doctor who puts a patient on chemotherapy for cancer foresees but does not intend the unpleasant side-effects.[80] Here (for example), the side-effect of chemotherapeutic nausea is not the means of making the cancer recede, just as the barrister's tiredness is not the means of preparing the brief. A perfectly foreseeable result, in these examples, does not equal intention. Intention and foreseeability often coincide, but they do not necessarily coincide.

---

[78] Finnis (n 63 above) 332.
[79] McGee, 'Finding a way through the ethical and legal maze' (n 56 above) 365.
[80] ibid 365.

The legal difficulty with all this, for English lawyers, is the decision of the House of Lords in *R v Woollin*,[81] in which it was said that where the charge is murder, and in the rare circumstances where a simple direction about intention is not enough, the jury should be directed that they are not entitled to find the necessary intention unless they feel sure that death or serious bodily harm was a virtual certainty (barring some unforeseen intervention) as a result of the defendant's actions, and that the defendant appreciated that this was the case.[82]

McGee observes that if the House, in *Woollin*, were saying that virtual certainty was identical to intention, 'it must respectfully be concluded that they were in error'.[83] But that is not what they were saying. The language used was certainly unfortunate and misleading. But it does not follow from their words that a jury *must* find that a virtually certain result is intended (only that they are entitled to do so). Hence the House were not definitely guilty of missing the point of McGee's examples.[84]

This is a strange debate, for whatever *Woollin* says or doesn't say, the intention/foresight distinction is well entrenched in English criminal law. It has been deployed, for instance, as a defence to murder in the classic double-effect case of death by an overdose of opiates where the intention was to provide adequate analgesia, but with the foreseeable and foreseen consequence of death.[85]

Keown and, less explicitly, Finnis, contend that there is no intention to kill in a case like that of Tony Bland because the doctor aims not to kill but to relieve the patient from futile, burdensome treatment.

We have already been over the problems with Keown's reliance on futility and burdensomeness in the context of the discussion about the sanctity of life. McGee wonders whether Keown might insist, in order to get around these difficulties, that the intended purpose is only the withdrawal of futile treatment—rather than the patient's death (which is merely foreseen). Yet this doesn't work either, as McGee observes:

> This would be like saying that, although I foresaw as certain that I would cause grievous bodily harm to my enemy if I shot him, I only intended to shoot him, not cause the grievous bodily harm. Further, it would commit Keown to the absurd

---

[81] *R v Woollin* [1999] 1 AC 82; cp *R v Moloney* [1985] AC 905 and *Hyam v DPP* [1975] AC 55.

[82] ibid 96 (Lord Steyn).

[83] McGee, 'Finding a way through the ethical and legal maze' (n 56 above) 366.

[84] C Foster, J Herring, T Hope and K Melham, 'The double effect effect' (2011) 20 *Cambridge Quarterly of Healthcare Ethics* 46; A McGee 'Intention, foresight and ending life' (2013) 22 *Cambridge Quarterly of Healthcare Ethics* 77; C Foster, J Herring, T Hope and K Melham, 'Intention and Foresight—From Ethics to Law and Back Again' (2013) 22 *Cambridge Quarterly of Healthcare Ethics* 86.

[85] See, for instance, the trial of Dr Moor: news.bbc.co.uk/1/hi/health/321212.stm (accessed 31 January 2014).

tautology that the purpose of withdrawing the treatment is withdrawing the treatment. There must be some purpose other than the side effect and other than the act itself which is capable of constituting the reason for the action in order for the distinction between intention and foresight to acquire a grip.[86]

These are, I think, potent reasons for saying that the asserted analogy between palliative care and the withdrawal of life-sustaining treatment is poor, and accordingly that the House of Lords were right in saying that there was a true intention to kill. It is hard to resist the conclusion that Keown and Finnis are simply confusing intention and desire.

The legal advice of Keown and Finnis, then, is insufficient to reassure the doctors that they are safe from a murder charge. The House of Lords still had work to do.

Having posed the doctors' problem (sanctity of life had to be honoured, and there was an intention to kill), the House set about constructing the defence. The first point in the skeleton argument was that withdrawal was an omission and not an act.

## C. Acts and Omissions

Whether one thinks that there is a distinction of moral weight between acts and omissions is largely a matter of intuition. And accordingly the place that you accord to intuition in your moral reasoning will determine the weight, if any, that you accord to the distinction.

There is a mass of thought experiments designed to make us question the intuition (which most of us have), that acts and omissions are morally different. The most famous are the 'trolley problem'[87] and its many variants.[88] Here is another—James Rachels' 'Wicked Uncle' example.[89]

Scenario 1: A Wicked Uncle will be entitled to a huge amount of money should X, a tiny baby, die. The uncle is given the job of bathing X. He pushes X under the water and drowns her.

---

[86] McGee, 'Finding a Way Through the Ethical and Legal Maze' (n 56 above) 373. See, further, A McGee, 'Ending the Life of the Act/Omission Dispute: Causation in Withholding and Withdrawing Life-sustaining Measures' (2011) 31 *Legal Studies* 467.

[87] J Thomson, 'Killing, Letting Die and the Trolley Problem' (1976) 59 *The Monist* 204.

[88] FM Kamm, 'Harming some to save others' (1989) 57 *Philosophical Studies* 227; FM Kamm, 'The Doctrine of Double Effect: Reflections on Theoretical and Practical Issues' (1991) 16 *Journal of Medicine and Philosophy* 571; A Lanteri, C Chelini and S Rizzello, 'An Experimental Investigation of Emotions and Reasoning in the Trolley Problem' (2008) 83 *Journal of Business Ethics* 789; J Mikhail, 'Aspects of the Theory of Moral Cognition: Investigating Intuitive Knowledge of the Prohibition of Intentional Battery and the Principle of Double Effect' (2002) *Georgetown Law and Economics Research Paper* (762385).

[89] J Rachels, 'Active and Passive Euthanasia' (1997) *Bioethics: An Introduction to the History, Methods, and Practice* 77.

Scenario 2: The circumstances are identical, but this time, fate is on the uncle's side. Just as he is reaching out his hand to push X under, X knocks her head on the side of the bath. This renders her unconscious. She goes under the water. X could save her, at no risk to himself, by lifting up her head. He doesn't. X dies.

Most think that the uncle's culpability is identical in each of these scenarios. Yet legally the consequences are very different. In scenario 1 the uncle is guilty of murder: there is an act, done with an intention to kill, and it has in fact killed. But in scenario 2 there is no legal liability at all in English law.[90] There is no duty of safe rescue.[91]

Problems like this have caused many to agree with Julian Savulescu who asserts, with characteristic forthrightness: 'There is no moral distinction between killing and letting die, despite many people having intuitions to the contrary'.[92]

Yet the intuition persists. Most of us, even though we understand the utilitarian calculus, are more reluctant to kill one in order to save five when the killing has to be by way of an act instead of an omission.[93] Psychopaths, who are natural, intuition-ignoring utilitarians (and who are therefore much more likely than average to see no difference between acts and omissions)[94] are not generally regarded as model citizens. Nor, and this gets nearer to *Bland*, are they regarded legally as the reasonable men whose views tend to be the benchmark used by English lawyers.[95]

Whether rightly or wrongly, the acts/omissions distinction is firmly embedded in English law. To abandon the distinction would be to say that the intuitions that insist that it is important (vertiginously old intuitions, with a complex and perhaps crucial relationship with our embodiedness and our relationality)[96] are irrelevant, and that they should always be trumped

[90] Unless it could be argued that by agreeing to bath the child the uncle had accepted a duty of care: see *R v Instan* [1893] 1 QB 450; *R v Stone and Robinson* [1977] QB 354.

[91] See *R v Khan and Khan* [1998] Crim LR 830.

[92] blog.practicalethics.ox.ac.uk/2013/10/winchester-lectures-kamms-trolleyology-and-is-there-a-morally-relevant-difference-between-killing-and-letting-die/#more-7096 (accessed 30 January 2014): see too J Savulescu and I Persson, 'McMahan & Withdrawal of Life-prolonging Aid' (2005) 46 *Philosophical Books* 11; J Savulescu, 'Editorial: Abortion, Infanticide and Allowing Babies to Die, Forty Years On' (2013) 39 *Journal of Medical Ethics* 257.

[93] See, for example: J Greene, 'Emotion and Cognition in Moral Judgment: Evidence from Neuroimaging' in J-P Changeux et al (eds), *Neurobiology of Human Values* (Heidelberg, Springer Verlag, 2005) 57; MD Hauser, F Tonnaer, and M Cima, 'When Moral Intuitions are Immune to the Law: A Case Study of Euthanasia and the Act-Omission Distinction in the Netherlands' (2009) 9 *Journal of Cognition and Culture* 149.

[94] M Cima, F Tonnaer and MD Hauser, 'Psychopaths Know Right From Wrong but Don't Care' (2010) 5 *Social Cognitive and Affective Neuroscience* 59.

[95] Nor are people with unusually high levels of testosterone who, similarly, are more utilitarian than normal: DR Carney and MF Mason, 'Decision Making and Testosterone: When the Ends Justify the Means' (2010) 46 *Journal of Experimental Social Psychology* 668.

[96] DW Light and G McGee, 'On the Social Embeddedness of Bioethics' in R DeVries and J Subedi (eds), *Bioethics and Society. Constructing the Ethical Enterprise* (Upper Saddle River NJ, Prentice Hall, 1998).

by utilitarian arithmetic of some kind. That is far from an unarguable position, and of course it is argued cogently by many (such as Peter Singer and Julian Savulescu), but it is not self-evidently true. One question that its proponents must answer is: what value system makes one say that one should kill one (even if that involves an act) in order to save five? In listening to that answer one should check carefully to see whether intuitions are, after all, at work in the justification.

The classification as an omission of the withdrawal of life-sustaining treatment from Tony Bland has attracted relatively little criticism.[97] Yet the classification is not indisputable. A positive decision to withdraw feeding had to be made, after anxious discussion. A hand grasped the naso-gastric tube and pulled it out. If, with an intention to kill, a layman had walked into the hospital ward and pulled out the tube, so causing death by the same mechanism, this would certainly have been regarded as an act for the purposes of the law of murder.

This suggests that the acts/omissions distinction is not really doing the work that the House said that it was. I suggest that the distinction was not essential to the decision. The difference between the position in *Bland* and the situation involving the homicidal layman who comes into the ward was simply a policy one: the doctors should not be liable; the layman should. It was necessary to clothe that policy in legal language, but the language of acts and omissions is inadequate: policy keeps on showing its legs. The language of duty is more satisfactory. We look at duty shortly.

But first, to pave the way for the definitive decision about duty, the House decided that the naso-gastric feeding was 'treatment'.

## D. Feeding by Way of Naso-gastric Tube is Treatment

In his early comment on *Bland*, John Keown trenchantly asked: 'What is being treated?'[98] He wants us to reply, with embarrassing absurdity: 'The human condition of needing nourishment'.

---

[97] John Finnis, whom one might have expected to dissent from this categorisation, objects not to the categorisation itself, but to the weight that is placed upon it. He writes: 'by relying *simply* on the distinction between an action (or 'positive action') and an omission, the rejection of this remarkable submission [a submission that there is no relevant distinction between the administration of a lethal dose of medication to an incompetent patient and the withholding of a necessary nutrient or medicine from such a patient], though welcome, leaves the law confessedly "misshapen" and "almost irrational"': 'Bland: Crossing the Rubicon' (1993) 109 *Law Quarterly Review* 329, 333. Keown agrees: 'It matters not … whether the shortening [of a patient's life] is brought about by an act or an omission. Intentionally shortening a patient's life by withholding treatment, or food, water or warmth, is no less wrong than injecting a lethal poison': J Keown, 'Restoring moral and intellectual shape to the law after Bland' (1997) 113 *Law Quarterly Review* 481.

[98] J Keown, 'Doctors and patients: hard case, bad law, "new" ethics' (1993) 52 *Cambridge Law Journal* 209, 210.

His question has great rhetorical force, but it does not necessarily invite the answer he wants. A better answer is: naso-gastric feeding is treatment for the manifestation of PVS which is inability to feed oneself. A good deal of sophisticated medical treatment is symptomatic treatment.

A more substantive criticism, again articulated by John Keown, is that naso-gastric feeding is feeding that does not necessitate sophisticated medical knowledge, and that accordingly it should be regarded as basic care. He writes:

> Whether the insertion of [a] feeding tube via the nose (a naso-gastric tube) is a medical intervention is questionable, for it can be performed by nursing staff and even by appropriately trained lay carers. In any event, *once the tube has been inserted by either method and is already in place* (as it has been in those *PVS* cases where courts have granted declarations condoning the withdrawal of tube-feeding), it is difficult to see how the mere pouring of food and water down it can realistically be described as 'medical treatment'. What *medical* skill is pouring thought to involve? And what is being *treated*? Why is feeding, albeit by tube, not thought to be part of the basic care which the doctor owes to the patient?[99]

On the question of the obligation to provide basic care, the position has been muddied rather than clarified by later authorities. Thus in *Burke v GMC*,[100] Lord Phillips MR, giving the judgment of the court, said:

> So far as ANH [artificial nutrition and hydration] is concerned, there is no need to look far for the duty to provide this. Once a patient is accepted into a hospital, the medical staff come under a positive duty at common law to care for the patient. The authorities cited by Munby J at paragraphs 82 to 87 under the heading 'The duty to care' establish this proposition, if authority is needed. A fundamental aspect of this positive duty of care is a duty to take such steps as are reasonable to keep the patient alive. Where ANH is necessary to keep the patient alive, the duty of care will normally require the doctors to supply ANH.[101]

The Court of Appeal thus decided on the obligation to provide ANH not on the basis of whether it was, or was not, 'basic care', but on the basis of the fundamental (although of course not absolute) duty to keep a dependent patient alive. Discharge of that duty might require sophisticated medical involvement—for instance in intubating a patient and connecting her to a ventilator in order to provide what is the most basic of all human needs—oxygen. The existence of that duty would seem to render otiose the debate about whether tube feeding is 'treatment' in the sense of being something that requires great medical sophistication.

Indeed, I suggest, that debate is otiose for two other reasons. First: the debate was necessary only because the House of Lords in *Bland* decided

---

[99] J Keown, 'Beyond Bland' (n 73 above) 68. See too GT Laurie and JK Mason, 'Negative treatment of vulnerable patients: Euthanasia by any other name?' [2000] *Juridical Review* 159.

[100] *R (on the application of Burke) v General Medical Council* [2005] EWCA Civ 1003,

[101] ibid [32].

that they should rely on the *Bolam* test in deciding whether or not Tony Bland's clinicians owed a duty to him to maintain naso-gastric feeding. That reliance was misconceived. We come to that issue below. And, second, the *Bland* situation is now covered by the Mental Capacity 2005. The only pertinent question is whether the proposed action or inaction is in the patient's best interests.[102] There is no room in the holistic determination demanded by the Act for any discussion of whether or not the action/inaction is 'treatment'.[103]

## E. The *Bolam* Test is Relevant in the Determination of Best Interests

If naso-gastric feeding was 'treatment', the reasoning went, the propriety of its continuation or withdrawal was quintessentially a matter of professional judgement. Even if it was right to deploy *Bolam* at the time in the way that it was deployed, it was plainly not right to deploy it now.

In *Re F (Mental Patient: Sterilisation)*[104] the House of Lords had decided that the *Bolam* test should apply to the determination of a patient's best interests.[105] This, and *Bland* itself, were the high points of medical paternalism. *Bolam* and best interests do not go well together. *Bolam* is a test (both of substantive law and evidence) forged in the crucible of clinical negligence litigation, which is used by courts to decide whether a claimant has proved that a clinician should be liable for compensatory damages. It is not really about the ascertainment of *facts* at all. Yet there is, at least in theory, a single, right or wrong answer to the question: 'Is intervention X in the patient's best interests?' Inquiries into best interests are, at least notionally, fact-finding exercises to which the *Bolam* test is constitutionally unsuited. If X is actually in the patient's best interests, it is wholly irrelevant whether or not there is a responsible body of medical opinion which believes that it is not.

That was finally recognised in *Re S (Adult Patient: Sterilisation)*.[106] Butler-Sloss LJ said:

> I would suggest that the starting point of any medical decision would be the principles enunciated in the Bolam test and that a doctor ought not to make any

---

[102] See Mental Capacity Act 2005, s 1(5).

[103] See Mental Capacity Act 2005, s 4.

[104] *Re F (mental patient: sterilisation)* [1990] 2 AC 1.

[105] Thus, for instance, Lord Goff said, at 78: '[T]he doctor has to act in the best interests of the assisted person. In the case of routine treatment of mentally disordered persons, there should be little difficulty in applying this principle. In the case of more serious treatment, I recognise that its application may create problems for the medical profession; however, in making decisions about treatment, the doctor must act in accordance with a responsible and competent body of relevant professional opinion, on the principles set down in Bolam'. See too Lord Bridge at 52, Lord Brandon at 66–68, and Lord Griffiths at 69.

[106] *Re S (adult patient: sterilisation)* [2001] Fam 15. See, too, the disapproval of applying *Bolam* principles to essentially moral questions in *Montgomery v Lanarkshire Health Board* [2015] UKSC 11, especially per Lady Hale at [114]–[115].

decision about a patient that does not fall within the broad spectrum of the Bolam test. The duty to act in accordance with responsible and competent professional opinion may give the doctor more than one option since there may well be more than one acceptable medical opinion. When the doctor moves on to consider the best interests of the patient he/she has to choose the best option, often from a range of options. As Mr. Munby has pointed out, the best interests test ought, logically, to give only one answer.

In these difficult cases where the medical profession seeks a declaration as to lawfulness of the proposed treatment, the judge, not the doctor, has the duty to decide whether such treatment is in the best interests of the patient. The judicial decision ought to provide the best answer not a range of alternative answers. There may, of course, be situations where the answer may not be obvious and alternatives may have to be tried. It is still at any one point the best option of that moment which should be chosen. I recognise that there [are] distinguished judicial dicta to the contrary in the speech of Lord Browne-Wilkinson in *Airedale NHS Trust v Bland* [1993] AC 789, 884. The passage in his speech was not however followed by the other members of the House. Hale J in *In re S (Hospital Patient: Court's Jurisdiction)* [1995] Fam 26, 32 followed the same approach. She said that, in accordance with the Bolam test, it followed that a number of different courses may be lawful in any particular case. That may be so, but I do not read *In re F (Medical Patient: Sterilisation)* [1990] 2 AC 1, upon which she relied, as relieving the judge who is deciding the best interests of the patient from making a choice between the available options. I respectfully disagree with Lord Browne-Wilkinson and Hale J. I have had the opportunity to read Thorpe LJ's judgment in draft and I agree with his analysis. As I have set out earlier in this judgment, the principle of best interests as applied by the court extends beyond the considerations set out in the *Bolam case* [1957] 1 WLR 582. The judicial decision will incorporate broader ethical, social, moral and welfare considerations.[107]

Thorpe LJ said there:

The Bolam test was of course developed in order to enable courts to determine the boundaries of medical responsibility for treatment that has gone wrong, and usually disastrously wrong. So at first blush it would seem an unlikely import in determining the best interests of an adult too disabled to decide for him- or herself. True the decision relates to whether or not the adult should receive medical treatment but that is not treatment already delivered but treatment prospectively available and the medical opinion under judicial review is likely to be forensic rather than from a doctor as part of a treatment package. That said there can be no doubt that the speeches in In re F determined that the Bolam test is relevant to the judgment of the adult patient's best interests when a dispute arises as to the advisability of medical treatment. But subsequently there has been some divergence of

---

[107] ibid 27–28.

judicial opinion as to the extent of the contribution that the Bolam test makes to the determination of best interests. Of course the issue that was decided in In re F was essentially the issue of jurisdiction rather than a review of best interests on the merits. But, as I said recently in *In re A (Medical Treatment: Male Sterilisation)* [2000] 1 FCR 193, the evaluation of best interests is akin to a welfare appraisal. For, as Lord Goff had said in *In re F (Mental Patient: Sterilisation)* [1990] 2 AC 1, 83: '... I can see little, if any, practical difference between seeking the court's approval under the parens patriae jurisdiction and seeking a declaration as to the lawfulness of the operation.' Subsequently, Sir Stephen Brown P in *In re G (Adult Patient: Publicity)* [1995] 2 FLR 528, 530 said: 'The jurisdiction is not strictly the exercise of a parens patriae jurisdiction but is similar to it and the speech of Lord Brandon in the case of In re F (Mental Patient: Sterilisation) [1990] 2 AC 1 does in fact provide the foundation for that approach. In re F was a case of sterilisation not a case of a persistent vegetative state patient and to that extent it is in a different sphere of gravity. Nevertheless, it is a case where a declaration in relation to the provision of certain medical treatment of an important nature was under consideration and it is clear that the result of the decision in In re F was that a case of this nature did give to the court a jurisdiction which has been referred to as patrimonial and not strictly "parens patriae" but similar in all practical respects to it.'

It seems to me to be a distinction without a difference, by which I mean that the parens patriae jurisdiction is only the term of art for the wardship jurisdiction which is alternatively described as the inherent jurisdiction. That which is patrimonial is that which is inherited from the ancestral past. It therefore follows that whilst the decision in *In re F* signposted the inadvertent loss of the parens patriae jurisdiction in relation to incompetent adults, the alternative jurisdiction which it established, the declaratory decree, was to be exercised upon the same basis, namely that relief would be granted if the welfare of the patient required it and equally refused if the welfare of the patient did not.

I would therefore accept Mr Munby's submission that in determining the welfare of the patient the Bolam test is applied only at the outset to ensure that the treatment proposed is recognised as proper by a responsible body of medical opinion skilled in delivering that particular treatment. That may be a necessary check in an exercise where it would be impossible to be over scrupulous. But I find it hard to imagine in practice a disputed trial before a judge of the Division in which a responsible party proposed for an incompetent patient a treatment that did not satisfy the Bolam test. In practice the dispute will generally require the court to choose between two or more possible treatments both or all of which comfortably pass the Bolam test.[108]

Although the Court of Appeal cannot, of course, overrule the House of Lords, this, for all practical purposes, was the end of *Bolam*'s employment in best interests determinations.

---

[108] ibid 29–30.

## F.  Continued Feeding was Not in Tony Bland's Best Interests

Lord Mustill was, with respect, surely wrong to say that Tony Bland had no interests of any kind.[109] Perhaps even the dead have interests (in, for instance, their bodies and their memories being treated with respect). In *Bland* in the Court of Appeal, Hoffmann LJ said that the fallacy in the argument that Tony Bland had no interests

> is that it assumes that we have no interests except in those things of which we have conscious experience. But this does not accord with most people's intuitive feelings about their lives and deaths. At least a part of the reason why we honour the wishes of the dead about the distribution of their property is that we think that it would wrong them not to do so, despite the fact that we believe that they will never know that their will has been ignored. Most people would like an honourable and dignified death and we think it wrong to dishonour their deaths, even when they are unconscious that this is happening. We pay respect to their dead bodies and to their memory because we think it an offence against the dead themselves if we do not.[110]

Patients in PVS undoubtedly have rights (and correspondingly interests) under Article 8 of the ECHR.[111] The better view is that they have Article 3 rights too.[112]

---

[109]  ibid 897.

[110]  ibid 829.

[111]  See, for instance, *NHS Trust A v M* [2001] Fam 348, and *R (Burke) v General Medical Council* [2005] QB 424. See too the discussion in A MacLean, 'Crossing the Rubicon on the human rights ferry' (2001) 64 *Modern Law Review* 775.

[112]  In *NHS Trust A v M* (n 111 above) the President held that Article 3 was not engaged because one cannot suffer inhuman or degrading treatment if one is not aware of it. This conclusion was rejected by Munby J in *Burke* (n 111 above) at paras 131–51. He said, at paras 149–51:

'In my judgment treatment is capable of being "degrading" within the meaning of Article 3, whether or not it arouses feelings of fear, anguish or inferiority in the victim. It is enough if judged by the standard of right-thinking bystanders—human rights violations obviously cannot be judged by the standards of the perpetrators—it would be viewed as humiliating or debasing the victim, showing a lack of respect for, or diminishing, his or her human dignity.

That this is indeed the effect of the Strasbourg jurisprudence is, I think, borne out by the Court's recognition in *Keenan v United Kingdom* (2001) 33 EHRR 913 in the passage at para [112] which I have already quoted that: "there are circumstances where proof of the actual effect on the person may not be a major factor. For example ... treatment of a mentally ill person may be incompatible with the standards imposed by Article 3 in the protection of fundamental human dignity, even though that person may not be able, or capable of, pointing to any specific ill-effects." I respectfully agree, therefore, with what Hale LJ said in *R (Wilkinson) v Broadmoor Special Hospital Authority* [2001] EWCA Civ 1545, [2002] 1 WLR 419. Having referred to *Herczegfalvy v Austria*, she continued at para [79]: "One can at least conclude from this that forcible measures inflicted upon an incapacitated patient which are not a medical necessity may indeed be inhuman or degrading. The same must apply to forcible measures inflicted upon a capacitated patient. I would hesitate to say which was worse: the degradation of an incapacitated person shames us all even if that person is unable to appreciate it, but in fact most people are able to appreciate that they are being forced to do something against their will even if they are not able to make the decision that it should or should not be done".'

Although Munby J's judgment was criticised by the Court of Appeal, the Court of Appeal seem to have endorsed this conclusion about Article 3: see *R (Burke) v General Medical Council* [2006] QB 273, para 39.

If the Article 8(1) right of a patient in PVS is engaged, one cannot refuse to consider, in deciding whether or not there is an overall breach of Article 8 in the withdrawal of treatment, all the countervailing societal interests that fall within 8(2). An infringement of an individual's Article 8 right may be justified if it is

> in accordance with the law and is necessary in a democratic society in the interests of national security, public safety or the economic wellbeing of the country, for the prevention of disorder or crime, for the protection of health or morals, or for the protection of the rights and freedoms of others'.[113]

While the House in *Bland* refused to acknowledge that it was relevant to consider the good that the resources spent on maintaining Tony Bland could do if spent on other patients, that nettle will have to be grasped some time. It seems plainly arguable that other patients' interests in that funding fall within the 'public safety', 'economic well-being of the country', 'protection of health or morals' and 'protection of the rights and freedoms of others' criteria in Article 8(2). There is, too, a growing awareness that altruism (and perhaps altruism to the point of death), might be a personal interest that can be articulated in terms of Article 8(1).[114] The relevant altruism might be the release of funds that could save others, or the relief of the distress of others (for instance the family), caused by seeing the patient in PVS.[115] The family's/carers' distress at the maintenance of a patient in PVS might also be relevant 8(2) criteria.

All that said, the answer the House gave in *Bland* was the answer that the Mental Capacity Act 2005 would give.

Yet it does not necessarily follow from *Bland*, as some have argued,[116] that if the diagnosis of PVS is correct, treatment should be withdrawn. Every case is fact sensitive, and while the perpetual absence of any awareness whatever is of course an enormous fact, it should not be conclusive.[117] Best interests determinations should be more nuanced than that. As substituted judgement creeps increasingly into the English law[118] it may be that a strongly expressed previous opinion by the patient that life should continue, even in PVS, perhaps coupled with similar views from the family, would be regarded as determinative of best interests.

---

[113] Article 8(2).

[114] See *Re G (Children)* [2012] EWCA Civ 1233, paras 29–30; J Herring and C Foster, 'Welfare means rationality, virtue and altruism' (2012) 32 *Legal Studies* 480.

[115] Lord Mustill's observations about the relevance of the family's distress (see 897) should be revisited in the light of Article 8.

[116] See, for instance, A Grubb 'Commentary' [1995] 3 *Medical Law Review* 83.

[117] See, for example, J Boyle 'A case for sometimes tube-feeding patients in persistent vegetative state' in J Keown (ed), *Euthanasia Examined* (Cambridge, Cambridge University Press, 1995) 195.

[118] See the heading '*Bland*: the aftermath', below.

## G. There was No Duty to Continue Feeding (and Indeed, Some Thought, there was a Duty Not to Continue Feeding)

This was the easy part, given the findings. The alternative would have been a direction that vitalism was the governing principle of English medical law, and a finding that withdrawal of treatment that conferred no benefit was murder.

It is perhaps unfortunate that the House could not have come straight to this—the only real—point. That they did not do so can only be explained by a worry about overstepping the constitutional mark and embarking on judicial legislation. But surely that worry was misplaced. Certainly in the law of tort it is trite to observe that the categories of negligence are not closed— which is a cautious way of saying that the courts are happy to extend the boundaries of the duty of care to accommodate new circumstances. There is no compelling reason why a similar approach should not be taken to public law duties. *Bland* was, after all, a legal pot pourri, in which private law ideas (such as the *Bolam* test) were used, without embarrassment, to solve a public law problem (liability for murder). If the boundaries of acceptable conduct were to be drawn using a test from the law of negligence, why not adopt private law's elastic conception of the ambit of the governing duties? It would have saved a lot of trouble and a lot of paper.

## IV.  *BLAND:* THE AFTERMATH

Although the House's reasoning was tortuous, it had the advantage (despite the protestations of Lord Mustill, John Finnis and John Keown), of leaving the criminal law of murder more or less undistorted. The decision was right on its facts, and it has not led to the dilution of the notion of the sanctity of life, as some feared. The potentially malignant elements (notably the use of the *Bolam* test) were soon abandoned, and the Mental Capacity Act 2005 now mandates a holistic yet legally much more straightforward approach to cases like Tony Bland's.

*Bland* was revisited by the Supreme Court in *Aintree University Hospitals NHS Foundation Trust v James.*[119,120] Lady Hale gave the judgment of the court. The starting point, she said, was that there is 'a strong presumption that it is in a person's best interests to stay alive'. That is what the doctrine

---

[119] *Aintree University Hospitals NHS Foundation Trust v James* [2013] UKSC 67.

[120] Other important considerations of *Bland* are in *Frenchay Healthcare NHS Trust v S* [1994] 2 All ER 403; *Re G* [1995] 3 *Medical Law Review* 80; *Swindon and Marlborough NHS Trust v S* [1995] 3 Med LR 84; *Re D* (1997) 38 BMLR 1; *Re H (adult: incompetent)* (1997) 38 BMLR 11. For the position in Scotland, see *Law Hospital NHS Trust v Lord Advocate* (1996) 39 BMLR 166, and the Adults with Incapacity (Scotland) Act 2000. For the position in Ireland, see *Re a Ward of Court (withholding medical treatment)* [1995] 2 ILRM 401.

of the sanctity of life amounts to in modern best interests cases, and it is a formulation with which Finnis and Keown should not quibble. The presumption can be rebutted by it being shown that it is not in the person's best interests to stay alive. That was the position in *Bland:* it is the statutory position under the 2005 Act too. But one should be careful how one approaches the question of whether continued existence is in the person's best interests: 'It is tempting', she said, 'to approach the case as if the question is whether it would be in Mr. James's best interests to withhold those treatments should they become necessary in order to sustain his life. But is that in fact the right question?'[121] It was not, she said. She looked again at *Bland*, and concluded:

> The focus is on whether it is in the patient's best interests to give the treatment, rather than on whether it is in his best interests to withhold or withdraw it. If the treatment is not in his best interests, the court will not be able to give its consent on his behalf and it will follow that it will be lawful to withhold or withdraw it. Indeed, it will follow that it will not be lawful to give it. It also follows that (provided of course that they have acted reasonably and without negligence) the clinical team will not be in breach of any duty towards the patient if they withhold or withdraw it.[122]

This is a change of emphasis. Whether it is a significant change will depend on what the courts decide about the role, if any, of substituted judgment in the determination of best interests. There are elements of substituted judgment in the 2005 Act. Section 4(6) provides that the decision-maker

> must consider, so far as is reasonably ascertainable;

> (a)  the person's past and present wishes and feelings (and, in particular, any relevant written statement made by him when he had capacity;
> (b)  the beliefs and values that would be likely to influence his decision if he had capacity; and
> (c)  the other factors that he would be likely to consider if he were able to do so.

Lady Hale said that the relevant test is still best interests rather than substituted judgement, but that the best interests test 'accepts that the preferences of the person concerned are an important component in deciding where his best interests lie'.[123] This is entirely consistent with the Act's policy of maximising patient autonomy, but there is a good deal of judicial work still to do. The courts need to identify the version of substituted judgement that is to be used (should we be concerned with the judgement of the patient as they were when they were healthy, looking notionally at the person they now are? Or with the judgement of the person in their disabled condition, assessing the value of their compromised life?) And they need to say how the

---

[121] *Aintree* (n 119 above) [17].
[122] ibid [22].
[123] ibid [24].

substituted judgement criterion interrelates with the other factors in the best interests checklist in section 4.[124]


## V. CONCLUSION

*Bland* has weathered fairly well. It looks slightly fussy and obsessively legalistic in this more pragmatic age. It did not answer all the questions pertinent to end of life decision-making, and some of those that it did answer it got wrong. It was light on the metaphysics, but none the worse for that. To some extent it has now been overtaken by a simpler, sleeker legal model. It will be remembered for its legal earnestness, for the seriousness of its moral deliberations, for its brave avoidance of easy answers, for its attempts to map the boundary between medical law and medical ethics, for its steadfast insistence on the centrality of the best interests test, and for its reluctance to acknowledge openly that it was making decisions on the basis of policy.

---

[124] C Foster, 'Taking an interest in best interests' (2013) 163 *New Law Journal* 15.

# 6

# *R v Cambridge Health Authority, ex parte B (A Minor)* (1995): A Tale of Two Judgments

JESSE WALL

## I. INTRODUCTION

*EX PARTE B* is a tale of two judgments. Laws J, at first instance, criticised the Cambridge Health Authority for merely tolling 'the bell of tight resources' when refusing to fund the treatment of a young patient with leukemia.[1] Bingham MR, in the Court of Appeal, exercised deference towards the Health Authority's discretionary power to make 'difficult and agonising judgments'.[2]

Following the decision by the Court of Appeal in *ex parte B*, the role that medical law has in determining how healthcare resources are distributed is clearly limited. Simply put, a health authority can lawfully exercise their discretionary powers to 'provide' to the extent they 'consider necessary to meet all reasonable requirements' services for the diagnosis and treatment of illness,[3] provided that a decision does exceed the loose constraints of 'reasonableness'. As Foster observed, 'although individual decisions about resource allocation are ethically difficult and emotionally agonising, they are legally undemanding'.[4]

After a brief overview of the two decisions, I will explain how the main legal issue in both of the judgments in *ex parte B* concerns the standard of review that is adopted by the courts in reviewing the decision of the Health Authority. I will then explore the factors that help calibrate the standard of review, and compare how these factors shaped the different approaches

---

[1] *R v Cambridge Health Authority, ex parte B (a minor)* (1995) 25 BMLR 5, 17 (QB).
[2] *R v Cambridge Health Authority, ex parte B (a minor)* (1995) 23 BMLR 1, [1995] 2 All ER 129, [1995] 1 WLR 898 (CA).
[3] National Health Service Act 1977, s 3(1).
[4] C Foster, 'Simple rationality? The law of healthcare resource allocation in England' (2007) 33 *Journal of Medical Ethics* 404, 406.

taken by Laws J and Bingham MR. Finally, I will make a brief comparison between the ethics of allocating limited healthcare resources and the role of medical law in governing how healthcare resources are allocated. Although individual decisions about resources allocation are 'legally undemanding', the reasons for why medical law takes such an abstinent stance require an explanation. This chapter aims to provide an explanation.

## II. OVERVIEW

Patient B had acute myeloid leukaemia. The leukaemia had gone temporarily into remission following chemotherapy, a course of total body irradiation and a bone marrow transplant. After suffering a relapse, Patient B's physicians were of the opinion that no further remedial treatment should be provided and that Patient B had six to eight weeks to live.

Patient B's father sought alternative medical opinions. He obtained advice suggesting that further remedial treatment could be administered in two stages: a course of chemotherapy (costing £15,000, having a 10 to 20 per cent estimated chance of success), and if the chemotherapy was successful, a bone marrow transplant (costing £60,000, having a 10 to 20 per cent estimated chance of success). Patient B's father requested the Health Authority responsible for Patient B's care to fund the treatment. The Health Authority refused and the Authority's decision was judicially reviewed.

Laws J at first instance quashed the Health Authority's decision on two grounds. First, Laws J held that since the Authority had 'taken a decision which interferes with the applicant's right to life' the Authority is required to provide 'a substantial public interest justification for doing so'.[5] The Health Authority had failed to provide a substantial justification as it had not adequately explained 'the priorities that have led them to decline to fund the treatment'.[6] Secondly, Laws J also held that the Health Authority failed to have regard for Patient B's family's views (as a surrogate for Patient B's views).[7] This was a relevant consideration that the authority failed to consider, in determining whether the proposed treatment was in Patient B's best interests. In quashing the decision, Laws J also criticised the Health Authority for viewing the proposed treatment as 'experimental' and for not viewing the proposed treatment in terms of an initial £15,000 expenditure.

Hence, four issues arose on appeal to the Court of Appeal. Bingham MR (with Brown P and Brown LJ concurring) found in favour of the Authority on all four grounds. First, the Court held that Patient B's physician, and thereby the Authority, was 'as vividly aware as he could have been of the

---

[5] *Cambridge Health Authority* (QB) (n 1 above) 13.
[6] ibid 17.
[7] ibid 15–16.

fact that the family, represented by B's father, were urgently wishing the authority to undertake this treatment'.[8] Secondly, the Authority could not be criticised for describing the proposed treatment 'experimental', as the treatment 'was not one that had a well-tried track record of success' and 'was at the frontier of medical science'.[9] The third finding is one of the most noteworthy findings: Bingham MR held that the Authority could not be criticised for failing to explain 'how a limited budget is best allocated to the maximum advantage of the maximum number of patients' since the court is not in a position to assess these 'difficult and agonising judgments'.[10] Fourth, the Court found that the Authority was correct to view the decision to fund treatment as a decision to allocate funds for both stages of the treatment, since 'they would have to continue if, having expended the £15,000, it proved successful and the call for the second stage of the treatment came'.[11]

### III. GROUNDS OF REVIEW AND STANDARDS OF REVIEW

There are a number of grounds upon which a court can find that a decision of a healthcare authority is unlawful. A healthcare authority, in making a decision, will be exercising a power that has a statutory basis. The court, in reviewing the decision, is able to determine whether the authority's decision was pursuant to a purpose that is consistent with the purpose of the statutory power, and whether the considerations that led the authority to make the decision are accurate and relevant to the statutory power.[12] Hence, the Court of Appeal in reviewing the decision of the Cambridge Health Authority, was asked to determine whether the Health Authority failed to consider the wishes of Patient B's family, whether the Health Authority erred in considering the treatment to be 'experimental', or erred in considering the radiation therapy and transplant as a single treatment.

There are also broader grounds upon which a court can review a decision. Where a healthcare authority identifies a set of relevant and accurate considerations that culminate in a decision, the court may also review the weight afforded to the considerations.[13] A decision may be unlawful where some of the considerations that led to the decision were given irrational, unreasonable or disproportionate weight in the decision-making process. The assumption here is that the decision-maker would be stepping outside their statutory powers if the decision-maker were using the power irrationally,

---

[8] *Cambridge Health Authority* (CA) (n 2 above) 136.
[9] ibid 137.
[10] ibid.
[11] ibid 138.
[12] P Craig, 'The Nature of Reasonableness Review' (2013) 66 *Current Legal Problems* 131, 136–37.
[13] ibid 137.

unreasonably or disproportionately. In this way, the judicial review of the weight afforded to the reasons and considerations behind a decision is a more abstracted version of the court reviewing the consistency of the specific decision with the purpose of the statutory power and the relevancy of considerations that lead to the decision.[14]

For Laws J, the failure of Health Authority to explain the priorities that had led them to decline to fund the treatment meant that the Health Authority could not identify a set of considerations sufficient to justify a decision which interfered with Patient B's right to life.[15] In other words, given the importance of sustaining Patient B's chance of life, for the decision of the Health Authority to refuse treatment to be a lawful decision, there must be a set of considerations that have sufficient importance to outweigh the importance of sustaining the patient's chance of life. The Court of Appeal also reviewed the weight afforded to the considerations that led to the decision to refuse treatment. However, the Court of Appeal considered the decision not to fund the treatment to be a reasonable, and therefore lawful, decision despite the lack of detail in the Authority's explanation of the priorities that weighed against funding the treatment.

The two judgments concerned the same ground of review: whether the decision-maker afforded the appropriate weight to the considerations that led to the decision. However, where the judgments differ is in the degree of intensity with which the court reviewed the decision of the Health Authority. Laws J doubted 'whether the decisive touchstone for the legality of the respondents' decision was the crude *Wednesbury* bludgeon',[16] approached the review with a greater degree of scrutiny, and applied (what has become known as) a standard of proportionality. This standard of review 'demands a reasoned justification' from the decision-maker 'for the choice it has made'.[17] Bingham MR, in contrast, approached the review with a greater degree of deference, and applied a reasonableness standard. Under this standard of review, the decision would be unlawful if 'it is beyond the range of responses open to a reasonable decision-maker'.[18]

The two decisions are noteworthy in terms of the different degrees of intensity adopted in reviewing a decision of a health authority whether to fund a treatment. The Court of Appeal decision is a landmark decision for the proposition that the courts will exercise a significant degree of deference when reviewing a discretionary resource allocation decision.[19] As I will explain, this is especially the case where the resource allocation decision is pursuant to sections 1 and 3 of the National Health Service (NHS) Act 1977.

---

[14] ibid 137–38; P Craig, 'Proportionality, Rationality and Review' [2010] *New Zealand Law Review* 265, 278.

[15] *Cambridge Health Authority* (QB) (n 1 above) 17.

[16] ibid 11.

[17] Craig, 'Proportionality' (2010) n 14 above, 272.

[18] *R v Ministry of Defence ex parte Smith* [1996] QB 517, 554.

[19] JA King, 'The Justiciability of Resource Allocation' (2007) 70 *Modern Law Review* 19, 199.

The different degrees of scrutiny adopted in the two judgments reflect the different priority given by Laws J and Bingham MR to factors that influence the degree of intensity or deference that a court adopts in reviewing a decision. We shall now turn to consider the factors relevant to determining the intensity with which a court will review a decision of a healthcare authority to fund a treatment, and compare how these factors determined the approaches taken by Laws J and Bingham MR.

IV. CALIBRATING THE STANDARD OF REVIEW

As I will explain in this section, (A) the impact of the decision on the individual—removing Patient B's remaining chance of life—is a factor that motivates an intense judicial review of the Health Authority's decision since judicial review aims to safeguard individual interests against the misuse of public power. Yet, there are also three related factors that prompt a significant degree of deference towards the Health Authority's decision. These concern B.(i) the degree of polycentricity in decisions to fund healthcare treatments, B.(ii) the need to evaluate healthcare outcomes and B.(iii) the scope of the statutory duty. It is the combination of these later three factors that explain why the Court of Appeal applied a deferential standard of review despite the impact of the decision on the individual. Note that these three factors are cascading reasons for the court to apply a more deferential standard of review. Put briefly, it is because a decision whether to fund a treatment is (i) a polycentric decision that the health authority must (ii) evaluate healthcare outcomes (iii) as part of their broad statutory discretion, that the court is unable to examine the decision with any degree of intensity.

## A. Intensity and the Impact of the Decision on the Individual

It was accepted that, without the funding for the further remedial treatment, Patient B would have a matter of weeks to live. For Laws J at first instance, the decision was an infringement of Patient B's right to life: 'The decision in this case has, to the knowledge of the decision-maker, materially affected for the worse, the applicant's chances of life. I hold that the applicant's right to life is assaulted by it'.[20]

In the Court of Appeal, Bingham MR also highlighted the seriousness of the decision:

[T]his is a case involving the life of a young patient and that that is a fact which must dominate all consideration of all aspects of the case ... No decision affecting human life is one that can be regarded with other than the greatest seriousness.[21]

---

[20] *Cambridge Health Authority* (QB) (n 1 above) 14.
[21] *Cambridge Health Authority* (CA) (n 2 above) 136.

It is clear that the consequences of the Health Authority's decision were significant for Patient B. Where a decision of a public authority has the effect of placing a significant or severe burden on the individual or has the effect of impeding the interests that are of real importance for the individual, the courts will review the decision with greater scrutiny. This reflects an institutional strength of judicial review: the adversarial process provides the court with the vantage point to properly assess the impact of a decision on the interests of an individual applicant. By reviewing the lawfulness of discretion exercised under statutory powers, judicial review can function to safeguard individual interests from the administrative machinery of the government.[22] Hence, the courts are 'institutionally competent'[23] at safeguarding individual interest, and will adopt a more intense level of scrutiny of a decision where the decision has a greater or more severe impact.

For some commentators, viewing the impact on the individual's interests through a human rights framework 'permits the court to shift the terrain on which a resource allocation decision is considered',[24] enables the courts to 'perform their constitutionally-assigned task of protecting human rights'[25] and 'give[s] effect to those clearly defined and enduring values which lie beyond the purviews of statute'.[26] According to these commentators, where a statutory decision interferes with a human right, the courts ought to rigorously scrutinise the decision and 'assert their authority and expertise over and above the expertise of policymakers'.[27]

One of the key points on which Laws J and Bingham MR differ in their analysis is the emphasis placed on the extent to which the impact of the decision on the individual intensifies the standard of review. Although Bingham MR recognised the seriousness of the decision, he avoided the language of 'human rights', and emphasised that the function of the court is 'strictly confined' to 'the lawfulness of decisions'.[28] In comparison, the analysis of Laws J focuses on Patient B's right to life, finding that

> certain rights, broadly those occupying a central place in the European Convention on Human Rights and obviously including the right to life, are not to be perceived merely as moral or political aspirations ... They are to be vindicated as sharing with other principles the substance of the English common law.[29]

---

[22] E Palmer, 'Resource Allocation, Welfare Rights—Mapping the Boundaries of Judicial Control in Public Administrative Law' (2000) 20 *Oxford Journal of Legal Studies* 63, 70; D Oliver, 'Is the *Ultra Vires* Rule the Basis of Judicial Review?' [1987] *Public Law* 543, 545.

[23] AL Young, 'In Defence of Due Deference' (2009) 72 *Modern Law Review* 554, 577.

[24] BM Sheldrick, 'Judicial review and the allocation of health care resources in Canada and the United Kingdom' (2003) 5 *Journal of Comparative Policy Analysis: Research and Practice* 149, 157.

[25] Young, 'In Defence' (2009) n 23 above, 575; TRS Allan, 'Human Rights and Judicial Review: A Critique of "Due Deference"' (2006) 65 *Cambridge Law Journal* 671–95.

[26] Palmer, 'Resource Allocation' (2000) n 22 above, 70–71; J Laws, 'Law and Democracy' [1995] *Public Law* 72, 92.

[27] Sheldrick, 'Judicial review' (2003) n 24 above, 157.

[28] *Cambridge Health Authority* (CA) (n 2 above) 136.

[29] *Cambridge Health Authority* (QB) (n 1 above) 12.

Given the rights infringement, Laws J subjected the decision of the Health Authority to an intense standard of review. This call for 'the most anxious scrutiny' of administrative decisions that may infringe the right to life preceded Laws J in *Ex parte B*,[30] and the approach taken by Laws J in requiring a 'substantial objective justification on public interest grounds'[31] for the infringement roughly mirrors the contemporary standard of review for European Convention rights infringements.[32]

The difference between Laws J and Bingham MR can be explained, in part, in terms of the difference of emphasis placed on the impact of the decision on the individual. At face value, the 'rights-based' approach taken by Laws J appears to be the orthodox approach to calibrating the standard of view. More precisely, however, Laws J and Bingham MR differ in terms of the weight they attribute to impact on the individual vis-a-vis other factors that are relevant to the standard of review applied. For Laws J, given that the significance and severity of the impact of the decision on the individual applicant is a factor that motivates intense scrutiny, the rights dimension of the case was sufficient to side-line the (below) factors in favour of deference, and enable the courts to 'assert their authority and expertise'. For Bingham MR, the impact on the individual is one of a number of factors that are relevant to calibrating the standard of review, and under such an approach a court may exercise self-restraint even when the right to life is engaged.

## B. Factors in Favour of Deference

The following three factors that favour deference towards a decision of a health authority stem from the statutory powers that a health authority exercises. Since the discussion will often refer to these statutory provisions, the relevant extracts are set out here. Under section 13 of the NHS Act, the Secretary of State can, and does, delegate the duties under section 1 and section 3 to health authorities. As a result, Section 1(1) imposes on health authorities a duty:

> to continue the promotion in England and Wales of a comprehensive health service designed to secure improvement—
>
> (a)  in the physical and mental health of the people of those countries, and
> (b)  in the prevention, diagnosis and treatment of illness,
>
> and for that purpose to provide or secure the effective provision of services in accordance with the Act.

---

[30] *Bugdaycay v Secretary of State for the Home Dept* [1987] 1 All E.R. 940, 952 (HL).
[31] *Cambridge Health Authority* (QB) (n 1 above) 12.
[32]  *R v Headteacher and Governors of Denbigh High School, ex parte Begum* [2006] UKHL 15, [30]–[34], [66]–[67], [94].

Section 3 requires that the Secretary of State (through health authorities) must:

> Provide ... to such extent as he considers necessary to meet all reasonable requirements ...
>
> (e)  such facilities for the prevention of illness, the care of persons suffering from illness and the after-care of persons who have suffered from illness as he considers are appropriate as part of the health service;
> (f)  such other services as are required for the diagnosis and treatment of illness.

In broad terms, the difference between the standards of review applied in the two judgments reflects the tension between the duty on health authorities to respect Patient B's right to life (under Article 2 of the European Convention) and the general duties to continue to promote a comprehensive health service (under section 1(1) of the NHS Act).

### (i)  The Degree of Polycentricity

A polycentric decision is a decision that affects 'a large and complicated web of interdependent relationships, such that a change to one factor produces an incalculable series of changes to other factors'.[33] A decision to fund a treatment is a polycentric decision since the allocation of funds toward a treatment reduces the funding available to a series of other treatments, services and programmes. The general concern is that, 'given the limitations of the adversarial process ... courts lack both the information and the capacity to assess the broader ramifications' of polycentric decisions.[34] This is a question of relative institutional competence. Similar to the courts' relative strength at safeguarding individual interests, this concern highlights a weakness of the 'judicial process as an institutional mechanism'[35] for solving polycentric problems.

Laws J at first instance was aware that the decision of the Health Authority was polycentric: 'I quite accept ... that the court should not make orders with consequences for the use of Health Service funds in ignorance of the knock-on effect on other patients'.[36] As was Bingham MR in the Court of Appeal:

> It is common knowledge that health authorities of all kinds are constantly pressed to make ends meet ... Difficult and agonising judgments have to be made as to how a limited budget is best allocated to the maximum advantage of the maximum number of patients. This is not a judgment which the court can make.[37]

---

[33] JA King, 'The Pervasiveness of Polycentricity' [2008] *Public Law* 101, 104; LL Fuller, 'The Forms and Limits of Adjudication' (1978) 92 *Harvard Law Review* 353, 397.

[34] Sheldrick (n 24 above) 152; J Allison, 'The Procedural Reason for Judicial Restraint' (1994) PL 452–73.

[35] JA King, 'Institutional Approaches to Judicial Restraint' (2008) 28 *Oxford Journal of Legal Studies* 409, 410.

[36] *Cambridge Health Authority* (QB) (n 1 above) 17.

[37] *Cambridge Health Authority* (CA) (n 2 above) 137.

Yet, all administrative decisions affect a series of interdependent relationships. As Palmer explains, 'it is axiomatic that prioritization over the use of resources lies at the heart of administrative decision-making'.[38] Since all administrative decisions have 'knock-on' effects, the problem of polycentricity is best understood as a problem of degree. The greater the number of possible knock-on effects, the more varied, diverse and incommensurable the knock-on effects are; and the more of the knock-on effects that the primary decision-maker is responsible for, the more polycentric the decision will be.

A decision whether to fund a treatment pursuant to sections 1 and 3 of the NHS Act 1977 is a decision with a high degree of polycentricity. The duty on a health authority is to promote a series of different aims: to provide facilities for the prevention of illness, secure improvement in diagnosis and treatment of illness, provide after-care for persons who have suffered from illnesses, and provide any such other services required for the diagnosis and treatment of illness. This series of duties equates, in practice, to a health authority being unable to further the aims that they are responsible for 'as much as they would like'. As Bingham MR explained in the judgment, health authorities

> cannot pay their nurses as much as they would like; they cannot provide all the treatments they would like; they cannot purchase all the extremely expensive medical equipment they would like; they cannot carry out all the research they would like; they cannot build all the hospitals and specialists units they would like.[39]

A decision pursuant to sections 1 and 3 will have a high degree of polycentricity, since it will have the effect of prioritising one healthcare aim over a number of other varied and incommensurable healthcare aims that health authorities are also duty-bound to promote.

A court has limited competence to review such a decision. In part because the court may lack the information and insight into the healthcare needs of patients and effect of various healthcare services. This concern had earlier been expressed by the Court of Appeal in *Re J*:

> I would stress the absolute undesirability of the court making an order which may have the effect of compelling a doctor or health authority to make available scarce resources (both human and material) to a particular child, without knowing whether or not there are other patients to whom those resources might more advantageously be devoted.[40]

In part this concern arises also because the judicial task is to adjudicate between the two conflicting interests *of the parties* to the dispute. To administer a policy—to further a set of aims by allocating entitlements between a population of persons—requires a skill set that is distinct from the judicial skill set.

---

[38] Palmer (n 22 above) 73.
[39] *Cambridge Health Authority* (CA) (n 2 above) 137.
[40] *Re J (a minor)* [1992] 4 All ER 614, 625 (CA).

Where Laws J and Bingham MR differ in terms of the standard of review adopted in *ex parte B* concerns whether the polycentricity of the decision discourages judicial engagement in the decision. For Laws J, since the decision has a significant and severe impact for Patient B (as above), the court is required to *engage* with the polycentric decision. As a result, the Health Authority is required to explain the priorities that led to their decision not to fund Patient B's treatment. Hence, Laws J held that for the Health Authority

> merely to point to the fact that resources are finite tells one nothing about the wisdom or, what is relevant for my purposes, the legality of a decision to withhold funding in a particular case. I have no evidence as to what kinds of case, if any, might be prejudiced if the respondents were to fund B's treatment. I have no idea where in the order of things the respondents place a modest chance of saving the life of a ten-year-old girl.[41]

In contrast, for Bingham MR, since 'difficult and agonising judgments ... as to how a limited budget is best allocated' are 'not a judgment *which the court can make*' (emphasis added),[42] the Health Authority could not be criticised for its failure to bring evidence of the competing priorities that it decided to advance at the expense of Patient B's treatment. In brief, Bingham MR viewed the high degree of polycentricity as a factor in favour of exercising deference towards the decision of the Health Authority. Laws J viewed the polycentric decision as something the Court ought to be able to review, namely whether the appropriate weight was attributed to the various other healthcare aims that the Authority was also duty-bound to promote.

## (ii) The Evaluation of Healthcare Outcomes

Let us momentarily follow through on Law J's suggestion that reviewing the Health Authority's decision involves reviewing the healthcare needs that were prioritised at the expense of the treatment of Patient B.[43] For simplicity's sake, let us remove the polycentricity and only compare Patient B with a notional 'Patient C'. We know that Patient B's *condition* was that she had acute myeloid leukaemia and had between six and eight weeks to live, the cost of the proposed *treatment* was £75,000, the healthcare *outcome* was for the leukaemia to go into remission, the proposed treatment had a 4–6 per cent *probability* of succeeding, and that Patient B sought the treatment. The comparison would then be with Patient C's best interests, medical condition, cost of treatment, healthcare outcome and probability of success. This comparison between Patient B and Patient C requires both medical and evaluative judgement; medical judgement as to the patients' condition and

---

[41] *Cambridge Health Authority* (QB) (n 1 above) 16.
[42] *Cambridge Health Authority* (CA) (n 2 above) 137.
[43] *Cambridge Health Authority* (QB) (n 1 above) 16–17.

prescribed treatment, and evaluative judgement as between the healthcare outcomes for both patients.

As far as the medical judgement is concerned, both Laws J and Bingham MR accepted that it is no part of the judicial function 'to make medical judgments',[44] 'express opinions as to the likelihood of the effectiveness of medical treatment, or as to the merits of medical judgment'.[45] However, Laws J added an important qualification: that the court must 'make such findings of fact as are necessary to enable me to determine whether there has been an error of law in the decision-making process under review'.[46] As discussed, the court's review of an administrative decision will include the review of relevance and accuracy of the considerations that formed the basis of the decision. Although Laws J and Bingham MR refrained from expressing opinion as to 'the merits of medical judgment', they were able to determine whether the proposed treatment could be accurately described as 'experimental', given the clinical evidence, and to determine whether the chemotherapy and bone marrow transplant ought to be viewed (for funding purposes) as separable treatments.

Where evaluative judgement is required is in how we prioritise one healthcare outcome (in light of the probability of the outcome) over a competing healthcare outcome (also in light of the probability of the outcome). Decisions as to whether a service or treatment is funded are driven by this evaluation between these possible healthcare outcomes. It is in exercising this evaluative judgement—that requires an examination of the relative weight of competing and incommensurate healthcare aims—that a health authority exercises *discretion*.

It is clear from sections 1 and 3 of the NHS Act that, insofar as the Secretary of State (or delegated authorities) must provide services and treatments 'to such extent as he considers necessary to meet all reasonable requirements', this evaluative task or prioritising services and treatments over others is a task for the Secretary of State (or delegated authorities). The extent to which a healthcare outcome has priority (in light of its probability and vis-a-vis competing outcomes) is a question of weight that is a question that is 'quintessentially within the discretion of the primary decision-maker'.[47] Although the reasonableness of the weight attributed to a consideration by the healthcare authority will always be subject to review by the courts,[48] legislation (and regulations) have allocated the evaluative task to the health authority. As Auld LJ subsequently held: 'The precise allocation and weighting of priorities is clearly a matter of judgment for each

---

[44] ibid 9.
[45] *Cambridge Health Authority* (CA) (n 2 above) 136.
[46] *Cambridge Health Authority* (QB) (n 1 above) 9.
[47] Craig, 'The Nature' (2013) n 12 above, 148.
[48] ibid 149.

authority, keeping well in mind its statutory obligations to meet the reasonable requirements of all those within its area for which it is responsible'.[49]

The considerations that formed the basis of the decision not to fund Patient B's treatment are a combination of medical and evaluative assessments. The court retains the ability to review the relevance and accuracy of the considerations that form the basis of an authority's decision, despite the considerations being of a specialist or technical nature. Although the courts also retain the ability to review the reasonableness of the evaluative assessment between different healthcare outcomes, this evaluative task falls within the statutory discretion of Secretary of State (and delegated authorities). Health authorities therefore exercise discretion in order to make a series of these evaluative assessments, and given their statutory authority to do, the courts are reluctant to review the discretion with intensity.

### (iii)  The Scope of the Statutory Duty

The third factor in favour of deference to the decision-maker is the scope of the statutory duty that the decision-maker is exercising. The duty exercised by the Health Authority in *ex parte B* was a 'general duty'. Section 3 sets out a duty to provide services and facilities, only 'to such extent as [the authority] considers necessary to meet all reasonable requirements'. The duty to provide facilities only applies as far 'as [the authority] considers appropriate as part of a health service'. The duty in section 1 is to promote, rather than provide, a 'comprehensive health service'. This section has been interpreted as a requirement that the authority 'pays due regard to that duty' whilst recognising that the 'fact that the service will not be comprehensive does not mean that he is necessarily contravening either section 1 or section 3'.[50]

Sections 1 and 3 provide the primary decision-maker with a wide discretion as to how to allocate public healthcare resources. These 'general', 'discretionary' or 'target' duties can be contrasted with 'specific' duties.[51] According to Lord Nicholls, 'the more specific and precise the duty the more readily the statute may be interpreted as imposing an obligation of an absolute character'[52] and the more likely it is to be enforceable by individual against the primary-decision maker. In comparison, the

> broader and more general the terms of the duty, the more readily the statute may be construed as affording scope for a local authority to take into account matters such as cost when deciding how best to perform the duty in its own area.[53]

---

[49] *R v North West Lancashire Health Authority, ex parte A, D & G* [2000] 1 WLR 977, 991.
[50] *R v North and East Devon Health Authority ex parte Coughlan* [2001] QB 213, 230.
[51] King, 'The Justiciability' (2007) n 19 above, 214.
[52] *R (on the application of G) v Barnet London Borough Council* [2003] UKHL 57, [2004] 2 AC 208, [13].
[53] ibid.

Without constraints, standards or limits on the discretion of the decision-maker, there remains little basis for the court to impose any substantive duty toward any particular individual. In comparison to *ex parte B*, consider the decision in *ex parte Tandy*.[54] Here, the local education authority had reduced the hours of home tuition for a sick child from five to three hours weekly. The House of Lords interpreted the duty to provide 'suitable education' under section 298 of the Education Act 1993 so as to impose a 'specific' or 'mandatory' duty on the education authority.[55] Since section 298 imposed a specific duty, the education authority could not 'avoid performing a statutory duty on the grounds that it prefers to spend the money in other ways'.[56] In *ex parte B* there were no specific duties owed to Patient B, only the general and discretionary duties under sections 1 and 3 of the NHS Act. Whereas section 298 of the Education Act sets out an education *standard*, sections 1 and 3 of the NHS Act set out a series of healthcare *aims*. Without any statutory standards or allocative principles to limit the discretion of the Health Authority, there is no standard against which to criticise the Authority's pursuit of healthcare aims.

There may be, however, regulatory standards that ought to form part of a health authority's decision-making process. For example, in *ex parte Fisher* the Health Authority refused to fund on a regular basis a drug (Beta Interferon) for multiple sclerosis patients until the results of a clinical trial were known.[57] The Secretary of State had issued a (non-mandatory) policy asking health authorities to develop and implement procedures for the use of the drug. The court held that the Health Authority failed to rationally account for their departure from the policy.

Moreover, where a health authority has a general discretion to exercise, this discretion is accompanied by the obligation on the health authority not to exercise their discretion in a fettered, fixed or rigid way. In *ex parte Fisher*, since there was no longer to be a clinical trial, the court also held that the Authority had fettered its discretion to fund the drug since the condition precedent for the funding (the clinical trial) could not be met in any circumstances. Similarly in *R (Rodgers) v Swindon NHS Trust*,[58] the policy of the Health Authority was not to fund a breast cancer drug (Herceptin) except where a patient presented an exceptional case for treatment. The court held that policy was irrational since the Authority was unable to identify any 'clinical circumstances' that could represent an exceptional case for treatment.[59]

---

[54] *R v East Sussex County Council, ex parte Tandy* [1998] AC 714; [1998] 2 All ER 769.

[55] Palmer (n 22 above) 79.

[56] *R v East Sussex County Council, ex parte Tandy* [1998] 2 All ER 769, 777 (Lord Browne-Wilkinson).

[57] *R v North Derbyshire Health Authority, ex parte Fisher* (1997) 10 Admin LR 27 (QB).

[58] *R (Rodgers) v Swindon NHS Primary Care Trust* [2006] EWCA Civ 392.

[59] ibid [67], [73].

*Ex parte Fisher* and *Rodgers* concern the judicial review of *policies* that health authorities formulate in order to determine which treatments will be provided. As for a decision as to the 'particular circumstances of the individual patient', and with regard to the 'competing demands' on a health authority's budget, the Court of Appeal in *Rodger* affirmed the deference exercised by the Court of Appeal in *ex parte B* by suggesting that 'it would be very difficult, if not impossible' to say that any particular decision was irrational.[60] It is because the questions of priority as to healthcare outcomes and aims are questions that fall within the broad discretion of healthcare authorities, without any particular standards to adhere to or specific duties to perform, that decisions as to which particular services and treatments ought to be provided are subject to a deferential standard of review.

As mentioned, these three factors in favour of deference toward the decision-maker are cascading factors. It is now possible to view these factors together. If the statutory duty of a health authority is a specific duty, 'the intention of Parliament is clearer and courts can proceed confidently in enforcing financially onerous duties';[61] whereas, if the duty is a broad and general duty, it is 'a statutory indication from Parliament that the matter is entrusted principally to the administrative decision-maker',[62] at least in part because 'the allocative impact of the judgment could be greater in view of the number of claims that might come forward'.[63]

## V. THE ETHICAL SUB-TERRAIN

When we explore the ethics of how healthcare resources *ought* to be allocated we encounter a structurally similar set of issues. We encounter: the impact that the decision not to fund a treatment can have on the interests or moral properties of a patient; the various moral duties or obligations that a healthcare provider owes to patients; and the need to formulate a way to assess which healthcare needs ought to have priority over others. To better understand the legal landscape, it is worth briefly mapping the ethical sub-terrain.

We all have a set of interests or moral properties 'simply by virtue of our humanity'.[64] For most, these interests are the basis of our human rights,[65]

---

[60] ibid [58].

[61] King (2007) (n 19 above) 215.

[62] ibid 219.

[63] ibid 215.

[64] J Tasioulas, 'On the Nature of Human Rights' in G Ernst and J-C Heilinger (eds), *The Philosophy of Human Rights: Contemporary* (Berlin, De Gruyter, 2012) 26; T Endicott, 'The Infant in the Snow' in T Endicott, J Getzler and E Peel (eds), *Properties of Law* (Oxford, Oxford University Press, 2006) 348, 362.

[65] Tasioulas, 'On the Nature' (2012) n 64 above, 26; J Raz, 'Human Rights Without Foundations' in S Besson, J Tasioulas (eds), *The Philosophy of International Law* (Oxford, Oxford University Press, 2010) 321.

and as Laws J observed, 'of all human rights, most people would accord the most precious place to the right to life itself'.[66] The right to life, as a *right*, provides powerful reasons for others to act in a particular way. If human rights are to feature in an ethical analysis, the recognition that a patient has a right to life imposes duties or obligations on providers of public health-care. In either case, the interests or moral properties that each patient has by virtue of their humanity form considerations or obligations that ought to feature in our moral reasoning about the allocation of healthcare resources.

A public healthcare provider therefore owes moral duties or obligations to a large population of patients. Given that the public healthcare authorities have finite resources, a public healthcare provider 'cannot provide all the treatments they would like',[67] and some way of identifying which treatments ought to be provided, at the expense of other treatments, is required.

Ethicists disagree as to how this evaluation ought to be performed. The ethical approach that was adopted by the Health Authority in *ex parte B*, and is currently practised by National Institute for Health and Clinical Excellence, aims to maximise healthcare *outcomes*. In particular, healthcare resources are allocated in order to maximise the 'quality of life' and the 'life-years' of the patient-population. What is ethically relevant when allocating limited healthcare resources, according to this approach, are the comparative healthcare outcomes of the various possible applications of the resources. This approach has been accused of making 'value judgments about people's lives'[68] and being 'contrary to basic morality and contrary to human rights'.[69] The underlying concern is that maximising healthcare outcomes forces a value-based comparison between people in order to determine which patient is 'worthy' of treatment.[70]

It is true that the current practice makes a value-based comparison between people. In fact, *any* way of identifying which treatments ought to be provided makes a value-based comparison between people. If we were to flip a coin, treat the first person to the hospital or refuse to treat people with red hair, we would be making a value-based comparison between people (assigning value to: heads over tails, front of the queue over the back of the queue, blonde hair over red hair). What is of critical importance is the values we base the comparison on.

If we were to base the comparison on what the patients have done, or will do, with their lives, then we would be 'making value judgments about people's lives'. Given that all patients have the right to life or a set of interests 'simply by virtue of their humanity', basic morality and human rights

---

[66] *Cambridge Health Authority* (QB) (n 1 above) 6.
[67] *Cambridge Health Authority* (CA) (n 2 above) 137.
[68] M Quigley, 'A NICE fallacy' (2007) 33 *Journal of Medical Ethics* 465.
[69] J Harris, 'It's not NICE to discriminate' (2005) 31 *Journal of Medical Ethics* 373, 375.
[70] Quigley, 'A NICE fallacy' (2007) n 68 above, 465.

require us 'to treat [all patients] with equal concern and respect'.[71] We will ultimately end up treating patients differently *on the basis that* the treatment of their condition will provide different healthcare outcomes. To the extent we can separate a person from their healthcare condition, such an approach becomes a very *impersonal* interpersonal comparison, that says nothing about the worthiness or otherwise of the person.

There are alternative ethical approaches to the current approach of maximising aggregate longevity and quality of life. These represent a different set of values which we can use to identify which treatments ought to be provided. For instance, we may seek to achieve a minimum standard of health or a minimum life-expectancy for all patients, we could treat the patients who face the most immediate threat to life or most immediate ill-health,[72] or distribute healthcare resources equally between all potential patients.

If we were to adopt one these alternative approaches, we would be limiting or replacing the healthcare *aim* (of maximising healthcare outcomes) with a minimum healthcare *standard* or a principle of healthcare allocation. In terms of an ethical analysis, we would be shifting from a position where the *consequences* of decision determine the soundness of the decision, to a scenario where the adherence to *duties* or *principles* would determine whether a resource allocation decision was ethically sound. In legal terms, we would be shifting from a healthcare authority exercising a general and discretionary duty, to a healthcare authority exercising a specific and standard-based duty.

Hence, the structure of the ethical debate underlies the legal debate. We ought to take the right to life seriously whilst recognising that healthcare providers are caught by a 'large and complicated web' of duties to patients. Evaluative judgement is therefore required to identify which treatments ought to be provided. This evaluative judgement can be oriented toward particular outcomes and consequences, and if so, a discretionary power must be exercised to determine how these outcomes can be maximised over a large population of patients. Alternatively, the evaluative judgement can be determined (entirely or in part) by ethical standards or principles that would take the legal form of duties owed to particular patients.

## VI. CONCLUSION

What healthcare treatments and services are funded determines the content of public healthcare. Medical law ultimately defers to the judgement of public healthcare authorities as to how healthcare resources are allocated.

---

[71] A Parkin, 'Allocating Health Care Resources in an Imperfect World' (1995) 58 *Modern Law Review* 867, 876; R Dworkin, *Taking Rights Seriously* (London, Duckworth, 1977) 226.

[72] R Cookson and P Nolan, 'Principles of justice in health care rationing' (2000) 26 *Journal of Medical Ethics* 323, 324.

As *ex parte B* demonstrates, this deference is despite the life or death consequences of funding decisions. I have sought to explain this deference with reference to three related factors. First, a decision to fund a treatment is a decision with a high degree of polycentricity, which the courts have limited institutional competence to review with any degree of intensity. Secondly, a decision to fund a treatment is driven by an evaluative judgement about healthcare outcomes, which is a discretionary judgement placed within the hands of the Secretary of State (and delegated authorities). Thirdly, the general scope of the duties imposed on the decision-maker limits the ability of the courts to criticise a healthcare authority's pursuit of healthcare aims.

This legal arrangement is premised upon the ethical assumption that the allocation of healthcare resources ought to be towards the aim of maximising the longevity and quality of life of all patients. This is a contestable ethical assumption, but is not an assumption 'contrary to basic morality'. At the moment, health authorities exercise a general duty to determine how resources are allocated in accordance with this aim. If we were to restrain the pursuit of this aim of maximising healthcare outcomes by imposing a standard or principle of allocation, health authorities would be under a specific duty to adhere to the standard or principle.

As for Patient B herself, an anonymous donor paid for the further remedial treatment to be provided in a private clinic. The treatment prolonged her life for two further years.

# 7

# R v Bournewood Community and Mental Health NHS Trust, ex parte L [1999]: Bournewood Fifteen Years On

GENEVRA RICHARDSON

## I. BACKGROUND

THE MENTAL HEALTH Act 1983 (MHA) creates a statutory framework for the provision of care and treatment for mental disorder. It permits detention in hospital and treatment without consent if necessary. In medical law terms it provides an exception to accepted principle.[1] In 1997 Mr L, who suffered from autism and profound mental disability, became very agitated at his day centre and since his carers could not be contacted he was readmitted to the behavioural unit at Bournewood hospital where he had previously been an inpatient. His consultant decided not to admit him compulsorily under the MHA because he was not objecting to being in hospital. Instead she admitted Mr L informally under section 131(1) of the Act. His carers, Mr and Mrs E, considered that he was being held unlawfully and applied to the High Court on his behalf. The trial judge held that section 131 preserved the common law jurisdiction in respect of informal patients and that Mr L's admission was therefore lawful. This was reversed by the Court of Appeal who held that section 131 applied only to patients who had the capacity to consent and had consented to admission. Since Mr L did not possess this capacity his admission was unlawful. The hospital appealed to the House of Lords.[2]

The *Bournewood* case concerned a significant problem affecting a large and highly vulnerable patient group, a problem which has yet to be fully resolved 15 years later. The Mental Health Act, for good or ill, provides a

---

[1] For a useful account of the scope of the Mental Health Act, see P Bartlett and R Sandland, *Mental Health Law: Policy and Practice*, 4th edn (Oxford, Oxford University Press, 2014).

[2] *R v Bournewood Community and Mental Health NHS Trust, ex parte L* [1999] 1 AC 458.

statutory framework for the imposition of hospital detention and treatment in the absence of consent. The powers are described at length and are accompanied by a range of safeguards relating to both detention and treatment and, in the main, they have been found to comply with the requirements of the ECHR. Care and treatment for mental disorder can, however, be provided without the use of these powers and for the vast majority of mental health patients it is so provided.[3] The presence of a mental disability does not necessarily imply the absence of mental capacity so most people seeking treatment for a mental disability will simply consent to that care and treatment in exactly the same way as they would for any other medical treatment. A proportion of people with mental disabilities who require medical treatment of whatever sort will, however, lack the mental capacity required by law to consent to that treatment.[4] In such cases, Mental Health Act powers might be available to provide the necessary authority if the required treatment is for mental disorder. But if those powers are either unavailable or not used then, at the time of the *Bournewood* case, treatment could only be provided under the common law doctrine of necessity. Today it would be provided under powers contained in the Mental Capacity Act 2005 (MCA). In practice in the 1980s and 1990s significant numbers of incapable patients in psychiatric facilities were treated under these common law powers. They would be 'detained' in hospital for their own safety but, not being subject to the MHA, they would not be covered by the safeguards provided by that Act. As early as 1985 the Mental Health Act Commission recognised this problem and asked for its remit to be extended to 'de facto' detained patients.[5]

It was claimed on behalf of Mr L that he was de facto detained in Bournewood hospital. He lacked the mental capacity to consent to his admission and he was not placed under MHA powers. The fact of Mr L's 'detention' was fiercely contested but the extent of his vulnerability was never denied. And in this respect Mr L's situation provides a poignant illustration of the dilemmas presented; highly vulnerable people experiencing severe restrictions on their liberty without any effective safeguards.

In its written submission to the House of Lords the Mental Health Act Commission estimated that there were 48,000 'informal' admissions to hospital each year where the patient lacked mental capacity and was subject to severe restrictions on their liberty. They also estimated that on any day there would be 22,000 informal, incapable patients resident in hospital

---

[3] It is hard to produce precise figures here. In their 11th Biennial Report the Mental Health Act Commission estimated that 90% of all admissions were informal: Mental Health Act Commission, *11th Biennial Report 2003–2005: In Place of Fear* (London, TSO, 2006) [xxiii].

[4] GS Owen, G Richardson, A David, G Szmukler, P Hayward and M Hotopf, 'Mental capacity to make treatment decisions in patients admitted to a psychiatric hospital—cross sectional study' (2008) 337 *British Medical Journal* 448.

[5] Mental Health Act Commission, *Fifth Biennial Report 1991–1993* (London, HMSO, 1993) 56–57. And see *Bournewood* (n 2 above) 482 (Lord Goff) where he also mentions the concerns expressed by 'the authors of authoritative textbooks on the subject'.

in England and Wales compared to 13,000 patients detained under the Act.[6] Understood in the context of these figures the Court of Appeal's judgment carried enormous consequences. As Lord Goff explained, large numbers of patients who were not then subject to MHA powers would have to be detained. This would impose considerable resource burdens on mental health services, on the professionals who had to administer the Act and on the mental health review tribunals. The Department of Health expressed considerable concern, as did a number of professional bodies. Further, if the ruling were extended to patients resident in nursing homes the numbers (and legal complications) would be greatly increased.[7]

In *Bournewood*, therefore, the House of Lords were presented not just with a question of fine statutory interpretation but with the resolution of a tension running deep throughout the law's whole approach to the treatment of mental disability. The first half of the twentieth century had seen increasing emphasis on the provision of informal treatment for those with mental disorders. People requiring treatment for mental disorder should not invariably be placed under compulsion but should access care and treatment voluntarily. Formal powers were to be provided with the necessary safeguards but informal care was to be encouraged.[8] This approach was reflected in the express retention of informal admission in section 131:

> Nothing in this Act shall be construed as preventing a patient who requires treatment for mental disorder from being admitted to any hospital or mental nursing home in pursuance of arrangements made in that behalf and without any application, order or direction rendering him liable to be detained under this Act, or from remaining in any hospital or mental nursing home in pursuance of such arrangements after he has ceased to be so liable to be detained.[9]

The Court of Appeal's decision that Mr L's detention was unlawful not only opened the way for MHA safeguards to be applied to a vulnerable group of patients and brought with it significant resource implications, it also threatened to undermine the whole emphasis on informal care. Whichever way it went the House of Lords' judgment was destined to be controversial.

## II. THE HOUSE OF LORDS' DECISION

On the crucial question of the meaning of section 131(1) the House of Lords were unanimous. The Court of Appeal had interpreted the section as applying only to those who had the mental capacity to consent to hospital

---

[6] Mental Health Act Commission, *Eighth Biennial Report 1997–1999* (London, HMSO, 1999) [4.6] and see *Bournewood* (n 2 above) 481 (Lord Goff).

[7] Mental Health Act Commission, *Eighth Biennial Report 1997–1999* (London, HMSO, 1999) [4.6].

[8] *In Place of Fear* (n 3 above) [xxiii].

[9] Mental Health Act 1983, s 131.

treatment. Only capable and consenting patients could be admitted without resort to the Act. Argument before the House of Lords provided evidence of the section's legislative history going back to its origins in the recommendations of the Percy Committee which preceded the Mental Health Act 1959.[10] On the strength of this history the House of Lords disagreed with the Court of Appeal and concluded that the section was intended to cover both 'voluntary patients', those having capacity and consenting, and 'informal patients', those who lacked capacity but who did not object. Where the requirements of the principle of necessity were met such informal patients could properly be admitted under the common law. There was no need to resort to the Act. This was a unanimous decision but in the case of Lord Steyn it was reached with considerable reluctance. He was greatly troubled by the consequences, considering that 'the law would be defective if it failed to afford adequate protective remedies to a vulnerable group of incapacitated mental patients'.[11] In Lord Steyn's view a reversal of the Court of Appeal would lead to 'compliant incapacitated patients' losing almost all the basic protections under the Act and the 'result would be *an indefensible gap* in our mental health law'[12] (emphasis added). Thus the *Bournewood* Gap was born and it has remained a significant feature in the landscape of mental health law reform ever since.

On the question of detention the decision is less clear cut. Lord Goff considered that Mr L had not been unlawfully detained for the purposes of the tort of false imprisonment. He was compliant with his treatment, made no attempt to leave the hospital and was housed on an unlocked ward. His responsible doctor explained that if he had expressed a desire to leave she would have had to consider whether detention under the Act was necessary. In Lord Goff's view all the restrictions imposed on Mr L were justified under the common law principle of necessity.[13] Lord Lloyd and Lord Hope agreed in general terms with Lord Goff but made no specific reference to the question of detention. Lord Nolan considered that Mr L had been detained.

> [Mr] L. was closely monitored at all times so as to ensure that he came to no harm. It would have been wholly irresponsible for those monitoring him to let him leave the hospital until he had been judged fit to do so.[14]

In Lord Nolan's view, detention was wholly justified within the principle of necessity. Lord Steyn also concluded that Mr L was detained:

> The truth is that for entirely bona fide reasons, conceived in the best interests of L., any possible resistance by him was overcome by sedation, by taking him to hospital, and by close supervision of him in hospital. And, if L. had shown any sign of wanting to leave, he would have been firmly discouraged by staff and,

---

[10] *Bournewood* (n 2 above) 482–84.
[11] ibid 494.
[12] ibid 493.
[13] ibid 486 89.
[14] ibid 491.

if necessary, physically prevented from doing so. The suggestion that L. was free to go is a fairy tale.[15]

The decision of the Court of Appeal had presented a considerable dilemma to the government; the judgment of the House of Lords in June 1998 relieved that pressure. The *Bournewood* Gap had been recognised and advertised but the immediate pressure from the courts to fill it had been lifted. During the hearing counsel for the Secretary of State had assured their Lordships that law reform was 'under active consideration'.[16] In fact the Law Commission had already embarked on a lengthy project which led eventually to the Mental Capacity Act 2005.[17] And in November 1998 the government appointed an Expert Committee to advise ministers on the reform of mental health law in England and Wales,[18] the start of a long and sometimes acrimonious process culminating in the amendment of the MHA 1983 in 2007.[19] But neither process was designed directly to address the position of those vulnerable patients within the *Bournewood* Gap. Before any concrete steps were taken to resolve their lack of protection further judicial intervention was required.

### III. *HL v UNITED KINGDOM*[20]

Following the House of Lords' decision an application to the European Court of Human Rights was made on Mr L's behalf alleging, among other things, a breach of Article 5. In October 2004 the ECtHR finally delivered its judgment in *HL v United Kingdom*. The court was unanimous in its view that Mr L had been detained and that this detention was in breach of both Article 5(1) and 5(4) of the Convention. On the question of detention the Court considered it key that

> the health care professionals treating and managing the applicant exercised complete and effective control over his care and movements from the moment he presented acute behavioural problems on July 22, 1997 to the date he was compulsorily detained on October 29, 1997.[21]

And they endorsed Lord Steyn's view that the applicant was under continuous supervision and control and was not free to leave. Any suggestion to the contrary was, in the Court's view, fairly described by Lord Steyn as 'stretching credulity to breaking point' and as a 'fairy tale'.

---

[15] ibid 495.
[16] ibid 497.
[17] The project started in 1989 and its final report on the subject was published in 1995: Law Commission, *Mental Incapacity*, Law Com No 231 (London, HMSO, 1995).
[18] See Report of the Expert Committee, *Review of the Mental Health Act 1983* (London, Department of Health, 1999).
[19] The history is recounted by Bartlett and Sandland (n 1 above) and by B Hale, *Mental Health Law*, 5th edn (London, Sweet and Maxwell, 2010).
[20] *HL v United Kingdom* (2005) 40 EHRR 32.
[21] ibid 25.

Having reached that conclusion, the Court had to determine whether such detention—deprivation of liberty in the terms of the Convention—was compliant with Article 5. Again the Court was unanimous. They were struck by the absence of procedural rules to govern the admission and detention of compliant incapacitated people under the common law and they concluded that this absence of procedural safeguards failed to protect against arbitrary detention. It was neither 'in accordance with a procedure prescribed by law' nor 'lawful' as required by Article 5(1). In addition, the absence of an adequate mechanism for the review of the legality of detention under the common law amounted to a breach of Article 5(4) which stipulates that

> Everyone who is deprived of his liberty by arrest or detention shall be entitled to take proceedings by which the lawfulness of his detention shall be decided speedily by a court and his release ordered if the detention is not lawful.

This judgment was highly significant in 2004 and remains so in 2014. In the first place the interpretation of deprivation of liberty in the context of 'compliant incapacitated' people was always going to be complex and controversial. In *HL* the Court found a deprivation of liberty on the facts but failed to give any very useful general guidance. In the face of this uncertainty our domestic courts, as will be seen below, have struggled to find generally applicable principles to govern the interpretation of this fundamental concept in the context of care for those with severe disabilities. Secondly, the conclusion that detention under the common law principle of necessity failed to meet the requirements of Article 5(1) presented the government with an obligation to introduce fairly radical reform. Had the non-compliance been restricted to Article 5(4) the introduction of an adequate mechanism for court review might have been sufficient, but the judgment found the entire process of admission to be unlawful. A fundamental review was therefore required, reigniting all the concerns expressed following the Court of Appeal decision in 1997.

## IV. STEPS TO PLUG THE GAP

By the time the *HL* decision was published the government had already introduced its Mental Capacity Bill. An earlier version of the Bill had been considered by a Joint Scrutiny Committee in 2003 prior to the ECtHR decision, and that committee had recommended that something be done to fill the *Bournewood* Gap.[22] The Bill as introduced, however, made no obvious provision. It must be assumed that the government were confident that they would win in Strasbourg, that the Court would find there to have been no deprivation of liberty. Whatever their reason, when faced with the

---

[22] See, Joint Committee on the Draft Mental Incapacity Bill, Session 2002–03, vol 1, HL Paper 189-1, HC 1083-1, [223]–[226].

*HL* judgment, the government had no plan B. The Department of Health undertook to consult widely on how best to meet its obligations under the Convention and, as a stop-gap measure, amendments were introduced to the Bill to ensure that the authority provided to non-judicial actors did not extend to the deprivation of liberty.[23] As originally passed, therefore, the Mental Capacity Act contained no '*Bournewood*' provisions and expressly excluded the deprivation of liberty from the authority it provided.

The consultation process revived all the seemingly intractable arguments about the proper balance between informality and safeguards.[24] There was a fear that the ECtHR decision would lead to a far greater use of formal powers and would work against the desire to integrate mental health services into mainstream healthcare: 'The judgment of *HL v The United Kingdom* has cast into doubt the continuing policy commitment towards informal treatment which has been held by all United Kingdom governments since the founding of the NHS'.[25] But at the same time there was the realisation that in the interests of an exceptionally vulnerable population of patients the *Bournewood* Gap had to be filled.

In 2006 the Department of Health published its plans for the amendment of the MCA 2005 via the Mental Health Bill, which was then before Parliament and became the Mental Health Act 2007.[26] The MCA, thus amended, now provides for deprivation of liberty in three circumstances: when authorised by the Court of Protection; when covered by the Deprivation of Liberty Safeguards (DoLS); and as an interim measure in certain emergency circumstances.[27] The DoLS scheme, which was designed to be the primary mechanism, came fully in to force in April 2009. Since then it has attracted persistent criticism from numerous sources.[28]

---

[23] See Mental Capacity Act 2005, ss 6(5), 11(6) and 20(13).
[24] Department of Health, *Bournewood Consultation: the approach to be taken in response to the judgment of the European Court of Human Rights in the 'Bournewood' case* (London, Department of Health, 2005).
[25] Mental Health Act Commission (n 3 above) [xxiv].
[26] Department of Health, *Bournewood Briefing Sheet* (London, Department of Health, 2006) and Ministry of Justice and Department of Health, *Impact Assessment of the Mental Capacity Act 2005 Deprivation of Liberty Safeguards to accompany the Code of Practice and Regulations* (2006).
[27] See Hale (n 19 above) 16.
[28] P Bowen, *Blackstone's Guide to The Mental Health Act 2007* (Oxford, Oxford University Press, 2007); G Richardson, 'Mental capacity at the margin: The interface between two Acts' (2010) 18 *Medical Law Review* 56; Care Quality Commission, *The operation of the Deprivation of Liberty Safeguards in England, 2010/11* (London, Care Quality Commission, 2012) 3; RM Jones, *Mental Health Act Manual*, 14th edn (London, Sweet & Maxwell, 2011); RM Jones, *Mental Capacity Act Manual*, 5th edn (London, Sweet & Maxwell, 2012); R Hargreaves, *The Deprivation of Liberty Safeguards* (London, Mental Health Alliance, 2011). And see, the House of Commons Health Committee *Post legislative Scrutiny of the Mental Health Act 2007*, First Report of Session 2013–14 HC 584 (TSO, London) paras 106–7, and most recently the House of Lords Select Committee on the Mental Capacity Act 2005, *Mental Capacity Act 2005: post-legislative scrutiny*, Report of Session 2013–14 (London, TSO, 2014).

## V. THE DEPRIVATION OF LIBERTY SAFEGUARDS

In the first place the DoLS are extremely cumbersome. Their initial introduction was achieved by way of the addition of sections 4A and 4B, Schedule A1, and Schedule 1A to the Act, and the Code of Practice designed to guide practitioners through their use runs to 120 pages.[29] The scheme provides for the relevant supervisory body to authorise the deprivation of liberty of an individual in a hospital or care home.[30] In order to be eligible for DoLS an individual must meet six qualifying criteria and six assessments must be undertaken by suitably qualified people.[31] Both the supervisory body and the managing authority have duties to monitor and review deprivations of liberty and there are provisions enabling people to raise concerns with those bodies.[32] Ultimately the person concerned or their representative can apply to the Court of Protection. In conception the scheme attempts to provide adequate safeguards while retaining a degree of informality and maintaining a distinction between DoLS patients and those detained under the MHA. In practice it has few friends.

The most persistent difficulties centre on three issues all of which were foreshadowed in *Bournewood* itself: resource burden and administrative complexity; the relationship between the DoLS and the MHA; and the definition of deprivation of liberty. In addition the DoLS apply only to hospitals and care homes, not to the supported living arrangements now commonly used to house people in the community. A deprivation of liberty in the case of a person living in such supported accommodation requires direct authorisation from the Court of Protection.[33]

### A. Resource Burden

As already described the House of Lords in *Bournewood* were very conscious of the resource burden that would be imposed on mental health services.[34] In the event, the numbers themselves are interesting. The Impact Assessment published by the Department of Health in May 2008 to accompany the introduction of the DoLS estimated that there would be 5000 DoLS authorisations in 2009–10, falling to 1,700 by 2015–16.[35] In practice the numbers of applications have increased year on year, in 2013–14 13,000 applications

---

[29] *Deprivation of Liberty Safeguards* (London, TSO, 2008).
[30] Provision is also made for 'urgent authorisation' by the managing authority, Hale (n 19 above) 16.
[31] These are explained in the Code of Practice (n 29 above).
[32] ibid ch 8.
[33] See the Code of Practice (n 29 above) [10.11].
[34] *Bournewood* (n 2 above) 481.
[35] Department of Health (n 26 above).

were completed, a 10 per cent increase on the previous year, and the number of authorisations significantly exceeds the Department's expectations. During 2013–14 a total of 8,500 authorised deprivations of liberty were active.[36] The financial costs involved are hard to calculate[37] but there is general agreement that the procedures are complex and the administrative burden considerable.[38] In recognition of continuing problems the Department of Health established a Mental Capacity Act Steering Group 'to agree a joint programme of action to continue to implement the Mental Capacity Act and the Deprivation of Liberty Safeguards'.[39] However, the House of Lords Select Committee on the Mental Capacity Act 2005 which published its Report in February 2014 concluded that the DoLS are not fit for purpose and that better implementation would be insufficient to address the fundamental problems identified in the evidence it received.[40] The Committee therefore recommended that the government undertake a comprehensive review of the DoLS legislation with a view to replacing its provisions. In response the government has asked the Law Commission to undertake a review of the legislative framework.[41]

## B. The MCA/MHA Interface

The DoLS were introduced as a consequence of the *HL* judgment in Strasbourg and were designed to plug the *Bournewood* Gap. At the time of the House of Lords judgment in 1998 there was only one relevant statutory framework, the Mental Health Act 1983. Decisions on behalf adults who lacked mental capacity were taken in their best interests under the common law. With the passing of the Mental Capacity Act 2005 most of those common law powers have been codified and we now have two statutory frameworks covering the provision of care and treatment for mental disorder in the absence of patient consent. The introduction of the DoLS extended the

---

[36] *Mental Capacity Act 2005, Deprivation of Liberty Safeguards Assessments, England—2013–14, Annual Report* (HSCIC, 2014).

[37] A Shah, M Pennington, C Heginbotham and C Donaldson, 'Deprivation of Liberty Safeguards in England: implementation costs' (2011) 199 *British Journal of Psychiatry* 232.

[38] See Clare et al, *Understanding the Interface between the Mental Capacity Act's Deprivation of Liberty Safeguards and the Mental Health Act* (University of Cambridge 2013): www.CIDDRG.org; and see Ministry of Justice supplementary written evidence to the House of Lords Mental Capacity Act 2005 Committee 2013, oral and written evidence, vol 2, p 1229, (www.parliament.uk/documents/Mental-Capacity-Act-2005/mental-capacity-act-2005-vol2.pdf).

[39] Ministry of Justice (n 38 above) vol 1, 513.

[40] House of Lords Select Committee (n 28 above) chapter 7.

[41] *Valuing every voice, respecting every right: making the case for the Mental Capacity Act* (Cm 8884, 2014) para.7.27. The precise terms of reference have yet to be agreed.

MCA by providing authority to detain in a form designed to comply with Article 5. On the one hand this move to plug the *Bournewood* Gap clarified the detention powers and introduced procedural safeguards but, at the same time, it created a problem of overlapping jurisdictions. There are now two statutes, the MHA and MCA DoLS, providing the power to detain an adult who is suffering from a mental disorder, lacks mental capacity and needs treatment for that disorder. In such cases a choice has to be made between the two Acts, thus creating additional confusion and uncertainty for mental health and social care professionals, carers, lawyers and the people with mental disabilities themselves. This overlap has been the subject of academic and practitioner comment, empirical research and frequent litigation in the Court of Protection.[42] It is a sad reflection on policy making in this area that successive governments have failed to stand back and consider the whole landscape. Responsibility is spread across government departments, political priorities change and junior ministers come and go. Most recently the minister responsible in the Department of Health had to admit to the House of Lords Select Committee that he had never heard of the *Bournewood* Gap.[43] While at a personal level this might be excusable—he only took up the role towards the end of 2012 and could be moved to another Department at a minute's notice[44]—people with mental disabilities and those who care for them deserve better. A fundamental overhaul is required, not yet more valiant attempts to plug the gaps. The uncompromising recommendations of the House of Lords Select Committee were therefore welcome and it must be hoped that the government's subsequent request to the Law Commission will be broadly interpreted.[45]

## C. Defining Deprivation of Liberty

In *HL* the Strasbourg court disagreed with the House of Lords in *Bournewood* and held that Mr L had been deprived of his liberty for the purposes of Article 5(1). The introduction of the DoLS was specifically designed to achieve compliance with Article 5 and the term 'deprivation of liberty' used in the MCA is expressly defined by reference to its meaning in

---

[42] See, for example, Bartlett and Sandland (n 1 above); Richardson (n 28 above); Clare et al (n 38 above); *Mental Capacity Law Newsletter* (39 Essex Street Chambers), www.39essex.com/newsletters/; House of Lords Select Committee (n 28 above); *GJ v The Foundation Trust* [2009] EWHC 2972 (Fam) and *AM v South London & Maudsley NHS Foundation Trust and The Secretary of State for Health* [2013] UKUT 0365 (AAC). The Mental Health Act Code of Practice which deals with the interface is currently under revision.

[43] House of Lords Select Committee written and oral evidence (n 38 above) vol 2, p 1241.

[44] In fact this particular minister was Shadow Secretary of State for Health for the Liberal Democrats 2006–10.

[45] House of Lords Select Committee (n 28 above) and government response (n 41 above).

Article 5(1).[46] Unfortunately, as suggested above, *HL* itself provided little by way of general guidance as to the nature of that definition. One much cited passage serves to illustrate the difficulties: '[t]he distinction between a deprivation of, and a restriction upon, liberty is merely one of degree or intensity not one of nature or substance'.[47] Since then an extensive case law, both European and domestic, has grappled with the concept and has evolved three essential components of a deprivation of liberty under Article 5: a) the objective component of confinement, b) the subjective component of lack of consent, and c) the attribution of responsibility to the state. In the context of mental disability the application of any such definition to those whose care and safety require severe restrictions on their liberty has been particularly problematic. If in such a case the person lacks the mental capacity to consent but nonetheless appears compliant with their situation, can they be said to be deprived of their liberty under Article 5(1)? To meet these situations the Court of Appeal developed a concept of 'relative normality': the restrictions imposed on the person should be compared, not with those experienced by the population at large, but with those likely to be experienced by people with similar disabilities.[48] Only if the conditions were more restrictive than those experienced by the latter group would they amount to a deprivation of liberty.

The concept of relative normality provided a means of resisting the extension of DoLS to the many and various situations where, in the interests of their own safety, people are housed in highly restrictive conditions. But at the same time it suggested that a different notion of liberty was to be applied to people with disabilities. Both *Cheshire West* and *P and Q (MIG and MEG)* were appealed to the Supreme Court, providing the first opportunity since *Bournewood* for the UK's most senior court to consider the meaning of deprivation of liberty in the context of severe mental disabilities. The judgment was eagerly anticipated, not least by the House of Lords Select Committee.[49] In March 2014 it was delivered.[50] Lady Hale gave the lead judgment. Having emphasised the universality of human rights, 'human rights are for everyone, even the most disabled members of our community',[51] she reviewed the Strasbourg case law. Although certain aspects of the cases under appeal had not been dealt with by that court, Lady Hale considered that certain features had consistently been regarded as key, namely that the person concerned 'was under continuous supervision and control and was

---

[46] Mental Capacity Act 2005, s 64(5).
[47] *HL v United Kingdom* (n 20 above) [89].
[48] *In re MIG and MEG* [2011] EWCA Civ 190, and *Cheshire West and Chester Council v P* [2011] EWCA Civ 1257 (on appeal see n 50 below).
[49] House of Lords Select Committee (n 28 above).
[50] *P v Cheshire West and Chester Council* and *P and Q v Surrey County Council* [2014] UKSC 19.
[51] ibid [1].

not free to leave'.[52] She also expressed agreement with the suggestion that neither the person's compliance, nor the relative normality of the placement, nor the purpose behind it was relevant. When applied to the cases under appeal Lady Hale concluded that all three individuals had been deprived of their liberty under Article 5(1). Of the seven-person court, three other judges agreed with her in all three cases, while the remaining three agreed in the case of *Cheshire West* but dissented in relation to *P and Q*.

Eagerly awaited though this judgment has been, the Supreme Court was never going to be able to provide a fully comprehensive definition to cover all cases involving people with mental disabilities. What it has done is to dispel some confusion. We now know what the key features of a deprivation of liberty are, that they apply equally to those with and without disabilities and that certain factors are irrelevant and should not be taken into account. That the cases of P and Q were on the very margin and divided the court illustrates the real dilemmas involved in applying the concept of deprivation of liberty to situations where 'the best possible arrangements have been made'.[53] The decision of the majority has certainly extended the reach of Article 5 beyond that articulated by the Court of Appeal and far beyond the current reach of the DoLS and must as a consequence add weight to the calls for reform of both their nature and scope.[54] The conditions in which a person is housed and cared for may be the best possible in all the circumstances but if they involve depriving that person of her liberty then some mechanism for independent review is essential to ensure that they remain in that person's best interests.

## VI. THE WAY FORWARD?

The need for a comprehensive overview of mental disability law was mentioned earlier, but what might be the parameters of such a review? The *Bournewood* case drew attention to a significant gap in the law's provision for people with mental disabilities. After the decision of the Strasbourg court in *HL* the government had to take steps to fill that gap. The steps it took by way of the DoLS may have achieved compliance with Article 5,[55]

---

[52]   ibid [49], quoting from *HL v United Kingdom* (n 20 above) [91].

[53]   ibid [56] (Lady Hale).

[54]   See, in particular, the recommendations of the House of Lords Select Committee (n 28 above). The restriction in the application of the DoLS to hospitals and care homes was always contentious and is increasingly hard to justify. The Association of Directors of Adult Social Services has estimated that as a consequence of the *Cheshire West* judgment there will be 138, 165 applications for DoLS in 2014–15 and 28,605 applications to the Court of Protection outside DoLS, see *Mental Capacity Law Newsletter July 2014*, Issue 48: www.39essex.com/ docs/newsletters/mc_newsletter_july_2014_compendium.pdf.

[55]   But see *MH v United Kingdom* [2013] ECHR 1008, for possible implications for the DoLS.

but they have in turn exposed the underlying tensions arising from the creation of two distinct statutory regimes, one for mental disorder and one for incapacity. These two regimes are based on very different principles and designed with different goals in mind but the fact remains that there is considerable overlap leading to significant problems in both principle and practice.[56] One solution to this dilemma is that suggested by the fusion project, the introduction of a single statute that would combine the tasks currently performed by the MHA and the MCA.[57] Such a proposal would abandon all specialist mental health legislation and replace it with an expanded capacity or guardianship framework. At a practical level there would be no *Bournewood* Gap and no problem of interface between two schemes. At the level of principle the existing discrimination against mental disorder would be removed because all those who lacked capacity, from whatever cause, would be treated under the same Act and according to the same principles. Similarly, all those who retained capacity, whether or not they had a mental disorder, would fall outside the Act and would be subject to the ordinary principles of medical and criminal law. Such a scheme is under active consideration in Northern Ireland but has recently been rejected in Victoria.[58]

Whatever the merits of the fusion project, as originally conceived it was based on a structure of substitute decision making. If an individual lacks the mental capacity required by law to make a particular decision that decision can be taken by others on her behalf in her best interests. Both the MCA and the DoLS adopt just such an approach and similar substitute decision-making structures are common to guardianship regimes in many jurisdictions, but they are now under challenge.[59] In the world of disability rights internationally the emphasis has moved from substitute to supported decision making. The UN Convention on the Rights of Persons with Disabilities (CRPD), which the UK has signed and ratified, best epitomises this radical shift in approach.[60] Decisions are no longer to be made, however benignly, on behalf of the person with disability. Instead she is to be supported and encouraged to make her own decisions.[61] In its purest form there

---

[56] See Richardson (n 28 above).

[57] See J Dawson and G Szmukler, 'Fusion of mental health and incapacity legislation' (2006) 188 *British Journal of Psychiatry* 504 and 'A model law fusing incapacity and mental health legislation—is it viable; is it advisable?' (2010) *Journal of Mental Health Law* (Special Issue).

[58] See the Victoria Law Reform Commission's report on Guardianship, at www.lawreform. vic.gov.au/projects/guardianship-final-report.

[59] Mental Disability Advocacy Centre (2013) *Legal Capacity in Europe*, at: mdac.info/en/ resources/legal-capacity-europe-call-action-governments-and-eu.

[60] There is a growing literature here see, for example, P Bartlett, 'The United Nations Convention on the Rights of Persons with Disabilities and Mental Health Law' (2012) 75 *Modern Law Review* 752, and G Richardson, 'Mental Disabilities and the Law from Substitute to Supported Decision-Making' [2012] *Current Legal Problems* 1.

[61] UN Convention on the Rights of Persons with Disabilities, article 12.

is no point beyond which the law can refuse to recognise a decision.[62] It can no longer deny the legal validity of a decision because of an absence of mental capacity.

Over recent years the debate concerning the implications of the CRPD for our domestic law has grown.[63] The Convention prohibits all discrimination on grounds of disability and has been interpreted as outlawing specialised mental health legislation which permits compulsory hospitalisation and treatment.[64] In this respect it appears to be at odds with Article 5(1)(e) of the ECHR which expressly permits the detention of persons of unsound mind.[65] The CRPD has also been interpreted as prohibiting substitute decision-making structures based on the presence of a disability, and a review of the position under the MCA has been submitted to the Ministry of Justice.[66] More specifically, the approach adopted by the CRPD shines a different light on the dilemmas exposed by *Bournewood* and its aftermath. *Bournewood* and the DoLS that followed were primarily concerned with 'compliant incapacitated' patients. If by that is meant patients who do not have the mental capacity at law to decide to be in a hospital or care home then such a notion would have no meaning under the Convention. The CRPD does not recognise the concept of incapacity at law. However impaired their decision-making ability everyone is entitled to the support necessary to enable them to make a decision themselves. Thus if the *Bournewood* dilemma were to be expressed in CRPD-compliant terms, the issue might turn on the level of support necessary to enable a person with severe mental disabilities to reach a decision about whether to come into hospital or to be a resident in a care home. The decision would be made by the person, not on her behalf and in her best interests by a substitute decision maker. The practical and indeed moral dilemmas presented by such an approach if applied strictly are far reaching[67] but the underlying principle

---

[62] A Dhanda, 'Legal Capacity in the Disability Rights Convention: Stranglehold of the past or Lodestar for the Future?' (2006) 34 *Syracuse Journal of International Law and Commerce* 429.

[63] See, for example, see D Lush, 'Article 12 of the United Nations Convention on the Rights of Persons with Disability' (2011) 1 *Elder Law Journal* 61 and now 'The 2nd World Congress on Adult Guardianship' (2013) 3 *Elder Law Journal* 43–49. See also P Fennell and U Khaliq, 'Conflicting or Complementary Obligations? The UN Disability Rights Convention and the European Convention on Human Rights and English law' [2011] *European Human Rights Law Review* 662, G Richardson, 'Mental Capacity in the Shadow of Suicide: What can the law do?' (2013) 9 *International Journal of Law in Context* 87 and Victoria Law Reform Commission (n 58 above).

[64] Annual Report of the High Commissioner for Human Rights to the UN General Assembly, presented January 2009: A/HRC/10/49 [49-9].

[65] See Fennell and Khaliq (n 63 above).

[66] See Committee on the Rights of Persons with Disabilities (2014) *General Comment No 1 Article 12*. And for the report to the MoJ see, Essex Autonomy Project (2014) *Achieving UN CRPD Compliance*.

[67] See Richardson (n 63 above).

is refreshing. People with impaired decision making are to be recognised as persons before the law in the same way as everyone else and must be given the support they need to enable them to exercise full legal capacity. The resources currently expended on the operation of the complex structure of substitute decision making created by the DoLS would be transferred to the provision of the structures necessary to enable supported decision making. Plainly, such an approach is not without problems of its own. These include the precise nature of acceptable supports, the boundary between support and coercion and the enduring problem of conflicts of interest. Nonetheless, a shift in thinking from substitute to supported decision making reduces discrimination towards people with mental disabilities and encourages recognition of their equal status. The DoLS would need to be radically restructured and if the logic of the CRPD were to lead to the repeal of the MHA our problems of interface would disappear at a stroke.

# 8

# Re MB (An Adult: Medical Treatment) [1997] and St George's Healthcare NHS Trust v S [1998]: The Dilemma of the 'Court-Ordered' Caesarean

MARIE FOX AND KIRSTY MORETON*

## I. INTRODUCTION

THE REFUSAL BY a pregnant woman of medical treatment that may save her life, or the life of her viable fetus, poses one of the most intractable dilemmas for decision making in both health law and medical practice. In this chapter we return to *two* landmark cases concerning this dilemma—*Re MB (An Adult: Medical Treatment)*,[1] and *St George's Healthcare NHS Trust v S and R v Collins and Others ex parte S*,[2] which purported to resolve important questions raised by a series of earlier cases, where the court had authorised caesarean section operations notwithstanding the absence of consent. We suggest that the pivotal contribution of our landmark cases to health law jurisprudence lies in affirming the core values of self-determination and respect for bodily integrity by upholding a competent adult pregnant woman's right to refuse to consent to any medical treatment, 'even though the consequences may be death or serious handicap of the child she bears, or her own death'.[3] However, we acknowledge that this right carries with it ethical implications, and are thus prompted to reflect on Lord Donaldson's obiter observation in *Re T (Adult: Refusal of*

---

* We would like to acknowledge the helpful feedback we received from Jonathan Herring, James Lee, Sheelagh McGuinness, Leon McRae and Stephen Smith.
[1] *Re MB (An Adult: Medical Treatment)* [1997] 2 FCR 541.
[2] *St George's Healthcare NHS Trust v S; R v Collins and Others ex parte S* [1998] 3 All ER 673, [1998] *Family Law* 526 (CA).
[3] *Re MB* (n 1 above) 553.

*Medical Treatment)*, that such cases present a 'novel problem of considerable legal and ethical complexity'.[4]

We shall begin by examining the backdrop to these cases: a series of seven
caesarean section cases heard by the High Court in the 1990s[5]—a time when
patient autonomy was more contested than it is today. Specifically, we will
argue that *Re MB* and *St George's* deserve their landmark status for their
role in underlining the prevailing trend towards the recognition of patient
autonomy in general and that of pregnant women in particular. This contrasts starkly with the paternalism that characterised the earlier cases, starting with the High Court decision in *Re S (An Adult: Medical Treatment)*,
which permitted treatment in the best interests of the pregnant woman and
her fetus notwithstanding the absence of consent.[6] Furthermore, although
*Re MB* and *St George's* appeared for more than a decade to have marked
an end to the litigation on non-consensual caesareans, we shall consider a
recent upsurge of interest in this issue and the application of our landmarks
in the recent high-profile cases of *Re AA*[7] and *In re P*.[8]

Our critical analysis of the implications of these landmark cases has
three strands. First, drawing upon feminist scholarship that emphasises the
importance of upholding bodily integrity, we contend that the judicial discourse in *Re MB* and *St George's* was symbolically and politically important
in dispelling then prevalent assumptions that cast doubt upon the capacity
of pregnant women. Moreover, by confirming the ruling in *Paton v British
Pregnancy Advisory Service Trustees*,[9] that the fetus lacks legal personality
and that to find otherwise would result in 'an unwarranted invasion of the
right of the woman to make the decision',[10] the rulings clarify that in the
event of maternal/fetal conflict the interests of the pregnant woman prevail.

Nevertheless, given that no case has actually upheld a woman's right to
refuse a caesarean section *before* the operation has taken place, the second
strand of our argument is to query whether the value of the judgments in
*Re MB* and *St George's* ultimately is more rhetorical and symbolic, rather
than contributing to changing the practical medical reality for pregnant
women. We posit that the reason for this disconnect may be revealed by
exploring the ethical dilemmas that apparently underpin the reasoning of

---

[4] *Re T (Adult Refusal of Medical Treatment)* [1992] 4 All ER 649, 652–53 (Lord Donaldson).
[5] The seven cases were: *Re S (An Adult: Medical Treatment)* [1992] 2 FCR 893; *Tameside
& Glossop Acute Services Trust v CH* [1996] 1 FCR 753; *Norfolk & Norwich Healthcare
(NHS) Trust v W* [1997] 1 FCR 269; *Rochdale Healthcare (NHS) Trust v C* [1997] 1 FCR
609; *Re L (An Adult: Non-Consensual Treatment)* [1997] 1 FCR 609; *Re MB* (n 1 above) and
*St George's* (n 2 above).
[6] *Re S* (n 5 above).
[7] *Re AA* [2012] EWHC 4378 (COP).
[8] *In re P* [2013] EWCOP 4581, J Copping, 'Judge says mother can be forced to have emergency caesarean' (11 December 2013) *The Telegraph*.
[9] *Paton v British Pregnancy Advisory Service Trustees* [1979] QB 276, [1978] 2 All ER 987.
[10] *Re MB* (n 1 above) 555 (Butler-Sloss LJ).

the Court in both cases as they address the 'delicate and difficult question'[11] of the lack of fetal status in law whilst acknowledging the increased 'personal responsibilities'[12] a pregnant woman owes to her fetus. In seeking to unpack the implications of this for the bodily integrity of pregnant women, we suggest that this tension demonstrates the difficulty that law faces in dealing with conjoined embodiment and accommodating the intertwined interests of the pregnant woman and her fetus.

Finally, we draw upon a different strand of feminist theory—the ethics of care—to posit an alternative approach to health decision making, which we suggest can be usefully employed to help reconcile the tensions between standard notions of bodily integrity and conjoined embodiment. We suggest that in this context an approach grounded in care ethics may serve to deflect the legal preoccupation with fetal status versus maternal rights, by instead centering decision making firmly within the *relationship* between the pregnant woman and the fetus. We deploy this approach to explore the ethical as well as legal obligations of pregnant women and the duties imposed on health professionals who care for them, and to help address the difficulties in determining the best interests of the pregnant woman deemed incompetent. We conclude by suggesting that, notwithstanding the seemingly clear stance on women's autonomy established by our two landmark cases, recent media controversy over the issue of 'forced' caesareans demonstrates that they failed fully to resolve the thorny issues that were posed back in the 1990s. While an approach grounded in care ethics may also fail to bring resolution, we argue that it is valuable in highlighting the complexity of decision making in these cases and alerting us to the need to move beyond the law in seeking solutions in such cases.

## II. THE LANDMARK CASES

### A. Background

*Re MB* and *St George's* occurred at a time when important questions were being raised in health law concerning patient autonomy; specifically the right to refuse medical treatment. The 1992 case of *Re T*[13] also involved a pregnant woman who, following a car accident and having consulted with her mother—a Jehovah's Witness—refused a blood transfusion. In his judgment Lord Donaldson stressed the value of self-determination, stating that:

> An adult patient who … suffers from no mental incapacity has an absolute right to choose whether to consent to medical treatment, to refuse it or to choose one

---

[11] ibid 556.
[12] *St George's* (n 2 above) 691.
[13] *Re T* (n 4 above).

rather than another of the treatments being offered … This right of choice is not limited to decisions which others might regard as sensible. It exists notwithstanding that the reasons for making the choice are rational, irrational, unknown or even non-existent.[14]

Importantly, a possible caveat to this absolute right lay in his obiter observation that '[t]he only possible qualification is a case in which the choice may lead to the death of a viable foetus'.[15] Significantly, and notwithstanding Lord Donaldson's emphasis on the importance of self-determination, T was deemed in the circumstances to lack capacity and was transfused, although she had by then miscarried. *Re T* thus sets the scene for the cases to follow in which pregnant women's refusal of treatment was over-ridden. Indeed Lord Donaldson's mooted exception was tested just two months later, in the first of a line of seven caesarean cases heard over a six-year period. In *Re S* a 30-year-old woman refused a caesarean on religious grounds.[16] Due to the concerns of the obstetrician when she was six days overdue that the woman and fetus would die without surgical intervention, the Health Authority applied to the High Court for an emergency declaration that it would be lawful to perform the caesarean. The application was extremely urgent and appeared to be based solely on the medical evidence as to the risks, without any consideration of the woman's capacity at all. Although there was no reason to doubt her competence, the court declared, apparently on the basis of Lord Donaldson's caveat, that her refusal should be overridden in the 'vital interests of the patient and her unborn child'.[17] The decision attracted sustained criticism[18] and indeed Butler-Sloss LJ in *Re MB* would later deem it 'a decision the correctness of which we must call into doubt'.[19] However, Kenyon Mason and Graeme Laurie observe that for a time *Re S* appeared to have set a precedent.[20] The fact that four subsequent High Court cases heard in quick succession in 1996–97 turned on the issue of the pregnant woman's capacity,[21] might undermine this point by indicating that the judges in subsequent cases doubted the validity of the reasoning in *Re S*.[22] Yet, Mason and Laurie are surely right that the underlying rationale—protection of fetal interests—remained the same, as in each of the four cases the Court held that the pregnant woman lacked capacity to

---

[14] ibid 652 (Lord Donaldson).

[15] ibid.

[16] *Re S* (n 5 above).

[17] ibid 894.

[18] See A Grubb, 'Commentary on Re S' (1993) 1 *Medical Law Review* 92; M Thomson, 'After Re S' (1994) 2 *Medical Law Review* 127.

[19] *Re MB* (n 1 above) 556.

[20] K Mason and G Laurie, *Mason and McCall Smith's Law and Medical Ethics*, 9th edn (Oxford, Oxford University Press, 2013) 90.

[21] See *Tameside, Norfolk, Rochdale* and *Re L* (n 5 above).

[22] We thank Jonathan Herring for clarifying our thinking on this point.

refuse and ruled that the surgery should be performed in the woman's best interests.[23]

This brings us to the landmark cases, which together mark the first time that the complex issues surrounding court-ordered caesareans were judicially considered in any depth. Before we outline the facts, we shall explain our choice to analyse both cases in this chapter. Although *St George's* is the more recent case and the only judgment to hold that the woman was competent and that her refusal of treatment should have been respected, the ruling is very fact-specific. Furthermore, the facts actually pre-date those in *Re MB*, having occurred 10 months earlier in April 1996. As such, Rosamund Scott notes that the first instance decision in *St George's*, which was the subject of such stinging criticism in the appeal, occurred in the 'legal limbo' between *Re S* in 1992 and *Re MB* in 1997.[24] In our view, therefore, *Re MB* may be considered of greater precedential value given the vital obiter statement of Butler-Sloss LJ pertaining to the position of competent women. Consequently, although *St George's* makes a crucial contribution to the jurisprudence in this field, particularly as regards the intersection with mental health legislation and its promulgation of policy guidelines for healthcare professionals, at its core it powerfully reaffirms the stance in *Re MB*. We therefore suggest that it is productive to consider both judgments and that taken together the rulings constitute a legal landmark.

## B. *Re MB*

### (i) Facts and Decision

*Re MB* involved an appeal by the patient, 23-year-old MB, against a High Court declaration that it was lawful for a consultant gynaecologist to perform any necessary medical treatment, including a caesarean section, notwithstanding her refusal to consent. It also held that reasonable force could be used in the course of such treatment. During a routine antenatal appointment when MB was 40 weeks pregnant, her fetus was discovered to be presenting in the footling breech position. This obstetric complication would, during vaginal delivery, present a 50 per cent risk of death to the fetus due to the potential for prolapse of the umbilical cord, which could obstruct the fetal blood supply leading to brain damage or death.[25] There was however, little physical danger to MB herself. A caesarean section was indicated, to which MB agreed. However upon her admission to hospital and over the course of five days, she repeatedly refused to provide blood samples or allow

[23] See *Tameside, Norfolk, Rochdale* and *Re L* (n 5 above).
[24] R Scott, *Rights, Duties and the Body: Law and Ethics of the Maternal-Fetal Conflict* (Oxford, Hart Publishing, 2002) 165.
[25] *Re MB* (n 1 above) 545.

a veneflon to be inserted for the administration of the anaesthetic, whilst continuing on at least five occasions to consent to or request the caesarean section itself. Consultant psychiatrist Dr F attributed her resistance to a phobia of needles. He acknowledged that MB understood and accepted the reason for the caesarean but claimed that due to her phobia 'at the moment of panic ... her fear dominated all' and 'that at the actual point she was not capable of making a decision at all, in the sense of being able to hold information in the balance and make a choice'.[26] Anaesthesia administered by mask was suggested and MB agreed, but later withdrew her consent, causing the operation to be cancelled for a second time. Late that evening the Health Authority applied to the High Court for the declaration, which Hollis J granted on the grounds that MB was overcome by her needle phobia, that the case was in line with the earlier judgment of *Re L*,[27] and that MB was incapable of considering the matter lucidly.[28] MB appealed on four grounds: that the judge was wrong to find on the evidence that she lacked the capacity to refuse; that the judge failed to make a finding in her best interests; that the evidence did not establish that the proposed treatment was in her best interests; and that it was unlawful at common law to use force on a mentally competent patient to impose medical treatment upon her.[29]

Dismissing the appeal, Butler-Sloss LJ began by confirming that the relevant general principles were first, as in *Collins v Wilcox*[30] *(approved in Re F)*,[31] that generally it is a criminal and tortious assault to perform physically invasive medical treatment without the patient's consent. Secondly, she applied the ruling in *Sidaway v Board of Governors of the Bethlem Royal Hospital*[32] that a mentally competent patient has an absolute right to refuse medical treatment. Thirdly, she confirmed the *Re F* holding that medical treatment could be given in an emergency, even if there was no consent due to lack of capacity, subject to the treatment being necessary and no more than was reasonably required in the best interests of the patient. The court then tackled the key questions of capacity, best interests and fetal status. On capacity it upheld the rebuttable presumption of capacity asserted in *Re T*[33] and the three-stage test for assessing capacity derived from *Re C*.[34] Butler-Sloss LJ stated categorically that a competent woman

---

[26] ibid 546.

[27] See *Re L* (n 5 above), which also concerned a patient suffering from needle phobia.

[28] *Re MB* (n 1 above) 548.

[29] ibid.

[30] *Collins v Wilcox* [1984] 1 WLR 1172.

[31] *Re F (Mental Patient: Sterilization)* [1990] 2 AC 1.

[32] *Sidaway v Board of Governors of the Bethlam Royal Hospital* [1985] AC 871.

[33] *Re T* (n 4 above) 874 (Lord Donaldson)—'The right to decide one's own fate presupposes a capacity to do so. Every adult is presumed to have that capacity, but it is a presumption which can be rebutted'.

[34] *Re C (An Adult: Refusal of Treatment)* [1994] 2 FCR 151. Thorpe J (at 156) stated that 3-stage test for capacity was: 1. Comprehending and retaining treatment information, 2. Believing it, 3. Weighing it in the balance to arrive at a choice.

'may for religious reasons, other reasons, for rational or irrational reasons or for no reason at all, choose not to have medical intervention'.[35] Yet, on the facts the court held, in accordance with the psychiatric evidence, that MB was suffering from 'an impairment of her mental functioning which disabled her', rendering her 'temporarily incompetent' due to panic caused by her phobia of needles.[36] It adopted a wide construction of 'best interests', which was 'not limited to best medical interests' but could include psychiatric and relational interests.[37] Finally, on the question of fetal status, counsel for the Health Authority had submitted that there should be a balancing of maternal and fetal interests even in competent patients. Although obiter, as MB had been declared incompetent, the court held—contrary to the assertion in *Re T*—that it was not within its jurisdiction to take the interests of the fetus into account.[38] Having reviewed case law from the UK,[39] the US,[40] the ECtHR,[41] and UK legislation,[42] it concluded that in accordance with *Paton* the fetus 'cannot have a right of its own at least until it is born'.[43] While acknowledging the 'ethical dilemma' which remained, the Court was clear that it was not a 'court of morals',[44] and was ill equipped to deal with the 'illogical' outcome that fetal interests receive certain protection under the criminal law yet the fetus 'is not protected from the (irrational) decisions of a competent mother'.[45]

## C. *St George's Healthcare NHS Trust v S*

### (i) Facts and Decision

As noted above, the facts in *St George's* occurred before those in *Re MB*; however the appellate judgment was handed down 15 months after that in *Re MB*. The case involved an appeal and application for judicial review

---

[35] *Re MB* (n 1 above) 553.
[36] ibid 554.
[37] ibid 555.
[38] ibid 556.
[39] See *Re F (In Utero)* [1988] FCR 529; *C v S* [1988] QB 135; *Burton v Islington Health Authority* [1992] 2 FCR 845.
[40] See *Raleigh Fitkin-Paul Morgan Memorial Hospital v Morgan* 201 A 2d 537 (1964); *Jefferson v Griffin Spalding County Hospital Authority* 274 SE 2d 457 (1981); *Crouse Irving Memorial Hospital Inc v Paddock* 485 NYS (1985); *Re Madyyun* 573 A 2d 1259n (1986); *Re AC* 533 A 2d 611 (DC 1987).
[41] See *Bruggemann and Scheuten v Federal Republic of Germany* (1977) 3 EHRR 244; *Paton v United Kingdom* (1980) 3 EHRR 408; *H v Norway* (Application No 17004/90), 19 May 1992, 73 DR 155; *Open Door and Dublin Well Woman v Ireland* (1992) 15 EHRR 244.
[42] Offences Against the Person Act 1861; s 1 Infant Life Preservation Act 1929; s 1 Abortion Act 1967; s 1 Congenital Disabilities (Civil Liability) Act 1976.
[43] *Paton* (n 9 above) 279.
[44] *Re MB* (n 1 above) 556.
[45] ibid 557.

of, amongst other things, a declaration obtained by St George's Healthcare NHS Trust that dispensed with the need for S's consent to the performance of a caesarean section. The facts were that 28-year-old S was, at 36 weeks pregnant, diagnosed with pre-eclampsia and advised to have labour induced to avert 'real danger' to her health and life and that of the fetus. She understood the advice but rejected it, as she wanted her baby to be born naturally. She was seen by a social worker and two doctors and again refused their advice, after which she was admitted to a mental hospital against her will for assessment under section 2 of the Mental Health Act 1983. Although S had previously been diagnosed with moderate depression, at no time throughout her detention in hospital was she given any treatment for mental illness or disorder. Subsequently, also against her will, she was transferred to another hospital. She articulated her reasons for refusal of treatment in the following terms:

> I have always held very strong views with regard to medical and surgical treatments for myself, and particularly wish to allow nature to 'take its course', without intervention. I fully understand that, in certain circumstances this may endanger my life. I see death as a natural and inevitable end point to certain conditions, and that natural events should not be interfered with. It is not a belief attached to the fact of my being pregnant, but would apply equally to any condition arising.[46]

In light of her continued refusal, the hospital applied ex parte to the court for a declaration, which was granted and that evening S delivered a baby girl by caesarean section. S was returned to the mental hospital, and two days later her detention under section 2 of the Act was terminated and, against medical advice, she discharged herself.

Upholding her appeal, the Court of Appeal found insufficient evidence on which to question S's competence.[47] On the issue of autonomy, Judge LJ drew upon *Airedale NHS Trust v Bland*[48] to confirm that 'even when his or her life depends on receiving medical treatment, an adult of sound mind is entitled to refuse it'.[49] Having considered fetal status the Court concluded that 'whatever else a 36 week old foetus is, it is not nothing';[50] yet affirmed Butler-Sloss's obiter statement in *Re MB* that fetal interests could not be taken into account in such cases. Judge LJ was categorical that pregnancy does not diminish a woman's entitlement to consent to or refuse medical treatment, recognising that a forced invasion of a competent woman's body, even for the best of motives, would result in 'irremediably

---

[46] *St Georges* (n 2 above) 681.
[47] ibid 684.
[48] *Airedale NHS Trust v Bland* [1993] 1 All ER 821, 860. This case is discussed in chapter 5 of this volume.
[49] *St George's* (n 2 above) 685.
[50] ibid 687.

damaging the principle of self-determination', even to the point that 'the principle of autonomy would be extinguished'.[51] The unique contribution of the judgment in *St George's* lies in its condemnation of the (mis)use of the mental health legislation. The court found that S's detention under the Mental Health Act 1983 was unlawful by virtue of what Judge LJ deemed the 'prohibited reasoning', evidenced in the assumption that because a woman is exhibiting a thinking process which is 'unusual, even apparently bizarre and irrational and contrary to the views of the majority of the community at large' she must be therefore mentally disordered and lacking capacity.[52] This holding was important in counteracting an earlier trend of using mental health legislation to compel women to undergo caesareans, as seen in the case of *Tameside*.[53] The Court was keen to stress that a patient detained under section 2 of the Mental Health Act was not deprived of all autonomy and could only be compulsorily treated for conditions connected with the mental disorder, and that pregnancy was not such a condition.

## D.  Application of *Re MB* and *St George's*

In terms of the subsequent application of *Re MB* and *St George's*, some commentators suggested that the ruling in *St George's* had settled the legal position.[54] Certainly a significant feature of both cases was the promulgation of guidelines,[55] intended to provide 'more certainty for healthcare professionals faced with the uncertainties thrown up by the common law'.[56] These judicial guidelines have been utilised in numerous professional policy documents.[57] Their value lies in emphasising that only when questions of competence arise should the case be brought before the courts. Also they stress that it is expedient that any potential issue be identified early so as to avoid, if possible, emergency applications to the court with all the inherent dangers of weak evidence, time pressures and possible lack of representation or involvement of the patient.

In practice, the rulings and accompanying guidance served to put an end to this spate of litigation since, until 2012,[58] only one case—*Bolton Hospitals NHS Trust v O*—was reported.[59] Citing both *Re MB* and *St George's*,

---

[51]  ibid 688.

[52]  ibid 691.

[53]  *Glossop* (n 5 above).

[54]  J Herring, 'Compelling Caesarean Sections' (1999) 140/141 *Law & Justice Christian Law Review* 43.

[55]  *Re MB* (n 1 above) 561–62; *St George's* (n 2 above) 701–2.

[56]  Mason (n 20 above) 92.

[57]  See, eg, Nice Guidance CG 132: *Caesarean section* (November 2011) available at: www.nice.org.uk/guidance/cg132/chapter/guidance.

[58]  *Re AA* (n 7 above).

[59]  *Bolton Hospitals NHS Trust v O* [2003] 1 FLR 824, [2002] EWHC 2871 (Fam).

Butler-Sloss LJ ruled that the patient's refusal of a caesarean in this case was due to panic, triggered by post-traumatic stress in the operating theatre, and could be overridden.[60] Then, in December 2013 the case of a 35-year-old pregnant Italian national, Alessandra Pacchieri, attracted international attention,[61] generating headlines such as '[c]hild taken from womb by caesarean, then put into care'.[62] Her case, known as *Re AA*, had been heard 15 months earlier in the Court of Protection.[63] *Re MB* (but notably not *St George's*) was cited in the case,[64] which concerned an urgent application by Mid-Essex NHS Trust to the Court of Protection for a declaration that it would be lawful to perform a caesarean without her consent upon Ms Pacchieri, who been compulsorily detained for five weeks prior to the hearing, under section 3 of the Mental Health Act 1983.[65] The court found that she was suffering from a significant psychotic mental disorder and remained 'seriously mentally ill and incapacitated'.[66] Due to the risk of uterine rupture should she go into natural labour,[67] it held that it was in Ms Pacchieri's best interests[68] that the surgery should be performed and that reasonable restraint could be used to 'achieve the operation safely and successfully'.[69] Mostyn J deemed that AA's case fell 'squarely within the guidelines' given in *Re MB*, adding that 'harsh though it is' the interests of the fetus were not the concern of the court as it had no legal standing, so that the decision must be made solely within the parameters of the Mental Capacity Act 2005.[70] In particular, Mostyn J sought to follow the interpretation of best interests laid out by Butler-Sloss LJ in *Re MB* that 'it must be in the best interests of a woman carrying a full-term child whom she wants to be born alive and healthy that such a result should if possible be achieved'.[71] Further, he echoed her words regarding the psychiatric consequences of refusal, in that AA 'was likely to suffer significant long term damage if there was no operation and the child was born handicapped or died'.

Similar reasoning informed the subsequent case of *Mrs P*, a 36-year-old woman with a 'very high risk pregnancy' who was suffering from a mental

[60] ibid.

[61] The story of the court-ordered caesarean section broke in the media at this time, in relation to subsequent adoption proceedings in relation to the child. See *Re P (A Child)* [2013] EW Misc 20 (CC).

[62] C Freeman, 'Child taken from womb by caesarean, then put into care' (30 November 2013), *The Telegraph*.

[63] *Re AA* (n 7 above).

[64] ibid.

[65] ibid para 2.

[66] ibid.

[67] ibid para 4.

[68] In accordance with the provisions of the Mental Capacity Act 2005.

[69] *Re AA* (n 7 above) para 8.

[70] ibid para 1.

[71] *Re MB* (n 1 above).

illness which caused her to refuse treatment.[72] In each case the woman was found to lack capacity, and the courts declared that a caesarean could be performed in her best interests.[73] After sifting through the sensationalist reporting surrounding the cases,[74] which was heightened by the subsequent care and adoption proceedings concerning Ms Pacchieri's daughter,[75] the decisions reached in both cases seem uncontroversial. Each featured a woman with a serious and sustained mental illness—in Ms Pacchieri's case a psychotic disorder,[76] whilst Mrs P had been diagnosed with paranoid schizophrenia[77]—and both clearly lacked capacity to consent to or refuse treatment. Yet both the media disquiet and subsequent public discussion revealed the underlying tensions that the landmark cases had failed to fully resolve, and it is to these tensions that we now turn.

### III. ANALYSIS OF THE IMPLICATIONS OF THE DECISIONS IN THE LANDMARK CASES

#### A. Autonomy and the Capacity of Pregnant Women: Rhetoric or Reality?

As noted above, one reason why *Re MB* and *St George's* have come to be regarded as a legal landmark is a matter of timing—they were decided at a crucial juncture in the evolution of contemporary health law and were instrumental in reinforcing a more pro-patient trend, particularly in the context of refusing treatment. As many commentators have traced, 1997 marked the beginning of a trend towards a more pro-patient standard in consent law generally, as developing jurisprudence asserted the rhetoric of patient autonomy and the right to have risks of treatment disclosed.[78] In some notable High Court decisions in the 1990s the seeds of a more

---

[72] *In re P* (n 8 above).

[73] ibid.

[74] See for example, L Davies, 'Italian woman who was given forced caesarean section: I want my baby back' (3 December 2013) *The Guardian*; Hamilton, 'Forced C-Section was "the stuff of nightmares": Social Services condemned for forcibly removing unborn child from woman' (1 December 2013), *The Independent*; C Carter, 'Social Workers invaded my body and stole my baby, says mother forced to have a caesarean' (5 December 2013), *The Telegraph*.

[75] *Re P (A Child)* [2013] EW Misc 20 (CC).

[76] *Re AA* (n 7 above).

[77] *In re P* (n 8 above).

[78] J Herring, 'Caesarean Sections and the Right of Autonomy' (1998) 57 *Cambridge Law Journal* 429, 438; J Herring, 'The Caesarean Section Cases and the Supremacy of Autonomy' in M Freeman and A Lewis (eds), *Law and Medicine: Current Legal Issues Volume 3* (Oxford, Oxford University Press, 2000); R Bailey-Harris, 'Patient Autonomy: A Turn in the Tide?' in M Freeman and A Lewis (eds), *Law and Medicine: Current Legal Issues Volume 3* (Oxford, Oxford University Press, 2000) 127; J Herring, 'The Loneliness of Status' in F Etbehaj et al (eds), *Birth Rites and Rights* (Oxford, Hart Publishing, 2012); J Coggon and J Miola, 'Autonomy, Liberty and Medical Decision-Making' (2011) 70 *Cambridge Law Journal* 523.

patient-centred test were sown,[79] and subsequently endorsed by appellate courts. In this regard the Court of Appeal rulings in our landmark cases were crucial in affirming that it is contrary to law to carry out a caesarean against the wishes of a competent woman even if her decision seems odd or morally repugnant, or completely unsupported.[80] Jonathan Herring sees the rulings as vindicating 'the supremacy of autonomy' at least where refusal is concerned,[81] while Rebecca Bailey-Harris casts the decision in *St George's* as marking *the* significant shift in the balance of power between health professional and patient. She construes the decision as 'concerned primarily with the power of the patient against the medical profession, rather than any conflict between mother and unborn child'.[82] However, more accurately, in our view, John Harrington characterises these cases as staging 'a conflict between medical power and patient autonomy and between the rights of the pregnant woman and the interests of the foetus'.[83] In this sense their landmark status is partly attributable to the complexity they pose for judges confronted with adjudicating on these two issues that lie at the very core of modern health law.

As Bailey-Harris notes, from a feminist perspective the decision in *St George's* has many positive features. In endorsing *Re MB* it 'put paid to any notion that women's mental condition in advanced pregnancy is synonymous with incapacity', as well as ruling out the use of mental health legislation to detain individuals merely because they displayed irrational or bizarre thinking.[84] She thus suggests that the conflicts that Harrington identifies have been resolved in favour of according the patient, rather than the doctor, power to determine her own treatment and deeming the pregnant woman to be in the same position as other patients when it comes to refusal of medical treatment.

Clearly there is indeed much to welcome in this, particularly given the importance of bodily integrity in guaranteeing women's equality and citizenship status. Drucilla Cornell has shown in the abortion context that denying women access to safe abortion effectively reduces them to their maternal functions and denies women the conditions of individuation or self-determination that men enjoy.[85] Similarly we would suggest that

---

[79] *Smith v Tunbridge Wells Health Authority* [1991] 5 Med LR 334; *Smith v Salford Health Authority* [1994] 5 Med LR 321.

[80] A Morris, 'The Angel in the House: Altruism and the Pregnant Woman' in A Morris and S Nott (eds), *Well Women: The Gendered Nature of Health Care Provision* (Aldershot, Ashgate Publishing, 2002); A Plomer, 'Judicially Enforced Caesareans and the Sanctity of Life' (1997) 26 *Anglo-American Law Review* 235.

[81] Herring (n 78 above).

[82] Bailey-Harris (n 78 above) 127.

[83] J Harrington, 'Time as a Dimension of Medical Law' (2012) 20 *Medical Law Review* 491, 508–9.

[84] Bailey-Harris (n 78 above) 134.

[85] D Cornell, *The Imaginary Domain: Abortion, Pornography and Sexual Harassment* (Abingdon, Routledge, 1995) ch 2.

the earlier court-ordered caesarean cases effectively reduced the women involved to their maternal functions by treating them as fetal incubators. Against this backdrop, the statements in *Re MB* and *St George's* are thus crucial in contesting this ideology and in vindicating the bodily integrity and equal citizenship of pregnant women.

Nevertheless, we would highlight two troubling features of the rulings. First, as we suggest below, the vision of individual autonomy promoted in these cases is problematic, with commentators such as Mason and Laurie warning of the dangers of an unstinting focus upon individual autonomy. They note that 'medical jurisprudence would, in general, do well to reflect on the extensive moral steps which are being taken when it accepts the cult of self-determination as its dominant principle'.[86] We argue below that this dominant principle, rooted as it is in individualised conceptions of bounded and separate bodies, is particularly ill equipped to accommodate the complex ethico-legal dilemmas to which pregnant embodiment can give rise.

Secondly, it is important in these cases to go beyond the rhetoric of the judges to examine what happens to these women *in practice*[87] and what their lived experience of the law is. In this regard we view our landmark cases as giving rise to several concerns. *St George's* remains the only case to have actually upheld the pregnant woman's right to refuse a caesarean, and, as is clear from the recital of facts above, it was a highly fact-specific decision which turned on S's ability to clearly articulate and defend her views, coupled with the highly problematic actions of the various professionals who managed her treatment. Significantly, all of the caesarean cases except our two landmark cases were heard at first instance, and clearly it is more difficult for judges to determine that the woman was in a position to refuse treatment while the life of the fetus remains in the balance. As Vanessa Munro points out:

> Typically, in appeal cases, the issue transcends the complexities of unascertainable bodily boundaries manifest in the first instance hearing ... The decision to enforce surgery having already been taken and the procedure having been performed, the party appears before the court once more as a separate and distinct legal person existing within a separate and bounded bodily confine.[88]

Clearly then it would be a brave first instance judge who, confronted with an emergency situation, would chose to uphold the woman's right to refuse treatment in the face of medical evidence that a possible outcome was death. Thus a key factor in the first instance decisions is the insidious pressure of

---

[86] Mason (n 20 above) 618; see also M Brazier, 'Do No Harm—Do Patients Have Responsibilities Too?' (2006) 65 *Cambridge Law Journal* 397.

[87] I Kennedy, 'Consent, Adult: Refusal of Consent, Capacity' (1997) 5 *Medical Law Review* 317; S Fovargue and J Miola, 'Policing Pregnancy: Implications of the *Attorney-General's Reference (No 3 of 1996)*' (1998) 6 *Medical Law Review* 265.

[88] V Munro, 'Square Pegs in Round Holes: The Dilemma of Conjoined Twins and Individual Rights' (2001) 12 *Social and Legal Studies* 459, 474.

adverse public reaction should a judge respect the woman's choice with the upshot that she or her fetus dies.[89] Elizabeth Wicks rightly argues that a key tenet of Judge LJ's dicta in *St George's* is that 'the autonomy of each individual requires continuing protection even, perhaps particularly, when the motive for interfering with it is readily understandable, and indeed to many would appear commendable'.[90] However it remains questionable whether such an approach would be so readily adopted by a High Court judge.[91] This is particularly unlikely given Lieve Gies' observation that the narratives in the first instance cases are replete with a sense of emergency and panic.[92] Harrington illustrates how this pressure to reach decisions within radically compressed time spans—which in the series of 1990s Caesarean cases ranged from 15–30 minutes—produces not only inadequate argumentation, representation etc,[93] but an 'urgency ... established rhetorically in the terms of the judgments themselves' with judges careful to present a precise time line and emphasising the life and death nature of the decisions.[94]

Such time pressures in turn facilitate judicial manipulation of the concept of capacity to enable the courts to conclude, in every case bar *St George's*, that the pregnant woman lacked the competence to refuse medically sanctioned intervention. This underlines Michael Thomson's contention that to understand these cases we need 'to contextualise medical responses to reproductive issues, and medical recourse to law, as still involving issues of professional assertion and validation'.[95] In line with the gendered deployment of psychiatric discourse in health law, judges uncritically endorse expert medicine pertaining both to the risks of refusing treatment and to the woman's state of mind, deeming her wishes to be unintelligible.[96] As Ann Oakley and Martin Richards note, the politics of obstetric practice intensify deference to professional opinion, with caesareans playing 'a special role in the clinician's claim to unique expertise'.[97] Furthermore, the requirement

---

[89] L Gies, 'Contesting the Rule of Emotions? The Press and Enforced Caesareans' (2000) 9 *Social and Legal Studies* 515, 523.

[90] *St George's* (n 2 above) 688, Judge LJ.

[91] E Wicks, 'The Right to Refuse Medical Treatment under the European Convention on Human Rights' (2001) 9 *Medical Law Review* 17, 30.

[92] Gies (n 89 above) 523.

[93] M Thomson, 'After *Re S*' (1994) 2 *Medical Law Review* 127.

[94] Harrington (n 83 above).

[95] M Thomson, *Reproducing Narrative* (Aldershot, Ashgate Publishing, 1998) 201. See also S Bewley and L Foo, 'Are Doctors Still Improving Child Birth?' in Etbehaj et al (n 78 above).

[96] J Bridgeman, 'Old Enough to Know Best?' (1993) 13 *Legal Studies* 69; K Keywood, 'Re-thinking the Anorexic Body: How English Law and Psychiatry "Think"' (2003) 26 *International Journal of Law and Psychiatry* 599; R Cain, 'A View You Won't Get Anywhere Else"? Depressed Mothers, Public Regulation and 'Private' Narrative' (2009) 17 *Feminist Legal Studies* 123.

[97] A Oakley and M Richards, 'Women's Experiences of Caesarean Delivery' in J Garcia et al (eds), *The Politics of Maternity Care* (Oxford, Clarendon Press, 1990); see also H Lim, 'Caesareans and Cyborgs' (1999) 7 *Feminist Legal Studies* 133, 140.

that a pregnant woman should submit to intervention in the best interests of her fetus chimes with wider social and common sense understandings, in which 'the notion of maternal sacrifice is a core element in the prevailing cultural construction of motherhood' so that '[a] bad mother is a woman who is not prepared to sacrifice her own well-being for the foetus she is carrying'.[98] These cultural and medical norms combine to cast the actions of the pregnant woman who refuses recommended medical treatment as aberrational and beyond comprehension, leaving it open to judges to find her incompetent to decide, thereby legitimising violation of her bodily integrity.

## B. Implications for Fetal Status: The Dilemma of 'Conjoined Embodiment'

Notwithstanding these problems, *Re MB* and *St George's* remain symbolically significant in reaffirming the pregnant woman's autonomy and clearly prioritising her interests over those of the fetus, which are deemed to lack legal weight. As Thomson has noted, the earlier cases from *Re S* onward seemed contrary to both statutory authority in the Abortion Act 1967 (as amended) and the Congenital Liabilities (Civil Disability) Act 1976 and to common law rulings that the fetus lacked status in UK law.[99] Against this backdrop it was crucial that in *Re MB* the ruling of the Court of Appeal in *Paton* that the fetus 'cannot … have a right on its own at least until it is born and has a separate existence from its mother'[100] was reaffirmed. To decide otherwise would have risked unravelling the uneasy compromise underpinning British abortion law and leading English law towards greater recognition of the fetus as a legal person.[101] Butler Sloss LJ was clear that: 'the court does not have the jurisdiction to take the interests of the foetus into account in a case such as the present appeal and the judicial exercise of balancing those interests does not arise'.[102]

Yet this rhetoric, which entrenches the view of the fetus in utero as a non-person in law and validates the autonomy of pregnant women, co-exists, as we have seen, with a readiness for courts *in practice* to breach the woman's bodily integrity in the name of the fetus. We would argue that this entails precisely the balancing exercise that Butler-Sloss LJ disavows. In part we attribute this disconnect between rhetoric and reality to the inability of

---

[98] Gies (n 89 above) 527. See also A Diduck, 'Legislating Ideologies of Motherhood' (1993) 2 *Social and Legal Studies* 461.

[99] Thomson (n 93 above) 131. See *Paton v British Pregnancy Advisory Service* [1979] QB 276; *B v Islington HA* [1991] 1 QB 638.

[100] *Paton* (n 9 above) 279, George Baker P.

[101] Thomson (n 93 above) 132.

[102] *Re MB* (n 1 above) 556, Butler Sloss LJ.

conventional legal discourse, grounded as it is in the distinctness of persons, to accommodate conjoined embodiment, including pregnancy. Scott has pointed to the difference that the body makes, observing that:

> There is something different ... about a duty which necessarily *inheres in* the body. It is very rare that one may have the opportunity to assist another in a way which makes serious and invasive demands of one's body—in effect to use one's body to help or save another.[103]

Indeed the position is still more complicated than the pregnant woman using 'her' body for someone else—as Iris Marion Young notes, the pregnant subject 'experiences her body as herself and not herself. Its inner movements belong to another being, yet they are not other, because her body boundaries shift'.[104] This complex conjoined and shifting embodiment means that as Isabel Karpin notes, 'the woman's body is seen as neither container nor separate entity from the foetus. Until the baby is born the foetus *is* the female body. It is part of her body/self'.[105] Conventional views of both autonomy, which is seen as the exercise of self-determination over a sovereign body, and of bodily integrity, which is similarly conceived as affording protection from the invasion of others,[106] are ill equipped to accommodate such complexity. Similarly, law has struggled with defining the fetus—a living, human and embodied entity but one encased within the woman's body—what Hilary Lim has referred to as 'a complex vision of 'indwelling'.[107] This struggle is vividly encapsulated in the conflicting decisions and approaches taken by the Court of Appeal and House of Lords in the case of *Attorney General's Reference (No 3 of 1994)*.[108] The defendant stabbed his pregnant girlfriend, whom he knew to be 22–24 weeks pregnant. Initially no injury to the fetus was detected, but six weeks later the woman gave birth to a grossly premature baby. It then became apparent that when she was stabbed the knife has penetrated the uterus and injured the fetus. The child died after 120 days. In wrestling with the question of whether the fetus was a person in being for the purposes of homicide law, the Court of Appeal held:

> The foetus is taken to be a part of the mother until it has an existence independent of the mother. Thus an intention to cause serious bodily injury to the foetus is an intention to cause serious bodily injury to a part of the mother just as an intention to injure her arm or leg would be so viewed.[109]

---

[103] Scott (n 24 above) 424.

[104] IM Young, 'Pregnant Embodiment: Subjectivity and Alienation' (1984) 9 *Journal of Medicine and Philosophy* 45, 46.

[105] I Karpin, 'Legislating the Female Reproductive Body: Reproductive Technology and the Reconstructed Woman' (1992–93) 3 *Columbia Journal of Gender and Law* 3325.

[106] K Savell, 'Sex and the Sacred: Sterilization and Bodily Integrity in English and Canadian Law' (2004) 49 *McGill Law Journal* 1093.

[107] Lim (n 97 above) 140.

[108] *Attorney General's Reference (No 3 of 1994)* [1996] 2 All ER 10.

[109] ibid (Lord Taylor CJ).

However this conceptualisation of the relationship between pregnant woman and fetus was rejected by the House of Lords, with Lord Mustill stating that, notwithstanding the intimate biological and emotional bond between fetus and pregnant woman:

> [T]he relationship was one of bond, not of identity. The mother and the foetus were two distinct organisms living symbiotically, not a single organism with two aspects. The mother's leg was part of the mother. The foetus was not.[110]

Sara Fovargue and Jose Miola suggest that both the House of Lords' ruling that the defendant was guilty of unlawful act manslaughter and their conceptualisation of fetal status in order to reach that decision appear 'just and reasonable' on the facts.[111] However, they argue that the implications of the ruling, when combined with what they read as a similar judicial readiness to protect fetal interests in the caesarean cases we have been considering, has the 'potential to sanction the policing of pregnant women' in the interests of the fetus.[112] We would add that, as we discuss below, the caesarean cases pose still more troubling issues for law because the judgments are couched in terms that implicitly assume that the interests or rights of the pregnant woman and fetus inevitably conflict. Moreover, this policing of pregnancy in the interests of the fetus entails more than interference with the woman's rights to self-determination and to make choices about the management of her pregnancy. Rather, enforced caesarean surgery constitutes a particularly gross violation of the woman's bodily integrity—the perceived conflict between woman and fetus is literally embodied in law. Susan Faludi graphically illustrates this in her account of the forced 'treatment' of an incurably ill cancer patient whose unwanted Caesarean procedure was authorised by the District Court of Washington DC:

> [I]nstead of treating her cancer, they jammed a tube down her throat and pumped her with sedatives, a strategy to delay the hour of death. Carder tried to fight this 'treatment', her mother says, remembering how her daughter thrashed and twisted on the bed, fending off the doctors. She said no, no, no. Don't do that to me. But Carder lost the battle and was, quite literally, silenced. With the tube in place, she couldn't speak.[113]

Thomson notes that another US case involved the forcible restraint of a pregnant woman's wrist and ankles with leather cuffs.[114] Although details of such violence are absent from the English cases, despite the fact that

---

[110] ibid (Lord Mustill).
[111] Fovargue and Miola (n 87 above) 293.
[112] ibid 281.
[113] S Faludi, *Backlash: The Undeclared War Against Women* (London, Chatto & Windus, 1992) 433. See further A Young, 'Decapitation or Feticide: The Fetal Laws of the Universal Subject' (1993) 2 *Women: A Cultural Review* 288, 289.
[114] Thomson (n 93 above) 134.

the use of force is explicitly authorised in cases such as *Re MB*,[115] it is noteworthy that in *St George's* we are told that S 'had decided that to struggle physically and be overcome would be undignified. She therefore lay still offering no resistance when at about 17.20 she was sedated'.[116] As Judge LJ remarks, in terms which echo the language of rape cases, '[u]nder the pressures of an exhausting and emotionally charged situation and faced with the court order, MS ceased to offer any resistance. This was not consent but submission'.[117]

Furthermore, the procedure to which these women are compelled to submit is not only a troubling interference with their bodily integrity, but one carrying health risks that include infection, hemorrhage, urinary tract injury and a dramatically increased risk of maternal death. As Thomson concludes: 'With such a wide variation in obstetrical practice, broad conflict of opinion, and the high degree of risk involved in a caesarean section it makes unquestioning judicial acceptance of medical calls of necessity especially unsuitable'.[118] In a similar vein, Munro notes that legal perceptions of fetal/maternal conflict extend:

> not only to a question of the foetal right to life versus the maternal right to autonomy, but also to protecting the maternal right to life against the imposition of a surgical technique that carries with it substantial medical risks, even death.[119]

We suggest that such bodily risks are downplayed in the judgments, and that an emphasis on the embodied effects of caesarean procedures and accompanying risks would reveal a continuing preoccupation in health law with regulating women's bodies and inscribing gendered narratives, such as those rooted in notions of maternal sacrifice.[120] Carl Stychin has argued that starting instead from the viewpoint of the pregnant woman's embodied experience would allow for different approaches to the ethical questions that have engaged health lawyers.[121] This would offer a counter to conventional approaches to health law regulation premised on a mind/body split which deflects attention from lived experience and the question of how we inhabit and experience the world through our bodies and connection with

---

[115] Although in fact MB on hearing of the appellate decision signed the consent form the following morning so that no force was necessary.

[116] *St George's* (n 2 above).

[117] ibid.

[118] Thomson (n 93 above) 135.

[119] Munro (n 88 above) 473.

[120] Thomson (n 95 above) 198; M Fox and T Murphy, 'The Body, Bodies, Embodiment: Feminist, Legal Engagement with Health' in M Davies and V Munro (eds), *A Research Companion to Feminist Legal Theory* (Aldershot, Ashgate Publishing, 2013).

[121] C Stychin, 'Body Talk: Rethinking Autonomy, Commodification and the Embodied Legal Self' in S Sheldon and M Thomson (eds), *Feminist Perspectives on Health Care Law* (London, Cavendish, 1998) 255.

others.[122] Such an approach is particularly valuable in the context of pregnancy, where, as Munro notes:

> Despite the rhetoric of [the] legal model of separation ... the biological reality remains that the foetus is completely dependent upon the body of the pregnant woman for healthy development. In this sense the legal ascription of an environment of conflict may be contra-indicated by the experiential context.[123]

In the following section we suggest that starting with embodied experience, particularly in the context of pregnancy, is compatible with a different ethical approach to these cases rooted in notions of care and relationality.

## C. Conflicts of Personal and Professional Responsibility: Viewing Court-Ordered Caesareans Through the Lens of the Ethics of Care

To date we have discussed the impact of our landmark cases on the issues of self-determination, capacity and bodily integrity, and their implications for the thorny question of fetal status and law's conceptual difficulties with conjoined embodiment. Throughout we have affirmed the stance of the law in upholding a woman's right of self-determination in this matter. Yet it appears from both our landmark cases and the more recent caesarean rulings that no cases have yet 'moved the debate beyond the simple ethical/medical model',[124] so that legal thinking remains enmeshed in a conflict-driven model which pits the woman's rights against fetal interests. This is in line with the ethico-legal approaches taken in other cases that address conjoined embodiment. Thus, writing of surgically separating conjoined twins, Sally Sheldon and Stephen Wilkinson observe that 'law and ethics have developed along a model of physically separate, individual human beings with competing needs and interests'.[125] The problems with this model are compounded by the failure of judges to comprehend 'women's accounts of pregnancy, childbirth and the early maternal bond'.[126] In response to such concerns, and the individualised autonomy approach which, as we have seen, struggles to accommodate the embodied complexity of pregnancy, some feminist theorists have advocated an alternative—relational—approach, which at

---

[122] R Fletcher, M Fox and J McCandless, 'Legal Embodiment: Analysing the Body of Healthcare Law' (2008) 16 *Medical Law Review* 321, 335.

[123] Munro (n 88 above) 473.

[124] C Wells, 'On the Outside Looking in: Perspectives on Enforced Caesareans' in Sheldon and Thomson (n 121 above).

[125] S Sheldon and S Wilkinson, 'Conjoined Twins: the Ethics and Legality of Sacrifice' (1997) 5 *Medical Law Review* 149, 151.

[126] ibid.

least in some variants is grounded in an ethic of care.[127] Care theory places the establishment and maintenance of human relationships at the core of moral life,[128] and potentially at the heart of the law.[129] Consequently, we suggest that it is better equipped than the conflict model to accommodate relational aspects of social living, including the relationship between the pregnant woman and her fetus.[130] Within the realm of choices that facilitate a 'good' or valuable life, some choices may entail assumptions of duties or responsibilities as well as the assertion of rights, so that 'our understanding of autonomy need not be confined to the interests of individuals, but may also encompass the connections between individuals and others' lives'.[131] Moreover, in this context such approaches have the advantage of focusing on relationships rather than fetal status or personhood. A relational conception of autonomy has become increasingly influential in healthcare law,[132] and has focused attention on questions of connection to and caring for others which are downplayed under the conventional ethics and law model that Sheldon and Wilkinson outline. The ethics of care has at its core a moral imperative to become fully immersed, or in the terminology of Nel Noddings 'engrossed', in the situation and view of the other, to be compelled to act in accordance with this, and to appreciate a mutual recognition within relationship.[133] Importantly in this context, the ethics of care should not be seen as a self-sacrificing ethic synonymous with the construction of maternal self-sacrifice we have criticised above; rather 'mature care' as posited by Tove Pettersen,[134] seeks to reconcile individual interests with the needs of others to whom we are connected—a reconciliation that can be effected by examining the concrete particulars in question.

In attempting to apply care theory to the issue of court-ordered caesareans, we would suggest that the relationship between pregnant woman and fetus is best viewed, not as one of antagonism or conflict, but as one in which motherhood is seen as an 'ideology and practice which fosters a

---

[127] The term 'ethic of care' was first adopted by psychologist Carol Gilligan in an attempt to explain a difference that she observed in the processes of moral reasoning, most often demonstrated by women. See C Gilligan, *In a Different Voice: Psychological Theory and Women's Development* (Cambridge MA, Harvard University Press, 1982).

[128] V Held, *The Ethics of Care: Personal, Political and Global* (Oxford, Oxford University Press, 2006) 10.

[129] J Herring, *Caring and the Law* (Oxford, Hart Publishing, 2013) 2.

[130] Munro (n 88 above) 466.

[131] Scott (n 24 above) 253.

[132] E Jackson, *Regulating Reproduction* (Oxford, Hart Publishing, 2001) ch 1; J Herring, 'Forging a Relational Approach: Best Interests or Human Rights?' (2013) 13 *Medical Law International* 32.

[133] N Noddings, *Caring: A Feminine Approach to Ethics and Moral Education* (Berkeley CA, University of California Press, 1984).

[134] T Pettersen, 'The Ethics of Care: Normative Structures and Empirical Implications' (2011) 19 *Healthcare Analysis* 51.

vision of connection and continuity'.[135] When Butler-Sloss LJ in *Re MB* observes that 'however desirable it may be for the mother to be delivered of a live and healthy baby, on this aspect of the appeal, it is not a relevant consideration'[136] she alludes to the inability of the law as currently constructed to take account of such connection and relational interests. Rather, the law aims to protect the woman and fetus from 'third parties and each other'.[137] Yet Judge LJ in *St George's* also emphasises the 'profound physical and emotional bond between the unborn child and its mother'[138]—language that echoes that in the *Attorney General's Reference* case and suggests similar tensions between connection and separation. We agree with Scott that there remain unanswered ethical questions about how that relationship and the tensions it embodies can be accommodated.[139] In this regard we believe that a care-centred approach better reflects the reality of the embodied experience of pregnancy and the relationship it entails. As Celia Wells notes, 'the answers would be no easier, but the debate would acquire the integrity it currently lacks'.[140] In trying to frame a debate capable of accommodating greater nuance and complexity we think that three aspects of the caesarean cases are worth further exploration: the responsibilities of the pregnant woman, the duties of healthcare professionals and interpretation of the best interests test.

## (i) Competent Women and 'Personal Responsibility'

In *St George's* Judge LJ notes that 'while pregnancy increases the personal responsibilities of the woman it does not diminish her entitlement to decide whether or not to undergo medical treatment'.[141] Viewing these responsibilities through the lens of care suggests that they take the form of an ethical obligation to maintain the physical and emotional relationship established with her fetus which develops in a 'gradualist sense',[142] when the pregnant woman chooses to continue with her pregnancy and bring her fetus to term. For John Eekelaar this responsibility is grounded in a social morality that expects 'parents to make decisions which will frequently relegate their own interests beneath those of their children'.[143] This, of course,

---

[135] K de Gama, 'Posthumous Pregnancies: Some Thoughts on 'Life' and Death' in Sheldon and Thomson, *Feminist Perspectives* (n 121 above) 276.

[136] *Re MB* (n 1 above) 554.

[137] C Wells and D Morgan, 'Whose Foetus is it?' (1991) 18 *Journal of Legal Studies* 431.

[138] *St George's* (n 2 above) 695.

[139] Scott (n 24 above).

[140] Wells (n 124 above) 255.

[141] *St George's* (n 2 above) 691.

[142] See Scott (n 24 above) 43.

[143] J Eekelaar, 'Does a Mother have Legal Duties to her Unborn Child?' in P Byrne (ed), *Health, Rigths and Resources* (Oxford Kings Fund Press and Oxford University Press, 1998).

begs the question of whether one consequence of applying a relational ethic to pregnancy is that the woman *may* be morally required to subordinate some of her rights to self-determination in favour of the fetal interest in survival.[144] As Margaret Brazier contends '[t]he absolute dependency of the future child on its mother increases, not diminishes her moral responsibility for its welfare'.[145] Indeed, although Frances Kamm argues that even in cases where a woman 'voluntarily' conceives, this in and of itself does not constitute a moral commitment to continue supporting the fetus,[146] she too acknowledges that a tipping point may be reached whereby the fetus may be 'worse off' if a woman withdraws her support it than if it was never conceived. At this point the woman has a duty to aid that fetus, so long as the cost to her is not too great.[147] In this regard, while we share Scott's belief that it is desirable that the law and morality are compatible as far as possible,[148] we believe that a distinction must be drawn between acknowledging ethical obligations and legally enforcing them. Thus, while conceding the moral obligations of the pregnant woman who elects to continue with her pregnancy, we agree with Scott that the 'physical burdens and risk for the pregnant woman ... are extraordinary by comparison with the bounds of what people are normally expected to do for one another'.[149] Consequently, to legally compel the performance of such moral duties of care, especially when they entail sacrifice of the self is unjust. Furthermore, compulsion is likely to be counterproductive from a care perspective. On a theoretical level compulsion neglects the 'engrossment' in and responsiveness to, the woman's point of view. Practically such an approach is likely to undermine trust between patient and healthcare professional and deter women from seeking healthcare and advice.[150] Nevertheless, even if such obligations are not legally enforceable, we would suggest that acknowledging that ethical responsibilities exist more accurately reflects the recognition of the connection between the pregnant woman and fetus than disingenuous judicial rulings holding that the woman was 'temporarily incompetent'. Such a finding of incompetence will invariably favour surgery undertaken in the woman's 'best interests', although in most of the cases, as we note below, the nature of these interests had not been fully explored.

---

[144] E Kluge, 'When Caesarean Section Operations impose by a Court are Justified' (1988) 14 *Journal of Medical Ethics* 206, 209.

[145] M Brazier, 'Parental Responsibilities, Foetal Welfare, Children's Health' in C Bridge (ed), *Family Law Towards the Millennium* (London, Butterworths, 1997) 271.

[146] Frances Kamm, *Creation and Abortion: A Study in Moral and Legal Philosophy* (Oxford, Oxford University Press, 1992) 90.

[147] ibid, 89, 94.

[148] Scott (n 24 above) xxviii.

[149] R Scott, 'The Pregnant Woman and the Good Samaritan: Can a Woman have a Duty to Undergo a Caesarean Section?' (2000) 20 *Oxford Journal of Legal Studies* 407, 431.

[150] For instance, in deterring women from seeking medical advice and treatment, or as in *St George's* where S was forced to argue for custody of her child—see Gies (n 89 above) 528.

A further complication is the difficulty of ascertaining the woman's 'true' wishes in cases such as *Re MB*, given that, on one level, the woman clearly desired the relationship with the fetus to continue, while simultaneously expressing a contradictory wish. It may well be true that placing the maternal/ fetal relationship at the centre of decision making and striving to preserve this connection more accurately reflects the woman's longer-term autonomous wishes than adhering to her expressed refusal of consent, clouded as it was by the results of phobic panic. As Herring notes '[t]he wish to have the child born alive was one far more closely aligned to her vision of what she wanted her life to be than her desire to avoid the prick of a needle'.[151] However, to adopt such a position would be problematic. First, as we have seen, trying to second-guess a woman's 'true' wishes or interests and then legally compel them would, as Herring acknowledges, 'require a quite novel departure for the law by creating a unique obligation on a woman in pregnancy unlike any other obligations between two people'.[152] Moreover, while it is true that the conjoined embodiment of woman and fetus *is* a connection unlike most others, and that this in turn may generate obligations unlike any others,[153] the obligation to promote fetal welfare should not be seen as the *sole* responsibility of the pregnant woman. Focusing on the perceived threat that she poses to her fetus downplays how social inequalities and environmental factors may pose a greater threat to fetal wellbeing than the actions of an individual pregnant woman.[154] Secondly, we have seen that in practice the current legal position diminishes a woman's right to bodily integrity. This is also vividly illustrated in cases of posthumous pregnancy, where brain-dead women have been ventilated in order to enhance fetal survival, thereby reducing the woman's status to that of a 'fetal container'.[155] Thirdly, a more unusual scenario is where, although a woman has continued with the pregnancy and the fetus is near to term, she has not willingly become pregnant or willingly chosen to continue with the pregnancy (perhaps because of lack of access to abortion, for instance) and has no desire to form a relationship with the fetus or future child. There were hints of such a scenario in the *St George's* case, where it was observed that S 'responded that she was not interested in the pregnancy or the baby'[156] and that after the birth she 'developed strong feelings of revulsion and at first rejected her baby'.[157] It might appear that the absence of any caring relationship between the woman and fetus in such cases means that the ethics of care

---

[151] Herring (n 54 above) 54.
[152] Herring (n 54 above) 51.
[153] See Wells (n 124 above) 256.
[154] See for instance, M Thomson, *Reproducing Narrative* (Aldershot, Ashgate, 1998) Part III for a demonstration of the effects of the toxic workplace environment on the unborn.
[155] de Gama (n 135 above) 260.
[156] *St George's* (n 2 above) 680.
[157] ibid, 677.

has exhausted its usefulness, requiring us to fall back on the traditional renderings of autonomy. Heather Draper suggests that in such a scenario the woman would be placed in the same position as a 'stranger', in terms of the degree of responsibility that she would owe.[158] Yet, whilst Draper might be right that relational responsibilities cannot be morally imposed in the absence of relationship, we would argue that even this scenario may be construed as falling within the ethics of care. If, as a result of 'engrossment' in the woman's situation, it was revealed that her most important relationship was the one that she had with herself (remembering that 'mature' care has an element of self-care and should not necessarily be self-sacrificing) then the most *caring* response may be to acknowledge her refusal of treatment as a means of respecting her interest in her bodily integrity. However, inevitably such cases require that, along with respecting a woman's interest in self-care, we thereby accept that in a small number of cases, fetal death may be the outcome.

### (ii)  Competent Women and the Responsibilities of Healthcare Professionals

When a competent pregnant woman refuses medical treatment that would benefit her fetus the health professionals caring for her are clearly faced with a dilemma. Although, as discussed above, the fetus is not a legal person, health professionals nonetheless may feel as though they effectively have two patients and be conflicted about the care that they owe to the woman and her fetus if their interests are perceived to differ. Furthermore, they will be conscious that forcing treatment on an unwilling patient has the potential to undermine the doctor-patient relationship and deter pregnant women from seeking medical treatment. Carrie Murphy, commenting on the case of *Mrs P*,[159] questions whether forcibly treating a woman who is 'already feeling incredibly confused, alone and disempowered' can really be in her interests.[160] Such dilemmas may be still more pressing if the woman's life is in danger too—a scenario which causes Mason and Laurie to query what weight a court should accord to this factor when addressing the decision-making process in these cases. Whilst observing that for a competent woman it is legally irrelevant whether death is imminent, they acknowledge that it is 'asking a great deal of the health care team to stand by and watch their patient die a painful death'.[161] Maintaining an unswerving focus

---

[158] H Draper, 'Women, Forced Caesareans and Ante-Natal Responsibilities' (1996) *Journal of Medical Ethic* s 327.

[159] *In re P* (n 8 above).

[160] C Murphy, 'Judge Rules Mentally Ill Pregnant Woman can have an Immediate C-Section Against her Will': www.mommyish.com/2013/12/11/emergency-c-section-for-mentally-ill-woman.

[161] Mason (n 20 above) 90.

upon patient autonomy thus risks devaluing the moral agency of health professionals, limiting their role to mere disclosers of information.[162] Brazier notes that in consequence they are reduced to 'service providers obliged to deliver what is ordered'.[163] Conversely, because the power to decide on a woman's competence ultimately rests with those professionals[164] (or the courts, who typically cede to medical opinion), the temptation is to 'manipulate the threshold of capacity'[165] in order to save the life of the pregnant woman and/or her fetus. Thus Thorpe LJ explicitly acknowledges that given 'the inevitable pull to consider the life of both the mother and child ... there is an obvious risk of strained reasoning'.[166]

We suggest that adopting an ethics of care approach in such situations may help circumvent such 'strained reasoning'. Butler-Sloss LJ in *Re MB* stated that when faced with a competent woman's refusal 'doctors may not lawfully do more than attempt to persuade her'.[167] However, the form or degree of such persuasion was not elaborated upon. Katherine Wade argues that a form of 'mutual persuasion', which takes a relational approach to the responsibilities owed between doctor and patient might be appropriate in such cases.[168] Drawing on the work of Alasdair Maclean[169] she suggests a form of dialogue whereby 'patients should seek to persuade professionals that their decision is in keeping with their goals and values'[170]—the kind of immersion and real listening, that we would suggest accords with Noddings' concept of 'engrossment'.[171] This also takes account of Brazier's argument that 'empowered patients also have moral responsibilities' (although, she concedes that it is difficult to translate these into legal responsibilities) to respect the doctor's autonomy by listening to their reasoned persuasion in favour of the procedure.[172] Yet, appealing though the notion of 'mutual persuasion' is, it does presuppose the possession of a certain level of knowledge, confidence and ability to communicate on the part of the patient that may not accord with reality, and fails to recognise the danger that the inherent power imbalance in such relationships may result in persuasion tipping over into undue influence or coercion. Consequently, Scott advocates

---

[162] A McCall-Smith, 'Fetal Medicine: Legal and Ethical Implications' (1992) *Issues in Fetal Medicine* 163, 169.

[163] Brazier (n 86 above) 420.

[164] Mason (n 20 above) 90.

[165] Brazier (n 86 above) 419.

[166] Thorpe LJ, 'The Caesarean Section Debate' (1997) 27 *Fam Law* 663.

[167] *Re MB* (n 1 above) 554.

[168] K Wade, 'Refusal of Emergency Caesarean Section in Ireland: A Relational Approach' (2013) 22 *Medical Law Review* 1, 25.

[169] A Maclean, *Autonomy, Informed Consent and Medical law: A Relational Challenge* (Cambridge, Cambridge University Press, 2009).

[170] Wade (n 168 above) 25.

[171] Noddings (n 133 above) 17–21.

[172] Brazier (n 145 above) 399, 422.

a more nuanced approach, suggesting that where the woman's reason for refusal is 'serious', in that it has an 'intrinsic connection to the woman and her underlying interests in self-determination and/or bodily integrity', then no further persuasion is appropriate.[173] By contrast, a refusal for 'trivial' reasons would justify light persuasion to ensure that the woman is fully aware of the consequences of her decision.[174] Ultimately Scott's concession that the final decision must rest with the pregnant woman,[175] leads Wade to conclude that 'mutual persuasion' is not so much about altering the outcome of the decision as *'facilitat[ing]* good decision-making',[176] in that it respects that the relationship between the woman and healthcare professional is a bi-directional one and provides for opportunities for caring and understanding the view of the 'other'. We agree.

### (iii) Incompetent Women and Interpretation of the Best Interests Test

Finally, and perhaps most realistically given the current legal affirmation of the competent woman's right to self-determination, the ethics of care may be usefully employed as a tool to aid in the interpretation of the 'best interests' test, when a woman is deemed to lack capacity.[177] Thus, even if, as we suggest, reasoning from the ethics of care generates moral rather than legal obligations that are owed by the pregnant woman to her fetus, such reasoning can inform legal reasoning in the application of the best interests test if the woman is found incompetent. This is particularly pertinent given that a finding of incompetence was reached in all of the reported cases except *St George's*. Yet the limited reasoning on best interests in the first instance cases offers little guidance on how the test is to be interpreted or what weight should be given to its various aspects. What is clear from *Re MB*, however, as confirmed in subsequent cases,[178] is that best interests encompasses more than *medical* interests.[179] In the particular circumstances of these cases this stance may have been pragmatic, as many of them, including *Re MB*, did not involve danger to the woman's life or health that would have necessitated the procedure for medical reasons. Nevertheless there are clearly principled reasons to adopt a broader, more holistic approach.

---

[173] Scott (n 24 above) 238.

[174] ibid 239, 244.

[175] ibid 253.

[176] Wade (n 168 above) 25.

[177] In *Re MB* (n 1 above) 555. This has been upheld in the form of the Mental Capacity Act 2005, ss 1(5), 4.

[178] See for example, *Re A* [2000] 1 FLR 389; *Simms v Simms* [2002] EWHC 2734 (Fam); *Local Authority X v MN and KM* [2007] EWHC 2003 (Fam).

[179] *Re MB* (n 1 above).

Applying the ethics of care to best interests assessments would, in our view more accurately reflect the complexity of reproductive decision making, which is inherently relational.[180] As Munro notes, relational and care-based approaches 'highlight the unique potential for connection within the pregnancy experience, and its attendant incompatibility with the individualistic emphasis on rights and the prevailing model of conflict it encourages'.[181] Such approaches would ground the best interests assessment firmly within the woman's relationships—first and foremost her relationship with the fetus. There is some recognition of the centrality of this relationship in the judgments, as the courts grapple with the seemingly 'obvious' conclusion that it must be in the pregnant woman's best interests to have a healthy baby.[182] Yet, perhaps because of the difficulty of reconciling this with the lack of fetal status, and a failure to appreciate that care ethics may sidestep the issue by focusing on interconnectedness rather than the question of legal status or personhood, the courts seem to half apologetically resile from this stance. This is evident in *Re AA*, where Mostyn J states that '[a]lthough I am not allowed to consider the interests of the unborn child, it must be in the mother's interest to have a healthy baby'.[183] However, rather than adopting a relational approach to reach or defend the outcome, the courts opt for the safer route of grounding their reasoning in psychiatric justifications in order to lend the stamp of medical legitimacy to their judgments.[184] For instance, Herring demonstrates how, in the *Norfolk* case, the best interests assessment encompassed a belief in the psychological harm or guilt that the woman might experience if the fetus did not survive.[185] Similarly in *Re AA* Mostyn J notes that 'I think, looked at from her point of view, there is also significant mental health advantage in her unborn child not being exposed to risk during his or her birth'.[186]

Casting the decisions as about the woman's state of mind allows little scope for addressing other interests. In contrast, and in addition to according significance to the maintenance of the connection between a woman and her fetus, a relational approach to best interests could also be extended to consider the woman's obligations to other family members and the impact that her refusal may have upon those such as the putative father or her other children.[187] Interestingly, in *Re MB* Butler-Sloss LJ, perhaps unwittingly,

---

[180] de Gama (n 135 above).

[181] Munro (n 88 above) 476.

[182] See *Re MB* (n 1 above) 555 (Butler-Sloss LJ)—'It must be in the best interests of a woman carrying a full term child whom she wants to be born alive and healthy that such a result should, if possible, be achieved'.

[183] *Re AA* (n 7 above) transcript.

[184] Se *Re AA* (n 7 above) para 4, *Re MB* (n 1 above) 439.

[185] Herring (n 54 above) 47.

[186] *Re AA* (n 7 above).

[187] Maclean (n 169 above) 247.

considered wider relational justifications by noting that '[i]t is clear on the evidence that the mother and the *father* wanted this child to be born alive and Miss MB was in favour of the operation' (emphasis added).[188] Yet, to do so leads to the unsettling conclusion that the father's relational interests may be relevant when assessing whether a caesarean may be in an incompetent woman's best interests but (according to the reasoning in *Paton*[189]) may play no part in the decision-making process of a competent woman.

## IV. CONCLUDING THOUGHTS

We began by noting that the forced caesarean cases have been at the centre of two conflicts—between medical power and patient autonomy and between the rights of the pregnant woman and the interests of the fetus.[190] We have seen how this construction of the issue has caused pregnancy to be regarded as entailing conflict in maternal/fetal relations, thereby fostering an understanding of the fetus as 'an autonomous individual with the ability to enforce such rights ... and obscuring the contingent nature of foetal existence'.[191] In this chapter we have sought to argue that starting from the different vantage point of an embodied ethic of care changes this understanding of pregnancy. Feminist commentators have pointed to the need for multiple narratives of the female body, which complicate ideologies rooted in notions of maternal altruism and sacrifice. Thus, Karpin suggests that 'a feminist description might emanate from the standpoint of an empowered, enfranchised woman, with the capacity to make choices not only about whether to bring a fetus to term, but also about the management of her pregnancy'.[192]

Yet law, and the surrounding culture, has struggled with such images, especially if they may result in fetal death, leading Gies to highlight the difficulty in 'envisage[ing] a situation in which the subordination of the foetus to the autonomy and bodily integrity of a pregnant woman gains a solid moral and commonsensical status'.[193] As we have seen in the recent cases, judges continue to appeal to this common sense notion of what the pregnant woman must want.[194] In our view this remains the key issue,

---

[188] *Re MB* (n 1 above).
[189] *Paton* (n 9 above) 991 Sir George Baker states 'this husband cannot by law by injunction stop his wife having what is now to be a lawful abortion'. This reasoning could equally be applied to a father's attempts to compel a competent woman to undergo a caesarean to save the life of his child, in the face of her legal entitlement to refuse medical treatment.
[190] Harrington (n 81 above) 508–9.
[191] Thomson (n 25 above) 144.
[192] Karpin (n 105 above) 326.
[193] Gies (n 89 above) 533.
[194] See remarks of Mostyn J in *Re AA* (text at nn 71, 183, 186 above).

which the rulings in these particular landmark cases have failed to resolve, because it remains true that a focus on the pregnant woman's state of mind in practice allows judges to deem her incompetent if she repudiates such medical and common sense. Of course, feminist legal scholars have long been wary of looking to law for solutions,[195] but Carol Smart's warning about the need to de-centre law seems particularly apt in this context. As Miller argues:

> One cannot hope to protect the foetus by laws that punish the mother; one can only strive to protect the interests of the foetus by protecting the interests of the mother. It is far better to have a few tragic private wrongs than that the state imposed coercion of pregnant women becomes a part of our legal landscape.[196]

We agree. Therefore while starting, as we advocate, with a relational approach grounded in an ethics of care and the lived experience of pregnant embodiment suggests that a pregnant woman does owe moral obligations of care to the fetus she has chosen to gestate and give birth to, we would argue that it is imperative that law should refrain from enforcing these obligations by requiring the woman to submit to unwanted medical intervention in the interests of her fetus. Rather, law must be attentive to 'the relevance of context, connection and embodiment' as opposed to dealing in separation, abstraction and individualism, as is currently the case. As Munro notes, it is particularly unlikely in this context that applying individualistic and abstract rights analysis will achieve a lasting resolution.[197] Moreover, while recognising the centrality of the woman-fetal relation, law should also resist the temptation to individualise responsibility, since, as noted above, broader social and environmental conditions may be equally relevant to fetal wellbeing.[198] Rather, given the importance of bodily integrity to women's citizenship,[199] judges should be cautious about resorting too easily to a finding that the pregnant woman is incompetent to refuse treatment. De Gama has demonstrated how little space the current law allows to take account of relational interests when addressing a competent woman's right to refuse medical treatment.[200] In our view the better way to foster relational and caring decision making would be for law to create the conditions for women to receive education and information to enable meaningful dialogue

---

[195] C Smart, *Feminism and the Power of Law* (London, Routledge, 1989).
[196] L Miller, 'Two Patients or One? Problems of Consent in Obstetrics' (1993) 1 *Medical Law International* 97, 99.
[197] Munro (n 88 above) 461.
[198] Draper (n 158 above) 331.
[199] Cornell (n 85 above).
[200] de Gama (n 135 above) 277.

with health professionals at an early stage in the pregnancy in order to agree treatment plans which will lead to optimal outcomes for all concerned. To achieve this we would argue that there is a need for a more nuanced and contested understanding of the female body, and a variety of ideologies of motherhood and pregnancy, which recognise the importance of valuing both the intimacy associated with the connection between woman and fetus and the validity of a woman's desire for separation.[201]

[201]  R West, 'Jurisprudence and Gender' (1988) 55 *University of Chicago Law Review* 1; and R Scott, 'Refusing Medical Treatment During Pregnancy and Birth: Ethical and Legal Issues' in Ebtehaj et al (eds), *Birth Rites and Rights* (n 78 above).

# 9

# R v Department of Health, ex parte Source Informatics Ltd [1999]

MARK TAYLOR

## I. INTRODUCTION

R v DEPARTMENT of Health, ex parte Source Informatics Ltd[1] has helped to establish the scope and nature of the common law duty of confidence in personal information.[2] Specifically, Source has supported the proposition that a key feature of a breach of the duty of confidence is the disclosure of *identifiable* data. If 'data is the 21st century's new raw material',[3] then this is an important proposition. It suggests that those holding personal information might process it as they please, without any concern for a breach of any duty of confidence, as long as any data disclosed (to a third party) are anonymised. This is a suggestion that deserves to be resisted. It overlooks the ways that the processing of anonymised data might engage with an interest in informational autonomy. It underplays the impact that the anonymisation and subsequent use of abstracted or transformed data might have upon individuals. It undermines the foundation of the confidential relationship between patients and those in whom they have confided sensitive personal information. Fortunately, while Source does support the proposition that the identifiability of data is a key concern, it does not support the claim that it is the only or overriding concern. A close reading

---

[1] *R v Department of Health, ex parte Source Informatics Ltd* [1999] EWHC 510, [1999] 4 All ER 185 (QB); [1999] EWCA Civ 3011, [2001] QB 424, [2000] 1 All ER 786 (CA).

[2] The duty of confidence does also extend to cover the processing of other data in other circumstances, including for example government data (*Attorney-General v Jonathan Cape Ltd, Attorney-General v Times Newspapers Ltd* [1976] QB 752), commercial ideas (*R (on the application of Veolia ES Nottinghamshire Ltd) v Nottinghamshire County Council* [2010] EWCA Civ 1214) and trade secrets. Other cases key to establishing the scope of the duty of confidence in relation to personal information include *Coco v AN Clark (Engineers) Ltd* [1969] RPC 41, *Attorney-General v Guardian Newspapers Ltd (No 2)* [1988] 3 All ER 545 and *Campbell v Mirror Group Newspapers Ltd* [2004] UKHL 22, [2004] 2 AC 457.

[3] Francis Maude, *Open Data White Paper: Unleashing the Potential* (Cabinet Office, June 2012) 5.

of *Source*, and its significance for the common law duty of confidence today, helps instead to reveal how and why the common law might yet provide the protection to which people are entitled and hold those who anonymise and instrumentalise personal information to account for misuse. Conscionable use cannot be guaranteed simply through a process of anonymisation.

The summary to a 1999 report, on a merger proposed between IMS Health Inc and Pharmaceutical Marketing Services Inc (PMSI), began

> Pharmaceutical business information is vital to the pharmaceutical companies, enabling them to monitor their competitive position, identify areas of product development, focus their sales and marketing activity and remunerate their salesmen.[4]

This is no less true today than it was when it was written 15 years ago. At the time, PMSI owned Source Informatics Inc (Source). Before the merger between the two companies, Source had been in competition with IMS Health Inc to develop services that would gather pharmaceutical business information directly from dispensing pharmacies. This information would identify GPs and their dispensing habits and improve the quality of 'vital' business information. The merger report provided a contemporary note that the 'Department of Health has recently issued guidance that such services breach patient confidentiality, guidance which is subject to judicial review'.[5]

The merger report gives an insight into the significance of the information for the company owning Source. It is perhaps no great surprise that the Court of Appeal did not find there to be any *privacy* interests at stake that were entitled to protection. Source was a company keen to access information that would improve the efficiency and effectiveness of its business. The Department's motives for denying access were similarly economic; they were concerned the information would be used to improve marketing to GP practices and raise the NHS drugs bill. The case was fought between two parties with *financial* interests in the outcome. Nevertheless, the judgment and reasoning in *Source* has been understood to cast doubt on the possibility that anonymised data might ever engage an individual's interest in privacy. A position supported tangentially by the law of data protection.[6]

We now stand at the edge of a revolution in the processing of patient data. Companies are looking to capitalise on a growing market in health 'apps'.[7]

---

[4] *Summary of IMS Health Inc and Pharmaceutical Marketing Services Inc: A report on the Merger Situation* (Prepared by the Competition Commission at the request of the Secretary of State for Trade and Industry, last revised April 1999). Available in National Archives at: webarchive.nationalarchives.gov.uk/; www.competition-commission.org.uk/ims.htm.

[5] ibid.

[6] The EU Data Protection Directive 95/46/EC [1995] OJ L281/31 extends protection only to identifiable data. See, for example, Recital 26. This is discussed further later in the chapter.

[7] Research2Guidance report on health apps predicts that by 2017 worldwide mobile health market revenue will total US$26 billion: Research2Guidance *Global Mobile Health Market Report 2013–2017* (March, 2013).

There is an overt ambition to make further use of patient data gathered by the National Health Service.[8] Now is a very good time to revisit the reasoning offered in *Source* to determine whether, and in what circumstances, it truly does support any claim that the common law duty of confidence attaches responsibilities to the processing of personal information only so far as such information remains identifiable. If the common law duty of confidence can serve to proscribe unconscionable uses of data following anonymisation, and thus serve a function that the law of data protection does not provide, then I suggest this to be a possibility that should not be easily surrendered.

In what follows, having set out the circumstances and background in more detail, I first consider how the approach taken in *Source* might help us to understand the relationship between a 'reasonable expectation of privacy', any necessity for consent to use identifiable patient data, and the historic concern of the common law to prevent unconscionable use of information held in confidence. I then move to directly address the question of whether *Source* did establish that a breach of confidence, or to put it in modern parlance, the tort of misuse of personal information,[9] could be necessarily avoided through the anonymisation of data. The law of privacy is a whirlpool where common law, statute, European directive and human rights obligations meet and churn. In this maelstrom, a particularly clear understanding of the relationship between 'anonymisation' and 'reasonable expectations of privacy' could provide a welcome and important opportunity for the common law to regulate the use of personal information anonymisation notwithstanding.

## II. CASE HISTORY

On 28 May 1999 an application for declaratory relief was heard in the High Court by Mr Justice Latham. The application was made on behalf of Source Informatics Ltd (Source). It was a response to Department of Health guidance issued following a request from Source to General Practitioners (GPs) for GP consent to the collection of certain information relating to patient treatment from prescription data. The information was to be collected and provided to Source by pharmacists who receive information from GPs in identifiable

---

[8] 'We've got to change the way we innovate, the way that we collaborate, and the way that we open up the NHS'. Extract from a speech given by the Prime Minister, The Rt Hon David Cameron, at the FT Global Pharmaceutical and Biotechnology Conference, 6 December 2011. Full transcript available at: www.gov.uk/government/speeches/pm-speech-on-life-sciences-and-opening-up-the-nhs (last accessed January 2014).
[9] See, seminal comments of Lord Nicholls in *Campbell v MGN Ltd* [2004] UKHL 22, [14] and more recently *Vidal-Hall and Others v Google* [2014] EWHC 13 (QB).

form for the purposes of dispensing prescribed medication. GP consent was sought for pharmacists to disclose data relating to the prescribing habits of GPs; the identity and quantity of drugs prescribed. The information would not identify the patients to whom the drugs had been dispensed or any other diagnostic information. Pharmacists would be paid by Source for providing the information. Despite no patient-identifiable information being sought by Source, the guidance issued by the Department of Health indicated that such disclosure could constitute a breach of the common law duty of confidence owed by GPs to their patients. The policy document read:

> [U]nder common law and Data Protection Act principles, the general rule is that information given in confidence may not be disclosed without the consent of the provider of the information. In this instance, both patients and GPs may be regarded as providers of the data in question ... Anonymisation (with or without aggregation) does not, in our view, remove the duty of confidence towards the patients who are the subject of the data.[10]

Source objected to the content of this advice. The initial response was to agree steps to further reduce the possibility of patient identification. Source agreed to exclude certain data relating to rare drugs or drug combinations that might allow individual patients to be inferentially identified. When the issue was considered in court, it was assumed that it would be possible for Source to guarantee patient anonymity.[11] The key issue remaining was the legality of the advice that the anonymisation of data did not remove the duty of confidence towards the patients who are the subjects of the data. When Source was unable to persuade the Department to change their position on this point, it sought a declaration that the guidance issued was wrong in law and that 'disclosure by doctors or pharmacists to a third party of anonymous information, that is information from which the identity of patients may not be determined, does not constitute a breach of confidentiality'.[12]

Between the parties there was no disagreement on the question of whether the data, at the point when the pharmacists received it, was confidential. Nor was there any dispute as to whether the pharmacists, or GPs, had a duty of confidence in relation to the data while it was held in identifiable

---

[10] Extract of policy document provided in judgment: [1999] EWHC 510, [1999] 4 All ER 185, 187(d), [1999] Lloyds Rep Med 264.

[11] Although Brown LJ made clear that it was for Source 'to satisfy all interested parties that there will be no risk of identification in practice': *R v Department of Health, ex parte Source Informatics Ltd* [2001] QB 424, [8]. I do not intend here to unpick this assumption. While there are those who doubt the robustness of any process of anonymisation, given modern possibilities for inferential or jigsaw identification, it is not necessary here to engage in this debate. For my views on the significance of context to the possibility of identification—and therefore the viability of anonymisation *in context*—see MJ Taylor, *Genetic Data and the Law* (Cambridge, Cambridge University Press, 2012), especially chapter 6: 'Anonymity'.

[12] *R v Department of Health, ex parte Source Informatics Ltd* [2001] QB 424, [2000] 1 All ER 786 (CA), [5].

form. Argument centred on whether the specific uses of the data proposed, involving first anonymisation and then disclosure to a third party for a purpose that went beyond that consented to by patients, constituted a breach of the common law duty of confidence.

It was Mr Beloff QC's submission, on behalf of the applicants, Source, that the proposed use of the data could not constitute a breach of confidence for two principal reasons: (1) Once abstracted from identifiable data, anonymised data are not confidential: 'So far as the patient is concerned, the information will have become purely statistical, carrying with it no information of a personal or private nature'.[13] (2) It is an essential element in any successful action for breach of the common law duty of confidence that the claimant suffers detriment. Even *if* the abstracted data *were* considered by the court to be confidential, Mr Beloff submitted that no detriment could follow the disclosure of that information in anonymised form to Source. On behalf of the Department of Health, Mr Sales disputed both claims. The Department of Health focused on the purposes for which the identifiable and confidential information had been provided to GPs and submitted that any use of confidential data, 'other than the one for which actual or implied consent had been given, will amount to a misuse'[14] of confidential information. The claim was that misuse was made in both 'the manipulation of the information and its transmission to the applicants for the commercial benefit of the pharmacist'.[15]

At first instance, Mr Justice Latham was persuaded by the argument that the specific use of the confidential data by the pharmacists was 'unauthorised' by patients.[16] He said,

[i]n my judgment what is proposed will result in a clear breach of confidence unless the patient gives consent, which is not part of the proposal at present. Nor is it suggested that the patient can be said to have given implied consent.[17]

The decision was appealed and reversed by the Court of Appeal. Lord Justice Simon Brown gave the leading judgment, which was agreed without further comment by the Lords Justice Aldous and Schiemann. Brown LJ turned from the idea that the presence or absence of implied consent was of central importance. He relied instead upon the idea expressed by Bingham LJ in *Attorney General v Guardian Newspapers Ltd (No 2) (Spycatcher)* that the rational basis of the claim to a duty of confidence 'lies in the notion of an obligation of conscience arising from the circumstances in or through which the information was communicated or obtained'.[18]

---

[13] *R v Department of Health, ex parte Source Informatics Ltd* [1999] 4 All ER 185, 188(g).
[14] ibid, 189(b).
[15] ibid.
[16] ibid, 192(h).
[17] ibid, 192(j).
[18] *Attorney General v Guardian Newspapers Ltd (No 2) (Spycatcher)* [1990] 1 AC 109, 216.

He considered 'the one and consistent theme'[19] evident within the jurisprudence surrounding the common law duty of confidence to be that

> the confidant is placed under a duty of good faith to the confider and the touchstone by which to judge the scope of that duty and whether or not it has been fulfilled or breached is his own conscience, no more and no less.[20]

Thus, the question for Brown LJ was '[w]ould a reasonable pharmacist's conscience be troubled by the proposed use to be made of patients' prescriptions?' It was the view of Brown LJ that it would not. This decision, and the approach taken by the Court, are significant for at least two reasons: (1) the shift from the test (applied by the High Court) which focused on whether a patient had 'authorised' use to one which instead focused on whether the use would be considered 'conscionable' by a reasonable health professional. This suggests a move to focus upon professional judgement rather than patient choice; an apparent shift from patient autonomy to professional discretion. This is out of step with other, particularly more recent, developments in the law, which are concerned to protect an individual's 'reasonable expectation of privacy' and personal autonomy.[21] It requires consideration to determine if the Court took a wrong turn in *Source* and to assess the case's enduring significance. (2) It supported the general proposition that the disclosure of information from which the identity of patients may not be determined could not breach confidentiality. This suggests that, if confidential data are held lawfully, then the party holding the data can use the data, or disclose to a third party in anonymised form, for any purpose at all without risk of breaching any duty of confidence.

This data is increasingly valuable. A growing number of people are using health apps.[22] Private companies are collecting and aggregating the personal health information provided. The data held in public clinical databases are increasingly used to inform more than an individual's direct care and treatment.[23]

---

[19] *R v Department of Health, ex parte Source Informatics Ltd* [2001] QB 424 (CA), [31].
[20] ibid.
[21] This point is considered immediately below but Buxton LJ provides a concise history of the development of the law of confidence into a law of privacy in *McKennitt v Ash* [2008] QB 73 from 80[8].
[22] eMarketer, 'Fitness, General Health Are Leading Health Apps' (1 October 2013): www.emarketer.com/Article/Fitness-General-Health-Leading-Health-Apps/1010263.
[23] It should be recognised that the common law duty of confidence will not have an application to some disclosures of confidential patient data to the Health and Social Care Information Centre for purposes beyond direct care. The Information Centre will be responsible for some significant initiatives to improve use of patient data for indirect care and it has new powers to collect such data, under the Health and Social Care Act 2012, which set aside the common law duty. The analysis of the common law offered in this chapter will only have application in so far as it has not been set aside by the Health and Social Care Act 2012 or otherwise. For discussion of these new powers, see MJ Taylor and J Grace, 'Disclosure of Confidential Patient Information and the Duty to Consult: The Role of the Health and Social Care Information Centre' (2013) 21 *Medical Law Review* 415.

At a time when the extent of individual control over uses of data provided for primary care is already being questioned,[24] the scope of the duty of confidence has particularly important implications for the extent to which the common law can control the aggregation and further use of personal health information gathered under different circumstances.

## III. REASONABLE EXPECTATION AND ARTICLE 8 ECHR

In *Campbell v MGN Ltd*, Lord Nicholls recognised that the time had come to explicitly recognise that the common law duty of confidence protected 'the values enshrined in articles 8 and 10'[25] of the European Convention on Human rights (ECHR). The common law has been gradually developed by the courts to provide such protection as part of a more general commitment to provide adequate protection to the rights enshrined in the ECHR.[26] Article 8(1) of the ECHR recognises the need to respect private and family life. This need has now been absorbed into the cause of action for breach of confidence.

The form of Article 8 now structures legal argument in the law of confidence. An interference with private and family life must first be established (under Article 8(1)) before a court will go on to consider whether the interference can be justified (under Article 8(2)). Each of the judges in *Campbell* supports Nicholls LJ's suggestion that, when determining a prima facie interference: 'the touchstone of private life is whether in respect of the disclosed facts the person in question has a reasonable expectation of privacy'.[27] UK courts have recognised that a person's 'reasonable expectation of privacy' will not be adequately protected by *only* regulating the misuse of personal information within *pre-existing* relationships. Recognising now that 'privacy itself is a legal principle drawn from the fundamental value of personal autonomy',[28] the courts have extended the scope of the duty of confidence to protect

> not only those people whose trust has been abused but those who simply find themselves subjected to an unwanted intrusion into their private lives. The law no longer needs to construct an artificial relationship of confidentiality between intruder and victim.[29]

---

[24] See, for example, Randeep Ramesh, 'NHS patient data to be made available for sale to drug and insurance firms', *The Guardian*, Sunday 19 January 2014 (available online: www.theguardian.com/society/2014/jan/19/nhs-patient-data-available-companies-buy) (last accessed January 2014).

[25] *Campbell v Mirror Group Newspapers Ltd* [2004] UKHL 22, [2004] 2 AC 457, [17].

[26] In the context of a historical lack of a general right to privacy in the UK. See, for example, *Wainwright v Home Office* [2003] 3 WLR 1137.

[27] [2004] UKHL 22, [21].

[28] Sedley LJ in *Douglas v Hello! Ltd* [2001] QB 967, 1001, [126].

[29] ibid.

This fresh emphasis upon autonomy might suggest, as implied by the approach taken by the High Court in *Source*, that the relevant question is whether the use of personal information has been 'authorised'. However, it would be a mistake, albeit an easy mistake, to derive from this position that individuals must explicitly consent to each and every use of personal information. It would similarly be wrong to assume that an ambiguous general 'authorisation' could be relied upon to justify processing that fell outside an individual's reasonable expectation.


## IV. CONSENT AND AUTONOMY

In general terms, autonomy is respected if the capacity to act in a free and informed way is respected. *Requiring* that an individual seek free and informed consent from another before using his or her personal information for a particular purpose can serve to protect that other's autonomy. The *process* of seeking consent can both provide the relevant information, and an opportunity to exercise choice, that might otherwise be lacking. Seeking consent is not, however, the only—or necessarily even always the most appropriate—way to respect autonomy. In circumstances where another can already anticipate that personal information will be used in a particular way—ie they already possess the relevant information—and there are already appropriate means for them to exercise relevant choice, then use without *explicit* consent does not necessarily undermine his or her autonomy. Indeed, sometimes, it might be that an individual would positively prefer that things were done without having first to be asked. Lord Goff famously extended the scope of a duty of care to include the circumstance where

> an obviously confidential document is wafted by an electric fan out of a window into a crowded street, or where an obviously confidential document, such as a private diary, is dropped in a public place, and is then picked up by a passer-by.[30]

To destroy the wafted document (if return was not practicable); to open and read some of the diary (to facilitate return): both might be actions that would be inappropriate in other circumstances. To insist that they could *only ever* take place with an individual's explicit consent, regardless of the circumstances, would, however, pose more risk than succour to personal autonomy.[31]

---

[30] *Attorney-General v Observer Ltd* [1990] 1 AC 109, 281 E.

[31] Another example might be the use of information by a healthcare professional to support an individual's direct care or treatment without explicit consent. When a person provides personal information during a health consultation the health professional does not explicitly ask if it is permissible to use that information to inform the diagnosis or recommended care. To insist upon such explicit consent could undermine the autonomy of the person providing the information (eg if the circumstances of care changed dramatically, such as emergency admission and the question arose as to whether use of personal information for the purposes of avoiding adverse drug reaction had been explicitly authorised).

Before returning to this point, there is a more fundamental (but associated) problem with the suggestion that a respect for autonomy, *manifest as a respect for privacy*, will always require explicit consent. The Court of Appeal in *Source* underlined that English Law does not protect the right to control information per se. As Brown LJ put it, a patient 'has no right to control its use provided only and always that his privacy is not put at risk'.[32]

The duty of confidence protects informational autonomy by ensuring no *interference* with autonomy, rather than by *requiring* the exercise of autonomy. The modern formulation of the 'tort of misuse of personal information'[33] continues to emphasise that it is the *misuse* of information that is proscribed. The Court's approach may perhaps be explained by the fact that English law has historically been based on freedoms and not rights.[34] The language used by the Court of Appeal may have been more reminiscent of the historical roots of the common law duty of confidentiality but that does not mean that it cannot be reconciled with more modern developments in the law. On the contrary, it may offer a useful reminder of its inter-personal aspect.[35]

Discussion of the duty of confidence originally prompted regular reliance upon the ideas of 'trust and confidence'. Samuel Johnson had, in 1755, defined 'confidence' to mean the 'firm belief in another's integrity or veracity'.[36] Brown LJ connected with that history by emphasising that it was the conduct of the party who held the confidential information that was to be examined: to be protected was the expectation that the individual in receipt of personal information would act with integrity.

This use of the language of conscionability, albeit now perhaps somewhat dated, does usefully remind us that a *reasonable* expectation of privacy must take into account the responsibilities of the individual holding the data.[37] This does not assume an individual's ability exclusively to control what would be an appropriate use: 'To avoid taking unfair advantage of information does

[32] [2001] QB 424 (CA), [34].
[33] See, seminal comments of Lord Nicholls in *Campbell v MGN Ltd* [2004] All ER 67, [14] and more recently *Vidal-Hall and Others v Google* [2014] EWHC 13 (QB).
[34] See Brooke LJ in *Douglas v Hello! Ltd* [2001] QB 967, [64].
[35] This is *not* to suggest that the common law relies upon a pre-existing relationship between particular persons. It is only to emphasise that the law has always been concerned to regulate the use by one person of information that relates to another.
[36] Cited by Megan Richardson, Michael Bryan, Martin Vranken and Katy Barnett, *Breach of Confidence* (Cheltenham, Edward Elgar Publishing, 2012) 5.
[37] It would be possible for relevant responsibilities, eg of a health professional, to be taken into account at two different points: at the point when a reasonable expectation is initially determined, or, at the point when it is determined whether any breach of confidence is justified. It may make little difference to the outcome at which point they are taken into account. For reasons I do not have the space here to unpack I have considerable sympathy for the view expressed by Brown LJ that 'the equitable obligation of confidence ought not to be drawn too widely in the first place' (see para [52]).

not necessarily mean that the confidee must not use it except for the confider's limited purpose'.[38]

There may be times even when it is appropriate to use data in ways that the data subject expressly does not want.[39] What *is* important here is that what will constitute a reasonable expectation of privacy, and what will constitute a failure appropriately to respect informational autonomy, will depend upon the *context*. While a pre-existing relationship is no longer required, the nature of any relationship that does exist will inform an understanding of 'any obligation of conscience arising from the circumstances in or through which the information was communicated or obtained'.[40]

Turning to consider, in particular, the relationship between a patient and doctor or other health professional, it is clear that the law *does* typically expect a patient's authorisation to be explicitly sought before their personal information is used for purposes beyond their direct care and treatment. In *Z v Finland*, the European Court of Human Rights said that: 'any state measures compelling communication or disclosure of information without the consent of the patient call for the most careful scrutiny'.[41] This is, in large part, a product of the particular relationship between doctor and patient and the particular public interest that is recognised in preserving the confidentiality of that relationship.[42] Any use of personal information beyond direct care and treatment, that a patient does not know about, and has no opportunity to express a preference in relation to, risks an action for breach of confidence.[43] The Courts may find an equivalent duty of

---

[38] *El Dupont de Nemours Powder Co v Masland* (1917) 244 US 102, cited favourably by Brown LJ, [437].

[39] See *Hellewell v Chief Constable of Derbyshire* [1995] 4 All ER 473, [1995] 1 WLR 804. The police were entitled to make 'reasonable use' of a photograph, which they held in confidence, for the purposes of policing.

[40] *Moorgate Tobacco Co Ltd v Philip Morris Ltd (No 2)* (1984) 156 CLR 414, 437–38 cited favourably by Bingham LJ, *Attorney-General v Observer Ltd* [1990] 1 AC 109, 215. See, an example of context being taken into account in *W v Edgell* [1990] Ch 359 where the relevant duties of the doctor were described not simply as the duties that a doctor might ordinarily owe a patient. The Court 'declined to overlook the background to Dr Edgell's examination of W' (p 392). The scope of the duty of confidence owed was shaped by the context.

[41] *Z v Finland* (1998) 25 EHRR 371, 372.

[42] ibid. See also, eg *X v Y* [1988] 2 All ER 648, 653; *W v Edgell* [1990] Ch 359, 422–23.

[43] There are two (related) ways in which the particular relationship between doctor and patient might give rise to an expectation that a patient will be asked for consent before personal information is used for purposes beyond their direct care and treatment. The first relates to the potential impact upon the patient if he or she loses confidence in the confidentiality of the healthcare system. This point unavoidably anticipates later discussion of the relevance of detriment to an action but the courts have recognised there to be a public interest in maintaining such confidence (see ibid). The second relates to the fiduciary nature of doctor-patient relationship and the equitable roots of the duty of confidence. It would be inequitable for a doctor to take advantage of his or her position in relation to a patient and either make a profit out of the patient's trust or otherwise place himself in a situation of conflicting interests. For discussion of fiduciary duties (raised in another context), see comments of Millett LJ, *Bristol and West Building Society v Mothew (t/a Stapley & Co)* [1998] Ch 1, 18.

confidence in circumstances where individuals have a similar 'reasonable expectation of privacy'. Brown LJ suggested that such expectations might be appropriately safeguarded through the process of anonymisation. However, the adequacy of such protection should itself be recognised to be entirely context dependent.

## V. ANONYMITY

Deryck Beyleveld has convincingly argued that *Source* supported a '"narrow" conception of privacy, which implies that the right to privacy is not engaged in the use of personal data once it has been rendered anonymous'.[44] He contrasts this with the 'broad' conception of privacy that is recognised and protected by Article 8 of the ECHR: A concept that extends beyond the simple protection of identity to 'the development and fulfilment of one's own personality'.[45] I would agree that, if English common law is to protect the right to a private and family life recognised by Article 8, then it cannot protect a narrow concept of privacy. I would also agree that *Source* has given support to the position that neither the anonymisation of data, nor the use of data in anonymised form, can interfere with privacy. However, as Beyleveld recognises '[t]he Court did not go quite so far as to declare that once personal information is rendered anonymous it can, under no circumstances whatsoever, continue to attract a duty of confidence'.[46] I would agree with this but in fact go further. I would suggest the broader approach taken in *Source* to determining the scope of the duty of confidence must be understood to support such a possibility. It would be a mistake to believe that the transformation of personal information into anonymised form, and the subsequent use of data in such an anonymised form, could *never* represent a misuse of data from which an individual was entitled to protection: It is wrong to suggest that the use of anonymised data could *never* trouble the conscience of a reasonable person in receipt of personal health data.[47]

---

[44] D Beyleveld, 'Conceptualising privacy in relation to medical research values' in Sheila MacLean (ed), *First Do No Harm* (Aldershot, Ashgate, 2006) 151.
[45] *X v Iceland* (Application No 6825/74), [1976] ECHR 7, (1976) 5 DR 86, 87.
[46] Beyleveld (n 44 above) 153.
[47] That it might trouble the conscience of a reasonable health professional is supported to some extent by the reporting of professional concerns over the care.data programme. See, for example, Nigel Praities, 'Over 40% of GPs intend to opt themselves out of care.data scheme', *Pulse*, 24 January 2014, www.pulsetoday.co.uk/your-practice/practice-topics/it/over-40-of-gps-intend-to-opt-themselves-out-of-caredata-scheme/20005648.article#.Uu_ISXd_uJk; Anonymous GP, 'Why I'm opting patients out of the care.data scheme', *Pulse*, 12 November 2013, www.pulsetoday.co.uk/your-practice/comment/why-im-opting-patients-out-of-the-caredata-scheme/20005022.article#.Uu_IqHd_uJk (last accessed January 2014). It is important to recognise, however, that the care.data programme is an initiative relying on the powers to collect data granted under the Health and Social Care Act 2012. See eMarketer (n 22 above).

*Source* lends support to the, revised and current, Department of Health position that 'once information is anonymised it is no longer confidential'.[48] However, *Source* did *not* close the door on the possibility that *the anonymisation* of data, or the subsequent use of abstracted data in anonymised form, might engage an individual's duty of confidence. Such possibility is likely to depend upon persons being able to demonstrate a (potential) misuse of the information from which they are entitled to protection: A risk that Brown LJ did not perceive in the circumstances of *Source*.

## VI. RELEVANCE OF DETRIMENT

While he did not consider it necessary to decide the issue to dispose of the application, Mr Justice Latham addressed the question of the necessity that any successful action for breach of the common law duty of confidence would require that the claimant suffer detriment of some kind. Two questions are raised: (1) Is detriment a necessary element? (2) Can relevant detriment result from the disclosure of anonymised data? Noting that different views were expressed in *Attorney General v Guardian Newspapers (No 2)* Latham J first quoted Lord Keith of Kinkel and support for the idea that specific detriment need not always be necessary.[49] He then turned to recognise Lord Griffiths' view that 'The remedy has been fashioned to protect the confider not to punish the confidant and there seems little point in extending it to a confider who has no need of the protection'.[50]

Despite the apparent differences, Latham's view is that 'there may, in truth, be little or no difference between the [different views]'.[51] He considered that each of the judges 'recognised that there must be some effect on the confider from which the Court considers that he is entitled to protection'.[52] This is consistent with the position taken by Rose J and favourably cited in the Court of Appeal; detrimental use of the data is not required for a valid claim for breach if circumstances otherwise demonstrate that claimants are entitled to protection.[53]

It is suggested that the fact that the case was brought to protect financial interests was relevant to the Court finding there to be nothing at stake that was entitled to protection by the common law duty of confidence. The circumstances of *Source* did not demonstrate *how* or *why* the use of

[48] Department of Health, NHS Code of Practice, November 2003, 29.
[49] *Attorney General v Guardian Newspapers Ltd (No 2) (Spycatcher)* (n 18 above) 255 E, cited [1999] EWHC 510, [1999] 4 All ER 185, 193(b) (n 13 above).
[50] *Attorney General v Guardian Newspapers Ltd (No 2) (Spycatcher)* (n 18 above) 270 D, cited [1999] EWHC 510, [1999] 4 All ER 185, 194(b) (n 13 above).
[51] [1999] 4 All ER 185, 194(f) (n 13 above).
[52] ibid (n 13 above).
[53] Brown LJ specifically resisted the idea that the case turned on the issue of detriment. See *R v Department of Health, ex parte Source Informatics Ltd* (n 19 above) 440, [35].

anonymised information might interfere with an individual's reasonable expectation of privacy. Brown LJ directly challenged any such suggestion and expressed difficulty in 'understanding how the patient's autonomy is compromised by Source's scheme'.[54] However, when assessing whether there could be some effect from which the Court considers an individual to be entitled to protection, there is no reason to think that the issue of identifiability would be determinative. Indeed, the approach taken by Brown LJ more generally would suggest that it would not.

## VII. IDENTIFIABILITY IS NOT DETERMINATIVE

Brown LJ is clearly persuaded that the identifiability of data is a significant relevant consideration. He favourably cites the dictum of Bingham LJ in *W v Edgell*, in which Bingham notes that the doctor whose conduct was at issue could not have discussed the details of his patient in any published research, personal biography, or while 'gossiping with friends'[55] *unless* 'he took appropriate steps to conceal the identity of W [his patient]'.[56] The clear implication being that, were such steps taken, there would be no breach of confidence.

Brown LJ does not go so far as to say that the disclosure of anonymised information might *never* constitute a breach of confidence. It must be remembered that, for Brown LJ, the 'touchstone' by which to judge the scope of the duty of confidentiality—*what is determinative*—is whether the use would trouble the conscience of a reasonable professional holding the data.

Brown LJ cites favourably from Dr Gurry's *Breach of Confidence* that the

> courts have been less concerned with formal requirements, than with the *practical effects* of a confidant's misconduct, and, where these are such as to represent a lack of good faith on the part of the confidant, he will be liable for breach of his duty of confidence.[57]

This supports the idea that, *if* the anonymisation of confidential data and the subsequent use of anonymised data could be shown *in other circumstances* to have 'practical effects' supporting a claim of 'unconscionable use',[58]— effects which might be more subtle than overtly detrimental[59]—then the

---

[54] *R v Department of Health, ex parte Source Informatics Ltd* (n 19 above) 440, [34].

[55] *W v Edgell* [1990] Ch 359, 419.

[56] ibid.

[57] F Gurry, *Breach of Confidence* (Oxford, Oxford University Press, 1984) 258, cited [2001] QB 424, 438–39, [29].

[58] *El Dupont de Nemours Powder Co v Masland* 244 US 102 (1917), cited by Brown LJ, *R v Department of Health, ex parte Source Informatics* (n 19 above ) 436–37, [24].

[59] Latham J suggests that their Lordships in *Attorney General v Guardian Newspapers (No 2)*, (n 18 above), 'were aware of the fact that an unauthorized use of confidential information might have subtly and not overtly detrimental consequences': [1999] EWHC 510, [1999] 4 All ER 185 194(e) (n 13 above).

test applied in *Source* would be satisfied. The claim that the disclosure of identifiable data is not a necessary element in a successful claim for breach of confidence is further supported by dicta in the Australian case of *Smith Kline & French Laboratories (Australia) Ltd v Secretary to the Department of Community Services and Health*, also favourably cited by Brown LJ:[60]

> Sometimes the obligation imposes no restriction on use of the ... information, as long as the confided does not reveal it to third parties. In other circumstances, the confided may not be entitled to use it except for some limited purpose.[61]

To recognise that the party holding the data in confidential form might not, in some circumstances, *use the data* except for some limited purpose is to recognise that the disclosure of identifiable information is not always a necessary element of a successful claim. If unconscionable use by the party holding the data—without the disclosure of identifiable data—may be prohibited, then it would be perverse to hold that unconscionable use by a third party—without the disclosure of identifiable data—could not fall within the scope of the law's protection; particularly if data have been anonymised by the party holding the data in identifiable form, and transmitted to the third party in anonymised form, specifically for such a purpose.

Brown LJ suggested that *in this case*, through the use of only anonymised data, 'the patient's privacy will have been safeguarded, not invaded'.[62] Anonymisation is certainly likely to be an important and relevant safeguard in most cases. However, it would be wrong to take from this that anonymisation would always be a *sufficient* protection. Anonymised information is not useless.[63] All that is required is that a use of data, in the circumstances under which it is imparted or obtained, is shown to be a use from which—it could be convincingly argued—individuals were entitled to protection.

## VIII. ENTITLED TO PROTECTION

To assume that anonymisation could operate as a sufficient protection of an individual's privacy interest in all circumstances would, as Beyleveld argues, be inconsistent with a broad understanding of privacy. It would—and this is the point I wish to rest on particularly—completely fail to recognise the circumstances in which individuals might be 'entitled to protection' from the use of the data in anonymised form.

---

[60] *R v Department of Health, ex parte Source Informatics* (n 19 above) 436, [24].
[61] *Smith Kline & French Laboratories (Australia) Ltd v Secretary to the Department of Community Services and Health* (1991) ALR 679, 691–92, cited ibid.
[62] *R v Department of Health, ex parte Source Informatics Ltd* (n 19 above) 440, [35].
[63] As 'a general proposition, a duty of confidence will not be imposed to protect useless information' (Scott J in *Attorney General v Observer Ltd* [on appeal from *Attorney General v Guardian Newspapers (No 2)*] [1990] 1 AC 109 at 149).

One can imagine at least two uses that might 'trouble the conscience' of a reasonable person holding personal information (particularly in circumstances where such data had been entrusted to them for a particular purpose with no expectation of further use). The first is the circumstance in which an individual has a *moral* objection to their data being anonymised and used to support particular kinds of research. Beyleveld gives the example of the Catholic woman whose data is used to support medical research into contraception. I consider this a significant consideration but I will not focus here upon it.

The second circumstance is where the purpose of the processing is to generate information about the group to which an individual belongs. As well as any moral objections to such processing[64] an individual might be practically affected in a number of ways if processing gives rise to derived data that is subsequently associated with them as a member of a group (not through re-identification of them as an individual in the original dataset).

In each of these circumstances one can question the extent to which an individual must *learn* of the use in order to be entitled to protection. Certainly, particular detriment is likely to be associated with discovery. Individuals are likely to be less candid if they do not trust persons to only hold data in ways that they consider to be appropriate. In the context of healthcare, this may have significant adverse effects to the care and treatment that can be provided. In any event 'trust and confidence' are undermined if persons use data in ways that others do not consider themselves to have any reason to accept. However, practical effects from which an individual might be considered to be entitled to protection could follow the use of anonymised data even if an individual does not become aware of the disclosure.

Anonymised data is valuable, as it was valuable to Source, because it can help to inform strategic decisions. The aggregation of anonymised data will allow for the stratification of people possessing particular demographic, or clinical, features into different groups. The purpose of such stratification will be to inform decisions about how to treat different people differently. So far as these are business decisions, these may be choices about which products to offer to which people and on what terms. The intent will be to do what is best for the company. This may, or may not, coincide with the best interests of the individuals about whom the data is originally collected.

Whether such stratification, and the differential treatment consequent to it, falls within an individual's 'reasonable expectation', whether it is a use of data that would only be conscionable with their express permission, I would suggest depends on the precise circumstances. For example, if

---

[64] See, for an example of moral concerns raised by the processing of 'group' data: Amy Harmon 'Indian Tribe Wins Fight to Limit Research of Its DNA', *The New York Times* (21 April 2010).

further processing is intended simply to improve the quality of an individu-al's experience, or the experience of others, with no adverse consequences, however subtle, then that might be regarded in one way. If, on the other hand, the aim is to better target marketing materials, to stratify pricing strategies, to deny contractual opportunities to individuals that fall within particular groups, then there would be a strong claim that failure to put individuals in a position where they could reasonably anticipate such use, and act accordingly, would undermine their informational autonomy in way that was inconsistent with a reasonable expectation of privacy.[65]

## IX. DATA PROTECTION LAW

Source Informatics concerned the common law duty of confidence and not the law of data protection. Indeed, the case was decided shortly before the Data Protection Directive 95/46/EC had been implemented in the UK through the Data Protection Act 1998.[66] However, the Court was neverthe-less invited to consider data protection law. It was hoped that it would avoid inadvertently introducing unnecessary legal inconsistency when the 1998 Act did come into force. Arguments concerning the law of data protection were disposed of by the Court of Appeal relatively briefly. The Court rec-ognised, however, that the Data Protection Directive[67] sought to establish a framework ensuring the appropriate processing of 'personal data'. Article 2 of the Directive defines 'personal data' as meaning 'any information relating to an identified or identifiable natural person ("data subject")' and defines the 'processing of personal data' as

> any operation or set of operations which is performed upon personal data, whether or not by automatic means, such as collection, recording, organisation, storage, adaptation or alteration, retrieval, consultation, use, disclosure by trans-mission, dissemination or otherwise making available, alignment or combination, blocking, erasure or destruction.

The Department of Health's argument that the anonymisation of personal data should be understood to fall within the scope of the very broad defini-tion of 'processing' was rejected by the Court. Brown LJ, while not attempt-ing a definitive ruling on the matter, indicated there to be 'commonsense and justice'[68] in the submission that the Directive 'can have no more application

---

[65] It is in the expected 'commercialisation' of the data that there might be the biggest differ-ence in 'reasonable expectation' toward companies to whom health data is provided compared to health professionals. The responsibility to not undermine personal autonomy does, however, support the claim that even in obviously commercial contexts people should be made aware of the different uses of (even anonymised) data.
[66] The Data Protection Act 1998 came into force on 1 March 2000.
[67] EU Directive 95/46/EU.
[68] *R v Department of Health, ex parte Source Informatics Ltd* (n 19 above) 442, [45].

to the operation of anonymising data than to the use or disclosure of anony-mous data (which, of course, by definition is not "personal data" ...)'.[69]

There are current proposals to replace the Directive with a General Data Protection Regulation.[70] Even if these proposals are carried through to frui-tion, current proposals continue to concern only information relating to an identifiable person. The anonymisation of data would still not be explicitly brought within the definition of 'processing'.[71] It is possible that *Source* can be read to support the common law duty of confidence providing protection in circumstances that the law of data protection does not. Without this, English law would lose an opportunity to ensure that the abstraction of anonymised data from personal information only takes place under circumstances that persons have reason to accept.

## X. CONCLUSION

One of the most significant aspects of *Source* is that, arguably at least, the Court of Appeal chose not to adopt the line taken by Mr Justice Latham and did not focus upon the issue of consent or patient authorisation for particu-lar use of confidential data. To the extent that autonomy was protected, it was through protecting the *conditions* for autonomous action rather than by requiring an exercise of individual autonomy. This is a significant distinc-tion. It has implications for whether individuals need be involved in, or even always aware of, specific decisions relating to the use of confidential infor-mation. Whilst arguably true to the origins of the common law duty, consist-ency with the more modern development of breach of confidence requires that the reasonable expectations of the patient are taken into account when a court establishes the scope of the duty. The enduring significance of *Source* is that it emphasises the importance of also taking a professional's own responsibilities into account when performing this calculation. Reconciling these two aspects, and recognising that a *reasonable* expectation of a patient must take account of the responsibilities of the health professional holding the data, places the requirement to seek prior explicit consent of a data subject into a particular perspective. The circumstances must be considered to determine whether, given a responsibility to respect individual autonomy, it would be *reasonable* to use data for a particular purpose without first asking for consent. There will be times when it would not be appropriate to seek consent before personal information is used for particular purposes. However, there will also be times when it *would* be appropriate to seek con-

---

[69] ibid, 442, [44].
[70] See, for details, http://ec.europa.eu/justice/data-protection/ (last accessed January 2014).
[71] For an argument that it *should* be read in, see M Taylor, 'Health Research, Data Protection, and the Public Interest in Notification' (2011) 19 *Medical Law Review* 267–303.

sent before using even *anonymised* data. A respect for privacy requires that (practicable) steps are taken to ensure that individuals are aware of the use made of the data they provide. Brown LJ did not see this in *Source* because he did not see any potential practical effects from which persons may be entitled to protection. Even if this was true in *Source*, it need not be true always. People can be affected in significant ways through the use of data in anonymised form.

Anonymised data remain useful. They can be used in ways that engage an individual's interest in controlling the use of their information. Respecting personal autonomy, as manifest in a respect for a private and family life, would suggest that *conscionable* use would always seek to ensure that, unless there are overriding considerations, persons are put in a position of self-determination: any decision to disclose personal information should be taken in awareness of any subsequent use that a reasonable person would consider relevant to that initial decision to disclose. To limit the scope of the duty, not by reference to the question of 'practical effect' or 'conscionability', but by the issue of subsequent identifiability, encourages anonymisation as a method of undermining individual autonomy. In so doing, it risks the relationships that the duty of confidence should serve to protect. As we increasingly industrialise and 'up-scale' the extraction and anonymisation of data from personal records, including personal health records, the importance of recognising that the common law may provide a means to proscribe unconscionable use is more pressing than ever.

# 10

# *McFarlane v Tayside Health Board* [2000] and *Cattanach v Melchior* [2003]

LAURA HOYANO

## I. INTRODUCTION

THIS IS A tale of two negligent medical errors in the control of human fertility by public health services, with the same consequence for the patients, unwanted conception of healthy babies, occurring in two jurisdictions with common legal roots in tort law, but with diametrically opposed rulings on the scope of liability from their highest courts. One reflected the conventional philosophy underpinning medical tort law, corrective justice, and the other gingerly opened the door to an interloper, distributive justice, whilst allowing corrective justice to operate on part of the claim (with retributive justice implicitly tossed into the mix by two judicial chefs).[1] Perhaps surprisingly, the radical approach came from the House of Lords, in *McFarlane v Tayside Health Board*,[2] to which the Australian High Court responded in *Cattanach v Melchior*[3] by adhering to orthodox principles. Both Courts pondered the moral attributes of creating life and parenthood, but they were wary of the moral content and ethical dimensions of professional negligence law.[4] Neither Court had any women members sitting on the appeals.

## II. THE SEEDS OF 'WRONGFUL CONCEPTION' CASES

### A. Distinctions in Terminology: 'Wrongful Life', 'Wrongful Conception' and 'Wrongful Birth'

It is important first to distinguish the three types of legal action which might arise where medical negligence results in the birth of a child, as they raise

---

[1] *McFarlane v Tayside Health Board* [2000] 2 AC 59 (SC (HL)) 96–97 (Lord Hope), 106 (Lord Clyde).
[2] ibid.
[3] *Cattanach v Melchior* [2003] HCA 38, (2013) 215 CLR 1.
[4] S Jhaveri, 'Judicial Strategies in Recognising New Areas for Recovery in Negligence—Lessons Learned from Wrongful Conception Cases' (2013) 21 *Tort Law Review* 63.

distinct legal issues. Both case law and legal literature have used the terminology in different ways to mean different things.[5] The following taxonomy is gaining acceptance.

A '*wrongful life*' claim is advanced by the child who claims that he or she should never have been born. English[6] and Australian[7] law, like most common law jurisdictions,[8] have rejected 'wrongful life' actions in principle because they would violate the sanctity of human life, and the values of non-existence and a disabled existence are impossible for a court to compare.

After initial conflation, '*wrongful birth*' has acquired a meaning distinct from '*wrongful conception*' which follows a failed sterilisation of either parent, or flawed genetic counselling leading the parents to decide to have a child.[9] In 'wrongful birth' cases the negligence is causally related, not to the conception, but to the birth. The claimants may have wanted a child, but not *this* child, with a disability sufficiently serious to justify a lawful termination[10] had the problem been detected through proper treatment of the expectant mother (eg misdiagnosis of rubella)[11] or antenatal screening for fetal abnormality.[12] The mother usually claims (in retrospect) that she would have terminated the pregnancy had she received competent diagnostic services. This raises tricky causation issues as to her hypothetical decision;[13] although she might have a claim for loss of personal autonomy to have a choice regarding termination.[14] An alternative scenario may be failure to diagnose an undesired pregnancy in time for a lawful termination.[15] More rarely, a failed abortion procedure due to obstetric negligence may result in a live birth.[16]

---

[5] J Mason, 'Wrongful Pregnancy, Wrongful Birth and Wrongful Terminology' (2002) 6 *Edinburgh Law Review* 46.

[6] *McKay v Essex County Council* [1982] 2 All ER 771 (CA).

[7] *Harriton v Stephens* (2006) 226 ALR 391 (Aus HC); *Waller v James and Hoolahan* (2006) 226 ALR 457 (Aus HC).

[8] *Hergott v Bovingdon* 2008 ONCA 2; *Cherry v Borsman* (1992) 94 DLR (4th) 487 (BCCA).

[9] See *RH v Hunter* [1996] OJ No 2065 (liability), [1996] OJ No 4477 (quantum) (Ont CtJ).

[10] Under the Abortion Act 1967, s 1(1)(d).

[11] See *Rand v East Dorset Health Authority* (2000) 56 BMLR 39 (QB); *Hardman v Amin* (2000) 59 BMLR 58; *Salih v Enfield Health Authority* [1991] 3 All ER 400 (CA).

[12] See *Whitehead v Hibbert Pownall & Newton (a firm)* [2008] EWCA Civ 285, (2008) 102 BMLR 57; *Farraj v King's Healthcare NHS Trust* [2009] EWCA Civ 1203, (2009) 111 BMLR 131; *Lee v Taunton and Somerset NHS Trust* [2001] 1 FLR 419 (QB); *Lillywhite v University College London Hospitals NHS Trust* [2005] EWCA 1466, [2006] Lloyds Rep Med 268.

[13] *Arndt v Smith* [1997] 2 SCR 539; *Deriche v Ealing Hospital NHS Trust* [2003] EWHC 3104 (QB).

[14] *Chester v Afshar* [2004] UKHL 41, [2005] 1 AC 134.

[15] See *Groom v Selby* [2001] EWCA Civ 1522, (2001) 64 BMLR 47; *Greenfield v Irwin (a firm)* [2001] EWCA Civ 113, [2001] 1 WLR 1292; *Crouchman v Burke* (1997) 40 BMLR 163 (QB) 167; *CES v Superclinics (Australia) Pty Ltd* (1995) 38 NSWLR 47 (CA).

[16] See *Scuriaga v Powell* (1979) Sol Jo 40 (CA); *Cherry* (n 8 above); *Mlle X c Picard* Cour de Cassation Chambre Civile 1, 25 June 1991 D 1991 (Cours de Cassation Civile), 566.

Both of the index judgments discussed here, *McFarlane v Tayside Health Board* and *Cattanach v Melchior*, concerned wrongful conception, ie failed sterilisation. *McFarlane* originated in Scotland which has its own NHS and distinct tort system (known as delict), but the Law Lords stipulated that their ruling applied to common law tort elsewhere in the UK.[17] *Cattanach* originated in Queensland, but again in the federal Australian system the common law principles propounded by the Australian High Court would be expected to have national application.

## B. Failed Sterilisation Procedures: Causes, Frequency and Cost[18]

It is difficult to assess the call made on NHS funds by failed sterilisation claims, in 1999 or currently. The NHS Litigation Authority does not disaggregate clinical negligence claims within obstetrics and gynaecology; whilst that category comprises the highest value of claims,[19] it includes children severely damaged during birth.[20] The Department of Health's response to a parliamentary question from Mary Glindon MP on 14 October 2014 about what she termed 'wrongful birth' claims disclosed that between 2003 and 2013 there had been 164 successful claims (and 83 unsuccessful claims), with £77,716,648 paid out in damages to date; the value of the claims was not disaggregated by the wrongful birth/wrongful conception distinction. Of the 104 closed successful claims analysed by cause, 27 resulted from failed sterilisations, of which 24 resulted in births of healthy children.[21] Seven resulted from failed terminations resulting in the child being born alive. Given the ambiguous terminology of 'wrongful birth', one cannot be entirely confident that the remaining 70 claims for disability related to negligent antenatal screening. This lack of specific, regularly disseminated information dilutes the specific economic deterrent and incentivising effect of medical negligence liability[22] in an area of clinical practice where it is relatively easy to avert claims through competently performed procedures and post-surgical prophylactic precautionary advice, without the spectre of defensive medicine unjustifiably inflating prevention costs.

---

[17] *McFarlane (HL)* (n 1 above), 68 (Lord Slynn).

[18] I am indebted to Dr Annette Roberge for explaining the medical aspects of sterilisation procedures to me.

[19] NHS Litigation Authority, *Fact Sheet 3: Information on Claims* (as at 31 March 2013).

[20] National Audit Office, *Handling Clinical Negligence Claims in England (HC 403)* (3 May 2001) para 1.4.

[21] HC Deb 14 October 2014 (Written Question 208750). The total value of claims paid out including costs came to £95,208,477.

[22] A Towse and P Danzon, 'Medical Negligence and the NHS: an Economic Analysis' (1999) 8 *Health Economics* 93.

During the litigation of *McFarlane*, claims against the NHS in England were escalating by up to 25 per cent per annum, costing £235 million in 1996–97.[23] This rise is as explicable by significant under-claiming for iatrogenic harm in previous decades and patients newly willing to bring genuine claims, as by importation of a so-called 'compensation culture' of unmeritorious claims from the USA.[24] A 2012 Scottish study of clinical negligence noted previous research indicating a 'problem of underclaiming' where patients did not pursue their legal entitlements due to ignorance of the error, inability to access legal representation, or fear of retribution.[25] Scotland has not seen a sharp rise in clinical negligence claims in recent years, and the rate remains lower than in England.[26]

Sterilisation is one of the most common medical procedures in the world. Around 50,000 female sterilisations were performed in 1999 and subsequent years in the UK.[27] By the 1990s, sterilisation had become the predominant method of contraception in Great Britain, with nearly 40 per cent of women aged 40 protected by male or female contraceptive sterilisation (the division amongst sexes being approximately equal).[28] In 1999, when *McFarlane* was decided, an estimated 47,268 tubal occlusions and 64,422 vasectomies were performed in England in the NHS and charitable sectors.[29] In 1997, 8,357 vasectomies and 7,871 female sterilisations were carried out in Scotland.[30] Sterilisation is particularly favoured by couples who already have children, especially after a third birth.[31] Thus the McFarlane and Melchior parents were representative in electing sterilisation because they regarded their families as complete.

Establishing the cause of a failed sterilisation may not be straightforward.[32] By the time the child is born, it may be quite unclear what went awry in the procedure, requiring expert testimony.[33] The shorter the interval between

---

[23] ibid, noting changes in accounting policy had caused overestimation of growth rates and recurrent expenditure on medical negligence.

[24] R Lewis, A Morris and K Oliphant, 'Tort Personal Injury Claims Statistics: Is There a Compensation Culture in the United Kingdom?' (2006) 14 *Tort Law Journal* 158, 174–75.

[25] Scottish Government Social Research, *A Study of Medical Negligence Claiming in Scotland* (June 2012) para 1.11.

[26] ibid, paras 2.6, 3.28, 3.122, Figures 4, 7.

[27] R Varma and JK Gupta, 'Predicting Negligence in Female Sterilization Using Time Interval to Sterilization Failure: Analysis of 131 Cases' (2007) 22 *Human Reproduction* 2437, 2437; R Varma and JK Gupta, 'Failed Sterilisation: Evidence-based Review and Medicolegal Ramifications' (2004) 111 *British Journal of Obstetrics & Gynaecology* 1322, 1322.

[28] M Murphy, 'Sterilisation as a Method of Contraception: Recent Trends in Great Britain and Implications' (1995) 27 *Journal of Biosocial Science* 31, 35.

[29] Royal College of Obstetricians and Gynaecologists, *Male and Female Sterilisation* (April 1999, [revised January 2004 edn] Evidence-based Clinical Guideline Number 4) 6.

[30] *McFarlane (HL)* (n 1), 84.

[31] Murphy, 'Sterilisation as Contraception' (1995), n 28 above, 39–40.

[32] There is no system for investigating or reporting failures to a national registry, even if they are litigated: Varma and Gupta, 'Predicting Negligence' (2007) 2.

[33] Eg *Ahern v Moore* [2013] IEHC 72 (High Court of Ireland).

the procedure and the pregnancy, the more likely the cause is a negligent failure mechanism.[34] In a study of 500 medico-legal obstetrics and gynaecology cases litigated between 1984 and 1994, 40 per cent comprised gynaecological cases, failed sterilisation being the most common cause (19 per cent).[35]

The prevalent method of female sterilisation is either to sever the fallopian tubes, or to apply Filshie clips or rings to each one to cause necrosis of the captured tube tissue. The tube can reconstitute itself through recanalisation but this is an unlikely occurrence, even less likely where two clips are applied to each tube. The commonest negligent causes of failure are the surgeon clipping a ligament or other tissue rather than the fallopian tube, missing the anatomical markers for correct placement,[36] or failing to close the clip properly. Pregnancy may also result if the clip was correctly placed but eroded or migrated elsewhere through the passage of time, risks intrinsic to the technique and hence not attracting liability.[37] More rarely, a fistula may have formed, again without fault of the surgeon.

Figures as to the frequency of tubal occlusion failure vary. In a 2013 Irish case two experts agreed that the risk of failure due to clinical error plus natural causes was 0.5 per cent, or five patients in 1,000.[38] However, empirical studies suggest a considerably higher rate. Two large population-wide studies have reported the 10-year cumulative probability of pregnancy as 18.5 per 1,000 procedures in the United States,[39] and 8.4 per 1,000 in Québec.[40] The Royal College of Obstetricians and Gynaecologists in 2004 stated that the 10-year failure rate using Filshie clips was two to three per 1,000, compared to five per 1,000 for all techniques.[41] A study pooling 131 cases of known failed female sterilisations from the United Kingdom and Australia identified 88 negligent and 43 non-negligent failures,[42] which

---

[34] Varma and Gupta (2007) (n 27 above).

[35] C B-Lynch, A Coker and JA Dua, 'A clinical analysis of 500 medico-legal claims evaluating the causes and assessing the potential benefit of alternative dispute resolution' (1996) 103 *British Journal of Obstetrics and Gynaecology* (the sample comprised 488 cases from the UK and 12 from Hong Kong and the Republic of Ireland).

[36] Expert testimony in *Byrne v Ryan* [2007] IEHC 207, [2009] IR 542 (High Court of Ireland) [34], [37]–[38].

[37] ibid [36]–[37], [41]–[42], [44].

[38] *Ahern* (n 33 above).

[39] H Peterson and others, 'The Risk of Pregnancy after Tubal Sterilization: Findings from the US Collaborative Review of Sterilization' (1996) 174 *American Journal of Obstetrics Gynecology* 1161. The higher failure rate in the US is attributed to the later (1996) licensing of the more effective Filshie clip, commonly used in the UK, Canada and Australia.

[40] J Trussell, E Guilbert and A Hedley, 'Sterilization failure: sterilization reversal and pregnancy after sterilization reversal in Quebec' (2003) 101 *Obstetrics & Gynecology* 677.

[41] Royal College of Obstetricians and Gynaecologists, *Male and Female Sterilisation* (2004), Executive Summary, 2.

[42] Varma and Gupta (2007) (n 27 above) 1, 6.

may suggest that whilst the failure rate is relatively low, it is more likely to be attributable to clinical error than natural causes.[43]

Sterilisation of males is generally achieved by division of the vas deferens on each side, a much less invasive, and simpler, procedure than female sterilisation. According to Mason it is very uncommon for the procedure to be performed negligently.[44] Medical error usually consists of failure to close off the vas completely through stitches or cauterisation. However, sterility may not be achieved due to natural processes: there may be residual sperm in the distal genital tract, which can retain motility for up to seven months, following which there should be fertility tests; and the vas may spontaneously recanalise any time after the procedure. According to Mason, recanalisation occurs in about one in 2,500 cases, but accounts for a major proportion of litigated cases.[45] The standard of care requires patients to be warned of these possibilities.[46] The Royal College of Obstetricians and Gynaecologists reports a failure rate of approximately one in 2,000 after clearance to stop alternative means of contraception has been given.[47]

Lord Hope in *McFarlane* opined that cases of failed sterilisation should be rare 'if proper care is taken'.[48] The statistics just discussed show significant failure rates, usually due to medical error in performing the procedure or in post-operative advice. The issue for the courts is whether and how to use negligence law to incentivise higher standards of performance.

## C. The Legal Formulations for Unwanted Birth Cases

There are several ways in which medical negligence actions can be pleaded in unwanted conception and birth cases:

— negligent words, under *Hedley Byrne*,[49] for wrongly stating the frequency of failure of a procedure, advice following the surgery not to use contraception, failure to advise of the possibility of spontaneous reversal, or incorrect advice regarding a hereditary genetic condition following which the claimants decide to have a child;

---

[43] Varma and Gupta, 'Failed Sterilisation' (2004) (n 27 above), 1329. A general underreporting of non-negligent sterilisation failures in medical and legal databases is likely due to the absence of reporting mechanisms: Varma and Gupta (2007) (n 27 above) 6.

[44] JK Mason, *The Troubled Pregnancy: Legal Wrongs and Rights in Reproduction* (Cambridge, Cambridge University Press, 2007) 100.

[45] ibid.

[46] See *Thake v Maurice* [1986] QB 644 (QB, CA).

[47] Royal College of Obstetricians and Gynaecologists (n 29 above), Executive Summary, 2.

[48] *McFarlane (HL)* (n 1 above), 75.

[49] *Hedley Byrne v Heller & Partners Ltd* [1964] AC 465 (HL).

— negligent services under the 'extended *Hedley Byrne* principle'[50] for the same errors;

— negligent services, for a botched sterilisation, laboratory mistakes in handling sperm or DNA samples, a botched abortion, incorrect diagnosis that the mother was not pregnant,[51] or flawed antenatal screening for fetal abnormality;

— a standard personal injury cause of action; this may be brought by the patient, on the premise that the medical procedure inflicted physical harm, but becomes problematic in the case of a failed vasectomy, in respect of claims for the mother's pain and suffering;

— contract,[52] although this cause of action is not available where the sterilisation services were provided by the NHS.

## D. An Outline of the Facts and Litigation in *McFarlane* and *Cattanach*

George and Laura McFarlane had four healthy children. With a new house purchase they took on a larger mortgage, so Mrs McFarlane returned to work to meet their increased financial commitments. Having decided that their family was complete, Mr McFarlane underwent a vasectomy operation by a consultant surgeon on 16 October 1989 at a Scottish NHS hospital operated by the Tayside Health Board. In a letter of 23 March 1990, he was informed that 'your sperm counts are now negative and you may dispense with contraceptive precautions', which they had been using as instructed by the surgeon. In September 1991 Mrs McFarlane became pregnant and Catherine was born after a normal pregnancy and delivery. She was a healthy child and accepted into the family as an integral, loved member. The cause of the failure of the vasectomy was unknown, so the breach of the duty of care pleaded lay in the negligent misstatement that Mr McFarlane had become sterile.

The McFarlanes claimed personal injury damages for Mrs McFarlane's pain, distress and inconvenience caused by the pregnancy and birth, her lost wages during the final stage of her pregnancy, prenatal expenses, postnatal loss of income, and the costs of the child's maintenance until her age of majority. Mrs McFarlane claimed £10,000 for *solatium* (non-pecuniary damages); the couple together claimed pecuniary losses of £100,000. The defenders brought a preliminary application to ascertain whether damages

---

[50] *Henderson v Merrett Syndicates Ltd* [1995] 2 AC 145 (HL); *Williams v Natural Life Health Foods Ltd* [1998] 1 WLR 830 (HL); *McFarlane (HL)* (n 1 above), 77 (Lord Steyn).

[51] *Allen v Bloomsbury Health Authority* [1993] 1 All ER 651; *Groom* (n 15 above).

[52] See *Scuriaga* (n 16 above); *Cataford v Moreau* (1978) 114 DLR (3d) 585 (Qué SC). Lord Clyde expressly reserved his position on whether there might be a different result in contract than in delict: *McFarlane (HL)* (n 1 above) 99.

were available in principle, arguing that no compensable harm had resulted from the birth of the healthy baby. At first instance the Lord Ordinary, Lord Gill, agreed with this submission, based on the pleadings.[53] The Court of Session Inner House disagreed, unabashedly applying corrective justice in holding that all heads of damage claimed were compensable under ordinary principles of delict.[54] The House of Lords, splitting 4:1, partly reversed this ruling, taking a middle path that some heads of loss were recoverable, but not the maintenance costs—at least for a healthy child.

The subsequent course of the *McFarlane* doctrine is important for our analysis. In 2003 in *Rees v Darlington Memorial NHS Trust*, seven Law Lords repelled an attempt to have *McFarlane* reversed,[55] and applied its reasoning to a disabled mother of a healthy child, splitting 4:3 on that issue.[56] In the interval between *McFarlane* and *Rees*, a majority of the Court of Appeal had carved out an exception where a disabled child resulted from the failed sterilisation, in *Parkinson*.[57] In *Rees*, the Law Lords specifically disapproved of the way Hale LJ had interpreted and distinguished *McFarlane* ('deemed equilibrium' of benefits and burdens for a healthy child which was disrupted by the additional costs entailed by disability).[58] Nonetheless Lord Steyn, Lord Hope, and Lord Hutton thought that *Parkinson* was correct in the result,[59] and Lord Millett ruminated that he did not find the result 'morally offensive' but wished to keep the point open,[60] but Lord Bingham, Lord Nicholls and Lord Scott doubted its validity since its foundations had been demolished in *Rees*.[61]

Kerry Anne and Craig Melchior married relatively late, and had two daughters before deciding that their family was complete. An additional motivation for sterilisation was that Mr Melchior had a form of muscular dystrophy which he feared (mistakenly as it turned out) might be inherited by a son. A tubal ligation was performed by a gynaecologist, Dr Cattanach. Mrs Melchior told him that she believed that her right fallopian tube had been removed during an appendectomy many years earlier. Dr Cattanach did not

---

[53] *McFarlane v Tayside Health Board* (1997) SLT 211 (SC (OH)). The state of the pleadings may be the reason for the confusion amongst the Law Lords as to whether, for example, Mrs McFarlane was claiming for loss of her wages.

[54] *McFarlane v Tayside Health Board* (1998) SCLR 126 (Court of Session, Inner House (Second Division)).

[55] *Rees v Darlington Memorial Hospital NHS Trust* [2003] UKHL 52, [2004] 1 AC 309, [7] (Lord Bingham), [16] (Lord Nicholls).

[56] ibid.

[57] *Parkinson v St James and Seacroft University Hospital NHS Trust* [2001] EWCA Civ 530, [2002] QB 266.

[58] *Rees (HL)* (n 55 above) [28] (Lord Nicholls), [59] (Lord Steyn), [94] (Lord Hutton), [111] (Lord Millett), [147] Lord Scott.

[59] ibid [35] (Lord Steyn), [57] (Lord Hope), [91] (Lord Hutton).

[60] ibid [112] (Lord Millett).

[61] ibid [9] (Lord Bingham), [19] (Lord Nicholls concurring with Lord Bingham), [147] (Lord Scott).

check her medical records nor did he search for a right fallopian tube during the surgery, clipping only the left. He also did not recommend a hysterosal-pingogram which was likely to have disclosed a functioning fallopian tube. Four years later she gave birth to a healthy son, Jordan, after a pregnancy complicated by thrombosis leaving a disability limiting her employment prospects; she also suffered postnatal depression. The case was pleaded as one of negligent advice and failure to warn.[62] The High Court of Australia, also on a 4:3 split, upheld the ruling of the Queensland Court of Appeal[63] that the parents could recover damages for the inconvenience and maintenance costs of this healthy child (the only head of damage appealed). The majority rejected the reasoning in *McFarlane*. Judgment in *Cattanach v Melchior* was delivered after oral argument in *Rees*.[64]

The McFarlane and Melchior claimants were ordinary, typical Scottish and Australian parents, already happily raising healthy children. In each case, the child was born healthy and was accepted into a loving family, and the additional burdens of raising the extra child could be met from their own resources, with some sacrifice. One wonders whether the negative reaction of the Law Lords and the dissenting Australian Justices to the claims of these relatively affluent families against resource-deprived public health services might have been different had the situations before them been less ordinary, for example where:

— pregnancy posed extraordinary risks for the mother;[65] or
— the parents could not use other forms of contraception for medical or religious reasons;[66] or
— the parents wished to avert the risk of an inherited genetic abnormality;[67] or
— were already struggling to cope with a child with severe congenital abnormalities which they wished no other child of theirs to inherit;[68] or
— the parents and four children were already crammed into two bedrooms, and could not afford larger accommodation;[69] or

---

[62] *Cattanach (HCA)* (n 3 above) [13].
[63] *Cattanach v Melchior* [2001] QCA 246 (Qld CA).
[64] Counsel made supplementary written submissions regarding *Cattanach*.
[65] *Ahern* (n 33 above) (mother had genetic blood clotting condition making pregnancy 'perilous'; child born with severe abnormalities and died aged six months); *Crouchman* (n 15 above), 165 (mother had already had an ectopic pregnancy).
[66] See *Udale v Bloomsbury Area Health Authority* [1983] 1 WLR 1098, [1983] 2 All ER 522, 524; *Crouchman* (n 15 above), 165.
[67] See *Hunter* (n 9 above) (negligence regarding genetic counselling of parents led to birth of two boys with Duchenne muscular dystrophy).
[68] See *Fassoulas v Ramey* 450 So 2d 822 (Florida SC 1984), where the parents already had two children both of whom had severe physical deformities with high costs of medical care; two more children were born after the failed sterilisation, each with deformities (one severe, the other corrected with surgery).
[69] See *Parkinson* (n 57 above) [6].

— the financial strain leads to family breakdown;[70] or
— the parents were very impoverished,[71] and already had numerous children to support, as in one Québec case where they had had ten children within 11 years.[72]

Is *McFarlane* an exemplar of easy facts making bad law?

### III. ENGLISH AND SCOTTISH LAW ON WRONGFUL CONCEPTION PRIOR TO 1999

In *McFarlane*, the NHS decided to challenge 15 years of consistent authority[73] from the English Court of Appeal and Scottish courts at first instance which had applied the conventional professional negligence template to award compensation for

— the pain and suffering of pregnancy and delivery;
— the pain and suffering and any associated costs related to repetition of the failed sterilisation procedure;
— any financial losses associated with the pregnancy, such as prescriptions and lost income due to illness;
— the cost of the layette;
— any loss of earnings sustained by the main carer if previous employment had to be given up; and
— the child's maintenance costs, as consequential economic loss directly flowing from personal injury, being not only objectively foreseeable but directly contemplated by the parents and the surgeon. This included not just the cost of food and clothing but also necessary expanded accommodation, school fees and the like.[74]

As Auld LJ explained the rationale,

> [post-natal] economic loss may be unassociated with 'physical injury' in the sense that it stems from the cost of rearing a child rather than any disability in pregnancy or birth, but it is not unassociated with the cause of both, namely the unwanted pregnancy giving rise to the birth of a child

---

[70] See also ibid.
[71] See *Thake* (n 46 above), 652.
[72] See *Cataford* (n 52 above).
[73] *Emeh v Kensington and Chelsea and Westminster Area Health Authority* [1985] QB 1012 (CA); *Thake* (n 46 above) (leave to appeal to HL denied); *Allan v Greater Glasgow Health Board* 1998 SLT 588 (SC (OH)).
[74] *Udale* (n 66 above), 527–28; *Allen* (n 51 above); *Benarr v Kettering Health Authority* (1988) 138 NLJ 179 (QB) (private schooling fees awarded where siblings had been educated privately).

and so all the claims arose out of one cause of action.[75] During the 1990s the NHS had been routinely settling failed sterilisation cases where the clinician's negligence was not contested for comparatively moderate sums, such as £40,000 in March 1999.[76]

## IV. SEARCHING FOR THE RATIO IN *McFARLANE* AND *CATTANACH*

### A. Mapping the Speeches

In 2003 in *Rees*, Lord Steyn ruefully described analysis of the judgments in *McFarlane* as a 'gruesome task'[77]—notwithstanding that he himself had penned one of those maligned judgments. The majority speeches are characterised more by anxiety to avoid perceived pitfalls than by clarity in mapping their pathways across what they saw as a treacherous bog.

By way of a one-dimensional overview,[78] three Law Lords expressly concluded there was no duty of care to avert the maintenance costs which they characterised as pure economic loss, each using a different route: no assumption of responsibility (Lord Slynn); not 'fair, just, and reasonable' because liability would be disproportionate to fault (Lord Hope); and not 'fair, just, and reasonable' because of distributive justice (Lord Steyn). Lord Hope relied upon an offset of benefits and burdens which seemed to fit more readily into a 'no loss' than a 'no duty' analysis. Lord Clyde expressly rejected a duty of care analysis, preferring a 'no loss' analysis (which one would think would be a cause-in-fact issue), but then based his conclusion upon lack of foreseeability (the next step, cause-in-law). Lord Millett, having incisively analysed and refuted the analyses of the majority, then seemed to base his complete denial of any liability on the absence of any actionable damage.

Many lower court judges, academics, and Justices from Commonwealth courts have analysed the speeches in *McFarlane* in quest of the ratio. It is even unclear whether there was a measure of consensus on the recoverability of some of the financial losses. The table attempts to encapsulate the fate of each head of damage claimed according to each speech. The same exercise is undertaken for the judgments in *Cattanach v Melchior*, where only the award of the Queensland courts for maintenance costs was appealed.

---

[75] *Walkin v South Manchester Health Authority* [1995] 1 WLR 1543, 1529, [1995] 4 All ER 132 (CA). The personal injury rule still applies to the limitation period post-*McFarlane*: *Godfrey v Gloucestershire Royal Infirmary NHS Trust* [2003] EWHC 549 (QB).

[76] National Audit Office, *Handling Clinical Negligence Claims in England* (HC 403) 30 April 2001, p 7, reported as an example of a typical settlement for wrongful conception when no Filshie clip had been applied to the right tube.

[77] *Rees (HL)* (n 55 above) [28].

[78] LC Hoyano, 'Misconceptions about "Wrongful Conception"' (2002) 65 *Modern Law Review* 890.

*McFarlane v Tayside Health Board* [2000] 2 AC 59 (SC (HL)): searching for a ratio

| Head of damage | Mother's pain & suffering: pregnancy & delivery | Mother's prenatal medical expenses & associated loss of income | Mother's postnatal loss of income | Layette for newborn | Child's maintenance costs |
|---|---|---|---|---|---|
| Lord Slynn | YES: *damnum* (Scottish term for material prejudice to a legal interest) because unwanted events, even if not 'injury' or 'harm' in the ordinary sense (p 74) | YES: if caused directly and immediately by the pregnancy: by inference, assumption of responsibility for (consequential?) economic loss (pp 74, 76) | NO (by inference): no assumption of responsibility for 'pure economic loss', hence no duty of care owed | YES: presumably assumption of responsibility for (consequential?) economic loss (p 74) | NO: no assumption of responsibility for 'pure economic loss', albeit foreseeable (p 75), hence no duty of care owed because not fair just and reasonable (p 76) ↱ rejects set-off as benefits and burdens too difficult to calculate reliably (pp 74–75). |
| Lord Steyn | YES: personal injury because 'substantial discomfort and pain' were the physical consequences of negligence (pp 81, 84) | YES: economic loss consequential on personal injury within the spirit of his 'limited recovery principle' (p 84) | No discussion, but probably NO, by analogy to 'pure economic loss' reasoning | No discussion | NO: claim categorised as 'pure economic loss' in respect of both parents (p 79) ↱ but rejects Lord Slynn's assumption of responsibility test as a 'rationalisation' (p 83), and Lord Clyde's 'reasonable restitution' solution as 'unrealistic and formalistic' (p 82); |

| Lord Hope | YES, the harmful event was conception, by analogy to personal injury, with the pain and discomfort of pregnancy being | YES, if claimed (pp 87–88) | *YES but only if direct result of the effects of the pregnancy itself, subject to remoteness rules (p 89) | NO (p 97)<br>↑ reasons not given but presumably also 'pure economic loss' falling outside the duty of care | ↑ rejects set-off as not being 'the correct legal analysis' (pp 81–82)<br>↑ prefers **distributive justice** adjudicated by the 'instinctive' and 'inarticulate' reaction of 'commuters on the [London] Underground' (p 82)<br>↑ 'if necessary' the claim is not fair, just and reasonable (so presumably no duty of care) (p 82).<br><br>NO: claim is foreseeable but 'pure economic loss', so **distributive justice** comes into play (pp 96–97)<br>↑ **not fair, just and reasonable** because liability disproportionate to fault and impossible to calculate due to offsetting benefits, so those expenses fall outside the duty of care owed by the hospital (pp 96–97) |

*(continued)*

*McFarlane v Tayside Health Board* [2000] 2 AC 59 (SC (HL)): searching for a ratio (*continued*)

| Head of damage | Mother's pain & suffering: pregnancy & delivery | Mother's prenatal medical expenses & associated loss of income | Mother's postnatal loss of income | Layette for newborn | Child's maintenance costs |
|---|---|---|---|---|---|
| | consequential pain and suffering (pp 86–87); including any postnatal physical or emotional problems (p 89) | | | | ↑ but cites *Kealey:* reasons for surgery may be relevant to determining whether consequence was injury or a 'blessed event' (p 94) |
| Lord Clyde | YES: harmful event was conception (p 99) with consequential physical pain and suffering (impliedly equated with personal injury) (p 102)<br>↑ Only award to be made is *solatium* | NO (p 106) | NO (pp 98, 104) | NO (p 104) | NO: not a separate duty of care issue but rather existence and extent of loss (pp 99, 102);<br>↑ 'reasonable restitution' (*restitutio in status quo ante*) dictates no recovery 'to do justice between the parties' (pp 104–5), as liability for maintenance costs goes 'far beyond any liability... the defenders could reasonably have thought they were undertaking' (p 105) and **disproportionate** to culpability (p 106). |

| Lord Millett (dissenting) | Harmful event was conception, as an invasion of bodily integrity, so cause of action is technically complete (p 107). → BUT no actionable harm resulted from the failed vasectomy as the birth of a normal healthy child | NO (by inference) | NO (by inference) | NO unless parents disposed of baby equipment in reliance on misrepresentation in which case replacements recoverable as special damages (pp 114–15) | NO → not an issue of ➤ categorisation of nature of wrong (p 108) ➤ categorisation of claim ➤ categorisation of claim as pure or consequential economic loss (p 109) ➤ disproportionality of the loss to the wrong (p 109) ➤ motivation for seeking sterilisation (pp 109–10) ➤ set-off (p 111), ➤ break in chain of causation (p 112–13) or | → rejects set-off as being factors of a different character, and quantification of the benefit is impracticable (p 103). ↑ Suggests claim at outer reach of chain of causation (p 104). ↑ Suggests surgeon's knowledge of motivation for seeking surgery may be relevant (pp 98, 103, 104). |

*(continued)*

*McFarlane v Tayside Health Board* [2000] 2 AC 59 (SC (HL)): searching for a ratio *(continued)*

| Head of damage | Mother's pain & suffering: pregnancy & delivery | Mother's prenatal medical expenses & associated loss of income | Mother's postnatal loss of income | Layette for newborn | Child's maintenance costs |
|---|---|---|---|---|---|
| | is not a matter for compensation (p 111). <br><br> ➔ Pain and suffering of pregnancy and delivery also excluded as being inescapable preconditions of birth (p 114) <br><br> ➔ Would have solved the apparent conflict by awarding a conventional sum of £5,000 for loss of reproductive autonomy. | | | | ➔ remoteness of damage, as the causal connection was 'strong, direct and foreseeable' (p 114). |

*Cattanach v Melchior* [2003] HCA 38: searching for a ratio decidendi

| Head of damage | Mother's pain & suffering: pregnancy & delivery AWARD NOT APPEALED | Mother's prenatal medical expenses & associated loss of income AWARD NOT APPEALED | Mother's postnatal loss of income AWARD NOT APPEALED | Layette for newborn AWARD NOT APPEALED | Child's maintenance costs |
|---|---|---|---|---|---|
| Gleeson CJ (dissenting) | no comment | no comment | no comment | no comment | ↑ separate duty of care required for pure economic loss<br>↑ actionable damage must be the parent-child relationship ([27]) but to acknowledge this would be incompatible with international instruments' recognition of the family as the fundamental group unit of society [35], and to seek to assign an economic value to the parent-child relationship is neither reasonable or possible ([38]) |
| McHugh J and Gummow J | YES (by implication) Commented on the illogic in awarding these claims but contesting the maintenance costs ([91]) | YES (by implication) | YES (by implication) | YES (by implication) | ↑ Contra Gleeson CJ, the damage was not the formation of the parent-child relationship, but the expenditure resulting from the surgeon's negligence ([67]–[68])<br>↑ normal principles of recovery are not displaced by arguments from public policy [77] or set-off of separate legal interests ([90]), as illustrated by the failure to contest the hospital and medical costs and other claims ([91]). |

*(continued)*

*Cattanach v Melchior* [2003] HCA 38: searching for a ratio decidendi *(continued)*

| Head of damage | Mother's pain & suffering; pregnancy & delivery AWARD NOT APPEALED | Mother's prenatal medical expenses & associated loss of income AWARD NOT APPEALED | Mother's postnatal loss of income AWARD NOT APPEALED | Layette for newborn AWARD NOT APPEALED | Child's maintenance costs |
|---|---|---|---|---|---|
| Kirby J | YES<br>➔ Denial of any recovery would provide legal immunity to medical practitioners engaged in sterilisation procedures that is unprincipled and inconsistent ([149]) | YES—Rightly awarded [Option 5] | YES—Rightly awarded [Option 5] | YES—Rightly awarded [Option want 5] | ➔ claim is consequential on personal injury, **not pure economic loss**, contra Gleeson CJ so no need to satisfy special tests ([148]–[150])<br>➔ *McFarlane* distinguished because based upon *Caparo* which he regrets is not accepted by the Aus HC ([122])<br>➔ no issue of indeterminacy<br>➔ no offset of benefits and burdens of different kinds ([173]–[175])<br>➔ Followed his own judgment in *CES v Superclinics* that there was no reason grounded in public policy to deny full compensation for all losses ([112])<br>➔ public policy arguments against recovery are 'sheer judicial fantasy' as money, not love or preservation of the family unit, is what is in issue [145] |

| | | | | | |
|---|---|---|---|---|---|
| **Callinan J** | → YES Rightly awarded (implied)<br>→ concurs with Kirby J's immunity concerns ([295]) | YES Rightly awarded (implied) | YES Rightly awarded (implied) | YES Rightly awarded (implied) | → **corrective justice requires full compensation** [298]–[299], as otherwise tortfeasor would reap a windfall ([301])<br>→ no set off as not equivalents, albeit calculable ([297]) |
| **Hayne J (dissenting)** | YES<br>→ Would allow recovery for this head only, plus the thrown away costs of the failed procedure ([262])<br>→ Rejects the 'no actionable harm because incontrovertible 'blessing' argument' ([195]–[197]) | NO Wrongly awarded | NO Wrongly awarded | NO Wrongly awarded | → rejects all financial claims as law should not permit the commodification of the child ([261])<br>→ Set-off not incalculable [200] but public policy precludes making the calculation [250], [259]<br>→ recovery is not required to vindicate the parent's interest injuriously affected by the medical negligence because it would require the law to value the new life to parent whose interests conflict with child's [253], [260]<br>→ rejects the 'damage the child' public policy argument ([202]–[203])<br>→ possible exception for expenditure to meet a child's 'special needs' as this would not require valuing the child ([262]–[263]) |

*(continued)*

*Cattanach v Melchior* [2003] HCA 38: searching for a ratio decidendi *(continued)*

| Head of damage | Mother's pain & suffering; pregnancy & delivery AWARD NOT APPEALED | Mother's prenatal medical expenses & associated loss of income AWARD NOT APPEALED | Mother's postnatal loss of income AWARD NOT APPEALED | Layette for newborn AWARD NOT APPEALED | Child's maintenance costs |
|---|---|---|---|---|---|
| Heydon J (dissenting) | NO (by inference) <br> ↑ incapable of being characterised as a loss on public policy grounds because would permit parental conduct inconsistent with duty to nurture ([347]–[362], [404])) <br> ↑ harmful impact of litigation on child ([372]–[404]) | NO (by inference) | NO (by inference) | NO (by inference) | ↑ fear of inflated and perjured claims ([338]–[346]) <br> ↑ if there is a duty of care [not discussed], does not extend to this head of damage. |

## B. The Roads Not Taken

### (i) No Actionable Harm Resulted from the Failed Sterilisation

A difficulty some judges have had in identifying conception, pregnancy or childbirth as constituting legal harm is that they are normal, natural processes which themselves are not illnesses or diseases.[79] By extension, they have been reluctant to label the arrival and existence of a child as an actionable harm, thinking this would be inconsistent[80] with the common law's refusal to recognise wrongful life claims by a disabled child[81] because of the inherent value of existence and the unknowability of the alternative. One New Zealand judge declaimed melodramatically that to categorise 'regeneration of the species' as an injury was 'highly artificial' and 'stigmatise[d] possibly the highest expression of love between human beings', maternal affection.[82] Such emotive language conversely stigmatises the victim of the medical negligence who seeks reparation.

Initially public policy was invoked to justify transferring the 'no actionable loss' argument from wrongful life to wrongful conception claims, and confined to healthy babies.[83] However, as Peter Pain J pointed out in *Thake*, the state, through supporting family planning and abortion services, is neutral, recognising that for many people the birth of a healthy child is not always a blessing, and so they had freedom of choice.[84] The argument that pregnancy and birth could not constitute harm was thought to have been definitively rejected by the Court of Appeal in *Emeh*: since the purpose of sterilisation was to avoid the woman enduring the experience of pregnancy and birth, the negligence necessarily inflicted damage on her by subjecting her to it.[85] So a natural physical experience, if desired, constituted harm if undesired, where it was the tortfeasor's duty to prevent it from occurring.

---

[79] *McFarlane (OH)* (n 53 above); *McFarlane (HL)* (n 1 above), 114 (Lord Millett); *Jones v Berkshire Area Health Authority*, Unreported, 2 July 1986 (QB (Ognall J)), cited with approval, obiter, by Lloyd LJ in *Gold v Haringey Health Authority* [1988] QB 481 (CA), 484; *Cattanach (HCA)* (n 3 above), [347]–[362] (Heydon J). In Ireland the defendant conceded that the pregnancy and birth constituted harm in *Byrne* (n 36 above) [169], but later contested it (unsuccessfully) in *Ahern* (n 33 above).

[80] Morgan and White suggest that the net effect of the positions of the Australian High Court in *Cattanach* and the wrongful life cases (*Harriton* (n 7 above); *Waller* (n 7 above)) is that 'while birth is not always a blessing for those caring for the born, life is always a boon for the person living it, irrespective of the cost or burden of that life to or on others' (D Morgan and B White, 'Everyday Life and the Edges of Existence: Wrongs with No Name or the Wrong Name?' (2006) 29 *University of NSW Law Journal* 239, 248).

[81] This point was taken by Lord Steyn in *McFarlane (HL)* (n 1 above) 83, quoting *Trindade and Cane, the Law of Torts in Australia*, 3rd edn (Victoria, Oxford University Press, 1999) 434, in arguing for coherence—but without recognising the incoherence set up by his position that there was actionable physical damage in the birth of a healthy child.

[82] *XY v Accident Compensation Corporation* [1984] 4 NZAR 219, 380 (Jefferies J).

[83] The argument was first accepted in *Udale* (n 66 above) by Jupp J.

[84] *Thake* (n 46 above), 666–67.

[85] *Emeh* (n 73 above), 1025.

Notwithstanding this firm stance, the Health Board revived the 'no action-able harm' argument in *McFarlane*, contending that it was not inconsistent with it providing abortion and contraception services. It submitted that the harm was the parents' disappointed legitimate expectation that they could enjoy unprotected marital intercourse without the risk of increasing their family, and should be measured in that context, resulting in a nil or a nominal award.[86] Further, it was a fallacy to assume that the foreseeable expense caused by negligence was necessarily recoverable loss.[87]

In *AD v East Kent Health Authority*, Cooke J thought he discerned this 'no actionable harm' view in all of the speeches in *McFarlane*: 'they all con-note, as a matter of legal policy, moral repugnance to the idea that the birth of a healthy child can constitute injury, damage or loss',[88] and concluded this was why the maintenance costs were denied. However, the table mapping the reasoning of the Law Lords shows that this synthesis is unsustainable, as Lord Hope, Lord Clyde, Lord Steyn and Lord Slynn all concluded that there was a harmful event (*injuria* in Scots law) which constituted personal injury, or at least something analogous to it, and hence actionable harm. The various identifications of the harm will be discussed below. Only Lord Millett concluded that 'there is something distasteful, if not morally offensive, to treat the birth of a normal, healthy child as a matter for compensation',[89] concluding that 'the law must take the birth of a normal, healthy baby to be a blessing, not a detriment'.[90]

### (ii) No Duty of Care was Owed to the Partner of the Patient

Lord Clyde was prepared to accept that there was an obligation on the hospital to make reparation to Mrs McFarlane,[91] notwithstanding that her husband, not she, was the patient. This argument failed in *Goodwill*, but there the male patient was not in a relationship at the time of the surgery, so it was held there was no proximity between the surgeon and his (unidentifiable, and assumed to be innumerable) future sexual partners, and hence not to his later partner who became pregnant after being told by her own doctor that the vasectomy made contraception unnecessary.[92] That decision was before the *Hedley Byrne* cause of action was extended to third parties in *Spring v Guardian Assurance*[93] and *White v Jones*,[94] making it more difficult to argue

---

[86] *McFarlane (HL)* (n 1 above), 62, 64.
[87] ibid 64.
[88] *AD v East Kent NHS Trust* [2002] EWHC 2256, [2002] 3 FCR 658 (QB), [9] point (ii).
[89] *McFarlane (HL)* (n 1 above), 111.
[90] ibid 113–114.
[91] ibid 102.
[92] *Goodwill v British Pregnancy Advisory Service* [1996] 2 All ER 161 (CA).
[93] *Spring v Guardian Assurance plc and Others* [1995] 2 AC 296 (HL).
[94] *White v Jones* [1995] 2 AC 207 (HL).

that a woman whose current partner underwent a vasectomy to prevent her pregnancy was not owed a duty of care by the surgeon.[95]

To date the issue seems not to have been raised by the NHS in respect of the father in tubal occlusion cases.[96] As Gleeson CJ remarked in *Cattanach*, a father could not be 'ignored as a faintly embarrassing irrelevancy'.[97] Lady Hale did address the question in obiter in *Parkinson*, musing that the father should have a claim if he met his parental responsibility to care for the child, assuming he had a sufficient relationship of proximity with the tortfeasor, but it was unnecessary to express a concluded view then.[98]

In *Cattanach*, the issue also was left open. Hayne J was not prepared to assume that it was self-evident that the surgeon owed a duty of care to the non-patient partner, but as the argument was not taken by the defendant it was not pursued.[99]

### (iii) Novus Actus Interveniens *Due to the Decision to Keep the Child*

Contrary to the stance of some American courts,[100] English judges have consistently held that the mother's decisions to continue her pregnancy, and not to place the baby for adoption, did not break the chain of causation between the negligence and the maintenance costs, or constitute a failure to mitigate her losses. The doctor, in failing to prevent the pregnancy through sterilisation, placed the mother in that dilemma, compounding the deprivation of her reproductive autonomy,[101] and had no right to expect her to solve it by having an invasive abortion with its attendant risks, or by disowning responsibility for her child.[102] Moreover, often there will be no grounds for

---

[95] See E Jackson, *Regulating Reproduction: Law, Technology and Autonomy* (Oxford, Hart Publishing, 2001) 29–30.

[96] The position that no duty was owed to the woman's partner was argued by solicitors or the deceased mother (who were being sued for negligently failing to move the case forward for nine years from the birth, by which time the mother had committed suicide) against a previously absent father in *Whitehead* (n 12 above); Rix LJ thought that there was a 'difficult but realistically arguable claim' by the father for maintenance costs once he had shouldered parental responsibility for the disabled child ([67]), but he was in the minority on this point. See also *AD v East Kent NHS Trust* (n 88 above) (decided before the HL judgment in *Rees* (n 55 above)) refusing to allow the maintenance costs to be held in trust for the child's substitute carer, his grandmother, when the mother was a permanent patient in a psychiatric hospital where she had been impregnated.

[97] *Cattanach (HCA)* (n 3 above) [9].

[98] *Parkinson* (n 57 above) [294].

[99] *Cattanach (HCA)* (n 3 above) [189].

[100] Eg *Sorkin v Lee* 434 NYS 2d 300 (NYAD, 1980); *Williams v Van Biber* No WD 47567 (Missouri CA) (medical costs for baby's heart defect not causally related to the failed vasectomy; plaintiff's claim tried to set up 'a kind of medical paternity suit').

[101] OM Bradfield, 'Healthy Law Makes for Healthy Children: *Cattanach v Melchior*' (2005) 12 *Journal of Law and Medicine* 305, 317.

[102] *Emeh* (n 73 above), 1024.

a legal abortion under the Abortion Act 1967, even if the woman did consider it an option.[103] Australian case law is more ambivalent.[104]

Counsel for the Health Board eschewed the argument that the McFarlanes had broken the chain of causation by deciding not to take the option of abortion or adoption.[105] Nevertheless, they hinted that because the McFarlanes had 'not unreasonably' decided not to put place their daughter for adoption, that meant she was not an unwanted child and that broke the chain between the negligent procedure and her maintenance costs[106]—in essence, the same argument.[107] The McFarlanes replied that they were opposed to abortion and adoption on moral and cultural grounds, so it could not be said that they exercised any choice in dealing with a situation which they did not control.[108] This was one of the very few points on which the Law Lords were unanimous in *McFarlane*;[109] Lord Steyn said that he could not conceive of any circumstances in which the parents' autonomous choice not to take either of those routes could be questioned.[110] The logic is undeniable, because the very purpose of the sterilisation procedure was to avoid being forced to make such a choice by an unwanted pregnancy.

## C. Navigating Different Roads to the Desired Result

One difficulty in unpicking the reasoning in wrongful conception and wrongful birth cases is that the arguments tend to intersect with and elide into one another. The following roadmap therefore features many vertiginous roundabouts.

### (i) Identifying the 'Gist' Harm: The Surgery, the Conception, the Pregnancy, or the Child? Or the Parent's Loss of Reproductive Autonomy?

The divergent speeches in *McFarlane* exemplify the difficulty which courts worldwide claim in identifying the 'gist' damage to complete an action in

---

[103] See *Udale* (n 66 above), 526.

[104] *CES v Superclinics (Australia)* (n 15 above), in a heavily split court, Priestley JA said that the parents could have surrendered the child to adoption even if it was too late for abortion, and so after they decided to keep the child, the defendant was not legally responsible for the parents' financial costs.

[105] *McFarlane (HL)* (n 1 above), 81.

[106] ibid 63, 110.

[107] Noted by Lord Allanbridge, *McFarlane (IH)* (n 54 above), 142–43. Lord Millett thought it was a different argument (*McFarlane (HL)* (n 1 above) [113]), but given that its crux is the parents' decision to keep the child, it is difficult to discern this difference.

[108] *McFarlane (HL)* (n 1 above), 65, 89–90.

[109] ibid 74 (Lord Slynn), 81 (Lord Steyn), 97 (Lord Hope), 104, 105 (Lord Clyde), 111, 112–113 (Lord Millett).

[110] ibid 81.

negligence. It is submitted that the problem has been manufactured by identification of the conception or birth as the gist damage for the action. One drawback of the label 'wrongful birth' or 'wrongful conception' identified by McHugh, Gummow and Hayne JJ in *Cattanach* is that it focuses attention on the arrival of the baby, rather than on the botched sterilisation procedure which precipitated that chain of events.[111] Mason argues that the concerns about moral opprobrium which so beset the Law Lords are minimised if one accepts that the McFarlanes' action is not about damage due to Catherine's existence, but simply about the unwanted costs entailed in her arrival after the surgeon's error.[112] In other words, the dispute is not between a mother and her unwanted child, but between the patient and the negligent medical professional who interfered with her right to plan her family and her life.[113]

## (a) The Failed Surgery

Where the failed procedure is tubal occlusion, the gist damage clearly should be personal injury, viz, the incompetently performed surgery, as the surgeon's scalpel interfered with the patient's bodily integrity, but the agreed beneficial purpose for so doing was not achieved. In short, the breach of duty and the gist damage both occur in the operating theatre. This was accepted in *Udale v Bloomsbury Area Health Authority*.[114] A failed sterilisation is not in and of itself benign. It increases the risk of a dangerous ectopic pregnancy.[115] Had the defective surgery been detected before conception, there would have been compensable harm arising from the need to repeat the procedure, for being subjected again to the risks of surgery, the pain of recovery and any loss of income from time off work.[116] Under this analysis, there is no need to enter into Lord Millett's debate as to whether a natural event, be that conception or giving birth, could constitute personal injury; those events directly flow from antecedent harm, the negligent surgery.

As noted above, this is not such a neat solution where the failed procedure is a vasectomy, such that it needs to be argued that the doctor also owed a duty of care to the mother to avoid conception in order to claim her personal injury.

---

[111] *Cattanach (HCA)* (n 3 above) [57] (McHugh and Gummow JJ), [193] (Hayne J).

[112] Mason, *Troubled Pregnancy* (2007) n 44 above, 123.

[113] Bradfield, 'Healthy Law' (2005) n 101 above, 311.

[114] *Udale* (n 66 above), [1983] 1 WLR 1098, 1104, quoted with approval by Lord Hope, *McFarlane (HL)* (n 1 above), 87.

[115] Varma and Gupta (2004) (n 27 above), 1329.

[116] Conceded by the defendant in *Udale* (n 66 above), 1104 and in *Byrne* (n 36 above) [137]–[140]; damages for the second surgery were awarded in *Kealey v Berezowski* (1996) 136 DLR (4th) 708 (Ontario HC), 742. A close analogy, particularly to clip placement errors, is 'wrong site surgery': DC Ring, JH Herndon and GS Meyer, 'Case 34-2010—a 65-year-old Woman with an Incorrect Operation on the Left Hand' (2010) 363 *New England Journal of Medicine* 1950.

## (b) The Conception

Ignoring for the moment the fact that usually the act preceding conception is pleasurable for both partners, can it constitute gist damage when its consequence is unwanted? The point is of some significance, because the cause of action would immediately be complete regardless of any ensuing events, or whether the pregnancy and delivery were normal or difficult, or whether the child was healthy or disabled, or whether the mother opted for termination of the pregnancy.[117] This is the route which was taken by Lord Hope, because conception was the very thing she had been told would not happen to her after the sperm tests had been carried out following her husband's vasectomy, and it was attributable directly to the hospital's negligence. The implantation of semen within her fertile body by her husband whom both parties believed to be sterile was at least 'analogous' to personal injury.[118] Lord Clyde and Lord Millett were also of the view that the harm had occurred at conception.[119] Therefore three of five Law Lords held that the damage was the unwanted conception, but as Lord Millett, dissenting, did not regard that damage to be actionable, there was still no majority on that point.

## (c) The Pregnancy and Delivery

For Lord Slynn and Lord Steyn, the pain and discomfort of pregnancy constituted the physical consequences of the negligence, and hence impliedly the personal injury.[120] Justice Kirby concurred with this interpretation in *Cattanach*.[121] This postponement of the harm, at least until the pregnancy becomes a physical burden, raises the prospect that there would have been no actionable harm had the mother decided on an early abortion or had suffered an early miscarriage, regardless of her pain and distress occasioned by the termination of the pregnancy.

Witting objects to the pathologisation of normal pregnancy, claiming that it does not cause any deleterious changes in the claimant's physiology, 'designed' for childbearing and returning to its pre-conception state, which could qualify as 'orthodox' physical injury. On this basis he emphasises the novelty of the characterisation of pregnancy as harm in *McFarlane*.[122] It is difficult to accept this proposition as in any way realistic: the nausea, back

---

[117] *McFarlane (OH)* (n 53 above), 142 (Lord Allanbridge).

[118] *McFarlane (HL)* (n 1 above), 86.

[119] ibid 99 (Lord Clyde), 107 (Lord Millett).

[120] ibid 74 (Lord Slynn), 81, 84 (Lord Steyn). For analysis, see Jhaveri, 'Judicial Strategies' (2013) n 4 above, 66–67; D Nolan, 'New Forms of Damage in Negligence' (2007) 70 *Modern Law Review* 59, 71.

[121] *Cattanach (HCA)* (n 3 above) [148]–[149].

[122] C Witting, 'Physical Damage in Negligence' (2002) 61 *Cambridge Law Journal* 189, 192–94.

pain and stretch marks which often accompany pregnancy may be accepted by the woman as the price for a child, but that does not mean that when they occur they do not constitute illness, pain and physical changes, some permanent. Many personal injury claimants regain their pre-tort health but they do not lose their cause of action as a consequence. By Witting's analysis, rape which does not inflict physical traces is not personal injury, because a woman's body is 'designed' for sexual intercourse. The criminal law defines 'bodily harm' as any hurt or injury calculated to interfere with the health or comfort of the victim.[123] The law has long accepted that other physical acts such as tattooing and hair-cutting,[124] which are accepted as benign when consensual, constitute actual bodily harm, or tortious touching, when they are not. It is consent which renders the physical impact on the body non-injurious. It is that consent to the interference with the claimant's health and comfort which is lacking in wrongful conception cases. On this analysis, Lord Slynn and Lord Steyn were entirely orthodox in characterising unwanted pregnancy as physical harm and qualifying as personal injury in tort terms when the woman did not consent to being in that state.

(d) Loss of Reproductive Autonomy

An alternative formulation[125] is that the interest impaired by the failed sterilisation is the loss of procreative autonomy in determining the size of one's family, or whether to become a parent at all.[126] This identification of gist damage has at least four advantages. First, the principle of patient autonomy is both robust and familiar, and has long been firmly embedded in medical law, expressed in a myriad of requirements in order for health professionals to act lawfully. Secondly, it does not denigrate the intrinsic value of parenthood, but instead notes that society may value that which a particular individual chooses not to, a choice which society also values. Thirdly, it renders irrelevant which partner has undergone the failed sterilisation, because each possesses an independent legal right to reproductive autonomy. Fourthly, it sets up the argument for *restitutio in integrum* of all foreseeable losses as if their right and interest had been respected by the health professionals involved, so far as money could achieve this; this

---

[123] *R v Miller* [1954] 2 QB 282 (CA).

[124] *Director of Public Prosecutions v Smith (Michael Ross)* [2006] EWHC 94, [2006] 2 All ER 16 (QBD).

[125] Accepted in *Kealey* (n 116 above), 735. This argument has considerable academic support, eg N Priaulx, 'Joy to the World! A (Healthy) Child Is Born! Reconceptualizing "Harm" in Wrongful Conception' (2004) 13 *Social & Legal Studies* 5, expanded in N Priaulx, *The Harm Paradox: Tort Law and the Unwanted Child in an Era of Choice* (London, Routledge-Cavendish, 2007); E Jackson, *Regulating Reproduction* (2001) n 95 above, ch 1.

[126] R Dworkin, *Life's Dominion: an Argument about Abortion, Euthanasia and Individual Freedom* (Oxford, Oxford University Press, 1993) 159.

damages rule was relied upon by the McFarlanes in the House of Lords,[127] and has since been instantiated as a necessary consequence of patient autonomy of choice in *Chester v Afshar*.[128]

However, only Lord Millett accepted this argument in *McFarlane*, albeit in a rather backhanded way, after his rejection of the parents' 'subjective devaluation' of their unwanted offspring, discussed below. For Lord Millett, the proper measure of their loss was not the consequences of Catherine's conception and birth, but the loss of their freedom to limit the size of their family, an important aspect of their personal autonomy, which the law should respect by a conventional award of £5,000.

This one aspect of Lord Millett's dissenting judgment has found its way into the law, not in *McFarlane* but in *Rees*. Although the point was not put to counsel by the Bench in oral argument,[129] Lord Bingham, Lord Nicholls and Lord Scott adopted Lord Millett's reiterated proposal, increasing the 'conventional sum' to £15,000.[130] Lord Bingham was careful to stipulate that this award was not compensatory,[131] and hence it should not stand in place of the general damage award for the pain and suffering of the pregnancy and delivery; typically half that amount.[132] Lord Steyn and Lord Hope strongly objected to this 'heterodox solution' as going well beyond a 'gloss' on *McFarlane* which had rejected it, and as a matter which should have been left for the Law Commission to make recommendations to Parliament.[133] The House's conversion to the merits of a conventional award in *Rees* implies some unease with *McFarlane*'s general disregard of patients' rights to procreative autonomy.

## (ii) Setting Off Benefits and Burdens to Erase the Loss

The commercial concept of set-off, commonly applied to debts as between claimant and defendant, has been called in aid by courts worried that parents could obtain a net benefit from raising a child at the expense of the negligent

---

[127] *McFarlane (HL)* (n 1 above), 65, relying inter alia upon the personal injury case of *Pickett v British Rail Engineering Ltd* [1980] AC 136 (HL). The contrary argument is made by CJ Roederer, 'Wrongly Conceiving Wrongful Conception: Distributive vs Corrective Justice' (2001) 118 *South African Law Journal* 347, 350.

[128] *Chester* (n 14 above). Discussed in chapter 11 of this volume.

[129] The author attended the appeal as a retained consultant of the NHS Litigation Authority.

[130] *Rees (HL)* (n 55 above) [7]–[10] (Lord Bingham), [17] (Lord Nicholls), [123]–[126] (Lord Millett), [148] (Lord Scott).

[131] ibid [8].

[132] Currently in the region of £7,500 general damages for a failed tubal occlusion where there is no serious psychological impact or depression: Hon Mr Justice Ian Burnett and others, *Judicial College's Guidelines for the Assessment of General Damages in Personal Injury Cases*, 12th edn (Oxford, Oxford University Press, 2013) 3030. This is likely to be raised to £8,250 to incorporate the 10% general uplift recommended by Sir Rupert Jackson and accepted by the Court of Appeal in *Simmons v Castle* [2012] EWCA Civ 1288.

[133] *Rees (HL)* (n 55 above) [40]–[47] (Lord Steyn), [70]–[77] (Lord Hope).

doctor. One New Jersey court insensitively remarked that the parents desired to retain all the benefits in having an infant with Down's syndrome, whilst saddling the physicians with the disproportionate and enormous expense of raising the child, thereby reaping a windfall.[134] Lord Clyde and Lord Millett also indulged in 'windfall' rhetoric, stating that the decision of the Inner House meant that the McFarlanes would have the enjoyment of a child free of any cost to themselves and maintained at the expense of the NHS.[135] Lord McCluskey in the Inner House flipped the argument over, stating that he would find it even more anomalous if under Scots law the wrongdoer received 'the benefit of the child in order to eliminate his liability to make money reparation to the victim for the palpable loss resulting directly from the wrong inflicted'.[136]

Until *McFarlane*, when the notion of set-off had been applied in wrongful conception and wrongful birth cases, it had operated between benefits and burdens which had at least some measure of commensurability. In *Allen v Bloomsbury HA*, the pain of childbirth was set off against the pain of abortion where the woman was already pregnant at the time of the sterilisation procedure.[137] Another form of set-off, between antenatal suffering and the joy of a safe birth, was proposed by the Tayside Health Board, but firmly rejected by Lord Hope, as joy in the delivery room did not extinguish the prior suffering of pregnancy.[138] In *Thake*,[139] it was held that the physical strain, trouble and weariness of caring for a child was offset by the happiness of raising a healthy child, so the McFarlanes did not claim for their personal labour in raising Catherine.

In *McFarlane*, the Health Board argued for yet a further form of set-off: the maintenance costs should be treated as extinguished by 'the very substantial benefits' which the child brought to the parents, which 'caused the health board's mistake to recede into the historical background'.[140] Counsel for the McFarlanes objected that the birth was not viewed by the law as conferring an 'asset' upon the parents, but rather rights upon the child (for care and maintenance) as against the parents. The Health Board's argument was successful with Lord Gill at first instance.[141] It also appealed to Lord Hope, who concluded that since it could not be established that the child's maintenance costs exceeded the benefits of having her in the family, the economic loss ipso facto must fall outside the ambit of the duty of care.[142] Lord Steyn

---

[134] *Berman v Allan* 80 NJ 421, 404 A 2d 8 (1979).
[135] *McFarlane (HL)* (n 1 above), 105 (Lord Clyde), 114 (Lord Millett).
[136] *McFarlane (HL)* (n 1 above), 140–41.
[137] *Allen* (n 51 above).
[138] *McFarlane (HL)* (n 1 above), 87; also rejected by Lord Cameron in *Allan* (n 73 above), 583.
[139] *Thake* (n 46 above), 682–685; see also *Allen* (n 51 above).
[140] *McFarlane (HL)* (n 1 above), 63.
[141] *McFarlane (OH)* (n 53 above), 215–216.
[142] *McFarlane (HL)* (n 1 above), 97.

rejected set-off as the correct legal analysis of the position but then, rather perplexingly, regarded the benefit to the parents as relevant in an assessment of the justice of their claim.[143]

Lord Clyde used a commercial lawyer's logic to identify the fallacy in the set-off argument:

> [I]n attempting to offset the benefit of parenthood against the costs of parenthood one is attempting to set off factors of quite a different character against each other and that does not seem to me to accord, [sic] with principle. At least in the context of the compensation of one debt against another, like requires to be offset against like. In this analogous context of endeavouring to cancel out the maintenance claim one would still expect economic gain to be set off by economic loss. It may be that the benefit which the child represents to his or her parent is open to quantification, but there is no principle under which the law recognises such a set-off. A parent's claim for the death of a child is not offset by the saving in maintenance costs which the parent will enjoy …[144] Furthermore, in order to pursue such a claim against the risk of such a set-off, a parent is called upon in effect to prove that the child is more trouble than he or she is worth in order to claim. That seems to me an undesirable requirement to impose upon a parent and further militates against such an approach. Indeed, the very uncertainty of the extent of the benefit which the child may constitute makes the idea of a set-off difficult or even impracticable.[145]

The rhapsodic paeans to parenthood by affluent male judges are, it might be thought, somewhat unrealistic in their appraisal of the impact of an extra child on the typical family unit. In Lady Hale's typically pithy language, the labour does not end when the child is born.[146] She quoted Sir Nicholas Browne-Wilkinson VC, that the 'studied calm of the Royal Courts of Justice … is light years away' from the hectic milieu of the normal household of the multitasking mother.[147] Ironically, judicial discourse on the unmitigated joys of parenting an unplanned healthy child, and on the family as the bedrock of society, often result in those same children living in straitened financial circumstances, with parents strained by extra financial and childcare burdens because the medical and legal systems thwarted their conscientious family planning. Often, the marriage has broken down under the strain by the time the case gets to trial, especially where a disability is involved.[148] In the tragic case of *Whitehead* the mother of a child with spina bifida committed suicide when the case had still not been set down

---

[143] ibid 81–82.
[144] A widow's claim for loss of financial support is not set off by her being relieved of a tyrannical husband: *Cattanach (HCA)* (n 3 above) [297] (Callinan J).
[145] *McFarlane (HL)* (n 1 above), 103.
[146] *Parkinson* (n 57 above) [70].
[147] *Surtees v Kingston-upon-Thames Borough Council* [1991] 2 FLR 559 (CA), 583.
[148] *Parkinson* (n 57 above) [6]; *Fish v Wilcox and Gwent Health Authority* (1993) 13 BMLR 134 (CA), 135; *Hunter* (n 9 above) [28].

for trial after nine years.[149] As Lord McCluskey said in the Inner House in *McFarlane*:

> The 'principle' that the value of the child should be held to outweigh all the finan-
> cial outlay incurred bringing up a child might well appeal to those who can afford
> to make such outlay without any, or any undue, financial hardship. But even in
> our civilisation, there are some for whom an unwanted and unplanned pregnancy
> is a financial disaster and may bring an end to a chosen way of life with finan-
> cial and personal losses ... [The] unrealistic task [of putting the monetary value
> upon the birth] can be avoided ... simply by holding that the benefits accruing to
> the parents of a healthy child which they have conceived are benefits that, along
> with the likely disbenefits, accrue to them alone, but that such benefits should not
> accrue to the relief of the wrongdoer whose negligence has cost the pregnancy.[150]

There are further hazards in deploying a set-off argument of this kind. First,
it risks treating the child as a commodity, an asset to the parents.[151] Lord
Gill lamely noted in *McFarlane* that the existence of the child brought to
the parents 'the contingent benefit of financial support in later life'.[152] More
realistically, as Lax J observed in *Kealey*, in the modern skills-based economy, unlike in an agrarian society, children are no longer an economic unit
of production, but instead are an economic drain for many years.[153]

Secondly, it raises the prospect that the value of the child's presence might
be calculated as being less than the cost in rearing her, so that she represented an overall net loss to the family unit.[154] This concern is reinforced
by the reiterated emphasis of the majority (apart from Lord Slynn) that
Catherine was healthy.[155] We have the spectre of disabled children being
regarded as being more trouble than they are worth—especially if the child
is very severely disabled, incapable of meaningful interaction with her family. Lady Hale adroitly used the set-off argument in *Parkinson* to justify the
award of damages for the extraordinary maintenance costs attributable to
that child's disability. Her Ladyship interpreted the majority's speeches in
*McFarlane* regarding set-off as concluding that there was a 'deemed equilibrium' between the benefits and burdens of raising a child. This analysis
also applied to a disabled child, affording him the same worth, dignity and
status within the family, but the set-off argument, by some sort of 'disturbed

---

[149] *Whitehead* (n 12 above).

[150] *McFarlane (IH)* (n 54 above), 140.

[151] A concern of Hale LJ, *Parkinson* (n 57 above) [89], and Hayne J in *Cattanach (HCA)* (n 3 above) [248], [261].

[152] *McFarlane (OH)* (n 53 above), 216–17. The same argument was advanced by the NHS, on sexist assumptions that sons help their parents financially and daughters help out with the laundry and housework, in *Udale* (n 66 above), 529.

[153] *Kealey* (n 116 above), 731.

[154] An objection raised by Lord Gill in *McFarlane (OH)* (n 53 above), 215, and by Lord Millett in *McFarlane (HL)* (n 1 above), 111.

[155] No fewer than 55 times: Hoyano, 'Misconceptions' (2002) n 78 above, 891.

equilibrium', could acknowledge that he cost more.[156] We have seen that the deemed equilibrium metaphor was rejected in *Rees* (which, when applied to disabled parents, carried with it denigration of their parenting capacity),[157] unfortunately without discarding the offset argument altogether.

A final objection is that the set-off argument overlooks the claimants' right to weigh the balance between benefits and burdens of parenthood for themselves. One Washington Court concluded that great weight should be given to a couple's reason for undergoing sterilisation in ascertaining whether the subsequent birth constituted damage to the parents, as that

> calculation, untainted by bitterness and greed, or by a sense of duty to a child the parents have brought into the world, is usually the best available evidence of the extent to which the birth of the child has in fact been an injury to them.[158]

Reliance upon motivation has been criticised as overlooking the parents' own calculation that for them the burdens outweigh benefits,[159] and that it is irrelevant to any legal principle.[160] Lord Millett disputed the 'parental balancing' objection because parents could not be allowed 'by a process of subjective devaluation to make a detriment out of a benefit'[161] (an odd import from restitution law). For His Lordship, whilst parents were entitled to decide themselves where their own interests lay, society itself had to regard the balance of benefits and burdens as beneficial, as it would be 'repugnant to its own sense of values to do otherwise', and the law had to reflect that view.[162] This is difficult to reconcile with Lord Millett's earlier firm rejection of the set-off argument because it must 'either be superfluous or produce the very results which are said to be morally repugnant'.[163] It sits even more uneasily with the symbolic award he advocated for invasion of the parents' right to personal autonomy in determining the size of their family, as implicit therein is recognition of their right to choose not to acquire what society (and for Lord Millett, the law) deems to be a benefit.

In the final analysis, the question must be whether medical negligence law can reasonably demand that the parents bring into account, so as to eradicate their loss, the very 'benefit' which the medical procedure was legitimately intended to avoid. *McFarlane* does not provide the answer.

---

[156] *Parkinson* (n 57 above) [89].
[157] Hoyano (n 78 above), 900–901.
[158] *Hartke v McKelway* 707 F 2d 1544 (USCA, DC Cir, 1983) 1555.
[159] IJ Alvarez, 'A Critique of the Motivational Analysis in Wrongful Conception Cases' (2000) 41 *Boston College Law Review* 585, 606. See also *Mukheiber v Raath* (1999) 52 BMLR 49 (SCA of South Africa) [48], rejecting previous South African precedent that the court should judge the validity of the motivation against public policy: *Edouard v Administrator, Natal* 1990 (3) SA 581 (SCA of South Africa) 593.
[160] *Cattanach (HCA)* (n 3 above) [205]–[207] (Hayne J).
[161] *McFarlane (HL)* (n 1 above), 112.
[162] ibid 113–14.
[163] ibid 111.

*(iii)  Abracadabra: Slicing Up the Surgeon's Duty of Care to Transform
Consequential into Pure Economic Loss*

Lord Slynn, Lord Steyn and Lord Hope, having accepted that the surgeon
owed a duty to avert the unwanted pregnancy, birth and its immediate financial impact, were then faced with the predicament of finding a route to their
desired conclusion, that the costs of raising Catherine to adulthood were
not recoverable. Heretofore maintenance costs had been treated by English
and Scottish courts as loss consequential on personal injury. As Peter Pain J
said in *Thake v Maurice* 'every baby has a belly to be filled and a body to
be clothed. The law relating to damages is concerned with the reparation
in monetary terms and this is what is needed for the maintenance of the
baby'.[164] How, then, to sever the nexus between the physical harm resulting
in the birth, and the need to feed and clothe the child it produced?

Their solution was to winch the maintenance claim from personal injury
into the autonomous territory of pure economic loss,[165] which then might
require that the claimant set up a separate duty of care on the part of the
surgeon, distinct from the duty not to inflict personal injury.[166] Each judge
identified a different mechanism to accomplish this switching manoeuvre,
and then to block the duty of care.

Lord Steyn initially relied upon the fact that the case had been pleaded as
falling within the extended *Hedley Byrne* principle, overlooking that *Hedley
Byrne* had been applied to claims of psychiatric and physical injury where
negligent words or professional services did not figure[167]—but then said it
didn't matter whether the claim was characterised as *Hedley Byrne* or negligence simpliciter, because it was still economic loss for negligently performed
services, for which a separate duty of care was required.[168] As discussed
below, Lord Steyn then invoked distributive justice to thwart the duty of
care, using as a fall-back that it was not 'fair, just and reasonable' to impose
it on the NHS.

Lord Hope hived off the child-rearing claim from the mother to the
father—notwithstanding that both McFarlanes had advanced it—so as to
break the nexus between childbirth and those costs.[169] This is hardly ten-
able given the prevalence of families with two working parents, and that the

---

[164] *Thake* (n 46 above), 666. For a contrary view see S Todd, 'Wrongful Conception, Wrongful Birth and Wrongful Life' (2005) 27 *Sydney Law Review* 525, 531–32.

[165] My Oxford lecture on this topic features a cartoon of a judge manoeuvring a crane
(in the shape of a stork) whisking baby McFarlane from the personal injury bassinet to a pure
economic loss bassinet.

[166] Severance of the economic loss from the personal injury claim was first deployed by
Brooke J in *Allen* (n 51 above), 662, although he was then bound to follow *Emeh* (n 73 above)
in awarding the single parent her loss of earnings and maintenance costs.

[167] *Costello v Chief Constable of Northumbria Police* [1999] 1 All ER 550 (CA); *Swinney v
Chief Constable of Northumbria Police* [1996] 3 All ER 449 (CA).

[168] *McFarlane (HL)* (n 1 above), 77, 83.

[169] ibid 75.

family unit has foregone the enjoyment of the money used to support the unwanted child. Having come up with this self-limiting explanation, Lord Hope relied on the third stage of the *Caparo* duty of care test, holding that it was not fair, just, and reasonable to impose a disproportionate liability on the surgeon—'in the performance of a voluntary and comparatively minor operation' to allow couples to have unprotected intercourse, and the incalculable nature of the benefit of parenthood thwarted set-off,[170] already discussed.

Lord Slynn relied upon *Caparo* for the proposition that the existence of *any* duty of care is determined by the nature of the specific damage which actually results, so that the surgeon's duty of care has multiple salami-like slices.[171] This of course does not fit with other types of negligently performed surgery where a separate duty of care analysis is not required for future financial losses such as loss of income. Lord Slynn's next step was to conclude, without much explanation, that the surgeon had assumed responsibility to prevent pregnancy, but not for the expense of rearing the child.[172] Lady Hale demolished the logic of this argument in *Parkinson*: '[g]iven that the doctor clearly does assume some responsibility for preventing conception, it is difficult to understand why he assumes responsibility for some but not all of the clearly foreseeable, indeed highly probable, losses resulting'.[173] Lord Slynn himself was obliged to acknowledge that this was illogical.[174]

*McFarlane*'s insistence that costs arising due to negligent surgery resulting in personal injury must be labelled as (unrecoverable) pure economic loss sits oddly alongside *Adams v Bracknell Forest BC*. Here the House of Lords held that the failure of education professionals to ameliorate illiteracy due to a congenital learning difficulty (dyslexia) 'in a post-Cartesian world' constituted untreated personal injury, even without any evidence of psychiatric harm, and so the loss of earnings claim constituted consequential economic loss.[175] This inverts the conventional reluctance of tort law to attribute causal potency to omissions compared to positive acts such as botched medical procedures.

Lord Millett was refreshingly scornful about these stratagems by the majority in *McFarlane*:

> I do not consider that the present question should depend on whether the economic loss is characterised as pure or consequential. The distinction is technical

---

[170] ibid 91.
[171] ibid 75.
[172] ibid 76.
[173] *Parkinson* (n 57 above) [115].
[174] *McFarlane (HL)* (n 1 above), 74.
[175] *Adams v Bracknell Forest Borough Council* [2004] UKHL 29, [2005] 1 AC 76 [10], [19]–[20] (Lord Hoffmann), disapproving of *Anderton v Clwyd County Council* [1999] Fam Law 188, [1999] ELR 1 (CA) and other Court of Appeal rulings that failure to ameliorate dyslexia was pure economic loss under *Hedley Byrne* (n 48 above).

and artificial if not actually suspect in the circumstances of the present case, and is to my mind made irrelevant by the fact that Catherine's conception and birth are the very things that the defenders' professional services were called upon to prevent. In principle any losses occasioned thereby are recoverable however they may be characterised. Moreover the distinction has no moral content, and while ostensibly relied upon by some of those who have rejected the claim it can in reality have played no part in their belief that it would be morally wrong to accede to it.[176]

This objection seems unanswerable.[177]

### (iv) The Argument from Morality

Some judges have acknowledged that it was impossible to extradite morality from their reasoning. As Madam Justice Lax of the Ontario Supreme Court said in *Kealey v Berezowski*,

> A claim for child-rearing costs juxtaposes the private world of tort law with a world that is imbued with personal and public views of morality. It asks whether tort law is bold enough or foolish enough to embrace as a harm that which we so clearly regard as a good ... Courts have struggled with the novel question at issue in this case because, in the absence of legislative guidelines for assessing damages of this kind, they are driven back on standard principles of negligence law or on public policy. Both may be inadequate for the task.[178]

Lord Millett, unlike the other members of the panel, was forthright in describing the issue as setting up a moral problem for the court. Whilst observing that foreign judgments rejecting claims for the financial consequences of the birth of a healthy child were 'heavily dependent on moral sentiments',[179] he himself did not stint in describing some of the mooted solutions as being morally repugnant or offensive,[180] or as prompting an 'instinctive' negative reaction.[181] Lord Steyn proclaimed that 'judges' sense of the moral answer to a question, or the justice of the case, has been one of the great shaping forces of the common law' but then delegated that determination of moral acceptability on this issue to the 'inarticulate' 'ordinary citizen' on the London Underground.[182]

Justice Callinan in *Cattanach* called upon judges to be candid in acknowledging their social values and the way these had moulded or influenced their judgments instead of the application of strict legal policy, rather

---

[176] *McFarlane (HL)* (n 1 above), 109.
[177] Approved by McHugh and Gummow JJ, *Cattanach (HCA)* (n 3 above) [72].
[178] *Kealey* (n 116 above), 731.
[179] *McFarlane (HL)* (n 1 above), 108.
[180] ibid 109, 111, 114.
[181] ibid 109.
[182] *McFarlane (HL)* (n 1 above), 83.

than disavowing recourse to public policy.[183] All of the Australian Justices acknowledged the moral content to their decisions in the case—and reached diametrically opposed, and vehemently expressed, conclusions. So the judicial moral compass is not necessarily set differently in the Antipodes from the British Isles, but provides a very uncertain direction for the law.

### (v)  The Argument from Policy: Public, Social, or Legal?

The lower courts in England and Scotland had not shied away from analysing public policy in wrongful conception cases.[184] One line of such reasoning is that since the law permitted publicly-funded abortion services under specified circumstances, and sterilisation procedures were available from and funded by the NHS at the patient's request, it could not be contrary to public policy to hold that the normal liability rules applied when the procedures were performed negligently.[185] Another public policy argument is that to preclude recovery might provide an incentive for late abortions, whereas a damage award could enable the mother to keep the child.[186] Moreover, damages may help to alleviate hardship for the family unit,[187] making it easier for the unwanted child to be welcomed, and for the family to remain intact. One counterargument commonly offered is that the courts should not award damages because of the sanctity of human life, the inducement by the litigation to parents to assert a lack of love for their child, and the risk that the child would learn that she was so unwanted that doctors were paying for her maintenance.[188]

In contrast, the Law Lords in *McFarlane* rather curiously, were united in their reluctance to allow the public policy label to be applied to their disparate lines of reasoning, with Lord Steyn referring to it as 'quicksands',[189] and Lord Clyde trotting out the spavined nag about public policy being 'a very unruly horse'.[190] Lord Hope claimed that the question for the Court was one of law, not 'social policy'.[191] Only Lord Clyde attempted to explain his reluctance to resort to policy considerations: noting that they typically included ethical or moral elements; for each one raised, there was a countervailing consideration.[192] Lord Millett also asserted, enigmatically, that

---

[183] *Cattanach (HCA)* (n 3 above) [291].
[184] Eg *Emeh* (n 73 above); *Allan* (n 73 above), 583.
[185] *Allan* (n 73 above), 583; *Scuriaga* (n 16 above); *Thake* (n 45 above) (Peter Pain J).
[186] *Emeh* (n 73 above), 1021.
[187] *McFarlane (IH)* (n 53 above) 134 (Lord Justice-Clerk (Cullen)).
[188] *Udale* (n 66 above); *McFarlane (OH)* (n 53 above), 216–17 (Lord Gill), dismantled by Kirby J as 'sheer judicial fantasy' in *Cattanach (HCA)* (n 3 above) [143]–[145].
[189] *McFarlane (HL)* (n 1 above), 83.
[190] ibid 100.
[191] ibid 95.
[192] ibid 100.

legal policy was not the same as public policy, even though he thought that moral considerations might play a part in both; he essayed a definition of legal policy, that the court's task is to seek justice. However, his Lordship defined that search for justice as demanding that 'the dispute be resolved in a way that is fair and reasonable in accordance with the ordinary notions of what is fit and proper', whilst maintaining the coherence of the law by avoiding inappropriate distinctions.[193] The difficulty is to know how fairness and reasonableness can be adjudicated without reference to policy considerations—and indeed the 'fair, just and reasonable' criterion of the *Caparo* test for duty of care is commonly regarded as an analogue for the 'countervailing policy considerations' criterion of the *Anns* duty of care test still used in Canada, New Zealand and Australia. Hayne J in *Cattanach* suggested that none of the Law Lords had managed to escape public policy considerations.[194] This elliptical discourse corroborates Cane's observation that the word 'policy' is one of the most under-analysed terms in the modern legal lexicon.[195]

In *Cattanach*, McHugh and Gummow JJ astutely observed:

> It is a beguiling but misleading simplicity to invoke the broad values which few would deny and then glide to the conclusion that they operate to shield the [health authority] from the full consequences in law of Dr Cattanach's negligence.[196]

Their Honours skewered the distinctions drawn in *McFarlane* by the majority:

> The reliance upon values respecting the importance of life is made impossible by the reference to the postulated child as 'healthy'. The differential treatment of the worth of the lives of those with ill health or disability has been a mark of the societies and political regimes we least admire. To prevent recovery in respect of one class of child but not the other, by reference to a criterion of health, would be to discriminate by reference to a distinction irrelevant to the objects to be achieved, the award of compensatory damages to the parents. To suggest that the birth of a child is always a blessing, and that the benefits to be derived therefrom always outweigh the burdens, denies the first category of damages awarded in this case [which was not appealed]; it also denies the widespread use of contraception by persons such as the Melchiors to avoid just such an event.[197]

Possibly their Lordships in their painstaking disavowals of reliance on public policy had in mind the dictum of Lord Scarman in *McLoughlin v*

---

[193] ibid 108.
[194] *Cattanach (HCA)* (n 3 above) [217]–[219].
[195] P Cane, 'Another Failed Sterilisation' (2004) 120 *Law Quarterly Review* 189, 191.
[196] *Cattanach (HCA)* (n 3 above) [77].
[197] ibid [78], citing Hoyano (n 78 above), 900–901.

*O'Brian* (cited by Lord Gill[198] and by Lord Allanbridge[199] in the courts below), that

> The distinguishing feature of the common law is this judicial development and formation of principle. Policy considerations will have to be weighed: but the objective of the judges is the formulation of principle. And, if principle inexorably requires a decision which entails a degree of policy risk, the court's function is to adjudicate according to principle, leaving policy curtailment to the judgment of Parliament. Here lies the true role of the two lawmaking institutions in our constitution. By concentrating on principle the judges can keep the common law alive, flexible and consistent, and can keep the legal system clear of policy problems which neither they, nor the forensic process which it is their duty to operate, are equipped to resolve. If principle leads to results which are thought to be socially unacceptable, Parliament can legislate to draw a line or map out a new path.[200]

That said, Lord Scarman's warning related to the perils of departing from established principle on the ground of public policy, which encouraged Waller LJ to award damages for the full consequences of the failed sterilisation in *Emeh*.[201] The Law Lords showed no compunction about departing from a well-established line of authority, without leaving that task to Parliament, but instead relied upon other labels to justify doing so, one being distributive justice.

### (vi) The Contest Between Corrective Justice and Distributive Justice

To introduce briefly the Aristotelian concepts of justice in the context of torts, *corrective justice* is the idea that liability rectifies the injustice inflicted by the tortfeasor on the tort victim, by triggering a remedy which correlates to the victim's loss, and the tortfeasor's obligation to make good that loss.[202] Corrective justice is the default justification for compensation in negligence, operating according to a bipolar relationship between the doer and the sufferer of the injustice set up by the tort.[203]

*Distributive justice* has a contrasting structure of justification: the sharing of a benefit or burden (such as risk of liability) by potential parties, comparing their relative positions in terms of a distributive criterion, usually some notion of the common good. Distributive justice is chameleon-like, and is cited as justification for a seemingly limitless range of arguments in private law—even the set-off analysis, and abortion and adoption mitigation

---

[198] *McFarlane (OH)* (n 53 above), 216.

[199] *McFarlane (IH)* (n 54 above), 143.

[200] *McLoughlin v O'Brian* [1983] 1 AC 410 (HL) 430.

[201] *Emeh* (n 73 above), 1022.

[202] E Weinrib, 'Corrective Justice in a Nutshell' (2002) 52 *University of Toronto Law Journal* 349, 350–51.

[203] E Weinrib, *The Idea of Private Law* (Oxford, Oxford University Press, 1995 [revised edn 2012]) ch 6,

options for the parents, discussed earlier.[204] Weinrib maintains that considerations of distributive justice are 'inadmissible' in negligence and other areas of private law,[205] but other theorists such as Peter Cane think they operate in areas such as determining the boundaries of legal responsibility, prescribing when duties of care are and are not owed, and which harms within those duties should be considered by the law as wrongful losses.[206]

Lord Clyde, in giving 'reasonable restitution' as his reason for excluding maintenance costs as being disproportionate to culpability,[207] seemed to be alluding to a third category, *retributive justice* (although Lord Hope attributed the same disproportionality argument to distributive justice).[208] Retributive justice theory requires that a sanction be roughly proportionate to the moral gravity of the wrongdoer's conduct, and so tempers corrective justice.[209] Honoré notes that the argument for proportionality weakens when the tortfeasor does not pay for the compensation personally,[210] as is the case with medical staff employed by the NHS or consultants contracted to provide NHS services, who are entitled to indemnification by the Crown.[211] Lord Millett effectively refuted the disproportionality point, noting that 'it is a commonplace that the harm caused by a botched operation may be out of all proportion to the seriousness of the operation or the condition of the patient which it was designed to alleviate', the simplicity and inexpensiveness of the operation being irrelevant.[212] In any event, as the South African Court of Appeal tartly remarked, the answer to the disproportionality argument was that professional people must not act negligently[213]—in short that the solution lay in their hands.

Maintenance costs for an unwanted child, conceived as a consequence of medical negligence, would seem to fit precisely within the paradigm of corrective justice,[214] as Lord Steyn[215] and McHugh, Gummow, Kirby and

---

[204] Roederer, 'Wrongly Conceiving' (2001) n 127 above, 361.

[205] Weinrib, 'Corrective Justice' (2002) n 202 above, 355.

[206] P Cane, *Responsibility in Law and Morality* (Oxford, Hart Publishing, 2002) 186–91, 217–18.

[207] *McFarlane (HL)* (n 1 above) 105, 106.

[208] ibid 96–97.

[209] As conceived by T Honoré, *Responsibility and Fault* (Oxford, Hart Publishing, 1999) 83, 87.

[210] T Honoré, 'The Morality of Tort Law: Questions and Answers' in Honoree, *Responsibility and Fault* (Oxford, Hart Publishing, 1995) 89.

[211] NHS (Clinical Negligence Scheme) Regulations 1996 (SI 1996/251); *NHS Indemnity Arrangements for Clinical Negligence Claims in the NHS* (HSG 96/48). In Scotland Crown indemnity was introduced in 1989 and is currently funded by the Clinical Negligence and Other Risks Indemnity Scheme: Scottish Government, *A Study of Medical Negligence Claiming in Scotland* (n 25 above), para 1.1.

[212] *McFarlane (HL)* (n 1 above) 109.

[213] *Mukheiber* (n 159 above) [50].

[214] *McFarlane (HL)* (n 1 above), 81 (Lord Steyn).

[215] ibid 81.

Callinan JJ,[216] and Lord Bingham in *Rees*,[217] acknowledged: right and duty are exactly correlated, because the patient's right to competent sterilisation services is the basis of the surgeon's duty, and the scope of the duty includes avoiding exactly the kind of right-infringement of which the patient complains.[218] The chain of events and losses is clearly foreseeable from the outset of the surgery should it be negligently performed. On this view, it was the argument of the NHS for non-recovery which was novel, not the assertion of the claim by the parents.[219] As Lord Cameron explained, the notion is simple and in accordance with the ordinary principles of the law of damages: 'where the purpose of the physician's actions is to prevent conception or birth, elementary justice requires that he be held legally responsible for the consequences which in fact have occurred'.[220] Lord Hope, as a Scottish Law Lord, noted that the Inner House had given effect to what he termed the 'traditional civilian system of corrective justice', which provided a remedy in damages whenever there was a concurrence in *damnum* and *injuria*.[221] Yet Lord Hope did not suggest that his invocation of distributive justice was alien to the Scottish system of delict.

The argument from corrective justice is perhaps most compelling where the patient's motivations for seeking the sterilisation encompassed financial concerns. But it is not restricted to that scenario, because the patient had a right to competent medical services to prevent fertility and the surgeon had a duty to provide that service so as to protect the patient from all consequences of conception. Under this view, it does not matter whether the right/duty relationship was set up by tort or contract, ie whether the services were publicly or privately funded. Lord Bingham, a superlative tort lawyer, was an eloquent proponent of the precept that very potent considerations of public policy were required to override the rule of public policy which had first claim on the loyalty of the law: that wrongs should be remedied[222]— in short, corrective justice. Lamentably, Lord Bingham was absent from *McFarlane* but presided at the hearing of *Rees*. His Lordship's reasons, as always pellucid, for his adoption of a conventional award representing the parent's loss of reproductive autonomy are redolent of corrective justice:

> My concern is this. Even accepting that an unwanted child cannot be regarded as a financial liability and nothing else and that any attempt to weigh the costs of

[216] *Cattanach (HCA)* (n 3 above) [51], [57] (McHugh and Gummow JJ), [176] (Kirby J), [302] (Callinan J).
[217] *Rees (HL)* (n 55 above) [4].
[218] Weinrib (n 202 above), 352.
[219] Contrary to Todd, 'Wrongful Conception' (2005) n 164 above, 532.
[220] *Allan* (n 73 above), 584, quoting from *Sherlock v Stillwater Clinic* 260 NW 2d (1977) 174–75.
[221] *McFarlane (HL)* (n 1 above), 96.
[222] *X v Bedfordshire County Council* [1995] 2 AC 633 (CA), 663, reiterated in *Van Colle v Chief Constable of Hertfordshire Police; Smith v Chief Constable of Sussex Police* [2008] UKHL 50, [2009] 1 AC 225, [56] (dissenting).

bringing up a child against the intangible rewards of parenthood is unacceptably speculative, the fact remains that the parent of a child born following negligently performed vasectomy or sterilisation, or negligent advice on the effect of such a procedure, is the victim of a legal wrong ... I can accept and support a rule of legal policy which precludes recovery of the full cost of bringing up a child in the situation postulated, but I question the fairness of a rule which denies the victim of a legal wrong any recompense at all beyond an award immediately related to the unwanted pregnancy and birth. The spectre of well-to-do parents plundering the National Health Service should not blind one to other realities: that of a single mother with young children, struggling to make ends meet and counting the days until her children are of an age to enable her to work more hours and so enable the family to live a less straitened existence; the mother whose burning ambition is to put domestic chores so far as possible behind her and embark on a new career or resume an old one. Examples can be multiplied. To speak of losing the freedom to limit the size of one's family is to mask the real loss suffered in a situation of this kind. That is that a parent, particularly (even today) the mother, has been denied, through the negligence of another, the opportunity to live her life in the way that she wished and planned. I do not think that an award immediately relating to the unwanted pregnancy and birth gives adequate recognition of or does justice to that loss.[223]

It is possible to make a plausible case, as Peter Cane does, that the recoverability of maintenance costs issue falls squarely within distributive justice, whether that be analysed as a 'duty of care' question or 'scope of liability for harm' question—and so Lord Steyn and Lord Hope would be within safe territory in invoking distributive justice as the solution. Lord Hope contented himself with echoing Lord Hoffmann's formulation of distributive justice in the nervous shock case of *Frost* as 'a practical attempt to preserve the general perception of the law as a system of rules which is fair as between one citizen and another', conceding that distributive justice generated very general and necessarily imprecise principles.[224] For Lord Steyn, distributive justice was necessarily based upon moral views:

My Lords, to explain decisions denying a remedy for the cost of bringing up an unwanted child by saying that there is no loss, no foreseeable loss, no causative link or no ground for reasonable restitution is to resort to unrealistic and formalistic propositions which mask the real reasons for the decisions. And judges ought to strive to give the real reasons for their decision. It is my firm conviction that where courts of law have denied a remedy for the cost of bringing up an unwanted child the real reasons have been grounds of distributive justice. That is of course a moral theory. It may be objected that the House must act like a court of law and not like a court of morals. That would only be partly right. The court must apply

---

[223] *Rees (HL)* (n 55 above), [8].
[224] *McFarlane (HL)* (n 1 above), 96, citing *White v Chief Constable of South Yorkshire Police* [1999] 2 AC 455, 510–11, on appeal from *Frost v Chief Constable of South Yorkshire Police* [1997] 3 WLR 1194.

positive law. But judges' sense of the moral answer to a question, or the justice of the case, has been one of the great shaping forces of the common law. What may count in a situation of difficulty and uncertainty is not the subjective view of the judge but what he reasonably believes that the ordinary citizen would regard as right ... The truth is that tort law is a mosaic in which the principles of corrective justice and distributive justice are interwoven. And in situations of uncertainty and difficulty a choice sometimes has to be made between the two approaches.[225]

Unfortunately Lord Steyn's musings were not based upon any logic or principle derived from distributive justice, but rather upon a putative opinion poll of passengers on the London Underground, expressing 'an inarticulate premise as to what is morally acceptable and what is not'.[226]

In effect if not in words, this seems to have been an admission of defeat on Lord Steyn's part. Justice Kirby in *Cattanach* was acerbic, criticising Lord Steyn's elevation of 'a fictional character' to 'a modern Delphic oracle' as an attempt to objectify the foundation of his judgment so as to avoid the appearance of unreliable personal opinion.[227] Instead, His Honour called on the judiciary to be willing to take responsibility for applying the established judicial controls over the expansion of tort liability. He asserted that judges had no authority to adopt 'arbitrary departures' from basic tort doctrine of corrective justice, not least 'on the footing of their personal religious beliefs or "moral" assessments concealed in an inarticulate premise dressed up, and described, as legal principle or legal policy'.[228]

Certainly Lord Steyn's metaphor, if such it was, fell short of Lord Nicholls' standard of judicial explication:

> To be acceptable the law must be coherent. It must be principled. The basis upon which one case, or one type of case, is distinguished from another should be transparent and capable of identification. When a decision departs from principles normally applied, the basis for doing so must be rational and justifiable if the decision is to avoid the reproach that hard cases make bad law.[229]

After *McFarlane*, distributive justice became something of a judicial football. As Lady Hale acerbically remarked in *Parkinson*,

> The traveller on the Underground is not here being invoked as a hypothetical reasonable man but as a moral arbiter. We all know that London commuters are not a representative sample of public opinion. We also know that the answer will crucially depend upon the question asked and the amount of relevant information and argument given to help answer it. The fact that so many eminent judges all

---

[225] *McFarlane (HL)* (n 1 above), 82, 83.
[226] ibid 82.
[227] *Cattanach (HCA)* (n 3 above) [135]. Kirby J refers wryly to the Australian equivalent, the person 'on the Emu Plains omnibus' ([151], fn 301).
[228] ibid [136], [137], [151], [177].
[229] *Fairchild v Glenhaven Funeral Services Ltd* [2002] UKHL 22, [2003] 1 AC 32, [36].

over the world have wrestled with this problem and reached different conclusions might suggest that the considered response would be less emphatic and less unanimous.[230]

Brooke LJ, concurring in *Parkinson*, invoked the 'fair, just, and reasonable' criterion for the threefold test for duty of care, and then stated as a fall-back that

> if principles of distributive justice are called in aid, I believe that ordinary people would consider that it would be fair for the law to make an award in such a case, provided it is limited to the extra expenses associated with the child's disability.[231]

Walker LJ, dissenting in *Rees* in the Court of Appeal, surmised that on the basis of distributive justice ordinary people would think that it was not fair if a disabled person who found she could cope with parenthood should recover when mothers who might become disabled by ill-health through the pressure and stress of having another child, albeit healthy, would not.[232]

In *Rees*, Lord Steyn acknowledged that '[i]nvoking the moral theory of distributive justice, and the requirements of being just, fair and reasonable, culled from case law, are in context simply routes to establishing the legal policy'.[233] Yet we have seen that Lord Steyn in *McFarlane* expressly divorced distributive justice from 'public policy'.[234] His Lordship made no attempt to distinguish between legal and public policy. Lord Bingham, never loath to delve into tort theory, nonetheless contented himself in *Rees* with noting that Kirby J was 'surely right' to observe in *Cattanach* that '[c]oncern to protect the viability of the National Health Service at a time of multiple demands upon it might indeed help to explain the invocation in the House of Lords in *McFarlane* of the notion of "distributive justice"'—a more pragmatic and concrete view of distributive justice than that expounded in *McFarlane*.[235] Lord Millett refused to cling onto the theory as his ratio decidendis, candidly recognising that:

> The decision of the majority of the Court of Appeal [in *Rees*] is destructive of the concept of distributive justice. It renders the law incoherent and is bound to lead to artificial and indefensible distinctions being drawn as the courts struggle to draw a principled line between costs which are recoverable and those which are not.[236]

---

[230] *Parkinson* (n 57 above) [82].

[231] ibid 283.

[232] *Rees v Darlington Memorial Hospital NHS Trust* [2002] EWCA Civ 88 [2003] QB 20 [55].

[233] *Rees (HL)* (n 55 above) [29].

[234] *McFarlane (HL)* (n 1 above), 83.

[235] *Cattanach (HCA)* (n 3 above) [178] quoted at [6] of *Rees (HL)* (n 55 above). Lord Bingham complimented the members of the Australian High Court (but not the panel in *McFarlane*) for the clarity and sharpness of their differing opinions in *Cattanach*.

[236] *Rees (HL)* (n 55 above) [121].

It is suggested that all that can be drawn as a lesson for a tort lawyer from this dismal morass is that distributive justice is every bit as equivocal, ambiguous, unpredictable and obfuscating as policy reasoning, be it labelled as public, social, moral or legal policy. It is not an exogenous test, but it permits the judiciary to abdicate its responsibility to identify and explain intellectually rigorous and coherent principles as a basis for their decisions. Not only does distributive justice not tell us *how* to make decisions, but it fails to *explain* or justify those decisions, as the speeches in *McFarlane* exemplify.[237] As Callinan J pointed out,[238] the arguments from distributive justice were as capable of yielding the opposite result, because the doctor, public health authority, or insurer had deeper pockets. The case the Law Lords made for distributive justice to override corrective justice in relation to one head of claim, is entirely unconvincing, once the metaphorical rhetoric is stripped away.

## V. *McFARLANE* AND *CATTANACH*: LANDMARK CASES—ON ROCKALL?

*Cattanach v Melchior* was decided in a fevered political climate of anxiety about large and sudden increases in medical indemnity and public liability insurance premiums in 2002, leading to the federal government appointing a commission[239] to recommend legislation specifically to limit negligence liability and quantum of damages for personal injury and death.[240] The Australian medical profession swiftly manned the barricades in response to the High Court judgment, enabled by *McFarlane* to protest its injustice, claiming that many medical practices would be forced out of business due to unaffordable insurance premiums.[241] The Australian Medical Association described the ruling as a 'horror story'.[242] Australian legislators in three States responded[243] with alacrity to the implied invitations of the majority

---

[237] Hoyano (n 78 above), 905.

[238] *Cattanach (HCA)* (n 3 above) [301].

[239] Hon Justice Ipp, *Review of the Law of Negligence—Final Report* (Commonwealth of Australia September 2002).

[240] Although the panel reinterpreted its terms of reference as being concerned with legal doctrine, not affordability of the tort system: P Cane, 'Reforming Tort Law in Australia: a Personal Perspective' (2003) 27 *Melbourne University Law Review* 649.

[241] C Zinn, 'Doctor Who Botched Sterilisation Has To Pay Cost of Raising Child' (2003) 327 *British Medical Journal* 183; see also the press releases and media articles quoted by Bradfield (n 101 above), 301, 315.

[242] P Cane, 'The Doctor, the Stork and the Court: a Modern Morality Play' (2004) 120 *Law Quarterly Review* 23, 26.

[243] Civil Liability Act 2003 (Queensland) (excludes maintenance costs for failed sterilisation (s 49A), failed contraceptive procedures or advice (s 49B)); Civil Liability Act 2002 (New South Wales) s 71(1) (applies to all causes of action for birth of a child; excludes recovery for maintenance and loss of earnings); Civil Liabilities Act 1936 (South Australia) s 67 (excludes ordinary costs of raising a child in extensive list of causes of action). The statutes preserve the right to compensation for additional costs arising from disability of the child.

Justices that such a radical departure from ordinary tort principles of corrective justice must be made by legislative bodies to reverse its effects.[244]

*McFarlane* continues to foment litigation, not least because the reasoning in the five speeches can be taken in almost any direction by a litigant and judge due to their inconsistencies and evaded questions, as the courts 'stumble from one set of facts to the next' in Cane's memorable phrase.[245] The split House in *Rees* on the fate of *Parkinson* (3:3, with Lord Millett perched on the fence) has left the state of British law on wrongful conception and wrongful birth in an unstable state, with crucial uncertainty in the very category where the heaviest burdens are foisted by medical negligence on parents. The NHS Litigation Authority continues to settle cases for the maintenance costs of disabled children on the basis of *Parkinson*, although there is reason to believe that it might reconsider contesting that precedent, as it did *Rees*, given the significant sums involved.[246] The editors of *McGregor on Damages* say that the outcome of such a challenge is impossible to predict, as the Supreme Court could reject, endorse or expand the exception for disabled children to permit recovery of the full cost of care, with much depending on the exact composition of the Court should a claim come eventually to be heard by it.[247] This cynicism is warranted by the disarray in *McFarlane* and *Rees*.

Corrective justice is a model which has a good fit with medical negligence: by requiring compensation of patients, it compels health professionals and the system within which they work to take responsibility for their errors and the consequences for patients, and provides an economic incentive to scrutinise and adjust procedures to avert further adverse incidents. The peculiar hybrid of corrective and distributive justice produced by *McFarlane*, *Parkinson* and *Rees* fails to meet the objectives of either model. Under the current mélange, where the loss falls as a consequence of the negligent medical services is usually a matter of chance. This is the only area of medical negligence law where a proven breach of the standard of care, resulting in proven foreseeable damage, leaves most of the loss to fall on the patient. The current arbitrary line-drawing represented by *McFarlane* and *Parkinson* arguably provides inadequate deterrence and incentivising of risk avoidance.[248] It is noteworthy that the medical literature in the UK in 2007, eight years after McFarlane, still pointed to simple measures which needed

---

[244] Eg *Cattanach (HCA)* (n 3 above) [138], [162], [180] (Kirby J).

[245] Cane, 'Another Failed Sterilisation' (2004) n 195 above, 191.

[246] Eg In a wrongful birth case where antenatal screening failed to identify a bilateral absence of arms on the fetus, the case was settled for £1.8 million: 'Wrongful Birth Claim—Child Missing Upper Limbs Bilaterally: CW v NHS Hospital Trust' (2011) 17 *Clinical Risk* 234.

[247] H McGregor, M Spencer and J Picton, *McGregor on Damages*, 19th edn (London, Sweet & Maxwell, 2014) para 38-290.

[248] *Cattanach (HCA)* (n 3 above) [161] (Kirby J); Bradfield (n 101 above), 314 (Bradfield being Resident Medical Officer, the Alfred Hospital, Melbourne).

to be taken in the NHS not only to prevent failed sterilisations through pre-cautionary procedures in the operating theatre, but also to identify, record and explain them to reduce their incidence.[249]

Moreover, the model of distributive justice invoked in *McFarlane* fits ill with the corrective justice model applied so rigidly by the majority in *Chester v Afshar*. In both cases the autonomy of the patient to make choices about her bodily integrity was infringed by the negligence. In the 'gloss' on *McFarlane* inserted by *Rees*, the autonomy interest was acknowledged only by a symbolic sum of £15,000, with the most burdensome direct financial consequences of that infringement unrecognised. In *Chester* the surgeon was required to bear the full and heavy financial costs consequential on his failure to warn, even though they were not directly inflicted by his negligence, but merely by the eventuation of a standard background risk of the procedure. This was justified in *Chester* on the basis that otherwise the legal duty to warn, to protect the patient's autonomy, would be empty because it would hold no consequences. Taking the rationale of *McFarlane* and *Rees*, however, it would not have been empty if a conventional award had been made to Ms Chester, and the healthcare system (whether publicly or privately funded) would not have to bear the burden of a massive liability for injuries which were not inflicted by the surgery. *McFarlane* and *Chester* cannot be reconciled at a level of principle.

In the final analysis, the stated reasons for applying distributive justice in *McFarlane* and corrective justice in *Parkinson* are both internally and externally incoherent and make arbitrary distinctions. Justice Kirby described judgments in this area as 'overwhelming legal analysis with emotion', noting dryly that most judicial declamations in this area of discourse 'have been on the side of those who most vehemently denounce their making'.[250] Whilst this criticism may be a little too caustic, the judgments do represent how far negligence law has come adrift of principle,[251] supplanted by obscure pragmatism.[252]

For that reason, *McFarlane* should not be treated as a landmark case for medical law as a whole, but rather an outlier, consigned to be buffeted by the stormy seas of Rockall, whilst *Cattanach* has been wiped off the most populated parts of the map of Australia.

---

[249] Varma and Gupta (2007) (n 27 above).
[250] *Cattanach (HCA)* (n 3 above) [151].
[251] Hoyano (n 78 above), 892, quoted by Kirby J in *Cattanach (HCA)* (n 3 above) [128].
[252] J Steele, 'Scepticism of the Law of Negligence' (1993) 52 CLJ 437, also quoted by Kirby J in *Cattanach (HCA)* (n 3 above) [128].

# 11

# *Chester v Afshar* [2004]

## SARAH GREEN

*CHESTER v AFSHAR*[1] is not a landmark to be celebrated. In order to serve preconceived notions of justice, the House of Lords in that case sacrificed the coherence of the causal inquiry in negligence. It is only if the decision comes to mark a path not to be trodden again that it will prove to be of any value to the common law. It stands out as a case which is neither consonant with orthodox causal principles, nor justified by reference to any established exception to those principles. Quite simply, it does not fit. This is a good thing for the tort of negligence, but a bad thing for those affected by this anomalous and extraordinary decision.

In *Chester v Afshar*, the defendant performed elective surgery upon the claimant in order to alleviate her severe back pain. Although he did so without negligence, she suffered significant nerve damage and was consequently left partially paralysed. The defendant breached his duty of care by failing to warn his patient of the 1–2 per cent risk of such paralysis occurring as a result of the operation. The causal problem arose in this case because the claimant did not argue that, had she been warned of the risk, she would *never* have had the operation, or even that, duly warned, she would have sought out another surgeon to perform the operation.[2] Her argument was simply that, had she been properly warned of the inherent risks in the procedure, she would not have consented to having the surgery within three days of her appointment, and would have sought further advice on alternatives. The House of Lords (Lord Bingham and Lord Hoffmann dissenting) held Mr Afshar liable on the basis that, since the ultimate injury suffered by the claimant was a product of the very risk of which she should have been warned, it could therefore *be regarded* as having been caused by that failure to warn. In effect, therefore, what the House of Lords did was to vindicate the claimant's right of autonomy, despite the fact that a bare interference with such a right is by no means an established category of actionable damage in negligence.[3]

---

[1] *Chester v Afshar* [2004] UKHL 41.
[2] Cf *Chappell v Hart* [1998] HCA 55, (1998) 195 CLR 232.
[3] Although see *Rees v Darlington Memorial Hospital NHS Trust* [2003] UKHL 52, and D Nolan, 'New Forms of Damage in Negligence' (2007) 70 *Modern Law Review* 59, 70.

The majority (Lord Hope, Lord Steyn and Lord Walker) decided that, although Miss Chester could not recover on the basis of conventional principles of causation,[4] her claim should nevertheless be successful. This conclusion was supported by two principal arguments; that her injury lay within the scope of the surgeon's duty of care and that, were she to be denied recovery, such a duty to warn would be drained of meaningful content. With respect, neither of these claims adequately supports the radical departure from established principles of causation demanded by that conclusion. First, the fact that the injury fell within the scope of the surgeon's duty of care is not a *substitute* for causal involvement; rather, it is a *limiting* device which applies once causally relevant factors have been identified. So, a causally relevant factor can be deemed legally irrelevant because it causes a result which falls outside of a defendant's duty of care. It does not follow, however, that a factor which has no causal relevance to an outcome can be made legally relevant because that outcome (which was not caused by the factor in question) just happens to be the mischief against which the defendant's duty of care was intended to guard. This is a clear non sequitur, and is not, unsurprisingly, an argument that has been repeated elsewhere in the tort of negligence.[5] In *Chester*, the defendant's breach had not been established, on the balance of probabilities, to have played any historical role in the claimant's injury because, but for the failure to warn, she would have run exactly the same risk (the 1–2 per cent risk of cauda equina syndrome inherent in the procedure itself, however carefully performed) on a different day. The fact, therefore, that the failure to warn did not make Miss Chester any worse off renders the *scope* of the defendant's duty irrelevant: in negligence, individuals do not have a duty to compensate for damage that they do not cause.

Second, a finding of no liability which follows a failure to establish a factual causal link between a breach of a duty of care and the claimant's damage has no effect whatsoever on the content of that duty of care. The form of the negligence inquiry is such that a breach of a duty of care is a necessary but not sufficient element of a successful negligence claim. This inevitably means that duties will be breached with impunity from negligence liability, so long as no damage has thereby been caused (or at least so long as no damage can be established on the balance of probabilities to have thereby been caused). This does not detract from the point or the worth of the duty of care concerned. A patient's dignity and right to decide is

---

[4] Because she did not argue that, but for the failure to warn, she would not have had the procedure at any point. Had she done so successfully, she would have established causation on orthodox grounds: see *McWilliams v Sir William Arroll Co Ltd* [1962] 1 WLR 295 (HL).

[5] Although Lord Walker and Lord Steyn attempted to make an analogy with the causal exception in *Fairchild v Glenhaven Funeral Services Ltd* [2003] 1 AC 32, the two situations are, as we shall see below, far from analogous.

protected by the law of tort's recognition that a medical professional has a duty to warn, not by a court's readiness to override causal considerations in the claimant's favour. If a breach of that duty to warn causes the claimant no loss, then a finding of no liability does not violate that right. It merely serves as an acknowledgement that the patient's inability to exercise that right did not, on this occasion, cause any loss. In his dissenting judgment in *Chester*, Lord Bingham is very clear about the importance of this point:

> I do not for my part think that the law should seek to reinforce that right by providing for the payment of potentially very large damages by a defendant whose violation of that right is not shown to have worsened the physical condition of the claimant.[6]

It is of course trite that damage is the gist of a claim in negligence and, whilst Mr Afshar was negligent and Miss Chester damaged, the two were not connected in the way this axiom anticipates. The fact that both the negligence and the damage occurred within the same factual matrix was no more than coincidental. In this context, an outcome is described as coincidental if the breach of duty is not one which increases the general risk of that outcome materialising. An oft-cited example is that of the claimant who, having had his leg broken by the defendant, is being taken to hospital when the ambulance in which he is travelling is struck by lightning. The fact that the claimant is killed by the lightning strike is coincidental in terms of the defendant's actions, since breaking someone's leg does not generally increase the risk of their being killed by lightning. In *Chester v Afshar*, the risk which eventuated in the injury to Miss Chester (paralysis brought about by cauda equina syndrome), was integral to the surgical procedure she underwent, and was not a risk which was or could be increased by a surgeon's failure to warn a patient of its existence.

Professor Stapleton disagrees with this, and argues that an increase in failures to warn patients of such risks will lead to a greater number of surgical procedures being undertaken, which will then in turn lead to a greater number of cases of paralysis occurring.[7] Since the net result will be a greater *incidence* of such injuries, the relationship between the failure to warn and cauda equina syndrome is not coincidental. In so doing, Stapleton makes it very clear that it is the overall incidence of such injuries, and not the degree of risk of the injury occurring on any given occasion which will thereby be increased. Unfortunately, this is precisely the point which undermines her argument. If the tort of negligence were concerned chiefly with the incidence of injuries, and had as one of its avowed aims the optimisation of risks, this would be a persuasive argument. It is what Law and Economics

---

[6] *Chester* (n 1 above) [9].
[7] See J Stapleton, 'Occam's Razor Reveals an Orthodox Basis for Chester v Afshar' (2006) 122 *Law Quarterly Review* 426, 441.

scholars would argue for, but it is not the premise on which the English law of negligence rests; a tort which, in its current form, serves corrective ends at the expense of distributive values.[8] The question, therefore, of whether *this* defendant increased the risk of injury to *this* claimant trumps any macro-level considerations about damage across a population. In these terms, the eventuation of the risk of cauda equina syndrome in Miss Chester's unfortunate case was coincidental to Mr Afshar's failure to warn her. This was a fact acknowledged by all of those in the majority,[9] who nevertheless decided that there existed sufficient 'policy' concerns to impose liability in spite of it.[10]

The fact that the occurrence of the claimant's damage in *Chester v Afshar* was coincidental to the defendant's breach says something important about the correct way to analyse the case. One of the many remarkable features of this decision is that it is not generally thought to fit within any of the recognised analytical categories into which negligence cases divide. As such, it has been characterised as a 'failure to warn' case and is often analysed as if it were *sui generis*.[11] In actual fact, however, *Chester v Afshar* is a loss of a chance case. This of course describes its analytical form; it says nothing about whether a chance had *actually* been lost on those particular facts. Classifying *Chester* in this way not only achieves the most consistency in terms of the broader tort of negligence, but it also facilitates the clearest analysis of the issues alluded to above.

Loss of chance cases in negligence have historically been divided into two categories: those concerned with the lost chance of a financial gain, and those concerned with the lost chance of a better physical outcome. Since it appears to be the case that courts are willing to allow claimants to recover for the former but not for the latter, this means of classification could lead to some moral disquiet. This is unfortunate, not least because it is unnecessary. There is indeed a distinction to be made between two 'types' of factual

---

[8] This is an enormous question, and one well beyond the scope of the current discussion. Fortunately, the task has been tackled by those far better suited to the task than I: see J Gardner, 'What is Tort Law For? Part 1: The Place of Corrective Justice' (2011) 30 *Law and Philosophy* 1, E Weinrib, *The Idea of Private Law*, revised edn (Oxford, Oxford University Press, 2012), J Coleman, *The Practice of Principle* (Oxford, Oxford University Press, 2011) and A Beever, *Rediscovering the Law of Negligence* (Oxford, Hart Publishing, 2009).

[9] *Chester* (n 1 above) [22], [81] and [101]. See also R Stevens, *Torts and Rights* (Oxford, Oxford University Press, 2007), 165.

[10] ibid [22] (Lord Steyn), [87] (Lord Hope), [101] (Lord Walker).

[11] It is categorised as a 'Particular Causation Problem' in J Steele, *Tort Law: Text, Cases and Materials*, 2nd edn (Oxford, Oxford University Press, 2009), as 'Coincidental Loss' in R Stevens, *Torts and Rights* (Oxford, Oxford University Press, 2007), under the heading 'What Would Have Happened' in WVH Rogers (ed), *Winfield & Jolowicz on Tort*, 18th edn (London, Sweet & Maxwell, 2010) and in MA Jones and AM Dugdale (eds), *Clerk & Lindsell on Torts*, 20th edn (London, Sweet & Maxwell, 2010) at 2–14, the case is said to stand in a 'third category' of its own (the first one being made up of situations in which properly-advised claimants would have followed the same path regardless, and the second covering those who would have acted differently).

situation which have been presented to the courts as appropriate vehicles for a loss of chance claim. The true distinction, however, does not lie in whether the claim is for a lost chance of financial gain or for 'a lost chance'[12] of a better physical outcome. Rather, such claims should appropriately be classified according to the following criteria:

**Type 1:** Those in which the chance exists independently of the breach of duty,[13] so that the breach affects a claimant's ability to avail herself of that chance, but not the substance of the chance itself. These are genuine loss of chance cases. Here, the uncertainty with which the law is concerned is whether the claimant has been denied access to an opportunity which exists *independently of the relationship between the parties.* This is essentially a question of whether the claimant's autonomy has been infringed, and explains why it should be established on the balance of probabilities that the breach of duty made the claimant worse off by affecting her access or exposure to that chance. The consequent damages, however, will be calculated according to the magnitude of the chance itself, regardless of whether the likelihood of success is greater than 50 per cent.[14] This is because the uncertainty inherent in the chance itself is not affected by anything the defendant has done, and it is not, therefore, necessary for the law to resolve it one way or another: in legal terms, the chance is relevant only in terms of quantification.

**Type 2:** Those cases in which the chance and the breach of duty are interdependent because the breach affects the existence and content of the chance itself. These are not in fact loss of chance cases at all, because to claim that a chance has been lost here is to beg the question. The relevant issue is not whether the claimant can take advantage of an established opportunity (as it is in Type 1 situations) but whether such an opportunity would even have *existed* in the absence of the defendant's breach of duty. Proof on the balance of probabilities is necessary in this context, therefore, because the very uncertainty which the law has to resolve in such situations is whether the defendant's breach of duty has eradicated a chance that would otherwise have existed. In other words, has the defendant altered the claimant's course of events for the worse? Such cases present, therefore, the orthodox causation question. It is only as a consequence of claimants' attempted reformulation of this question, in anticipation of a no-liability result, that such factual situations have been represented as involving lost chances. On the basis of such a reformulation, however, every negligence scenario could be recast as one in which a chance has been lost, because the forensic process does not deal in certainties.

---

[12] A concept which is not without definitional difficulty, as we shall see below.

[13] See Lord Hope in *Chester v Afshar* [2004] UKHL 41, [81]: 'the risk of which she should have been warned was not created by the failure to warn. It was already there, as an inevitable risk of the operative procedure itself however skilfully and carefully it was carried out'.

[14] As long as it is more than speculative: see Stuart-Smith LJ in *Allied Maples v Simmons & Simmons* [1995] 4 All ER 907; [1995] 1 WLR 1602, 1614.

Once such a distinction is recognised, the apparent incoherence of the common law's current position disappears: genuine loss of a chance claims (Type 1 cases) are capable of success where it can be shown that the defendant's breach of duty affected the claimant's *access* to an independent opportunity. On the other hand, those which are simply orthodox claims are otherwise bound to failure (Type 2 cases in which the defendant's breach has not been established on the balance of probabilities to have changed the claimant's course of events for the worse) are not saved by re-labelling them as claims for lost chances. Since, as we shall see, most cases falling within the Type 2 category are medical negligence claims, it appears as if the law is skewed towards favouring material interests over issues of physical integrity. A correct analysis, however, reveals this not to be the case: *Chester v Afshar*, for instance, is both a medical negligence case and one which should properly be understood as having the potential to involve a lost chance. Although the present argument is that its result should have been one of no liability, this has nothing to do with the interest at stake, and everything to do with the particular physical sequence of events that transpired, in which, ultimately, no chance was actually denied to the claimant.

*Allied Maples v Simmons and Simmons*[15] is one of the clearest examples of a Type 1 case. The defendants therein were solicitors, whose negligence in drafting an acquisition contract had deprived the claimants of the opportunity to negotiate for more advantageous terms. The claimants, relying on the negligently-drafted agreement, believed they were protected from liabilities arising from the acquisition when in fact they were not. Had they known of their vulnerability, they would have attempted to acquire such protection from the vendor before the contract was concluded. The Court of Appeal decided in favour of the claimants, and determined that damages should be assessed by reference to the chance of a successful negotiation, had this been a possibility. It concluded that, as long as there was a real, as opposed to speculative chance of success, there was no need for a positive outcome to be more likely than not. These facts fall squarely within the Type 1 classification because the solicitors' breach of duty had no effect whatsoever on the substance or content of the chance itself; its existence was extraneous to, and independent of, the solicitors' actions. The phenomenon of the chance *eo ipso*, therefore, is of no relevance to the question of causation, but only to the subsequent question of quantification. The breach of duty did, however, affect the claimant's ability to avail itself of that chance, and it is this specific question of the defendant's effect on the claimant's autonomy which represents the true causal question. Consequently, it is the answer to

---

[15] *Allied Maples Group Ltd v Simmons and Simmons (a firm)* [1995] 4 All ER 907, [1995] 1 WLR 1602.

this question which must be (and was) established by the claimant on the balance of probabilities:

> On the evidence before him the judge was justified in concluding that the defendants' breach of duty did have a causative impact upon the bargain which the plaintiffs and the vendors struck. He was entitled to find that, if the plaintiffs had negotiated further, they had a measurable chance of negotiating better terms which would have given them at least some protection against the liability on assigned leases which they were to assume on the draft agreement as it then stood, and as ultimately signed.[16]

In such cases,[17] what the claimant has to prove is that the defendant's breach of duty has prevented her from taking advantage of an opportunity which exists independently of the claimant-defendant relationship and the interaction therein. This, therefore, becomes a straightforward, but specific, causal question: is it more likely than not that, but for the defendant's breach, the claimant would have *had access to* an opportunity from which she is currently excluded?

The difference between this type of case and those properly classified as Type 2 situations can be illustrated by reference to the two English decisions primarily associated with claims for lost chances. The first is *Hotson v East Berkshire Area Health Authority*,[18] and the second is *Gregg v Scott*.[19] In the first case, the claimant, a 13-year-old boy, fell from a tree and injured his left hip.[20] The defendant's hospital, from which he sought treatment, negligently failed to diagnose or treat him correctly for five days. Ultimately, the claimant suffered avascular necrosis of the epiphysis, involving disability of the hip joint with the virtual certainty that osteoarthritis would later develop. At trial, Simon Brown J found that, even had the injury been properly diagnosed and treated in a timely manner, there remained a 75 per cent risk that avascular necrosis would have developed in any event, but he awarded the claimant damages corresponding to the 25 per cent chance of which the defendant's negligence had supposedly deprived him. Whilst the Court of Appeal concurred, the House of Lords decided in favour of the defendant and held that the trial judge's finding that, at the time of the fall there had already been a 75 per cent chance of avascular necrosis developing, amounted to a finding on the balance of probabilities that the fall was the sole cause of the injury. The Court did not, however, expressly exclude the

---

[16] ibid 1620 (Hobhouse LJ).
[17] Other examples include *Kitchen v RAF Association* [1958] 1 WLR 563 and *Yardley v Coombes* (1963) 107 *Solicitors Journal* 575.
[18] *Hotson v East Berkshire Area Health Authority* [1988] UKHL 1, [1987] AC 750 (HL).
[19] *Gregg v Scott* [2005] UKHL 2.
[20] More specifically, his left femoral epiphysis.

possibility that 'loss of a chance', as it was presented therein, could ever form the basis of a successful claim in negligence.[21]

In *Gregg v Scott*, the claimant visited the defendant GP in November 1994, complaining of a lump under his left arm, which the defendant diagnosed as a benign lipoma. In failing to refer the claimant to a specialist at that point, the defendant was held to have been in breach of his duty of care. It was not until November 1995 that such a specialist saw the claimant, following a referral by another GP in August 1995. A biopsy carried out by order of the specialist surgeon revealed that the claimant actually had cancer in the form of non-Hodgkin's lymphoma. The trial judge found that the claimant's chance of being 'cured' (defined in this context as a period of 10 years' remission) was 42 per cent when he made his visit to the defendant, but that the nine-month delay, consequent upon the defendant's negligent failure to diagnose his illness correctly, reduced his chance of being cured to 25 per cent. As the claimant had only a 42 per cent chance of a cure in the first place, however, he was unable to prove on the balance of probabilities that the defendant's negligence caused him to be in a worse state than he would have been in, had his treatment not been delayed by nine months. In the light of this fact, the claimant argued that he had suffered the loss of a chance of being cured as a result of the defendant's negligence. In so doing, he invited the court to address a similar question to the one first considered by the House in *Hotson* as to whether or not such a loss should be recoverable.

By a majority of three to two (Lord Hope and Lord Nicholls dissenting), the House of Lords dismissed the claimant's appeal and held that it was (still) not prepared to extend loss of a chance claims to clinical negligence cases. In essence, Mr Gregg was told that he could not recover from Dr Scott because he could not prove on the balance of probabilities that the latter's negligence caused his life expectancy to be reduced. Whilst, on the facts as found by the trial judge, it had been established that the defendant's breach of duty had reduced the epidemiological likelihood of survival by 17 per cent, the House of Lords correctly refused to recognise this as actionable damage. As Lord Hoffmann put it: 'A wholesale adoption of possible rather than probable causation as the criterion of liability would be so radical a change in our law as to amount to a legislative act'.[22]

The court refused to depart from the orthodox approach of establishing a causal link between a defendant's breach of duty and a claimant's actionable damage on the balance of probabilities. In doing so, it recognised that the characteristic common to all causation problems is that of imperfect knowledge and, to use Lord Hoffmann's words once more: 'What we lack

[21] *Hotson* (n 18 above) 786.
[22] *Gregg* (n 19 above) [90].

is knowledge and the law deals with that lack of knowledge by the concept of the burden of proof'.[23]

In other words, although the law cannot expect to deal in certainties, the least it can do is expect a probability to be more likely than not. Common to both *Hotson* and *Gregg* is the fact that the claimants could not have established their claims on the basis of the orthodox approach to causation, since in neither case was it more likely than not that the claimant was any worse off as a result of the defendant's breach of duty. The formulation of both claims, misleadingly couched in terms of 'lost chances', was an attempt to sidestep the standard burden of proof on the basis that the claimants had lost something of value to them in having their 'already likely to suffer an adverse outcome' position made, by the defendant's breach, into 'even more likely to suffer an adverse outcome'. That this argument was made is, at least from a human interest point of view, easily understandable, since most individuals would class even the tiniest percentage chance of avoiding an adverse physical outcome as being something of significant value to them. In legal terms, however, such a 'chance' is less a prediction of what would have happened to a particular claimant than it is an approximation of the forensic margin of error:

> If it is proved statistically that 25 per cent of the population have a chance of recovery from a certain injury and 75 per cent do not, it does not mean that someone who suffers that injury and who does not recover from it has lost a 25 per cent chance. He may have lost nothing at all. What he has to do is prove that he was one of the 25 per cent and that his loss was caused by the defendant's negligence. To be a figure in a statistic does not by itself give him a cause of action. *If the plaintiff succeeds in proving that he was one of the 25 per cent and the defendant took away that chance*, the logical result would be to award him 100 per cent of his damages.[24] (emphasis added)

As the emphasis shows, what is uncertain in Type 2 cases is whether the claimant ever had a chance at all, and as this is an uncertainty which affects the legal conclusion to be drawn, it must be decided on the balance of probabilities.

As *Allied Maples* demonstrates, the claim that a breach of duty has caused the loss of a chance is not one that is alien to the law of tort. It is also definitively clear in the law of contract that claimants can recover damages which are calculated according to the percentage chance of making a particular gain, where the defendant's breach has denied them the opportunity of making that gain. In *Chaplin v Hicks*,[25] for example, the claimant

---

[23] ibid [79].

[24] *Hotson v East Berkshire HA* [1987] 1 All ER 210 (CA) 223 (Croom-Johnson LJ).

[25] *Chaplin v Hicks* [1911] 2 KB 786. This is the clearest statement of the point, but see also Lord Mackay in *Hotson v East Berkshire Area Health Authority* [1987] AC 750, 785 and H Reece, 'Losses of Chances in the Law' (1996) 59 *Modern Law Review* 188, 197.

was granted damages corresponding to the one-in-four chance that, had she been granted the appointment with the defendant to which her contract entitled her, she would have been chosen[26] as one of the 12 most attractive finalists in his beauty/talent competition. In these Type 1 situations, we can seek answers in relation to what the opportunity was, what it consisted of, and how might be assessed. All of these inquiries are conducted without reference to the defendant's breach, or to the relationship between claimant and defendant. Their answers, therefore, will tell us nothing about the interaction or causal link between the defendant's breach and the claimant's damage. Since, in these cases, there exists a chance independent of the relationship between the parties, from which the actions of the defendant could exclude the claimant, it is legitimate to ask whether, on the balance of probabilities, the actions of the defendant caused the claimant to 'lose a chance'. In other words, did the defendant prevent the claimant from availing herself of the discretely identifiable opportunity? In *Allied Maples*, for example, the claimants' relationship with their solicitors had no influence whatsoever on the content of the chance of their being able to elicit concessions from their vendor in the hypothetical world in which they could attempt this.[27] What was important to establish there was whether, on the balance of probabilities, the defendants had in fact denied the claimants the opportunity to take advantage of such a chance.

This sort of conclusion is not one, however, which can be made on the basis of Type 2 factual scenarios. In these situations, there is no such thing as an independently quantifiable opportunity which can be divorced from the question of whether the defendant's breach made the claimant worse off. In the Type 2 cases of *Gregg* and *Hotson*, for instance, the claimants' chances of avoiding an adverse physical outcome were inextricably bound up with the effects of the defendant's negligent diagnosis. The relevant 'chance' therefore is not assessable independently of the breach, since it is defined and determined by it. Given that there is nothing extraneous from which the claimant can be excluded, the question is not whether, on the balance of probabilities the claimant has been denied access to an opportunity, but whether the claimant ever had such an opportunity in the first place. This is the crux of the question in Type 2 cases, but is not even an issue in Type 1 cases. In the latter, the existence of the chance is a given, albeit that it needs to be quantified.

---

[26] Although, see A Burrows, *Remedies for Torts and Breach of Contract*, 3rd edn (Oxford, Oxford University Press, 2004) 54, fn 4 for the point that, had the Court of Appeal recognised that the contingency turned on the decision of the defendant himself, as opposed to an independent panel, no damages at all should have been awarded, on the basis of the principle that a court is entitled to assume that a defendant will make the decision most favourable to himself. See also A Burrows, 'Uncertainty about Uncertainty: Damages for Loss of a Chance' [2008] *Journal of Personal Injury Law* 31, fn 44.

[27] The fact that they could not attempt it in the real world explains why they had lost their chance.

The approach in *Allied Maples* made specific reference to the fact that the hypothetical outcome therein was partly dependent on how an independent third party might have behaved.[28] Although this has come to be regarded as a defining characteristic of the decision,[29] it is not obvious why it should be so. What matters in the context of Type 1 cases is not whether the independent chance to which the claimant wanted access is determined by the actions of third parties, but only whether it exists independently of the interaction between the claimant and the defendant. That this is true is demonstrated by *Chester v Afshar*, itself a Type 1 case, and one in which the relevant chance had no connection to human behaviour. The 'chance' in *Chester v Afshar* was the 1–2 per cent risk of developing cauda equina syndrome, and this risk was *inherent in the surgical procedure*. The same risk could of course be represented as a 98–99 per cent chance of the procedure *not* having this adverse outcome. As Stuart-Smith LJ makes clear in *Allied Maples*, it matters not how such an uncertainty is perceived: 'I can see no difference in principle between the chance of gaining a benefit and the chance of avoiding a liability'.[30]

It was this 98–99 per cent likelihood of avoiding injury which forms the independent chance element in *Chester*, analogous to the claimants' opportunity of negotiating a more favourable settlement in *Allied Maples*, or the young actress's prospects of gaining a lucrative contract in *Chaplin v Hicks*.[31] Just as in these cases, the magnitude of this chance was not affected by anything that occurred between the parties to the dispute in *Chester*: rather, their relationship determined only whether the claimant could avail herself of the chance[32] in question. Mr Afshar's failure to warn his patient meant that he performed her operation on Monday 21 November 1994 as opposed to a date sometime later. Consequently, Miss Chester ran the 1–2 per cent risk of developing cauda equina syndrome. (She also, and simultaneously, availed herself of the 98–99 per cent chance of avoiding that eventuality.) But for Mr Afshar's negligence, Miss Chester would probably, according to her own evidence, have run an identical risk, and taken an identical chance, on a different day. The breach of duty in this case, therefore, did not affect her ability to take advantage of an independent chance in the way that the breaches in *Allied Maples* and *Chaplin v Hicks* were found to have done. It remains a Type 1 case, however, because the breach *could* have had such an

---

[28] *Allied Maples* (n 15 above) 1609 (Stuart-Smith LJ).
[29] M Simpson, A Dugdale and M Jones (eds), *Clerk & Lindsell on Torts*, 20th edn (Sweet & Maxwell, London, 2010) 2–23.
[30] *Allied Maples* (n 15 above) 1611.
[31] On the version of facts as ultimately accepted by the Court, but see Burrows (n 26 above).
[32] The chance itself was independent of the relationship between, and the actions of, the parties, because it was, according to the evidence, an inherent risk of that particular procedure, and not affected in its magnitude by the way in which the surgery was conducted.

effect and *would* have done if, for instance, she could have shown that she would never have undergone the surgical procedure, thereby giving herself a 100 per cent chance of avoiding cauda equina syndrome.

Of course, it is true that, on 21 November 1994, Miss Chester was unfortunate enough to succumb to the relatively small risk of injury, and that the consequences for her were dire. This is, however, irrelevant in negligence terms. The tort is not one which seeks to compensate those who suffer loss as a result of misfortune: ideological considerations aside, it is staggeringly ill-equipped to do so. The causal element of the negligence inquiry is what binds it to corrective, as opposed to distributive, ends and for courts to choose to override this on an ad hoc basis is to do the common law a disservice:

> To be acceptable the law must be coherent. It must be principled. The basis on which one case, or one type of case, is distinguished from another should be transparent and capable of identification. When a decision departs from principles normally applied, the basis for doing so must be rational and justifiable if the decision is to avoid the reproach that hard cases make bad law.[33]

With the greatest of respect to those in the majority in *Chester*, it is neither 'rational' nor 'justifiable' in a Type 1 case to take account of what *actually happened* as a result of the chance taken by the claimant. The key question on such facts is whether the claimant had her access to that chance, and therefore her autonomy, denied by the defendant's actions. A defendant in such a case, in which the content of the chance in question is completely independent of his actions, should not be held liable for the way that chance turned out. The very fact that we know how things turned out suggests that no chance has been lost because, by definition, it must have been taken. To compare, as judges and commentators have done,[34] the 1–2 per cent a priori risk of injury with the 100 per cent ex post knowledge that the injury occurred is an inauthentic exercise. To state the truism that, had the operation been performed some days later, the injury would probably not have occurred (since it was 98–99 per cent likely not to have done so) but then to conclude from this that the defendant's breach thereby caused the injury because it exposed the claimant to an identical risk *which is now known to have eventuated*, is not to compare like with like. It would have been unlikely that injury would have resulted on 28 November, but *no more* unlikely than it was on 21 November. The only difference between the two events is that we (now) know what happened as a result of one of them, but it is an eventuality which is both independent of, and coincidental to, the defendant's actions.[35] Put simply, the

---

[33] *Fairchild v Glenhaven Funeral Services Ltd* [2003] 1 AC 32, 36 (Lord Nicholls).

[34] See, for example, Stapleton (n 7 above), and Lord Steyn in *Chester* (n 1 above) [21].

[35] This is to go an inferential step further than that anticipated by S Fischoff in Fischoff, 'Heuristics and Biases in Hindsight' in D Kahneman, P Slovic and A Tversky (eds), *Judgment Under Uncertainty: Heuristics and Biases* (Cambridge, Cambridge University Press, 1982), in which he discusses the phenomenon of situations being regarded as inherently deterministic once their outcome is known.

defendant made no difference to the claimant's normal course of events, and should therefore not be subject to negligence liability.

As was almost inevitable in a case concerning a contentious causation point, those in favour of departing from orthodoxy looked to the principle associated with *Fairchild v Glenhaven Funeral Services*.[36] This controversial *Fairchild* principle, which began life in *McGhee v National Coal Board*[37] and has most recently been scrutinised in *Sienkiewicz v Grief*,[38] was developed to deal with a situation where an employee has contracted a disease brought about by exposure to a harmful substance (in the eponymous case, mesothelioma and asbestos respectively). Where he has been exposed to that harmful substance by two or more employers in breach of their duty to protect him from it, each of those employers will be liable for his loss,[39] despite the inability of medical evidence to attribute the occurrence of the illness either to a particular period, or to cumulative exposure, so long as the exposure for which the employer was responsible was not insignificant. The traditional 'but for' test cannot be applied in such cases because, as the precise aetiology of mesothelioma is unknown, there is insufficient information available to implement it.[40] Essentially, under an application of this principle, a claimant need not prove on the balance of probabilities that a defendant's breach of duty caused her loss, as long as she can prove that the breach materially increased the risk that she would suffer that loss.

It is remarkable indeed that the two dissenting voices in *Chester* were the only constituents of the House of Lords in that case who also contributed to the unanimous decision in *Fairchild*. Apparently, therefore, they were both in favour of there being a principle of modified causation; it was just that neither of them saw *Chester* as being an appropriate case for its application. With respect, this is surely correct and the reasons for this are several. Primarily, the principle in *Fairchild* was established in order to deal with a situation very different to the one in *Chester*. The essence of that exceptional

---

[36] *Fairchild v Glenhaven Funeral Services Ltd* [2003] 1 AC 32.

[37] *McGhee v National Coal Board* [1973] 1 WLR 1. In this earlier case, the claimant suffered from dermatitis following exposure to brick dust, but the evidentiary gap on these facts arose because medical experts were unable to say whether this was attributable to the dust caused by the defendant's non-tortious exposure (during the claimant's working day) or by its tortious exposure (during the claimant's cycle ride home, caked in dust as a result of the non-provision of showers). Liability was ultimately imposed on the basis that the defendant's breach of duty had materially contributed to the risk of the claimant's developing dermatitis, and this was the principle transposed onto *Fairchild*, the case that made it (in)famous.

[38] *Sienkiewicz v Grief (UK) Ltd* [2011] UKSC 10.

[39] Jointly and severally if the injury is mesothelioma and the agent asbestos (s 3 Compensation Act 2006), and severally if the principle applies because the 'rock of uncertainty', as defined below, is present, but either asbestos or mesothelioma are not involved (*Barker v Corus* [2006] UKHL 20).

[40] This is the 'rock of uncertainty' identified in *Sienkiewicz* as the touchstone of liability under the exceptional *Fairchild* principle; see below.

principle is that it offers a solution when the problem faced by the court is one of an evidentiary gap. In other words, it was formulated to modify conventional causal principles where, otherwise, it would be impossible for a claimant to establish that the defendant's breach of duty was a factual cause of her injury. It is a principle which, in the intervening years, has received much scrutiny, and this aspect of it has been affirmed at the highest level:

> Of course, the *Fairchild* exception was created only because of the present state of medical knowledge. If the day ever dawns when medical science can identify which fibre or fibres led to the malignant mutation and the source from which that fibre or those fibres came, then the problem which gave rise to the exception will have ceased to exist. At that point, by leading the appropriate medical evidence, claimants will be able to prove, on the balance of probability, that a particular defendant or particular defendants were responsible. So the *Fairchild* exception will no longer be needed. But, unless and until that time comes, the rock of uncertainty which prompted the creation of the *Fairchild* exception will remain.[41]

Quite simply, this was not the problem in *Chester*; there was no 'rock of uncertainty'. Although there was disagreement between the majority and the minority as to what the answer to the causal question should be, every judgment indicated that it was possible to reach such an answer on the evidence, and this is exactly what the Court cannot do in cases to which the *Fairchild* principle properly applies.[42] The question for a court in a genuine *Fairchild*-type situation is 'given that there is insufficient information to conduct the causal inquiry in the conventional way, should that causal inquiry be modified?' In contrast, the essential issue in *Chester* was 'given that the conventional causal inquiry in this situation would yield an answer of no liability, should that causal inquiry be modified in circumstances such as these?' Moreover, liability under the *Fairchild* principle is based on defendants having materially increased the risk of their employees contracting mesothelioma,[43] whereas, in *Chester*, 'the failure to warn cannot be said in any way to have increased the risk of injury'.[44] The conceptual difference between the two is as obvious as it is significant.

The exceptional principle in *Fairchild* was adopted on the basis that, although the precise aetiology of mesothelioma was unknown, it was accepted therein that it had been caused by one single agent: asbestos. Although there are obiter dicta doubting the relevance of this point in *Sienkiewicz v Grief*,[45] which represents the Supreme Court's latest word on *Fairchild*, it remains,

---

[41] *Sienkiewicz v Grief* [2011] UKSC 10, [142] (Lord Rodger).

[42] Which also includes, most notably, *Barker v Corus* (n 39), and *Sienkiewicz v Grief* (n 41 above).

[43] *Fairchild* (n 36 above) throughout, but particularly [34] (Lord Bingham), [42] (Lord Nicholls), [67] (Lord Hoffmann), [114] (Lord Hutton) and [170] (Lord Rodger).

[44] *Chester* (n 1 above) [61].

[45] *Sienkiewicz* (n 41 above) [187].

with respect, a highly significant limitation on the reach of that principle. The longevity of *Wilsher v Essex Area Health Authority*,[46] a case in which the House of Lords denied an application of the principle[47] to a situation where the defendant's breach of duty had contributed one out of five possible causes of the claimant's injury, is testament to this.[48] The single agent limitation ensures that there is a link between the risk created by the defendant and the risk which actually eventuated in harm to the claimant. Without it, any defendant who exposed the claimant to a risk could face liability, and this contravenes the principle that negligence does not impose liability for the creation of a risk *simpliciter*. Furthermore, *Chester* is not just a case where the claimant's injury had several potential causes;[49] unlike *Wilsher*, the contribution made by the defendant's breach of duty was not even one of those potential causes. Therefore, if the principle in *Fairchild* is not applicable to a case such as *Wilsher*, then, a fortiori, it is not applicable to *Chester*.

In *Fairchild*, Lord Hoffmann was careful to emphasise that the principle affirmed therein should not be 'so broad that it takes no account of significant differences which affect whether it is fair and just to impose liability'.[50] It is only reasonable to suggest, therefore, that the subsequent application of that principle to a case with differences as significant as those in *Chester* is not what the architects of that principle intended. Indeed, despite the fact that Lord Bingham conceded in *Fairchild* that it 'would be unrealistic to suppose that the principle here affirmed will not over time be the subject of analogical and incremental development',[51] he made it clear that he would consider the imposition of liability in *Chester* to be a 'substantial and unjustified departure from sound and established principle'.[52] Since, in the intervening decade, appellate courts have shown no appetite for expanding the reach of *Fairchild*, *Chester* looks increasingly anomalous, and its justification on the basis of such a principle, whilst always tenuous, is now indefensible. *Chester v Afshar* was not even a hard case. It should not have made such bad law, and the fact that it did means that it is a landmark indeed. It can only be hoped that it attracts few visitors.

---

[46] *Wilsher v Essex Area Health Authority* [1987] 1 AC 1074.

[47] In its previous incarnation as the principle in *McGhee* (n 37). In deciding *Fairchild* subsequently, the House explicitly stated that *Wilsher* remained good law: *Fairchild* (n 36 above) [70] (Lord Hoffmann).

[48] The House refused to apply the principle to a situation where the defendant's breach of duty had contributed one out of five possible causes of the claimant's injury: *Wilsher* (n 46 above).

[49] Eg the pre-disposition of the claimant, the severity of the patient's condition, the skill of the surgeon, the nature of the surgery itself, but not, significantly, the day on which the procedure was carried out.

[50] *Fairchild* (n 36 above) [60]. Although he was not alone in his call for restraint: see [37] and [43] (Lord Nicholls).

[51] ibid [34].

[52] ibid [9].

# 12

# R (on the Application of Burke) v General Medical Council [2004]; Burke v United Kingdom [2006]

## Contemporaneous and Advance Requests: The Fight for Rights at the End of Life

SHAUN D PATTINSON

### I. INTRODUCTION

KEN MASON ONCE gave a lecture in which he sought to identify the five most significant UK medical law cases of the past 30 years.[1] His choice pre-dates the *Burke* litigation,[2] but even so I doubt that the decision of the Court of Appeal would now be one of his choices. In fact, Mason's selection includes only one of the 15 landmark cases in this collection.[3] There is simply a huge number of medical law cases illustrating the content of medical law, advancing legal principle and likely to feature in future development of the law. Why, then, does this chapter focus on *Burke*?

There are two particularly striking features of the *Burke* litigation. First, it was the seminal—and currently only—case dealing with a patient's request for artificial nutrition and hydration (ANH)[4] to be continued. Secondly,

---

[1] JK Mason, 'Law and Medical Ethics: Have We Learnt Any Lessons?' Unpublished lecture held in Edinburgh Law School on 31 October 1998. For discussion see GT Laurie, 'The Autonomy of Others: Reflections on the Rise and Rise of Patient Choice in Contemporary Medical Law' in SAM Mclean (ed), *First Do No Harm* (Aldershot, Ashgate Publishing 2006) 131.

[2] *R (on the application of Burke) v General Medical Council* [2004] EWHC 1879 (hereafter HC); [2005] EWCA Civ 1003, [2005] 3 FCR 169 (hereafter CA); *Burke v United Kingdom* (Application No 19807/06), 11 July 2006.

[3] Mason's selection: *Re B* [1981] 1 WLR 1421, *Gillick v Norfolk and Wisbech Area Health Authority* [1986] AC 112, *Re MB* [1997] 2 FCR 541, *Attorney-General's Reference (No 3 of 1994)* [1998] AC 245 and *R v Cox* (1992) 12 BMLR 38.

[4] The latest GMC guidance refers to 'clinically assisted', rather than 'artificial', nutrition and hydration: see General Medical Council, *Treatment and Care Towards the End of Life: Good Practice in Decision Making* (GMC, 2010) para 3. This chapter retains the language used in the *Burke* litigation.

its true significance results not so much from what it did, but rather from what it did not do. The first instance decision of Munby J sought to recognise circumstances in which a patient had a legal right to be provided with life-prolonging treatment, but was overturned by the Court of Appeal, whose judgment later received the support of the European Court of Human Rights (ECtHR). Many commentators have supported the overturning of Munby J—variously declaring that it was 'surely right' that his decision was appealed,[5] the decision was 'unsatisfactory'[6] and the outcome of the appeal was 'probably unsurprising'.[7]

It will be argued in this chapter that the first instance decision was interpreted uncharitably and that the Court of Appeal thereby missed the opportunity to give proper recognition to the rights of potentially vulnerable patients. Further, while the law is still some way from recognising a right to treatment of the form suggested by Munby J, it will be shown that the subsequent case law displays a willingness to grant greater weight to the previously autonomous wishes of an incapacitated patient than the Court of Appeal had been willing to countenance in *Burke*.

A preliminary terminological issue arises with regard to the distinction between possession of sufficient cognitive faculties to be able to make a decision with respect to the given situation and possession of the decision-making authority required for a legally valid decision.[8] A minimum condition of the latter is the ability to communicate, whereas a patient who lacks the ability to communicate may still be considered to have the 'locked-in' cognitive ability to make a decision.[9] Elsewhere, I have referred to cognitive decision-making ability as *competence* and legal decision-making ability as *capacity*.[10] In the *Burke* litigation, Munby J and the Court of Appeal use these labels exactly the other way around.[11] The terminology used in

---

[5] R Gillon, 'Why the GMC is Right to Appeal Over Life Prolonging Treatment' (2004) 329 *British Medical Journal* 810, 810.

[6] JK Mason and GT Laurie, 'Personal Autonomy and the Right to Treatment: A Note on *R (on the application of Burke) v General Medical Council*' (2005) 9 *Edinburgh Law Review* 123, 132.

[7] Emily Jackson, *Medical Law* (Oxford, Oxford University Press, 2013) 968.

[8] An example of this distinction between cognitive and legal decision-making ability is presented where a child with full understanding is denied the legal authority to refuse treatment in the face of parental consent, as in *Re W (A Minor) (Medical Treatment: Court's Jurisdiction)* [1993] Fam 64, esp [84] and [86].

[9] Munby J (HC [45]) notes that Lord Mustill in *Airedale NHS Trust v Bland* [1993] AC 789, 897 made reference to a 'patient suffering the mental torture of Guillain-Barré syndrome, rational but trapped and mute in an unresponsive body'.

[10] See further SD Pattinson, *Medical Law and Ethics*, 4th edn (London, Sweet & Maxwell, 2014) ch 5.

[11] See eg 'a patient who is incompetent, because unable to communicate, may otherwise be functioning with intellect and senses wholly unimpaired' (HC [45]) and '[a] patient is competent if he has the capacity to take logical decisions and the ability to communicate those decisions' (CA [10]).

*Burke* is now potentially confusing when referring to the two-stage test in the Mental Capacity Act 2005, which is a test for legal decision-making authority requiring an ability to communicate and would therefore be described as a competence test in their terminology. In this chapter, I will use my own terminology except when quoting.

## II. BACKGROUND

Leslie Burke had a degenerative brain condition that would eventually remove his ability to swallow and require him to receive ANH to survive. The evidence identified three stages that Burke might pass through: the first when he has capacity and is aware, the second when aware of his surroundings and predicament but unable to communicate (ie is 'locked-in'), and the third after lapsing into a coma.[12] Thus, his prognosis was that he would be, in my terminology, (1) capacitated, then (2) competent but incapacitated, and then (3) both incompetent and incapacitated.

Burke was concerned that the guidance of the General Medical Council (GMC)[13] would permit ANH to be withdrawn while he remained aware (ie stages 1 and 2) and he emphatically did not 'want to die of thirst'.[14] He therefore brought judicial review proceedings against the GMC, claiming that the guidance was incompatible with his rights under the European Convention on Human Rights (the Convention): Article 2 (the right to life), Article 3 (the prohibition of inhuman and degrading treatment) and Article 8 (the right to respect for private and family life). While Munby J was willing to declare that parts of GMC guidance were unlawful,[15] the Court of Appeal took a different view and Burke's subsequent application to Strasbourg was similarly unanimously dismissed.

Munby J's 225-paragraph judgment granted six declarations.[16] The first three declarations specifically concerned Burke and the other three concerned the GMC's guidance. According to the first declaration, any decision by Burke while he has *capacity*, or contained in a valid *advance directive*, requesting that he be provided with ANH is determinate that such provision is in his best interests, at least in circumstances where death is not imminent and he is not comatose. According to the second and third declarations, any such decision by Burke would also mean that a hospital that has assumed his

---

[12] HC [170]; CA [36].
[13] See General Medical Council, *Withholding and Withdrawing Life-prolonging Treatments: Good Practice in Decision-making* (GMC, 2002). See the replacement guidance: GMC (n 4 above) esp paras 119–122.
[14] HC [6].
[15] GMC (n 13 above) paras 13, 16, 32, 42 and 81.
[16] HC [225].

care must arrange for ANH, and a doctor who has assumed his care must either continue to arrange for the provision of ANH or arrange for his transfer to a doctor who will do so, in the period until Burke's death is imminent and he is comatose. The other three declarations specified paragraphs in the GMC guidance that were unlawful. The guidance was said, in particular, to fail 'to acknowledge the heavy presumption in favour of life-prolonging treatment and that such treatment will be in the best interests of a patient unless the life of the patient, viewed from that patient's perspective, would be intolerable'. Further, there were a number of situations where it would be unlawful to withdraw ANH from an incapacitated patient without judicial sanction.[17]

The Court of Appeal, in overturning Munby J's declarations, ruled that they had extended well beyond the law relating to the patient.[18] Mr Burke was not faced with doctors who wished to withdraw life-prolonging ANH against his will and, in the view of the Court, he had not made an advance directive/decision.[19] The Court ruled that Burke should have sought reassurance from the GMC, whose guidance was not unlawful. Lord Phillips, giving the judgment of the Court of Appeal, opined that the application had served no useful purpose. According to his Lordship, it had not been open to doubt that the common law (like Article 2 of the Convention) imposes a duty on those who care for a capacitated patient such as Burke to provide ANH as long as it prolongs his life and is in accordance with his expressed wishes.[20] Any doctor who brought an end to a patient's life by withdrawing ANH in such circumstances would be guilty of murder.[21]

The Court of Appeal, after allowing submissions from no fewer than seven interveners, firmly asserted that it was not the role of the Court to act as a 'general advice centre'.[22] Steps were taken to limit future judicial involvement to that of adjudicator of last resort. For a start, there remained no legal duty to obtain court approval before treating an incapacitated adult, even if that treatment involved the removal of ANH.[23]

The European Court of Human Rights ruled the application to be 'manifestly ill-founded'.[24] The Strasbourg court took the view that English law adequately protected Burke's rights under Articles 2, 3, 8 and 14. The Court considered itself 'satisfied that the presumption of domestic law is strongly in favour of prolonging life where possible, which accords with the spirit of the Convention'. Further, there was no duty to obtain judicial

---

[17] HC [202].
[18] CA [20]. The judgment of the Court of Appeal was given by Lord Phillips MR.
[19] CA [22].
[20] CA [39]–[40].
[21] CA [34].
[22] CA [20]–[21].
[23] CA [70].
[24] *Burke v UK* (Application No 19807/06), 11 July 2006.

authorisation for the withdrawal of ANH, as this would be 'prescriptively burdensome', and there was no discrimination in the exercise of the applicant's Convention rights contrary to Article 14, as neither a capacitated nor incapacitated patient 'can require that a doctor gives treatment which that doctor considers is not clinically justified'.

### III. WITHHOLDING AND WITHDRAWING LIFE-PROLONGING TREATMENT FROM CAPACITATED PATIENTS

Both Munby J and the Court of Appeal accepted that, while Burke has capacity, those who care for him have a duty to provide him with ANH for as long as it prolongs his life and is in accordance with his expressed wishes. There was, however, some divergence with regard to how they reached this conclusion and its ambit. The essential difference is that Munby J supported his conclusion by reference to Burke's rights, whereas the Court of Appeal relied entirely on the obligations imposed by the common law on those who accept the care of a patient.

Munby J examined both the common law and the Convention, as given domestic effect by the Human Rights Act 1998, to arrive at a set of legal and ethical principles.[25] His Lordship identified: the *sanctity of life* (protected by Article 2), *dignity* (protected by, in particular, Article 3) and *autonomy or self-determination* (protected by, in particular, Article 8). The right to die with dignity was derived from analysis of the case law, particularly the case law on Article 3, and was said to encompass the right to be protected from treatment and lack of treatment 'which will result in one dying in avoidably distressing circumstances'.[26] The right to autonomy or self-determination was given even greater emphasis. Various common law authorities—addressing the right of a patient with capacity to refuse treatment, contemporaneously and by advance directive—were cited as indicative of the 'absolute nature' of this right.[27] Autonomy was also shown to underpin Article 8, which was said to embrace 'such matters as how one chooses to pass the closing days and moments of one's life and how one manages one's death'.[28]

In contrast, the Court of Appeal ruled that the common law authorities cited by Munby J were concerned solely with the 'paramount right to refuse treatment' and 'the right to self-determination does not entitle the patient to

---

[25] HC esp [73].

[26] HC [166]. For analysis of the potential implications of Munby J's derivation of a right to die with dignity, see John Coggon, 'Could the Right to Die with Dignity Represent a New Right to Die in English Law?' (2006) 14 *Medical Law Review* 219.

[27] HC [75], citing cases such as *Re C* [1994] 1 WLR 290, *St George's Healthcare NHS Trust v S* [1999] Fam 26 and *Re B* [2002] EWHC 429 (Fam).

[28] HC [130], [166] and [178].

insist on receiving a particular medical treatment'.[29] There was, the Court of Appeal declared, a legal duty to provide ANH to a capacitated patient, because the case law shows that '[o]nce a patient is accepted into a hospital, the medical staff come under a positive duty at common law to care for the patient'.[30] This duty will not override the wishes of a capacitated patient who refuses ANH, but where a patient wishes to be kept alive by ANH 'this will not be the source of the duty to provide it'.[31]

There was thus a key difference between the approach at first instance and the approach on appeal: Munby J had concluded that while Burke had capacity he had the *right* to insist on receiving life-prolonging ANH, whereas the Court of Appeal concluded that Burke would merely be the *beneficiary of a duty* to provide such treatment, whose only right was to refuse it. Strasbourg did not engage with this issue; its concern was with ensuring that the content of Burke's rights was protected, rather than with the precise domestic means by which that outcome was achieved. The Strasbourg court was therefore satisfied with the Court of Appeal's ruling that it would be murder 'to withdraw life-prolonging ANH from a patient who ... [had capacity and] desired the treatment to continue'.[32]

There were two other significant differences between the approach of Munby J and the Court of Appeal.

*First*, the courts had a different response to a counterfactual situation in which during the final stages of Burke's life ANH would hasten his death, rather than prolong his life. Munby J's appeal to the patient's determinate right to autonomy indicates that, where it is the patient's wish, ANH should be provided in such circumstances.[33] In contrast, the Court of Appeal ruled that 'a patient cannot demand that a doctor administer a treatment which the doctor considers is adverse to the patient's clinical needs'.[34] The Court of Appeal's response thereby leaves the decision to the judgement of the doctor. But why should a patient's prioritisation of relief from thirst over a marginally extended life be rejected in favour of a doctor's prioritisation of marginally extending his life? As Foster has pointed out, the 'odd' position of the Court of Appeal means that '[p]recisely when the patient is at his most vulnerable the law abandons him'.[35] It is not purely a clinical decision; it is a decision to be made solely by reference to the patient's interests and therefore properly made by the patient. The Court of Appeal's approach

---

[29] CA [31].
[30] CA [32], noting that the relevant case law was cited by Munby J at HC [82]–[87].
[31] CA [32].
[32] *Burke v United Kingdom* (Application No 19807/06), 11 July 2006.
[33] HC [116].
[34] CA [55].
[35] C Foster, 'Burke: A Tale of Unhappy Endings' [2005] *Journal of Personal Injury Law* 293, 298.

could not be supported by appeal to the policy of prohibiting euthanasia. In law, acting on a patient's request for life-shortening ANH is not equivalent to acting on a patient's request for a lethal injection. It is well established that a doctor may lawfully administer palliative care in circumstances where this has the incidental effect of shortening the patient's life.[36]

*Secondly*, the Court of Appeal's focus was entirely on ANH, whereas Munby J's principles had an apparently wider reach. As preliminary matters, his Lordship expressly declared that he was not addressing situations concerned with the prioritisation or allocation of scarce resources, or the provision of experimental or untested forms of treatment, because those issues did not arise in the context of ANH.[37] This has been taken by some to imply that his Lordship's reasoning extends beyond ANH—to all ordinarily available life-prolonging treatment or, according to the Court of Appeal, even beyond life-prolonging treatment.[38] With respect, the Court of Appeal was being most uncharitable; Munby J's judgment was clearly shaped by the nature of Burke's particular concerns and the GMC's guidance on the withdrawal/withholding of ANH and 'life-prolonging treatments generally',[39] and he makes repeated references to 'life-prolonging treatment'.[40]

Many academic commentators reject the suggestion of a *right* to insist on ordinarily available life-prolonging treatment or even ANH. Gillon considers such an approach to support the 'non-beneficial and wasteful provision of life prolonging treatment in general and artificial nutrition and hydration in particular'.[41] Mason and Laurie similarly bemoan his Lordship's support for a rights-based approach over a communitarian/duty-based approach.[42] Neither work, however, defends the rejection of a rights-based autonomy focus, beyond pointing to professional discretion and finite resources. What is properly regarded as 'non-beneficial and wasteful' and whether we should adhere to a rights-based over a duty-based perspective are issues requiring much deeper analysis. Elsewhere, I have defended the theoretical pre-eminence of a particular rights-based approach.[43]

---

[36] This was accepted by both the HC at [104] and the CA at [63]. For discussion of the relevant case law see Pattinson (n 10 above), para 14-017.

[37] HC [27]–[28].

[38] CA [20]: 'it has been understood as bearing on the right to treatment generally, and not merely life-prolonging treatment'.

[39] HC [9].

[40] See eg HC [98] and [116].

[41] Gillon (n 5 above) 810.

[42] JK Mason and GT Laurie, 'Personal Autonomy and the Right to Treatment: A Note on *R (on the application of Burke) v General Medical Council*' (2005) 9 *Edinburgh Law Review* 123, esp 127 and 131.

[43] SD Pattinson, *Influencing Traits* (Aldershot, Ashgate, 2002) ch 1 and Pattinson (n 10 above) ch 16.

Munby J's particular approach was to give great weight to the right to self-determination, relying on *Pretty v UK*[44] to support the view that Article 8 embraces 'such matters as how one chooses to pass the closing days and moments of one's life and how one manages one's death'.[45] That was despite the fact that this view on the ambit of Article 8(1) had been rejected by the House of Lords in *Pretty* before the case reached the ECtHR,[46] and the case law on section 2 of the Human Rights Act 1998 suggests that the lower domestic courts remain bound by decisions of the higher courts even when they are inconsistent with subsequent decisions of the ECtHR.[47] In any event, Munby J's statement on Article 8 does now represent the view of the UK's highest appeal court, which has subsequently departed from its own judgment in *Pretty* in favour of that of the ECtHR.[48]

In my view, Biggs is right to insist that concerns about the expansionist potential of a rights-based approach could have been dealt with in *Burke* by simply restricting the rights claim to *Burke's* specific concerns.[49] The provision of ANH to someone in Burke's position, for as long as he is not comatose, raises no real resource allocation difficulties additional to those raised by the Court of Appeal's position. Other life-prolonging treatment and other conditions may raise additional complexities but, as Biggs points out, future cases could consider and develop safeguards to ensure that the rights of others are fully protected in those contexts.

## IV. WITHHOLDING AND WITHDRAWING LIFE-PROLONGING TREATMENT FROM INCAPACITATED PATIENTS

The Court of Appeal considered Munby J's declarations to go far beyond the 'current concerns of Mr Burke'.[50] The Court of Appeal was particularly concerned with the fact that Munby J's declarations dealt with the position of incapacitated patients, when 'Mr Burke is likely to remain competent until the final stages of his illness' and '[w]e do not understand Mr Burke's

---

[44] *Pretty v United Kingdom* (Application No 2346/02) (2002) 35 EHRR 1.

[45] HC [130], [166] and [178].

[46] *R (on the application of Pretty) v Director of Public Prosecutions* [2001] UKHL 61.

[47] See *Kay v Lambeth London Borough Council* [2006] UKHL 10 as subsequently interpreted and applied in, eg, *R (on the application of Purdy) v Director of Public Prosecutions* [2008] EWHC 2565, [45]; [2009] EWCA Civ 92, [54]; [2009] UKHL 45, [32]. I have argued elsewhere that such an approach to domestic precedents is both wrong in principle and contrary to the actual reasoning of Lord Bingham in *Kay*, see SD Pattinson, 'The Human Rights Act and the Doctrine of Precedent' (2015) 35 *Legal Studies* 142.

[48] *Purdy* [2009] UKHL 45, [36].

[49] H Biggs, '"Taking Account of the Views of the Patient", but only if the Clinician (and the Court) Agrees—*R (Burke) v General Medical Council*' (2007) 19 *Child & Family Law Quarterly* 225.

[50] CA [22].

current concerns to relate to this stage and, if they do, we think that they are premature'. With respect, Munby J's judgment makes it clear that:

> The claimant wants to be fed and provided with appropriate hydration until he dies of natural causes. He does not want ANH to be withdrawn. He does not want to die of thirst. He does not want a decision to be taken by doctors that his life is no longer worth living.[51]

Burke's expressed wishes refer to his life 'until he dies', which does mean that his concerns *did* relate to the final stage of his life. Indeed, as will be explained below, Burke should be understood to have been making an advance directive, which could not properly be dismissed as 'premature'.[52]

Perhaps, Burke's concerns were considered 'premature' because his medical prognosis was not entirely certain and his period in stage 2 might be only fleeting. Burke's period in stage 2 could, however, be lengthier than expected and it is worth remembering that the case law is littered with examples in which medical predictions of a speedy decline have been proven wrong.[53] Since the Court did hold as a matter of fact that Burke's condition might enter three stages, it was legitimate for Munby J to examine the relevant law on Burke's view on what should happen when he could no longer express a view.

Both Munby J and the Court of Appeal accepted that they were bound by authority to accept that the best interest test applies to incapacitated patients. The Court of Appeal, however, took issue with Munby J's approach to the best interest test. By way of context, it should be noted that the Mental Capacity Act 2005 was passed in the period between Munby J's judgment and the Court of Appeal's decision, and came into force over two years later. The Court of Appeal was firmly of the view that the provisions of the 2005 Act were in accord with 'the position at common law'.[54]

Munby J examined the case law in some depth, including that on patients in a permanent vegetative state (PVS) and incapacitated but sentient patients capable of being kept alive for an indefinite period by the provision of ANH. According to Munby J:

> There is a very strong presumption in favour of taking all steps which will prolong life, and save in exceptional circumstances, or where the patient is dying, the best interests of the patient will normally require such steps to be taken. In case of doubt that doubt falls to be resolved in favour of the preservation of life. But the obligation is not absolute. Important as the sanctity of life is, it may have to

---

[51] HC [6].

[52] For an earlier expression of this view see SD Pattinson, *Medical Law and Ethics*, 1st edn (London, Sweet & Maxwell, 2006) 484–86, esp fn 44.

[53] Consider eg the pessimistic, but ultimately incorrect, predictions of life-expectance for the patients in *Re C* [1994] 1 WLR 290 and *R v Portsmouth Hospitals NHS Trust ex parte Glass* [1999] 2 FLR 905.

[54] CA [57].

take second place to human dignity. *In the context of life-prolonging treatment the touchstone of best interests is intolerability. So if life-prolonging treatment is providing some benefit it should be provided unless the patient's life, if thus prolonged, would from the patient's point of view be intolerable.*[55]

The Court of Appeal, when quoting the judge, added that emphasis to the last two sentences. It was declared that there could be no objection to the above summary 'had it not contained the final two sentences, which we have emphasised'.[56] The Court of Appeal explained that it rejected the suggestion that 'the touchstone of "best interests" is the "intolerability" of continued life' and the situations of patients in PVS and the incapacitated but sentient kept alive by ANH were 'very different'. With regard to a patient close to death—which the Court of Appeal strangely claimed did not relate to Burke's 'legitimate concern at this stage of his life'[57]—not only was 'intolerability' said not to be the test of best interests, but the Court of Appeal expressly rejected the idea that there was a 'single test, applicable in all circumstances'.[58] So how are we to interpret and apply the best interests test in the final stages of life? The Court of Appeal refused to provide any guidance beyond asserting that 'it is best to confine the use of the phrase "best interests" to an objective test'.[59] This approach seemed to be articulated solely as a way of denying the need to attach particular weight to Burke's subjective understanding of the benefit of continued ANH. Burke's explicit desire to avoid dying of thirst and hunger indicates that he considers avoidance of that experience at the end of his life to be a benefit. From his point of view, the continued provision of ANH would be neither futile nor intolerable, but in his best interests.

The Court of Appeal's approach to the best interest test was rather too quick given that it did not examine any of the case law in depth and seems to assume that the application of an objective best interest test is self-explanatory without elaboration. When referring to the 2005 Act, the Court of Appeal asserted that 'section 4 does no more than require this to be taken into consideration when considering what is in the best interests of a patient'.[60] Subsequent case law has shown a willingness to grant greater weight to the previously autonomous wishes of an incapacitated patient than the Court of Appeal was willing to countenance.

In *Aintree University Hospitals NHS Foundation Trust v James*, the Supreme Court considered the application of the 2005 Act to a patient in a minimally conscious state.[61] David James had suffered multi-organ failure

[55] HC [116], as quoted in CA [61].
[56] CA [61].
[57] CA [56].
[58] CA [63].
[59] CA [29].
[60] CA [57].
[61] *Aintree University Hospitals NHS Foundation Trust v James* [2013] UKSC 67.

with severe brain damage and was dependent on artificial ventilation. The hospital trust sought declarations that it would be in James's best interests to withhold specified types of invasive treatment if his condition deteriorated. Lady Hale, with whom the other Supreme Court justices agreed, reaffirmed that the starting point is a strong presumption that it is in a person's best interests to stay alive, but that is not an absolute and 'there are cases where it will not be in a patient's best interests to receive life-sustaining treatment'.[62] Lady Hale noted that 'there has been some support for a "touchstone of intolerability" in those cases [not concerned with patients in PVS] where a balancing exercise is to be carried out'.[63] Her Ladyship was, however, faced with a conflict over the meaning of a related touchstone—'futility'—by the first instance judge and the Court of Appeal. The judge had asked whether the proposed treatment would be futile in the sense of ineffective or of no benefit to the patient. The Court of Appeal rejected that approach to the best interests test, ruling that the treatment would be futile if it would have no real prospect of curing or at least palliating the patient's condition. The Supreme Court sided with the first instance judge.[64] Treatment could be a benefit to a patient 'even when it did not cure or palliate, where the burdens were outweighed by the benefits of continued existence'.[65]

Significantly, the Court of Appeal rejected the suggestion in the Court of Appeal that the best interests test required an objective assessment of the patient's wishes and feelings. Lady Hale declared that:

> The purpose of the best interests test is to consider matters from the patient's point of view. That is not to say that his wishes must prevail, any more than those of a fully capable patient must prevail. We cannot always have what we want. Nor will it always be possible to ascertain what an incapable patient's wishes are … insofar as it is possible to ascertain the patient's wishes and feelings, his beliefs and values or the things which were important to him, it is those which should be taken into account because they are a component in making the choice which is right for him as an individual human being.[66]

There is much in *Aintree* that is inconsistent with the approach of the Court of Appeal in *Burke*. For a start, the refusal to accept that Burke had concerns about stage 2 was tantamount to replacing his actual wishes and feelings with the Court's own assessment of his wishes and feelings, which Lady Hale tells us we must not do. Indeed, the Court of Appeal had expressly rejected assessment of the best interest test from the patient's point of view in favour of an objective test, which is the converse of the position articulated by the Supreme Court. The Court of Appeal in *Burke* denied that intolerability and futility

---

[62] ibid [35].
[63] ibid [37].
[64] ibid, esp [40].
[65] ibid [40].
[66] ibid [45].

were notions capable of providing any guidance when assessing whether treatment was of some benefit to a patient in the final stages of his life, whereas
Lady Hale found utility in both notions. Lady Hale was not, of course, seeking to defend a right to treatment of the form advanced by Munby J, but she
gave a very different emphasis to the weight to be attached to the patient's
previous views on what is or is not of benefit to the patient. The approach
of the Supreme Court makes it much harder for the concerns of Burke to be
dismissed when he enters a minimally conscious state at stage 2. It seems to
me that it supports a far stronger presumption that ANH should be continued
until he dies than follows from the approach of the Court of Appeal.

## V. ADVANCE DIRECTIVES

Another reason given by the Court of Appeal as to why Munby J's declarations
went far beyond the current concerns of Burke was that 'they address the
effect of an advance directive, sometimes referred to as "a living will", when
Mr Burke has made no such directive'.[67] As indicated above, Burke was just
as concerned with his future as a locked-in but aware patient as he was with
the position in which he was in at the time of the litigation. Thus, he ought
to have been taken to be making an advance request to the effect that ANH
should continue until his death. The Court of Appeal were, perhaps, mis-
led by Munby J's statement that certain issues '[m]ay turn upon the precise
terms of the claimant's advance directive'.[68] But Munby J was not thereby
stating that Burke had not made an advance directive, but recognising that
the precise form of that directive could well have changed by the time (some
years hence) that Burke loses capacity.

The right to dignity and the right to autonomy were said by Munby J
to underpin the legal right to make a binding advance refusal, which he
extended to encompass a legal right to making a binding advance request
for ANH. According to his Lordship, an incapacitated patient's right to
dignity under Article 3 meant that if he has made

> an advance directive which is both valid and relevant to the treatment in question ...
> [then] his *decision to require the provision* of ANH which he believes is necessary to
> protect him from what he sees as acute mental and physical suffering is ... in principle
> determinative.[69]

This was another step too far for the Court of Appeal. It held that the common law position on advance requests was identical to that under the Mental
Capacity Act 2005.[70] The 2005 Act was said to regard advance requests as

---

[67] HC [22].
[68] HC [175].
[69] HC [169].
[70] CA [57].

an important consideration when assessing what is in the best interests of a patient (under section 4(6)(a)), but not to give advance requests the binding force granted to advance refusals under section 26. The Court of Appeal did not analyse section 26 in any depth. The section itself does not actually state that an applicable advance refusal is binding; rather section 26(1) states that a valid and applicable advance decision 'has the effect as if he had made it, and had had capacity to make it, at the time when the question arises whether the treatment should be carried out or continued'. In other words, all section 26 does is say that a valid and applicable advance refusal has the same effect as a valid contemporaneous refusal and it is the common law that says that a valid contemporaneous refusal is binding.[71]

Subsequent case law has confirmed that where the 2005 Act offers equivalent protection to the common law, its provisions replace the common law;[72] but the common law may nonetheless extend protection to persons beyond that offered by the Act.[73] Further, under section 3 of the Human Rights Act 1998, the provisions of the 2005 Act must be read to give effect, as far as possible, to the Convention rights. Thus, it remains possible for the courts to recognise advance requests for ANH to be given to patients in the final stage of their lives as having binding force. The case law as it stands does not support such a position, but we have already seen that the best interest test is now recognised as giving much greater weight to a patient's previous wishes than had been accepted by the Court of Appeal in *Burke*.

Consider *X Primary Care Trust v XB*.[74] Theis J was concerned not with an advance request for treatment as in *Burke*, but with an advance refusal; nonetheless, his Lordship's approach to the previous wishes of the now incapacitated patient is instructive. First, Theis J relied on oral evidence as to the patient's wishes to interpret references to 'non-invasive ventilation' in his written advance refusal to refer to an invasive ventilation device, which involved a tube being passed into his windpipe. Secondly, his Lordship declined to treat the words 'valid until' followed by a now expired date as indicating that the advance refusal was time-limited on the basis that such an interpretation did not represent the patient's view. Theis J thereby sought to give maximal recognition to the patient's actual will when interpreting his advance directive. This stands in complete contrast to the Court of Appeal in *Burke*, which was not even willing to interpret Burke's statements as an advance directive.

---

[71] See eg *Re T* [1993] Fam 95 and *Re B* [2002] EWHC 429.

[72] Eg *ZH v Metropolitan Police Commissioner* [2012] EWHC 604, [44].

[73] Eg *Re L* [2012] EWCA Civ 253, where the Court of Appeal confirmed that the court could intervene to protect an adult who *just* satisfies the 2005 Act's capacity test (and therefore falls outside of the Act), but is unable to exercise an autonomous choice because of factors such as coercion and undue influence.

[74] *X Primary Care Trust v XB* [2012] EWHC 1390.

## VI. THE NEED TO INVOLVE THE COURT

Munby J declared that there were a number of situations where it would be unlawful to withdraw ANH from an incapacitated patient without judicial sanction.[75] One such situation was where a doctor wishes to withdraw or withhold ANH where the evidence suggests that the patient when capacitated would have wanted it to continue in the relevant circumstances.[76] His Lordship was of the view that the ECtHR's decision on Article 8 in *Glass v UK*[77] had transformed what was previously only a requirement of good practice into a legal requirement.[78] According to the Court of Appeal, however, Munby J was simply wrong to postulate such a legal duty. *Glass v UK* was said to have considered the implications of the doctors' conduct in the light of Strasbourg's understanding of English law and the specific situation in *Glass* had concerned a child.[79] When it comes to incapacitated adults, the Court was said to have the power to declare the legal position but not to change it.[80] A declaration merely specifies what may take place with or without a declaration. There were situations where it was 'advisable' for a doctor to seek court approval. The House of Lords in *Bland* had given withdrawal of ANH from a patient in PVS as an example of where court approval should be obtained '*as a matter of good practice*'.[81]

The Court of Appeal thereby expressly rejected the idea that it had lawmaking functions,[82] at least in this context:

> So far as the criminal law is concerned, the court has no power to authorise that which would otherwise be unlawful ... Nor can the court render unlawful that which would otherwise be lawful. The same is true in relation to a possible infringement of civil law.[83]

The ECtHR saw no reason to doubt that this view was in accordance with Burke's Convention rights. The Strasbourg court was satisfied that a doctor was 'fully subject to the sanctions of criminal and civil law' and was therefore only recommended to obtain legal advice 'where a step is controversial in some way'. The Court declared:

> Any more stringent legal duty would be prescriptively burdensome—doctors, and emergency ward staff in particular, would be constantly in court—and would not necessarily entail any greater protection.

---

[75] HC [202].

[76] HC [214].

[77] *Glass v United Kingdom* [2004] 1 FLR 1019 (2004) 39 EHRR 15.

[78] HC [210].

[79] CA [75]–[80].

[80] CA [71].

[81] CA [71].

[82] Compare the interpretative theory of law, see eg R Dworkin, *Law's Empire* (Oxford, Hart Publishing, 1986), and the declaratory theory of law, see eg A Beever, 'The Declaratory Theory of Law' (2013) 33 *Oxford Journal of Legal Studies* 421.

[83] CA [71].

The ECtHR thereby accepted the debate as framed by the Court of Appeal, which focused on whether the need to involve the court was a matter of good practice or a legal requirement.

The Court of Appeal placed some emphasis on the Intensive Care Society's estimation that the application of Munby J's criteria would lead to around 10 applications a day being made to the courts.[84] Resource issues thereby seemed to have influenced Court of Appeal's view that Burke was not entitled to impartial adjudication if stage 2 were to give rise to a conflict between his desires and clinical opinion on the continued provision of ANH. Not only did Burke not have a right to ANH, he did not even have a right to judicial consideration of his case. The Court of Appeal's approach unfortunately meant that it did not consider it necessary to opine on when a step would be sufficiently controversial to render it good practice to seek a declaration. It was, however, apparent that its list would have been much shorter than Munby J's, because it suggested that Burke would not have brought his case before the court had he been 'well advised'.[85] The Court of Appeal should, at the very least, have recognised that patients in what we would now call 'a minimally conscious state' are more vulnerable when it comes to the withdrawal of ANH than patients in PVS.

## VII. CONCLUSION

The general direction of medical law over the last few decades has been away from medical paternalism towards patient autonomy.[86] *Burke* represents a notable exception, save for Munby J's 'path-breaking' judgment'.[87] The issue is not that patients must always have what they want, which Lady Hale was right to reject as an unrealistic goal. The Court of Appeal, however, left patients like Burke to live in fear that when they reach the point of being aware but unable to complain about their thirst and hunger—a point at which they could hardly be more vulnerable—their desire for continued ANH could be sacrificed on the basis of clinical opinion without the need for impartial adjudication. The recent Supreme Court decision in *Aintree* at least offers reassurance that the best interest test is to be interpreted from the viewpoint of such patients, giving their previously expressed wishes particular weight.

---

[84] CA [69].
[85] CA [13].
[86] See Pattinson (n 10 above), chs 4 and 5.
[87] P Fennell, 'The Right to Require Life-Prolonging Treatment' (2004) 12 *Medical Law Review* 306, 315.

# 13

# The Right to Die and the Right to Help: *R (on the Application of Purdy) v Director of Public Prosecutions* [2009] and Its Legacy

KATE GREASLEY

## I. BACKGROUND: EUTHANASIA AND ASSISTED DYING IN ENGLISH LAW

### A. Euthanasia

THE LABELS 'MERCY killing' and 'euthanasia' are commonly used to define a particular category of homicide whereby the perpetrator acts out of altruistic motives, and usually at the behest of the victim, to end the victim's intolerable suffering, typically as a result of terminal or chronic illness. Despite changing attitudes toward euthanasia in recent times, its legal status has remained unchanged. While euthanasia is generally viewed as set apart from other kinds of homicide, it is still dealt with under the usual law of murder or (if mitigating features apply) manslaughter. Murder is defined in English law as the killing of another human being with the intention to kill or cause serious bodily harm, and no exception is made where the killer's motive is to end the victim's suffering. In one scenario, however, an exception to the usual inference of an *intention* to kill is made: a doctor is not deemed to have intended a patient's death if she prescribes treatment for the purposes of relieving pain and suffering, but with the known side-effect of hastening that patient's death. This is known as the 'doctrine of double-effect', and effectively immunises doctors who provide lethal doses of pain medication to dying patients from murder or manslaughter liability.[1]

---

[1] See *Airedale NHS Trust v Bland* [1993] AC 789 (Lord Goff of Chieveley), [867]. Discussed in chapter 5 of this volume.

In contrast to positive acts of killing, which are almost always prohibited in English law, medical staff *are* permitted to withdraw life-sustaining treatment or to refrain from a life-saving intervention either where treatment is not deemed to be in an incompetent patient's best interests, or where a patient competently refuses consent for such treatment. The crucial difference between a positive act of killing and *omitting* to save a patient through medical intervention was underscored by the House of Lords in *Airedale NHS Trust v Bland*, where it was held that the doctors caring for a man in a permanent vegetative state were permitted to withdraw life-sustaining artificial nutrition and hydration which was deemed not to be in his best interests, but that they would not have been permitted to kill him through positive intervention by switching off his life-support machine.[2] As Lord Browne-Wilkinson clarified, 'the doing of a positive act with the intention of ending life is and remains murder'.[3]

Further to this, however, medical practitioners are legally prohibited from providing or continuing treatment wherever a competent patient refuses that treatment, whether or not it is thought to be in her best interests. Thus, in *Re B*, the doctors of a tetraplegic woman who was dependent on artificial ventilation to breathe and wished for it to be turned off were ordered by the Court to carry out her wishes, her mental capacity not being in question.[4] Delivering the judgment, Dame Butler-Sloss P expressed regret that the woman had made a decision that would result in the ending of her life, even imploring her to reconsider, yet concluded that the continued artificial ventilation against her wishes constituted an unlawful assault on her body. It is apparent from this that the legal permissibility of withdrawing life-sustaining treatment in many cases is simply the reverse-side of the law of medical consent. As is well known to medical lawyers, any non-consensual treatment of a competent patient will constitute an assault, even if that treatment is necessary to preserve the patient's very life (see also, *S v St George's Hospital Trust*).[5]

## B. Assisting and Encouraging Suicide

The legal regulation of assisting or encouraging another person to commit suicide is set apart from that governing euthanasia. The Suicide Act 1961 abolished suicide as a crime, but criminalised the act of assisting another to commit suicide as a separate indictable offence under section 2(1). Since

---

[2] ibid.
[3] ibid [885].
[4] *Re B (Adult, refusal of medical treatment)* [2002] 2 All ER 449.
[5] *S v St George's Hospital Trust* [1998] 3 All ER 673. Discussed in chapter 8 of this volume.

amended by the Coroners and Justice Act 2009,[6] section 2(1) provides that a person ('D') commits an offence if:

(a)   D does an act capable of encouraging or assisting the suicide or attempted suicide of another person, and

(b)   D's act was intended to encourage or assist suicide or an attempt at suicide.[7]

Section 1(c) of the 1961 Act provides that the offence is punishable with up to 14 years' imprisonment, although section 2(4) forbids any charges under the offence from being brought without the consent of the Director of Public Prosecutions (DPP). The existence and exercise of this prosecutorial discretion has been, and continues to be, a pivotal issue in the law of assisted suicide and, as we shall see, was a core issue in the *Purdy* decision itself. While section 2(1) criminalises all instances of encouraging or assisting suicide without exception, the prosecutorial record tells a different story. Before the *Purdy* litigation, no prosecution had yet been brought against a person who had assisted a loved one to travel abroad in order to end her life with the help of professionals at a specialised clinic (usually in Switzerland). In the *Purdy* judgment itself, it was noted (by Lord Hope) that only eight such cases of a known 115 had even been referred to the DPP for a decision on a possible prosecution.[8] In effect, the DPP had adopted an unofficial policy of declining to prosecute those who compassionately assisted in the suicide of loved ones who, owing to intolerable pain or suffering, had implored help to end their lives—what I will call 'compassionate assistance cases'. This specific kind of section 2(1) transgression was, at least informally, treated as being outwith the scope of the crime's mischief. In short, the DPP had instituted a policy of wilful blindness toward breaches of section 2(1) in compassionate assistance cases.

The reasons behind prosecutorial leniency in compassionate assistance cases are, of course, readily apparent. At least a large segment of public opinion, if not the wealth of it, vehemently opposes the penalisation of those who, in tragic circumstances, accede to the request of a loved one to assist them in dying, often at great personal cost. For supporters of a legal right to die, however, the unofficial policy of non-prosecution was not an acceptable solution. Objections to the state of the law ran along two main tracks. In the first place, it was argued that the very existence of criminal liability for assisting suicide in cases where the 'victim' requests help to end her suffering constituted an unlawful interference with that individual's rights under the

---

[6]   Coroners and Justice Act 2009, s 59(2).

[7]   At the time of the House of Lords judgment in *Purdy*, the relevant section, in its yet to be amended form, read that a crime is committed where one person 'aids, abets, counsels or procures' the suicide of another.

[8]   *R (on the application of Purdy) v Director of Public Prosecutions* [2009] UKHL 45 (Lord Hope), [30].

European Convention, including the Article 8 right to private and family life. In the second place, a significant amount of disquiet was expressed about the unofficial nature of the DPP's policy, which, it was argued, breached standards of fair warning and consistency in the law. These arguments were put to the House of Lords in *R (Pretty) v DPP*.[9] Diane Pretty, the appellant, suffered from motor neurone disease, an incurable and degenerative illness that was rendering her increasingly debilitated. Pretty had sought confirmation from the DPP that her husband would not be prosecuted if he assisted her suicide by accompanying her to a Swiss suicide clinic. When the DPP refused to give her that confirmation, she complained that his refusal to grant her certainty, along with the prohibition on assisting suicide in the 1961 Act, violated a number of her Convention rights. A key contention was that the Article 8 right to respect for private and family life encompassed the right to end one's life prematurely, in the manner and timing of one's own choosing.

The House of Lords rejected Pretty's claim that her desire to end her life engaged her right under Article 8 or any other Convention right. The value of personal autonomy protected by Article 8, it argued, did not encompass choosing one's own death. It was further judged that even if the right to private and family life was at stake, the government 'had shown ample grounds to justify the existing law and the current application of it'.[10]

Pretty subsequently applied to the European Court of Human Rights for review of the House of Lords decision. In *Pretty v UK*,[11] the ECtHR diverged from the House of Lords' conclusion on the engagement of Article 8, holding that Pretty's desire to end her life did indeed invoke her rights under that article. However, it went on to argue that insofar as Pretty's Article 8 right was infringed by the ban on assisted suicide, that infringement was justified under Article 8(2) of the Convention as a necessary and proportionate restriction which was in the public interest. The nature of that interest was, in the Court's words, 'to safeguard life by protecting the weak and vulnerable and especially those who are not in a condition to take informed decisions against acts intended to end life or to assist in ending life'.[12] The Court found that the need to protect vulnerable people from potential abuses that might occur were the general prohibition to be lifted justified the section 2(1) offence as 'necessary in a democratic society', notwithstanding that it placed limitations on the Article 8 rights of some, like Pretty.[13]

The Court was not persuaded by Pretty's further contentions that even if the law was directed at the legitimate aim of public protection, the blanket

---

[9] *R (on the application of Pretty) v Director of Public Prosecutions* [2001] UKHL 61.
[10] ibid (Lord Bingham), [30].
[11] *Pretty v United Kingdom* (2002) 35 EHRR 1.
[12] ibid [74].
[13] ibid [78].

ban on assisted suicide contained in section 2(1) was a disproportionate means of securing that aim. In determining that the blanket ban was indeed a proportionate measure, the Court drew attention to the fact that even though the law admitted of no exceptions, prosecutorial discretion meant that the DPP could refrain from prosecuting where clearly inappropriate. Consequently, the English law's prohibition of assisted suicide was judged to be compatible with Convention rights.

## II. THE *PURDY* DECISION

A few years following the *Pretty* litigation, the law's stance on assisted suicide came back under the spotlight. In December 2008, the DPP publicly announced his decision not to prosecute the family and friends of a 23-year-old rugby player, Daniel James, who had employed their assistance in ending his life after he had been left permanently paralysed by a training accident. James's parents had helped him to travel to a Swiss euthanasia clinic in order to die. The DPP took the novel action of promulgating the reasons that had informed his decision not to prosecute in this particular case.[14] Among them were the facts that James was possessed of full mental capacity and that his parents had not encouraged his suicide, but, rather, had persistently discouraged his wish to die, which greatly distressed them, before finally relenting and helping him.

Debbie Purdy first brought her case only shortly before the James statement was issued. Purdy suffered from multiple sclerosis, a progressive and incurable disease which works by attacking the nervous system. Like Diane Pretty, she anticipated a time when her life would become intolerable, and applied to the High Court for an order that her husband, Mr Puente, would not face charges under the Suicide Act if he accompanied her abroad to a suicide clinic. The High Court declined the order, whereupon Purdy took her case to the Court of Appeal, on similar grounds as had been argued in the *Pretty* case.[15] The Court of Appeal declined to hold that Purdy's Article 8 right was engaged by the legal prohibition on assisted suicide, despite the ECtHR ruling to the contrary, regarding itself as bound by the earlier House of Lords decision. A second, and somewhat separate, claim made by Purdy's counsel was that the DPP's refusal to clarify his policy on prosecuting section 2(1) offenders in compassionate assistance cases rendered the ban not in accordance with law, since there was insufficient fair warning of the repercussions of assisting suicide. The Court of Appeal also rejected this claim. The problem with the argument, in the view of Lord Judge CJ, was

---

[14] See K Starmer, 'Decision on Prosecution—The Death by Suicide of Daniel James' (9 December 2008): www.cps.gov.uk/news/articles/death_by_suicide_of_daniel_james.
[15] *R (on the application of Purdy) v Director of Public Prosecutions* [2009] EWCA Civ 92.

that liability under section 2(1) was perfectly clear. Hence, Purdy was not seeking clarification of the *law*, but was instead seeking assurance about the way in which prosecutorial discretion would be exercised in her husband's case. Although the Court expressed sympathy for the 'dreadful predicament' in which the couple found themselves, it did not accept the argument that the DPP's refusal to guarantee Mr Puente immunity from prosecution breached standards of foreseeability in the law.

Unsuccessful in the Court of Appeal, Purdy appealed to the House of Lords, where a markedly different decision was given.[16] Departing from its earlier decision in *Pretty*, the Court followed the Strasbourg ruling in upholding Purdy's claim that the general prohibition on assisted suicide infringed her Article 8 rights to private and family life, as well as holding, unanimously, that the DPP was under a legal duty to issue formal guidelines on the prosecution of section 2(1) offenders. Giving the main judgment, Lord Hope expressed his clear preference for the approach of the ECtHR in *Pretty*, which recognised that the right to private life and self-determination encompassed the right not to be 'forced to linger on in old age or in states of advanced physical or mental decrepitude which conflict with strongly held ideas of self and personal identity'.[17]

Like the Strasbourg court, the Lords therefore had next to consider whether the interference with the Article 8 right was 'in accordance with law' by being 'necessary in a democratic society', pursuant to Article 8(2) of the Convention. The Court's understanding of what was required for compliance with Article 8(2) was key to its conclusion that the DPP needed to formalise his policy. As Lord Hope explained, the Convention principle of legality requires rules to be sufficiently precise, accessible, and foreseeable to those affected by them. Hence, given that a Convention right was infringed by the section 2(1) offence, Ms Purdy was entitled to expect a considerable degree of certainty regarding the consequences of law-breaking. This, in turn, required that 'the law must indicate with sufficient clarity the scope of any such discretion conferred on the competent authorities and the manner of its exercise'.[18] In short, Lord Hope argued that the standards of foreseeability and clarity that are required of any law limiting a Convention right are equally required of *prosecutorial discretion* relating to that law.

The only question left to ask, therefore, was whether the DPP's policy as it stood provided clear enough guidance to Debbie Purdy and her husband to meet the Convention standard of legality. The Court's answer was that it did not. This part of its reasoning focused on the level of guidance contained in the Code for Crown Prosecutors—a written code outlining general guiding principles for prosecutors in the exercise of their discretion. The DPP argued

---

[16]  *R (Purdy)* (HL) (n 8 above).
[17]  *Pretty* (n 11 above) [36].
[18]  *Purdy* (n 8 above) (Lord Hope) [43].

that the guidance issued in the Code was sufficient to meet the relevant standards of clarity and foreseeability. The Law Lords disagreed. Since the Code applied indistinctly to all crimes, they said, it did not reveal enough about the likelihood of prosecution for the specific offence of assisting suicide, which would require an indication of the factors likely to be taken into account in those prosecutorial decisions. In this respect, the Daniel James decision was held up as a case in point. The DPP's release of a public policy statement explaining his decision not to prosecute James's assistants was regarded as testament to the fact that the general Code fell short of offering guidance that could explain offence-specific decisions. In conclusion, it was held that the DPP was required to 'promulgate an offence-specific policy' which outlined the circumstances tending in favour of and against the prosecution of those who assist or encourage suicide.[19]

All in all, the *Purdy* decision brought about no substantive change in the English law of assisted suicide. Section 2(1) of the Suicide Act remained in place and was not declared to be incompatible with any Convention rights. No legal exception to section 2(1) was recognised—at least formally speaking, it continued to apply equally to those who assisted in the deaths of terminally ill family members. The main outcome of the case was instead that a previously unofficial policy of deciding against prosecution in situations like Purdy's was ordered to be made more official through codification. At the core of the decision were two foundational premises: that the Article 8 right to private and family life is compromised by the criminalisation of assisted suicide, and that clarification of the prosecutorial policy was one of the things needed to bring that criminal prohibition in accordance with law.

### III. AFTERMATH AND THE *NICKLINSON* LITIGATION

In the wake of the House of Lords ruling in *Purdy*, a number of critical developments in the law of, and public debate about, assisted suicide unfolded. First, in response to the judicial ruling, the DPP penned the ordered 'Policy for Prosecutors in Respect of Cases of Encouraging or Assisting Suicide' ('the 2010 policy').[20] The policy listed a wide array of factors tending both towards and against a public interest in prosecuting section 2(1) offenders. Factors leaning in favour of prosecution included a victim's lack of capacity to form a voluntary, informed and settled intention to commit suicide; any pressure to commit suicide directed at the victim by the suspect, or non-altruistic motives harboured by the suspect, for example, the prospect of gaining financially from the death of the victim. On the other side, factors

---

[19] ibid [56].
[20] The policy in full can be found at: www.cps.gov.uk/publications/prosecution/assisted_suicide_policy.html.

tending against prosecution included evidence that the suspect was 'wholly motivated by compassion', that the suspect had sought to dissuade the victim from her chosen course of committing suicide, and that the suspect had reported the suicide to the police and fully assisted them with their enquiries. In the introduction, the 2010 policy clarified that it did not in any way 'decriminalise' the offence of encouraging or assisting suicide, and that nothing within it should be taken to amount to assurance that a person will be 'immune' from prosecution if he or she breaks the law in section 2(1). The policy also stated that the list of public interest factors provided was not 'exhaustive', and that each case would still be considered on its individual merits.

For many, Debbie Purdy's court battle was taken as yet another indication of the dire necessity of change in the law of assisted suicide. In September 2010, a commission was convened by Lord Falconer to consider at length whether the current legal situation was adequate, or whether there was a compelling case for law reform. Lord Falconer had already proposed a liberalising amendment to the law of assisted suicide during debate about the 2009 Coroners and Justice Act, which, if adopted, would have struck out certain forms of assisting suicide from the remit of section 2(1). That amendment was rejected by 194 votes to 141.[21] Now, with the momentum of *Purdy* behind it, the Falconer Commission spent over a year hearing evidence and arguments both for and against law reform, and making case study visits to jurisdictions like the Netherlands and Oregon in the United States, where the blanket ban on assisted dying has been lifted.

In a document that spanned 400 pages, the commission concluded that the current legal status of assisted dying was 'inadequate and incoherent' and that there was a strong case for providing the choice of assisted death to terminally ill people, within the confines of carefully worked out eligibility criteria and safeguards.[22] Key elements of these criteria included conditions that the patient must be at least 18 years of age, suffering from a terminal illness, and demonstrating a clear and settled intention to die, checked by the requirement of a minimum two-week gap between the initial request to die and the final act of death. It was also proposed that this final act must be taken, or at the very least assisted, by the patient herself. In other words, only assisted suicide, and not any form of voluntary euthanasia, was envisioned by the commission as apt for partial decriminalisation. The authority of the commission's conclusions were, however, somewhat compromised by suggestions that the commissioners were predisposed to advocating law reform. Nine of the twelve had publicly stated their commitment to a change in the law of assisted suicide at some point before the panel was convened. Moreover, the

---

[21] HL Deb vol 712 cols 596–643 (7 July 2009).
[22] 'The Commission on Assisted Dying' (2011), *Demos*: www.demos.co.uk/files/476_CoAD_FinalReport_158x240_I_web_single-NEW_.pdf?1328113363.

commission was not a government initiative, but was initiated and financed by two public figures (Terry Pratchett and Bernard Lewis), both of whom are avowed proponents of the legalisation of assisted suicide. In fact, a number of respectable organisations and individuals (the British Medical Association among them) refused to give evidence to the commission because of concerns about the terms on which it was proceeding.

Lastly, the House of Lords' decision in *Purdy* was significant in paving the way for the next and most recent saga of court challenge to the law of assisted suicide: the *Nicklinson* case. Tony Nicklinson was a man in his early fifties who, as a result of a stroke, suffered from what is known as 'locked-in syndrome'. The condition rendered him completely paralysed and unable to speak, with his entire bodily movements limited to blinking. Finding his condition unbearable, Nicklinson wished to end his life, though he required the help of others to do so. He initially took his case to the High Court, arguing that the very limited necessity (or, 'lesser of two evils') defence to murder in English law would be available to doctors who ended his life at his request. He also sought a declaration that the law of assisted suicide as it stood was incompatible with his Article 8 right to private life, as Pretty and Purdy had done before him. Predictably, the High Court rejected the argument that voluntary euthanasia could be a form of necessity killing and hence outwith the category of murder.[23]

Immediately after his claim was rejected in the High Court, Nicklinson took the decision to refuse all food, which shortly after led to his death. His wife, Jane, was given leave to appeal the ruling on his behalf, but was met with the same result in the Court of Appeal.[24] Regarding the Article 8 claim, Toulson LJ considered that the question of the compatibility of section 2(1) with the Convention right had already been determined by the judiciary 'at the highest level', but that he would have rejected Nicklinson's claim in any eventuality, on the ground that the UK had a wide 'margin of appreciation' under European law when framing its law of assisted suicide, and that legal change was a matter for Parliament.

Jane Nicklinson's last stop was the Supreme Court, which handed down judgment in July 2014.[25] Nicklinson's claims were joined together with those of another claimant, Paul Lamb, and a man anonymously referred to as 'Martin', both of whom suffered from conditions of severe paralysis similar to that of Tony Nicklinson, and wanted help to end their lives.[26]

[23] *R (on the application of Nicklinson) v Ministry of Justice* [2012] EWHC 304 (QB).
[24] *R (on the application of Nicklinson) v Ministry of Justice; R (on the application of AM) v Director of Public Prosecutions* [2012] EWHC 2381 (Admin).
[25] *R (on the application of Nicklinson and Another) v Ministry of Justice; R (AM) v Director of Public Prosecutions* [2014] UKSC 38.
[26] Martin's claims had in fact already been joined to the *Nicklinson* appeal at the earlier Court of Appeal stage.

Jane Nicklinson and Lamb argued that the current ban on assisted suicide, which made no exception for people in intolerable suffering and expressing a settled wish to die, was a disproportionate and hence unjustified interference with Lamb and Tony Nicklinson's Article 8 rights. Martin's argument was somewhat different, and reintroduced the issue of prosecutorial policy. In a continuation of the argument that gave rise to the judgment in *Purdy*, he claimed that the terms of the 2010 policy were still insufficiently clear, since it did not give specific guidance about the likely prosecution of healthcare professionals or carers who assisted people to die.

A full panel of nine Supreme Court justices considered the claims of the three appellants. Nicklinson and Lamb's appeals were dismissed by a majority of 7-2. Following the reasoning in the *Purdy* judgment, it was the Court's unanimous view that section 2(1) of the Suicide Act does indeed interfere with the Article 8 rights of British citizens who wish to control the manner and timing of their own deaths, but who require help to do so. However, the majority nevertheless rejected the appeals on the ground that it was for Parliament to decide whether the current law was inconsistent with those rights and to amend it accordingly. Four of the justices believed that the Court lacked the constitutional authority to make a determination on whether the law of assisted suicide was incompatible with Article 8, and that it should respect Parliament's own assessment on a matter about which it is better qualified to decide. The other five judges all accepted that the Court had the constitutional competence to make a declaration of incompatibility on an issue such as assisted suicide. However, three of the five (Lord Mance, Lord Neuberger, and Lord Wilson) thought that it would still be inappropriate for the Court to make such a declaration before giving Parliament an opportunity to reconsider and amend the law in light of the present judgment. Only two of the justices, Lady Hale and Lord Kerr, were prepared to issue a declaration of incompatibility, holding that, in making no exception for those who had expressed a settled and voluntary wish to die, the current ban was clearly incompatible with Article 8, since it constituted a disproportionate interference with the right.

On the Martin question, the judges were unified in siding with the DPP and holding that the 2010 policy did not need to be clarified any further in order to be in accordance with law. The Court drew a crucial distinction between the *Purdy* principle, which stated that the DPP must publish his policy to meet the Convention requirements of foreseeability, and the suggestion that the Court could dictate what needed to be in that policy. It concluded that requiring the DPP to indicate the relevant factors in prosecutorial decisions was the most the Court could do. In effect, therefore, the Court's ruling on Martin's claim established a limit on the main principle to come out of *Purdy*, and on the level of detail required for the DPP's policy to be sufficiently clear.

## IV. PROSECUTORIAL DISCRETION AND STANDARDS OF FORESEEABILITY

### A. Clarification or Advance Exemption?

As was seen, the central ruling in *Purdy*—subsequently endorsed by the Supreme Court in *Nicklinson*—was that the DPP fell under a legal requirement to publish his prosecutorial policy in relation to encouraging or assisting suicide in order to meet standards of clarity and foreseeability. An unofficial policy of wilful blindness when it came to the compassionate assistance cases was not good enough; interested parties such as Purdy and her husband had to be furnished with more information about what would influence the decision whether or not to prosecute assistants. In short, the claimants had demanded a right to anticipate with greater certainty what the outcome would be, and the House of Lords had acceded that demand.

By rejecting Martin's claim in *Nicklinson,* the Supreme Court appeared to impose a limit on the *Purdy* principle, whilst affirming its basic validity. While it was correct that the DPP must publicise his policy in order for the ban on assisted dying to be in accordance with law, it was not necessary for him or (by then) her to include specific guidance about how the prosecution service would treat assistants of suicide that are neither family members nor close friends of the 'victim'. The promulgation of general factors tending towards or against prosecution was sufficient to meet the applicable standards of foreseeability and clarity.

With the notable exception of Lord Hughes, the original *Purdy* principle was not doubted by the *Nicklinson* court. The crucial question surrounding that original principle was whether fair warning in the law requires fair warning of how prosecutorial discretion is likely to be exercised when section 2(1) offences are committed. From one perspective, the affirmative answer to that question given in *Purdy* may seem odd, given the continuing criminalisation of assisted suicide. In spite of the Court's insistence that the promulgation of the DPP's policy would not amount to a guarantee of immunity for any section 2(1) offenders, the rationale for the order seemed to rest on the need to provide greater certainty to those contemplating committing the offence. On the face of it, however, there is a certain tension between the argument based on foreseeability of prosecution and the retention of the section 2(1) offence without any formal exceptions. That tension might be drawn out through an analogy with advance reliance on an excuse.

Excuses in criminal law serve to reduce the liability or punishment of an offender based on mitigating factors which indicate that, while her act was still criminally wrong, it was less blameworthy than paradigmatic contraventions of the given prohibition.[27] If this is indeed the theoretical underpinning for excuses, it follows that the blame-reducing factors giving rise to an excuse cannot reduce blame in the same way if an offender relies on them in advance of the offence, especially so if that reliance is instrumental to her decision to commit the offence in the first place. Granting the offender the benefit of the excuse in such a scenario would effectively transform the excusatory factors from reasons for mitigation to a qualification of the offence where particular features were present. In a similar vein, it could be argued that by ordering formal clarification of factors tending against the prosecution of assisted suicide, the *Purdy* court was effectively ordering prospective assurance for section 2(1) offenders, where it was the case that *retrospective* lenience would probably be shown. Rather than amounting to prosecutorial leniency where the perpetrator was not thought to be blameworthy, the effect of the new policy, it might be argued, was that of creating an unofficial exception to the offence, in which circumstances those wishing to break the law might act in confidence of being shielded from liability.

Were this true, it would not in any way cut against the widely held view that the prosecution of assistants in cases like Debbie Purdy's is indeed wholly inappropriate; nor would it cast doubt upon the altruistic motivation of assistants in those cases. Nevertheless, if the particular features of *Purdy*-like cases are meant only to militate against a public interest in prosecution, not to qualify the offence, it might be thought that granting the offender prior assurance of their ameliorating impact is incongruent with the legal status of assisted suicide.

Giving his judgment in *Nicklinson*, Lord Hughes was drawn to this view of the *Purdy* principle, remarking that the House of Lords in *Purdy* had neglected a vital distinction between 'examination after the event of all the facts of a case and advance exemption from the law of particular kinds of offending'.[28] While he acknowledged that there must surely be section 2(1) offenders whom it is not in the public interest to prosecute, he pointed out that this is true of 'every offence in the criminal calendar'.[29] In his view, however, the DPP could not identify that category of persons in advance without 'crossing the constitutional boundary' and granting advance exemption to a group of potential offenders. Regarding standards of foreseeability, he argued that the only knowledge to which section 2(1) offenders were entitled was simply the knowledge that the prosecutor will examine all the facts of any given case, and decide on the merits of the case whether it is in the

---

[27] For developed accounts of the nature of excuses, see JL Austin, 'A Plea for Excuses' in JO Urmson and GJ Warnock (eds), *Austin, Philosophical Papers*, 3rd edn (Oxford, Oxford University Press, 1979) 85; J Gardner, 'The Gist of Excuses' (1997) 2 *Buffalo Criminal Law Review* 575; and J Horder, 'Excusing Crime' (Oxford, Oxford University Press, 2004).
[28] *Nicklinson* (n 25 above) (Lord Hughes) [276].
[29] ibid [277].

public interest to pursue prosecution.[30] In his view, it was not incumbent on the state to provide an answer to the question 'What is the likelihood of prosecution?' to someone contemplating assisting someone to commit suicide, as a matter of foreseeability in the law.

Purdy's demand for a clearer prosecutorial policy seemed to have even more the characteristic of an effective request for guaranteed immunity in her husband's case when viewed in the light of the DPP's track record in prosecuting similar cases. As Lord Hope highlighted in his judgment, at the time Purdy's case was being considered, no prosecution had yet been brought against an abettor of 'suicide-tourism', and only eight cases out of a known 115 had even been referred to the DPP for a decision on prosecution.[31] Similarly, in *Nicklinson*, Lord Neuberger underscored the DPP's evidence that there had, in fact, only ever been one successful prosecution under section 2(1). In that case, the defendant had provided petrol and a lighter to a vulnerable man known to be suicidal, and who suffered serious burns as a result.[32] The DPP had also informed the *Nicklinson* court that between 1998 and 2011, a total of 215 people in the UK had used the services of the Dignitas assisted dying clinic in Switzerland, and that no one had been prosecuted for providing assistance in connection with those cases.[33] Judging from this record, there seemed to be little practical doubt about what the prosecution decision would have been, had Purdy's husband assisted her in travelling abroad to die. If Mr Puente had been prosecuted, he would have been the first assistant out of hundreds to face such consequences in such circumstances.

Had even a very small number of compassionate assistants been prosecuted for their actions, Purdy's claim that the Director's policy was insufficiently clear would have been more credible. As it stood, her claim that there was a lack of clarity as to what would happen in her husband's case was true only formally speaking. In his *Purdy* judgment, Lord Neuberger even referred to the legal debate at hand as having a 'slight air of unreality', given that it should have by then been so clear to Ms Purdy that her husband would not be prosecuted, particularly in light of the Daniel James statement.[34] The informal policy was unmistakably clear; the only thing that did not exist was official assurance that her husband would not be prosecuted.

However, looking more closely at Lord Hope's majority judgment in *Purdy*, it might be suggested that it was not so much the clarity of the prosecutorial policy that was at issue, as the forward-looking need to ensure consistency of practice and protect against the arbitrary exercise of

---

[30] ibid [278].
[31] *Purdy* (n 8 above) (Lord Hope) [30].
[32] *Nicklinson* (n 25 above) (Lord Neuberger) [48].
[33] ibid.
[34] *Purdy* (n 8 above) (Lord Neuberger) [97].

prosecutorial discretion. Lord Hope reasoned that a law which confers discretion as to prosecution does not necessarily fall short of the requirement for foreseeability, provided that the 'scope of the discretion and the manner of its exercise' are indicated clearly enough to provide protection to individuals against 'arbitrary' interference.[35] Continuing this strain of reasoning in *Nicklinson*, Lord Neuberger explained the original *Purdy* principle in the following terms:

> The purpose of the DPP publishing a code or policy is not to enable those who wish to commit a crime to know in advance whether they will get away with it. It is to ensure that, as far as is possible in practice and appropriate in principle, the DPP's policy is publicly available so that everyone knows what it is, and can see whether it is being applied consistently.[36]

Consistency and non-arbitrariness are standards of justice that are, of course, applicable to prosecutorial decision-making. However, one might question whether those standards were really at issue with regard to section 2(1), particularly given the clear consistency of practice to date, which was readily acknowledged by the Court, and was in some sense even a presupposition of Purdy's argument (what she sought was formal acknowledgement of a certain prosecutorial practice which, *unofficially*, was consistently being followed). As the record had already shown, it was possible to have consistency without formal clarification; there was nothing that needed to be rectified in that respect. If the Court's reasoning was instead that a published policy would forestall the threat of future arbitrariness, the question might be raised as to why there was any greater need to protect against the arbitrary exercise of prosecutorial discretion in relation to assisting suicide, by demanding offence-specific guidance, than in relation to any other criminal offence.

## B. Distinguishing Assisted Suicide

This last point introduces another possible problem with the main principle advanced in *Purdy*. As Lord Hughes noted, it is true of every criminal offence that the prosecution service retains the discretion to decide against prosecuting offenders if it is deemed not in the public interest. But in the case of no other offence has it been suggested that the failure of the DPP to publish offence-specific guidelines for prosecution breaches standards of foreseeability and clarity in the law. It is not open to someone who is, for instance, contemplating committing theft, or assault, to demand greater clarity about the factors likely to influence the likelihood of prosecution

---

[35] *Purdy* (n 8 above) (Lord Hope) [41].
[36] *Nicklinson* (n 25 above) [141].

should they decide to commit the offence. What is different about section 2(1) of the 1961 Act?

This raises an interesting question about the uniqueness of assisted suicide as a criminal offence. In his *Purdy* judgment, Lord Neuberger drew attention to the fact that the DPP had in fact issued some statements of specific guidance in relation to the prosecution of other crimes.[37] He accepted the DPP's argument that in all such cases, the existing statements are for the benefit of the victims, not the offenders, but believed that it simply underscored the 'unusual features' of the section 2(1) offence that the potential 'victim' (Purdy) was the one seeking clarification in this instance. In his subsequent *Nicklinson* judgment, Lord Neuberger developed his explanation of the uniqueness of the section 2(1) offence and the special need for a clearly promulgated prosecutorial policy relating to it. He highlighted the particular 'importance of prosecutorial discretion in connection with assisting suicide', which owed partly to the 'public importance of' and 'public concern about' its exercise.[38] He also explained that it was because Purdy's Article 8 rights were engaged by the ban on assisted suicide (something which the *Purdy* court had acknowledged, in line with the ECtHR decision in *Pretty*) that she was entitled to clarity about the consequences of law-breaking.

The fact that Debbie Purdy herself had an interest—possibly, the main interest—in a more manifest policy can hardly be doubted. Lord Neuberger summarised the nature of that interest in *Purdy* when he said that a more detailed policy would be of 'practical value' to her, as well as providing her with some 'moral and emotional comfort' in the midst of her situation. Purdy's own stake in greater certainty as to whether her husband might be prosecuted for accompanying her to Switzerland was entirely apparent. Since her ability to end her own life depended on help from her husband, fear that he might not escape criminal liability clearly placed a limit on her exercise of self-determination, albeit indirectly.

It might be asked, however, whether it could not be just as true of other criminal prohibitions that, in certain circumstances, they have the effect of interfering with a protected right. Consider, for instance, theft carried out in circumstances in which the offender steals food in order to avoid almost certain starvation. In those conditions, the breach of the criminal prohibition on theft is the only way to protect the right to life, meaning that, in such conditions, the blanket ban on theft interferes with a protected right (Article 2 under the ECHR). Presumably, were the English Supreme Court ever to consider the claim that the blanket ban on theft is thereby incompatible with Convention rights, it would answer quite straightforwardly that because the

---

[37] *Purdy* (n 8 above) (Lord Neuberger) [104]. Specific detail of those other statements was set out by Lord Brown at para [84], and included statements about the prosecution of rape, of domestic violence, and of 'homophobic and transphobic hate crime'.

[38] *Nicklinson* (n 25 above) [39].

ban *in its blanket form* is justified and proportionate, no incompatibility results. (And one can imagine easily enough what the general thrust of the proportionality reasoning would be like: only a blanket prohibition on theft will be sufficient to protect private property.) But this would not preclude the operation of the basic *Purdy* principle. The blanket ban was deemed justified and proportionate there too, yet the Court was still of the opinion that offence-specific guidance on prosecution was needed to bring the prohibition into accordance with law. Following the *Purdy* principle, then, we might ask: could those who foresee needing to commit theft in order to advance a basic right not demand an offence-specific prosecutorial policy?

Of course, stealing to avoid imminent starvation is probably a prime example of the kind of theft it is not in the public interest to prosecute. But could it be correct that the mere potential for conflict between the blanket ban and a protected right (even one as important as the right to life) renders the prohibition on theft not in accordance with law in the absence of an offence-specific prosecutorial policy? It is difficult to imagine such an argument ever being ventured.

Some criminal offences, of course, have already been acknowledged by the ECtHR as interfering with Convention rights. In *A, B, and C v Ireland*, for example, the Court recognised that the right to private life under Article 8 was threatened by criminal liability for abortion, albeit Member States had a wide 'margin of appreciation' when it came to balancing that interference with their reasons for restricting abortion.[39] Again, however, tracing the line of reasoning developed in *Purdy*, it might seem to follow that those considering performing abortions outside of the confines of the law can claim entitlement to specific prosecution policies relating to criminal abortion offences.[40]

But there is more to the singling out of assisted suicide than the mere fact that it engages a Convention right, as Lord Neuberger indeed recognised in *Nicklinson*. As his Lordship understood it, section 2(1) was distinguished not just because the prohibition engaged Convention rights, but because, in many cases, the crime entails a 'unique combination of features, all of which point firmly towards a requirement for clear guidance'.[41] He enumerated those 'unique' features as follows:

> First, section 2(1) renders it a crime to assist someone else to do an act which is not itself in any way a crime. Secondly, the victim is not merely a willing participant, but the instigator. Thirdly, the victim's article 8 rights are interfered with *unless* the crime is committed. Fourthly, the person committing the offence will be a reluctant participant, motivated by compassion for the so-called victim, and not by emotions which normally stimulate criminal behaviour.[42]

---

[39] *A, B, and C v Ireland* [2010] ECHR 2032.
[40] These include the Offences Against the Person Act 1861, ss 58 and 59, and the Infant Life Preservation Act 1929, s 1.
[41] ibid [133].
[42] ibid.

The third feature—that the *'victim's'* rights will be interfered with unless the crime is committed—is a very uncommon feature of other criminal offences, although, it might possibly be true of some other crimes in the right conditions. Consider, for example, crimes of assault that are committed at the behest of the victim, but for which consent is no defence.[43] In cases such as these, the criminality of the act is unaffected by the victim's *consent in fact*, due to the legal inability to consent to harm above a certain degree (in English law, the threshold is that of 'actual bodily harm').[44] The contexts in which those crimes occur are most likely to be those of intimate relationships, making it at least arguable that in being unable to consent legally to harm above a certain threshold, the 'victim's' right to private life is compromised by the criminal offence. As in the case of assisted suicide, the basic infringement of the right would not be affected by the determination that the prohibition is justified for reasons of public policy; this would only mean that the infringement is in accordance with law.[45] However, were the law to acknowledge the *engagement* of the victim's rights to private life by such offences (for which a compelling case could surely be made), cases of this nature would mirror assisted suicide in respect of Lord Neuberger's third feature.

Lord Neuberger's fourth point is that the section 2(1) offenders are often 'reluctant' assistants to the crime, motivated by compassion rather than selfish interests. This can be every bit as true of voluntary and involuntary euthanasia as it is of assisted suicide, and, indeed, paradigmatically is. It is the case, as Lord Neuberger notes in his first point, that the act which section 2(1) renders it an offence to assist is not itself a crime, suicide itself having been decriminalised by the 1961 Act. However, I do not think it widely believed that the rationale behind the decriminalisation of suicide is that suicide is not a harm which ought to be avoided. If that were right, we would be hard pushed to explain all of the other, quasi-coercive methods typically used to prevent people from taking their lives, not the least: incarceration on psychiatric wards. Rather, support for the decriminalisation of suicide surely derives from the pointlessness or counter-productiveness of attaching criminal liability to those who take their own lives or attempt to do so (the latter group being in need of medical assistance, not criminal sanctions). If this is correct, the reasons for decriminalising suicide do nothing to ameliorate the reasons that exist for criminalising its assistance.

---

[43] See *R v Brown* [1994] 1 AC 212.

[44] ibid.

[45] In *R v Brown* (ibid), Lord Templeton considered and rejected the suggestion that the appellants activities, which involved inflicting minor wounds on one another for the purpose of sexual gratification, were within the remit of the right to private and family life, but argued that even if the appellants claimed to exercise such rights, Article 8 could not invalidate the prohibition, which was justified, in the court's view, to protect against a 'cult of violence'.

Lord Neuberger went on to say that it was because all four features are such likely elements of a section 2(1) offence that *Purdy* was decided the way it was. This suggests that it was not only the potential for such features to be present in a section 2(1) offence that caused Lord Neuberger to view it as so 'unique'—potential which might hold equally for a number of other offences—but the fact that the offence bears them out *typically*. When one person helps another to commit suicide, it almost always *is* the case that the 'victim' is not just a willing participant but the instigator, and that the helper acts with altruistic motives etc—or so he seemed to say. Thus, the singular nature of section 2(1) lay, for Lord Neuberger, not in its propensity to be carried out without real culpability, but in the fact that it is typically inappropriate to prosecute offenders. Of course, if prosecution of assisted suicide is not just exceptionally, but typically, inappropriate, the question might immediately be raised as to why it is apt for criminalisation at all—a broader debate that will be explored below. More than this, though, one might wonder whether underlying Lord Neuberger's remarks is a stronger claim about the general nature of assisted suicide: not just that offenders do not deserve punishment, but, perhaps, that they act within the boundaries of what is permissible—that their actions simply are not wrong. Insofar as this is believed, the burden of argumentation seems to shift to the defender of a criminal prohibition, with or without exceptions.

## V. THE WIDER DEBATE

The continuing debate over the decriminalisation of assisted dying focuses on a cluster of principled and pragmatic considerations, and has spawned a vast and still-proliferating literature.[46] In *R (Pretty) v DPP*, Lord Steyn neatly summarised the character of that debate in the following way:

> The arguments and counter-arguments have ranged widely. There is a conviction that human life is sacred and that the corollary is that euthanasia and assisted suicide are always wrong. This view is supported by the Roman Catholic Church, Islam and other religions. There is also a secular view, shared sometimes by atheists and agnostics, that human life is sacred. On the other side, there are many millions who do not hold these beliefs. For many the personal autonomy of individuals is predominant. They would argue that it is the moral right of individuals to have a say over the time and manner of their death. On the other hand, there are utilitarian arguments to the contrary effect. The terminally ill and those suffering great pain from incurable illnesses are often vulnerable. And not all families, whose

---

[46] See, among other things: J Keown, *Euthanasia, Ethics, and Public Policy: An Argument Against Legalisation* (Cambridge, Cambridge University Press, 2002) and J Keown (ed), *Euthanasia Examined* (Cambridge, Cambridge University Press, 1995); LW Sumner, *Assisted Death: A Study in Ethics and Law* (Oxford, Oxford University Press, 2013), and M Warnock and E MacDonald, *Easeful Death: Is there a Case for Assisted Dying?* (Oxford, Oxford University Press, 2008).

interests are at stake, are wholly unselfish and loving. There is a risk that assisted suicide may be abused in the sense that such people may be persuaded that they want to die or that they ought to want to die. Another strand is that, when one knows the genuine wish of a terminally ill patient to die, they should not be forced against their will to endure a life they no longer wish to endure. Such views are countered by those who say it is a slippery slope or the thin end of the wedge. It is also argued that euthanasia and assisted suicide, under medical supervision, will undermine the trust between doctors and patients. It is said that protective safe-guards are unworkable. The countervailing contentions of moral philosophers, medical experts and ordinary people are endless.[47]

It might be thought at first that the focus in *Purdy*—and, to an extent, in *Nicklinson*—on the narrow question of the DPP's obligation to pub-lish guidance detracted from many of the core issues surrounding assisted dying summarised by Lord Steyn. In fact, those considerations were at all times at the centre of discussion, and significantly informed the direction of legal argument. It was only because both courts had first acknowledged the extreme hardship endured by people in Debbie Purdy's position, owed largely to the criminal prohibition on assisted suicide, that the question of prosecutorial guidance was even at issue. Had the courts not recognised that individuals such as Purdy had a critical interest in a relaxation of the law, the legality of the prosecutorial guidance would not have been raised. Only once it made the prior determination that the ban interfered with Purdy's Article 8 right did the Court need to ask itself whether that interference was legal, and, as part of *that* inquiry, whether the exercise of prosecutorial dis-cretion needed to be predictable.

The conventional arguments against the partial decriminalisation of assisted suicide occupied just as important a place in the structure of legal argument. This was because the perceived need to protect vulnerable peo-ple from possible pressure to end their lives—pressure which might be augmented by the legality of assisted suicide—was acknowledged by all courts (the ECtHR, the House of Lords in *Purdy*, and the Supreme Court in *Nicklinson*) as the main legal justification for the general ban on assisted suicide. Without that justification, a simple determination that the ban interfered with Article 8 would have been the end of the matter, and the ban would have been declared incompatible with Convention rights. As it was, the 'legitimate aim' of protecting the vulnerable invoked the possible appli-cation of Article 8(2), making the remaining legal issue an inquiry about whether the ban met *all* of the conditions necessary to be 'in accordance with law', including proportionality, clarity and foreseeability.

In many ways, therefore, the structure of legal argument in *Purdy* and *Nicklinson* tracked the character of contemporary public debate about assisted suicide. That debate is no longer, in the main, a contest between

[47] *Pretty* (n 9 above) [54].

those who embrace an absolute principle of the sanctity of human life and those who do not, but instead a debate about how the interests some might have in a controlled death are to be balanced with the possible negative effects of relaxing the prohibition on assisted dying. In neither the court contests nor the public debate has the basic moral permissibility of helping someone like Debbie Purdy or Tony Nicklinson to die come under serious scrutiny.[48] Rather, the locus of argument has settled on the question whether it could ever be possible to provide codified exceptions to the ban on assisted dying without risking the kinds of abuses about which the Strasbourg court expressed concern in *Pretty v UK*, when it explained that it is 'the vulnerability of the class' of terminally ill people which 'provides the rationale for the law in question'.[49] The Court regarded those 'vulnerable' people as individuals who, in its words, 'are not in a position to take informed decisions against acts intended to end life or assist in ending life'.[50] In *Purdy*, Baroness Hale (as she then was) described the relevant class of people as those 'who are vulnerable to all sorts of pressures, both subtle and not so subtle, to consider their own lives a worthless burden to others'.[51]

Needless to say, defenders of partial decriminalisation usually dismiss such 'slippery slope' concerns as excessive risk-aversion or, perhaps, hysterical scaremongering. In so doing, they often point to examples of other jurisdictions where legalisation has taken place as evidence that the typical concerns are overstated.[52] Surely, if the right safeguards are only in place, and the appropriate conditions stipulated (perhaps along the lines of the Falconer Commission's recommendations), provision for legal assisted suicide in exceptional cases need not endanger any vulnerable people.

It can be a shortcoming of these rebuttals, however, that they fail to appreciate the full spectrum of the 'slippery slope' argument, which ranges from concerns about the direct manipulation and coercion of the terminally or incurably ill to more credible worries about the covert influence of decriminalisation upon general attitudes toward the severely disabled or dying, and, especially, upon the value such people place on their own lives. It is this second kind of slippery slope, far more so than the first, which presents itself as a plausible and potentially ineradicable side-effect of a change in the law. Which sorts of measures, it might be asked, could possibly protect against the operation of feelings of worthlessness or burdensomeness on an individual's clear and settled wish to die? Insofar as the legal availability of

---

[48] See *Nicklinson* (n 25 above) [90], where Lord Neuberger opined that the sanctity of life argument in fact does little other than 'replicate the concerns about the lives of the weak and vulnerable'.

[49] *Pretty v UK* (n 11 above) [64].

[50] ibid [74].

[51] *Purdy* (n 8 above) [65], quoted by Lord Mance in *Nicklinson* (n 25 above), at [81].

[52] See, for example: S Smith, 'Evidence for the Practical Slippery Slope in the Debate on Physician Assisted Suicide and Euthanasia' (2005) (13) *Medical Law Review* 17.

the option might inform such feelings, or any general attitudes that give rise to them, it is hard to imagine how such influences could possibly be screened out. A terminally or incurably ill individual whose belief that her life is no longer worth living has been partly informed by the law's hypothetical acceptance of her wish to die *can* surely look and sound the same as someone who finds her existence truly unbearable.

Lord Neuberger demonstrated a good understanding of the slippery slope concern in its more subtle form when explaining, in *Nicklinson*, that the worry about weak and vulnerable people 'has two aspects': the direct concern for those who lack the desire to die but who feel under some sort of duty to do so, and the additional fear that

> the extension of the law to permit assisted suicide would send a more general message to weak and vulnerable people, who would consequently be more at risk of committing, or seeking assistance to commit, suicide, while not having the requisite desire to do so.[53]

He went on to point out that despite statements in the Falconer Report to the effect that the evidence presented did not indicate any abuse of the law in the Netherlands, Oregon or Switzerland (all places which permit assisting suicide in restricted circumstances), 'negative evidence is often hard to obtain', and the concern could not, in his opinion, be dismissed as 'fanciful or unrealistic'.[54] Along similar lines, and in spite of her eventual judgment in favour of *Nicklinson*, Lady Hale accepted the argument that in a legally regulated framework, it may be still extremely difficult to distinguish those who act under undue pressures from those who do not.

For Lady Hale, however, as for the rest of the Supreme Court, the inquiry did not end with that concession. There was still the question of proportionality to consider. The applicants had contended that the section 2(1) ban was a disproportionate interference with their Article 8 rights partly for the reason that, although it legitimately aimed at protecting the vulnerable, a general ban without exceptions was 'more than was necessary' for that protection; a ban that permitted some exceptions within a regulated framework would work just as well. In the alternative, however, the applicants also put forward a different argument about proportionality, claiming that the blanket ban in section 2 did not strike a fair balance between their interests and those of the weak and vulnerable who might be improperly influenced to seek out death.[55] This introduced a possibility that was heretofore not widely considered in the legal debate about assisted suicide, and did not feature in the *Purdy* ruling. Perhaps it should not be a foregone conclusion that inappropriate pressures ought to be guarded against *at all costs*. Perhaps a

---

[53] *Nicklinson* (n 25 above) [86].
[54] ibid [88].
[55] ibid [83].

small risk that a system of legal exceptions could result in pressure on some to avail themselves of it is a price worth paying to provide an escape route for those who, like Debbie Purdy and Tony Nicklinson, find themselves trapped in an unbearable situation. Lady Hale broached this question of balance when she remarked, in *Nicklinson*, that forcing the appellants to stay alive for the sake of protecting *other people* may be asking too much of them.[56] As she said: 'no-one who has read the appellants' accounts of their lives and their feelings can doubt that they experience the law's insistence that they stay alive for the sake of others as a form of cruelty'.[57]

While Lady Hale ultimately thought that the universal ban was, in any event, more than was needed to protect the 'weak and vulnerable' from potential abuse (she regarded it as not being 'beyond the wit of a legal system to identify those people, those few people, who should be allowed help to end their own lives'[58]), her remarks seemed at least to make room for the possibility that some degree of risk could be an acceptable ramification of relaxing that ban. For those unconvinced that the slippery slope risk could ever be neutralised, the question over how the interests of those suffering intolerably balance against the possibility of undue influence is where the debate finally bottoms out. No doubt there are those who would balk at the notion that any amount of slippage should be accepted as the cost of legally permitted assisted suicide. On the other hand, many of those who were exposed to Tony Nicklinson's disturbing account of a toilsome and pained life, and his desperation to escape it, may find themselves, like Lady Hale, wondering whether the law's refusal to lift its ban in respect of such individuals can be justified on the basis of a speculative risk to some unknown others.

It must, I should think, be of consequence in this balancing exercise that those who find their lives unbearable and maintain a settled desire to die are not altogether prevented from enlisting assistance to bring their lives to an end. As has been seen time and again, it *is* the clear policy of the DPP to refrain from prosecuting close friends and family members who proffer that assistance (often by accompanying travel abroad) in circumstances like those of *Purdy* and *Nicklinson*, ban or no ban. However, the ban still has serious and restrictive implications for those who need or want help to end their lives. For one, only those people who possess friends or relations willing to assist them, and the means and ability to travel abroad, are able to die through the aid of professional healthcare workers.[59] The restriction of prosecutorial lenience (as far as we can be confident) to close friends and relations effectively precludes such individuals from enlisting the services

---

[56] ibid [313].
[57] ibid.
[58] ibid [314].
[59] Lord Neuberger highlighted some of these existing problems in *Nicklinson* (n 25 above) [109].

of healthcare professionals inside the United Kingdom, denying them the option of a peaceful death at home. One final, serious, result of this situation is that patients who foresee a time when their life will become unbearable, but when they will lack the physical capability to travel abroad, may make arrangements to seek a controlled death abroad at a time when their life still retains value for them, as Purdy argued she would be forced to do.

How these drawbacks are to be measured against the traditional concerns about undue influence (insofar as they are thought credible) is a problem going right to the heart of the assisted dying debate. The differing opinions of some of the judges in *Nicklinson* came down to how they viewed the implications of this play-off. Lord Mance conceded that there is a genuine question regarding the 'residual risk that is acceptable in this present context',[60] but was nonetheless of the view that it was more appropriate to leave Parliament to engage in that delicate balancing exercise, particularly given that no fresh, compelling evidence about those risks had been brought before the Court since the *Pretty* judgment. The proportionality question, he argued, ultimately required 'value judgments'—specifically, a judgment about 'how much risk would attach to and be acceptable in consequence of a relaxation coupled with the introduction of safeguards, and how such risks should be measured against the benefits to persons such as Mr Nicklinson and Mr Lamb'.[61] Given that this was the case, Parliament's assessment of 'the value of the evidence and the choices to be made in its light' was to be accorded particularly strong weight.[62]

Lady Hale regarded the situation quite differently. As she saw it, a certain justificatory structure fell into place once it was recognised, as it was in both *Purdy* and *Nicklinson*, that the general ban on assisted suicide compromised the applicants' Article 8 rights. The burden fell on defenders of the ban to show that it was justified—which included being proportionate—rather than on proponents of an exception to show that it would not entail too much risk to the vulnerable.[63] This, for Lady Hale, was a question of 'principle rather than evidence'.[64] When the definite interference with the right is pitted against unsubstantiated concerns over potential abuses operating even within the confines of a strict exception, the case for avoiding the interference by creating the exception ought to win out.

Lady Hale's principle may merit some further consideration. Whatever one makes of that principle, the question of how the interests of the 'Purdys'

---

[60] ibid [189]–[190]. Lord Mance noted that in a recent Canadian case concerning assisted dying, the Supreme Court of British Columbia had rejected the Canadian government's argument that its restrictive legislation was justified because its purpose was to eliminate all risk to vulnerable persons (see *Carter v Canada (Attorney-General)* 2012 BCSC 886).

[61] ibid [189].

[62] ibid.

[63] ibid [319]–[321].

[64] ibid [320].

and the 'Nicklinsons' stack up against the interests of those hypothetical few who may succumb to illegitimate pressure to take their lives is still a pertinent one for the law and ethics of assisted dying. Perhaps Lord Mance was correct when he proposed that this was essentially a matter of judging between values, rather than arguing about evidence. Although this balancing question was not addressed in the *Purdy* ruling, the *Purdy* conclusions laid the foundations for its centrality to legal argument about assisted suicide. By holding, for the first time in English law, that the 'right to die' was encompassed by Article 8, the *Purdy* court reset the terms of legal reasoning about assisted suicide, which then and subsequently centred on how far that right could be limited for the protection of others and whether such limits were indeed necessary. Whatever 'right to die' sceptics may have thought about the Article 8 conclusion, it is clear that, post-*Purdy*, the shape of legal argument to come will continue to be informed by the starting premise that prohibiting assisted suicide breaches a fundamental right.

# 14

# *Yearworth and Others v North Bristol NHS Trust* [2009]

LOANE SKENE

## I. INTRODUCTION

IN *JONATHAN YEARWORTH and others v North Bristol NHS Trust*,[1] the Court of Appeal for England and Wales held that six men who had deposited their semen for freezing before undertaking cancer treatment were entitled to be compensated when it was negligently destroyed. The Court said that the men had deposited the semen solely for their benefit and that constituted a bailment. That was a significant decision because the law in England and Wales, as in other common law countries, had previously not recognised that people from whom bodily material had been removed ('originators') could have proprietary rights in their bodies or bodily material. Those things were not capable of being 'property' (as stated in the Australian case *Doodeward v Spence*[2] and many earlier cases in the UK). No one could legally 'own' them, subject to the '*Doodeward* exception',[3] which enabled other people[4] to obtain legal rights to possess, control, or even sell such material, by undertaking 'work and skill' or conferring 'different attributes' on it. The bailment analysis in *Yearworth* provided a

---

[1] *Jonathan Yearworth and others v North Bristol NHS Trust* [2009] EWCA Civ 37 (*Yearworth*); available at: www.bailii.org/ew/cases/EWCA/Civ/2009/37.html.

[2] *Doodeward v Spence* (1908) 6 CLR 406; [1908] HCA 45 (*Doodeward*); this case is discussed in chapter 1 in this volume.

[3] This 'exception' was stated in *Doodeward* (n 2) [14] (Griffiths CJ). It has been adopted in many later cases in Australia, England and Wales; and also in English legislation: Human Tissue Act 2004 s 39(2)(c) 'material which is the subject of property because of an application of human skill' is excepted from the prohibition of commercial dealings in human material for transplantation. (The Human Tissue Act 2004 governs the removal, storage, and subsequent use of bodily material from the deceased: but only storage and use for living persons. The Human Tissue Act (Scotland) 2006 governs these matters in Scotland but does not have a similar provision.) Semen is not governed by the Human Tissue Act 2004, but by the Human Fertilisation and Embryology Act 1990.

[4] And presumably also originators if they have undertaken 'work or skill' or conferred 'different attributes' on their own removed material. However, there is no authority on this point.

right to the originators themselves to be compensated for the negligent loss of their bodily material without consideration of other matters.

This chapter explains the facts of *Yearworth*, the decision of the Court of Appeal and the implications of the case for the development of the law in this area.

## II. *YEARWORTH*: THE FACTS

The plaintiffs in *Yearworth* were six men who had been diagnosed with cancer. Before starting chemotherapy, they deposited their semen at the Southmead Hospital in Bristol. The defendant, the North Bristol NHS Trust, was responsible for that hospital. As stated in the judgments,[5] the men's semen (which contained their sperm) was produced and stored 'for their possible later use' [3], with some men authorising later use of the semen for 'treating a named partner' [6](b). Each man signed a consent form for his semen to be stored and the consent form stated that he could withdraw his consent or vary the terms of the consent at any time before his sperm was used [6](b). When the men sought to retrieve their stored semen after their chemotherapy, they found that it had been irretrievably damaged after 'the amount of liquid nitrogen in the tanks in which it was stored fell below the requisite level' [8]. All of the men were naturally distressed to hear this and they commenced an action in negligence. Five of the men alleged they had suffered a psychiatric injury as well as mental distress [10], as they were 'already in a vulnerable condition' [9]. The defendants accepted that the semen had been destroyed as a result of their negligence. However, it was acknowledged by the Court in the judgment that their claims had 'limitations or complications' and 'their worth in damages [would be] relatively small' [12].

## A. Claim for 'Personal Injury'

The five men who claimed to have suffered psychiatric injury as well as distress, argued that the Trust had acted in breach of its duty of care in the way it had stored their semen, and so caused them 'personal injury' as well as 'damage to their property'.[6] The Trust admitted the breach [13]; but it did not admit that the breach caused the men 'personal injury' (or 'damage to their property').

---

[5] References in this paragraph and later in the chapter are to paragraphs in the judgment, unless otherwise stated.

[6] One man had died before the proceedings and the administrator of his estate brought proceedings.

The men's 'personal injury' claim was quickly rejected.[7] The court held that causing harm to bodily material removed from the body could not be 'personal injury' because 'it would be a fiction to hold that damage to a substance generated by a person's body, inflicted after its removal for storage purposes, constituted a bodily or "personal injury" to him' [23].

## B. Claim for 'Damage to Property'

The men's claim for damage to their property, on the other hand was successful. Initially, the men had made this claim (as with the personal injury claim) 'solely by reference to the tort of negligence' [13].[8] However, they later presented arguments on bailment issues, at the request of the Court of Appeal.[9] This indicated the basis on which the Court's decision was ultimately made. The Court accepted that the deposit of the semen for later use constituted a bailment. The unit in which it had been deposited was liable 'under the law of bailment, as well as that of tort' [50]; the arrangements were 'closely akin to contracts' [57]; and 'modest recovery' could be awarded for 'mental distress' against a gratuitous bailee in such circumstances [59].[10]

The references to the law of bailment as the basis of the men's right to compensation have important legal implications. In order to succeed in a claim arising from a bailment of their semen, the men had to establish first, that the stored semen was property; and secondly, that they had either 'legal ownership' or a 'possessory title' to that property, which the Court 'for convenience' elided as 'ownership' [25].

The categorisation of the semen as property was thus the vital first step. In its path was the long-established '*Doodeward* principle' that, as a general rule, there is no property in a human body or bodily material.[11] However,

---

[7] If that argument had been accepted, damages could have been awarded for negligently causing personal injury and it would not have been necessary for the court to consider whether the semen was property or could be subject to proprietary rights.

[8] An action in contract would also have been possible but the service had been provided under the NHS, so that the men did not pay for their semen to be stored. There was therefore no consideration to found a contract.

[9] An action in bailment was an innovation in itself: 'Until the decision in *Yearworth*, there was debate as to whether a claim could be brought "in bailment", rather than conversion, trespass to goods or other relevant tort action': I Goold and M Quigley, 'Human Biomaterials: A Property Approach' in I Goold et al (eds), *Persons, Parts and Property. How should we regulate Human Tissue in the 21st Century?* 1st edn (Oxford, Hart Publishing, 2014). Goold and Quigley also draw attention to critical comments from other commentators on this point: J Lee, 'The Fertile Imagination of the Common Law: *Yearworth v North Bristol*' (2009) 17 *Torts Law Journal* 130; C Hawes, 'Property Interests in Body Parts: *Yearworth v North Bristol NHS*' (2010) 73 *Modern Law Review* 130.

[10] The matter of compensation was remitted to the County Court for determination.

[11] *Doodeward* (n 2 above).

that case dates back to the early twentieth century. Since then, many exceptional circumstances have been recognised in which bodily material has been
held to be subject to proprietary rights,[12] some of which were discussed by
the court. Moreover the court criticised the *Doodeward* principle itself. The
Court said that it was 'not content to see the common law ... founded upon
[a] principle ... which was devised as an exception to a principle, itself of
exceptional character, relating to the ownership of a human corpse' [45](d).
The principle was 'not entirely logical' and 'we prefer to rest our conclusions
on a broader basis' [45](d), (e). Also,

> developments in medical science now require a re-analysis of the common law's
> treatment of and approach to the issue of ownership of parts or products of a
> living human body, whether for present purposes (viz an action in negligence) or
> otherwise. [45](a)

The Court was therefore prepared to re-examine the law in this area.

The Court of Appeal held, on the facts of the case, that the men did have
'*ownership* of the sperm which they had ejaculated' (emphasis added).[13]
The term 'ownership' was used loosely. It might mean that the men had the
best title or 'all such rights as by law are capable of being exercised over
that type of property against all persons including the right to possession of
the property and any proceeds of its sale'.[14] Indeed, the men presumably did
have other rights as well as the right to possession, such as the right to use
their semen and to prohibit others from using it, and to have it destroyed.[15]
However, the Court did not say that directly. Instead, it elided ownership
with 'possessory title' and the basis for its decision in favour of the men was
that they had the possessory title.

Moreover, the Court said that the men had 'ownership of [their sperm]
*for the purposes of their claims in tort*' (emphasis added).[16] That is, they
had a right to possession which would found a claim in bailment if the
semen they had deposited for their later use was negligently destroyed. They
would also presumably have the right to sue in conversion for the wrongful
destruction of their 'property' (though that was not in issue in the case and
was not considered by the Court). A claim in conversion may be based on a

---

[12] The finding that bodily material can be property seems often to have been made for
pragmatic reasons; eg for the law of theft, consumer protection and forensic tests; see L Skene,
'The current approach of the courts [regarding proprietary interests in human bodily mate-
rial]' (2013) 40 *Journal of Medical Ethics* 1008–24; doi:10.1136/medethics-2012-100994, 20
February 2013.
[13] *Yearworth* (n 1 above) [45](f).
[14] *Concise Australian Legal Dictionary*, 4th edn (Chatsworth NSW, Lexis Nexis, 2011) 421,
definition of 'ownership'.
[15] Some of these rights may be limited by the Human Fertilisation and Embryology Act
1990, as noted in the judgment ([42](d), [44]); but the men nevertheless had those rights.
[16] *Yearworth* (n 1 above) [47].

right to possession (against anyone but the owner) as well as a right to full ownership (against anyone).[17]

In deciding that there was a bailment of the stored semen, the Court considered several points. First, the men deposited their semen on the basis that they *retained control* of it. 'The sole object of their ejaculation was that, in certain events, it might later be used for their benefit' [45](f)(ii). The men had 'negative control' over the use of their sperm–ie the right 'to direct that the sperm be not used in a certain way' [45](f)(ii); and they could 'require the destruction of the sperm', which is a 'fundamental feature of ownership' [45](f)(iii). It did not matter that their right to 'direct' the use of the sperm was limited by legislation regarding the use of stored semen in reproductive treatment: 'there are numerous statutes which limit a person's ability to use his property' [45](f)(ii). Although the sperm would have to be destroyed at the end of the storage period, no one other than the men had any rights in relation to the sperm.

Secondly, all parties intended that the semen would be available to the men *to use later*, either for their own treatment or possibly for use by someone else with their authority. (The Court said it was not required to consider cases where the intended use was for other people, such as donated products where a claim might be made by the 'donor' or even 'donees' specified by the donor [45](b), but the main point was that the semen was intended for later use, rather than for use *by the particular men*. If their intention was that the semen should be stored and available for use by another person[18] (and the storing party agreed), then it would seem as much to be a bailment as if it were stored for use by the men who generated the semen. Any indication of intended later use would negate the suggestion that the originator intended that the material should be regarded as 'abandoned'. The 'bailor' could then presumably claim in bailment as in *Yearworth* (or in contract, if the arrangement was for consideration); or the third party could claim as a representative of the bailor,[19] or even in his or her name, if the Contracts (Rights of Third Parties) Act 1999 (UK) applied, the person was named and the contract was made for his or her benefit.[20]

---

[17] See, eg, *Kuwait Airways Corporation v Iraqi Airways Company and Others* [2002] 2 AC 883 at [38]: 'a concomitant deprivation of use and possession'; RFV Heuston and RA Buckley, *Salmond and Heuston on the Law of Torts*, 21st edn (London, Sweet & Maxwell, 1996) 97–98.

[18] As in the case of *Hecht v Superior Court of Los Angeles County (Kane)* 20 Cal Rpt 2d 275 (1993) (cited in *Yearworth* at [40]. See also *Kate Jane Bazley v Wesley Monash IVF Pty Ltd* [2010] QSC 118 (*Bazley*) at [20], where a deceased man purported to bequeath his sperm by will for the purpose of redirecting its use after death, and the court held it was therefore property).

[19] Compare *Bazley* (n 18 above), 'rights of property in the bailor [may entitle] him *or his representative* to call for the property's return' [30] (emphasis added).

[20] Such a contract also limits the powers of the person entering the contract to amend it. This may be significant to the issue of 'control' which is the foundation of the bailor's own rights in bailment.

Thirdly, it was not only the men's intention when depositing their semen that it should be available for their later use. The men made their intention known to the party agreeing to store the semen, and the semen was *accepted on that basis by that party*. '[T]he Trust had promised ... to freeze and to store' the semen [3] for the future use of the men [6]. By choosing to take possession, it assumed the responsibility of safe keeping [48](c). There was a gratuitous bailment 'closely akin to contracts' [57].

In other words, the stored semen could not be regarded as 'abandoned tissue', even if semen might be so regarded in other circumstances. Counsel for the men differentiated stored semen from other 'products of the body which are removed from it with a view to their being abandoned–such as cut hair, excised tissue and amputated limbs' [19].[21] The Court of Appeal considered this other bodily material quite briefly but the Court accepted the principle of abandonment as extinguishing any property interest that might otherwise arise in such material. The Court referred to the American case, *Washington University v Catalona*[22] in which the university was held to be a donee and not a bailee because 'the donors had abandoned any possessory interest in the tissue'.[23] For this reason, researchers who have used tissue to develop a new product, such as a diagnostic test or cell line, may gain a proprietary interest in it and the originator will have no interest.[24]

One matter that was not explained in *Yearworth* was the legal source of the men's property right in the semen when they first deposited it for storage. It would seem from the principles of bailment that a 'condition precedent' to a bailment is that the bailor has a property interest in the thing to be bailed, but that matter was not discussed in the judgment. The court apparently regarded the bailment itself as establishing the rights of the men in the stored semen. But if the men had 'bailed' semen taken from a *third party* without consent for the men's later use, that 'bailment' would presumably not make the semen their 'property' so that they would be entitled to compensation if it was negligently destroyed; or to which they would be entitled to regain possession. They would need to have some type of prior legal entitlement to it, a property right that would found a bailment.

One answer to the question of how the men's property interest first arose might lie in the statements in *Doodeward* concerning the right to possession, and the suggestion in that case that a right to possession could have more than one legal basis. In addition to the 'work or skill'/'different attributes' test that can make bodily material property and confer a right of possession in favour of the person who worked on the material, it may be, as accepted

---

[21] Presumably semen would also normally fall into this category.

[22] *Washington University v Catalona* 437 F Supp 2d 985 (2006), US District Court, Eastern District of Missouri (a decision later affirmed by the US Court of Appeals, 8th Circuit: 490 F 3d 667).

[23] As stated by the Court of Appeal in *Yearworth* (n 1 above) [48].

[24] As held, for example, in *Moore v Regents of the University of California* 793 P 2d 479 (1990).

by two of the judges in *Doodeward* (Griffiths CJ and Barton J), that a person who is in possession of a thing is, without more, legally entitled to possession unless someone else can prove a greater right to possession.[25]

A right to *possession* in favour of originators (or their representatives) has been recognised in a number of Australian cases since *Yearworth*. In *Bazley*,[26] *Edwards*[27] and *Re H*,[28] widows were held not only to be entitled to possession of their deceased husband's stored semen, but also to use it in fertility treatment[29] or to have it destroyed. Moreover, the incidents of the originator's (or representative's) property rights could conceivably extend beyond those of possession, use and destruction, to include other rights within the 'bundle of rights' noted in the widely-quoted taxonomy of Honoré[30] to cover sale and other transactions for profit (though legislation on human tissue donation and fertility treatment commonly prohibits the sale of bodily material, gametes and embryos). As White J emphasised in *Bazley*, the Court in *Yearworth* recognised the 'rights of *property* in the bailor' [30] (emphasis added). Also, as noted above, the Court of Appeal in *Yearworth* elided 'legal ownership' and 'possessory title' [25]. Ms Edwards had an 'entitlement to *property*' [91]. Thus, there may be circumstances where an arrangement could be made for the use of at least some types of excised bodily material for profit (such as hair sold for wigs).

## III. DEVELOPMENTS SINCE *YEARWORTH*

Since *Yearworth* was decided, there has been extensive academic commentary on the case and its implications.[31] Some commentators have argued

---

[25] The third judge, Higgins J, was not persuaded that an earlier possessor had any greater right than a later possessor, despite the former having been unlawfully deprived of it in an earlier transaction. These aspects of *Doodeward* are discussed in chapter 1 in this volume.

[26] *Kate Jane Bazley v Wesley Monash IVF Pty Ltd* [2010] QSC 118.

[27] *Jocelyn Edwards; Re the estate of the late Mark Edwards* [2011] NSWSC 478.

[28] *Re H, AE (No 3)* [2013] SASC 196.

[29] Subject to legislation in some States on the posthumous use of stored gametes.

[30] See A Honoré, 'Ownership' in AG Guest (ed), *Oxford Essays in Jurisprudence* (Oxford, Clarendon Press, 1961). The so-called 'bundle of rights' includes rights to buy, sell, use, transfer to another, lend to another, and exclude others. An example of a person having some rights in 'the bundle' but not others is provided by *Yearworth*: a bailee of stored semen has the right to possession of the semen but not the right to sell or destroy it (without the consent of the bailor/originator).

[31] For example, Lee (n 9 above); SHE Harmon and G Laurie, '*Yearworth v. North Bristol NHS Trust*: Property, Principles, Precedents and Paradigms' (2010) 69 *Cambridge Law Journal* 476; Harmon, HE Shawn, '*Yearworth v. North Bristol NHS Trust*: A Property Case of Uncertain Significance?' (2010) 13 *Medicine, Health Care & Philosophy* 343; Hawes (n 9 above); J Wall, 'The legal status of body parts: A framework' (2011) *Oxford Journal of Legal Studies* 1; L Skene, 'Proprietary Interests in Human Bodily Material: *Yearworth*, Recent Australian Cases on Stored Semen and their Implications' (2012) 20 *Medical Law Review* 227; J Wall, 'The trespasses of property law' (2014) 40 *Journal of Medical Ethics* 19: doi:10.1136/medethics-2013-101439. There have been recent Special Issues in the *Journal of Medical Ethics* ((2013) vol 40(10)) and the *Journal of Law and Medicine* ((2013) vol 21)) on the regulation of human bodily material and a book on this topic was published in the UK in 2014: Goold et al (eds) (n 9 above).

strongly in favour of a property approach;[32] others have been more guarded or even opposed.[33] However, in considering the implications of *Yearworth* in the development of the law, it should be noted that the *Doodeward* principle was not totally rejected in *Yearworth*. The Court of Appeal noted the cases establishing that a human corpse and parts of a human corpse could be property in certain circumstances. It quoted *R v Kelly and Lindsay*[34] (which in turn cited *Doodeward*), that 'parts of a corpse are capable of being property ... if they have acquired different attributes by virtue of the application of skill, such as dissection or preservation techniques, for exhibition or teaching purposes' [36]; or

> perhaps on some future occasion ... even without the acquisition of different attributes, if they have a use or significance beyond their mere existence ... for example, they are intended for use in an organ transplant operation, for the extraction of DNA, or for that matter, as an exhibit in a trial' [36].[35]

But as noted above, that was not the basis for the Court's ultimate decision in *Yearworth*. Instead, the Court focused on the rights of the men as a result of the bailment of their semen.[36]

The Court of Appeal was certainly critical of the '*Doodeward* exception' and, as noted above, it based its decision on other grounds. However, as stated, the law still enables people to gain a proprietary interest in human bodily material by undertaking 'work or skill' or changing it so that it has 'different attributes'. Also, the *Doodeward* approach underlies section 39(2)(c) of the Human Tissue Act 2004, which applies in England, Wales and Northern Ireland and refers to the 'application of skill'.[37]

---

[32] For example, I Goold and M Quigley, 'Human Biomaterials: The Case for a Property Approach' in Goold et al (eds) (n 9 above); JW Harris, *Property and Justice* (Oxford, Clarendon Press, 1996) 351:'Every person ought to be regarded as the owner of any separated part of his body'; G Laurie, *Genetic Privacy, A Challenge to Medico-Legal Norms* (Cambridge, Cambridge University Press, 2002) 321: the 'next milestone [in medical law] will be the legal recognition of self-ownership'. Different types of property rights and the difference between regarding bodily material as property and treating it as property in some circumstances are discussed by L Skene, 'Raising issues with a property approach', ch 19 in Goold et al (eds) (n 9 above).

[33] J Herring and P-L Chau, 'Relational bodies' (2013) 21 *Journal of Law & Medicine* 294; L Skene, 'Raising issues' (n 31 above); J Wall (2014)(n 31 above). Herring, Chau and Skene have suggested that comprehensive legislation may be necessary to cover particular circumstances. The Human Tissue Act 2004 (which applies in England, Wales and Northern Ireland) and the procedures of the Human Fertilisation and Embryology Authority in the UK illustrate the type of regulatory structure that could be adopted.

[34] *R v Kelly; R v Lindsay* [1998] EWCA Crim 1578; [1999] QB 621.

[35] Quoting *R v Kelly; R v Lindsay* (n 34 above) 630 G–631 E (Rose LJ).

[36] The judgment considered only stored *semen*. A similar argument might be made regarding other bodily material deposited for later use, like blood removed for an autologous transfusion, or a child's umbilical cord blood removed for later use. Although semen might be regarded as in a category of its own because of the psychological pain of the loss of reproductive potential, there could equally be distress and suffering for people whose deposits of blood in such circumstances are lost.

[37] See (n 3 above).

In Australia, there have been a number of cases concerning legal rights in relation to stored semen,[38] but those cases have focused on the right of the widows of the deceased men and not of the men themselves. The Australian cases have followed *Doodeward* as State courts in Australia are bound by decisions of the High Court. Although the widows have been successful in their actions on the basis that they were entitled to possession of their deceased partner's semen (even if it was removed after his death), that entitlement arose because the semen was regarded as being stored (or collected) solely for their benefit. The storage and collection constituted the 'work or skill' required for the semen to become property under the *Doodeward* principle and the widows were entitled to possession because the doctors who stored or collected the semen were regarded as acting as their agents in doing so.[39]

In England, there have been other developments that might seem to indicate that the principles stated in *Yearworth* may not be applied more widely. In 2011, the Nuffield Council on Bioethics suggested that it may be better to concentrate on the rights that originators may want (the 'sticks' in the widely-cited 'bundle of rights')[40] instead of focusing on whether excised bodily material is 'property'.[41] The law could then distinguish 'between the property rights of the originator with respect to control and compensation (that is, compensation for misuse rather than recompense in the form of economic gain), and property rights with respect to income'.[42]

Alternatively, rights in removed bodily material could be regulated by privacy law instead of property law, as suggested by the Australian Law Reform Commission in 2003;[43] and adopted in legislation in New South Wales in 1998.[44]

---

[38] *Kate Jane Bazley v Wesley Monash IVF Pty Ltd* [2010] QSC 118; *Jocelyn Edwards; Re the estate of the late Mark Edwards* [2011] NSWSC 478; *Re H, AE (No 3)* [2013] SASC 196.

[39] See Skene (n 31 above).

[40] Honoré (n 30 above). The so-called 'bundle of rights' includes rights to buy, sell, use, transfer to another, lend to another, and exclude others.

[41] Nuffield Council on Bioethics, *Human Bodies: Donation for Medicine and Research* (October 2011) available at: www.nuffieldbioethics.org/sites/default/files/Donation_full_report. pdf (accessed 21 July 2014) 16–17, para 70. Similarly, Harmon suggests that 'the language of property is *Yearworth* is … being used as a metaphor', 'a means of extending some level of *control* to actors, including originators of tissue, in the new bioeconomy … and a pragmatic means of securing *justice*, of providing a remedy': Harmon (n 31 above) 346; see also Harmon and Laurie (n 31 above): 'property was only used as a convenient vehicle through which to achieve a certain outcome'.

[42] Nuffield Council (n 41 above) [7.20].

[43] Australian Law Reform Commission, *Essentially Yours: The Protection of Human Genetic Information in Australia* (Report 96, 2003), available at: www.alrc.gov.au/publications/ 1-introduction-inquiry/essentially-yours (accessed 22 July 2014). See Recommendations 8-2a ('personal information' should be defined to include bodily samples); 20-2 (federal privacy legislation should be used to regulate the holding of tissue samples, rather than human tissue legislation).

[44] Privacy and Personal Information Protection Act 1998 (NSW) s 4(2) which defines 'personal information' as including body samples.

There has been no movement since *Yearworth* towards using property law in regulating the use of human bodily material in *research*, which has traditionally been regulated on principles of altruism and autonomy, rather than property law,[45] and through ethical guidelines rather than legislation. The guidelines are continually under review and updated, both in the UK[46] and in Australia.[47] But there is also legislation: the Human Tissue Act 2004, which applies in England and Wales and Northern Ireland; and the Human Tissue Scotland Act 2006 which applies in Scotland; and, in all of the UK, including Scotland, it is an offence to hold bodily material intending to analyse its deoxyribonucleic acid (DNA) and use the results in research without consent from the person from whom the material was removed.[48]

## IV. CONCLUSION

*Yearworth* was the first case in which a deposit of human bodily material was held to be a bailment. That finding had important implications for the originators of the material. As bailors, they had a right to possession (a proprietary right), so that, on the ordinary principles of property law, they were entitled to be compensated if their bailed bodily material was negligently destroyed. That was a major change from the previous judicial reasoning regarding removed bodily material which was based on the *Doodeward* 'no property' principle. Applying that principle, property rights in bodily material could arise only by undertaking 'work or skill' on the material or changing it so that it acquired 'different attributes'. The property rights would then be in favour of the person who worked on the material and not the originator. In *Yearworth* the Court took the first step to acknowledge that originators have proprietary rights over bodily material removed from their bodies, at least in certain circumstances. However, it remains to be seen whether that finding will be applied more widely. As commentators have

[45] RE McWhirter et al, 'Body ownership and research' (2013) 21 *Journal of Law & Medicine* 323.
[46] Human Tissue Authority, Code of Practice–Consent (Code 1, 2009) at www.hta.gov.uk/_db/_documents/2006-07-04_Approved_by_Parliament_-_Code_of_Practice_1_-_Consent.pdf (accessed 22 July 2014); Human Tissue Authority, Code of Practice–Research (Code 9, 2009) at: www.hta.gov.uk/policiesandcodesofpractice/codesofpractice.cfm (accessed 22 July 2014). The Human Tissue Authority licenses more than 800 organisations that store and use human tissue for purposes such as research, patient treatment, post-mortem examination, teaching, and public exhibitions.
[47] National Health and Medical Research Council [Australia], *National Statement on Ethical Conduct in Human Research* (1998), Updated March 2014, Australia: Canberra, at: www.nhmrc.gov.au/_files_nhmrc/publications/attachments/e72_national_statement_march_2014_140331.pdf (accessed 22 July 2014).
[48] Human Tissue Act 2004, s 45; Human Tissue Scotland Act 2006, s 16 (bodily material from a deceased person).

noted, the Court's decision in *Yearworth* was essentially pragmatic with no examination of 'the moral foundations [on which] ... the finding of property is based'.[49] Similarly, the Court did not explore the legal basis on which the men were entitled to possession of the semen when they 'bailed' it to the Trust. Also, not surprisingly, there are continuing debates about whether property law is the most appropriate instrument to regulate issues relating to human bodily material.[50]

---

[49] Harmon and Laurie (n 31 above).
[50] See (n 31 above).

# 15

# *A, B and C v Ireland* [2010]

IMOGEN GOOLD

## I. INTRODUCTION

*A* *B AND C* is an appeal taken to the European Court of Human Rights (ECtHR) under Article 8 of the European Convention on ,Human Rights. It was held that the right to privacy under Article 8 did not confer upon the appellants a right to an abortion. However, Irish law was found to be non-complaint with Article 8 by failing to provide an accessible procedure through which a woman could establish whether she qualified to have a legal abortion in Ireland.

In some ways, *A, B and C v Ireland* is an anti-landmark case. For many, it represents a forgone opportunity to follow the ground-breaking approach to abortion taken by the United States Supreme Court in *Roe v Wade*, which recognised that abortion fell within the Constitutional right to privacy and so afforded American women the right to an abortion until the point of viability. While the US Court held that the balance between the right to privacy and the state's interest in protecting pre-natal life tipped in favour of the woman, the ECtHR chose to leave such balancing to the discretion of Member States. In doing so, the ECtHR refused to take the step of holding that European women have a right to abortion. In Paolo Ronchi's words, 'the hopes of those waiting for a European *Roe v Wade* were ... dashed'.[1] This decision has ramifications not only for Irish abortion law, and the regulation of abortion in Europe generally, but also more widely for how issues of morality (which often attend issues around medicine) are addressed in the European context.

## II. SOCIAL AND LEGAL CONTEXT

Ireland's abortion laws are some of the most restrictive in Europe, second only to those of Malta, which does not permit abortion on any grounds.[2]

---

[1] P Ronchi, 'Case Comment: *A, B and C v Ireland*: Europe's Roe v Wade still has to wait' (2011) 127 *Law Quarterly Review* 365, 369.

[2] Andorra and San Marino take an approach similar to that of Ireland.

Its laws are hence 'unusual, although not uniquely harsh'.[3] As in the United Kingdom, unlawful abortion in Ireland is a crime. Until 2013, abortion was criminalised under sections 58 and 59 of the Offences Against the Person Act 1861, which had the effect of prohibiting the procuring of an abortion and attempts to do so.[4] Contravention of this prohibition carried a sentence of imprisonment, which could be for life. Both judicial opinion and legislative measures made clear that the Act's effect was that there could be no lawful abortion.[5]

Change came in 1983 with the Eighth Amendment to the Irish Constitution, as a result of which Article 40.3.3 now reads:

> The State acknowledges the right to life of the unborn and, with due regard to the equal right to life of the mother, guarantees in its laws to respect, and, as far as practicable, by its laws defend and vindicate that right.[6]

Sheelagh McGuinness notes that this amendment was made in response to the decision in *Roe v Wade*[7] to make clear (despite its wording) that abortion was prohibited in Ireland at that time.[8] It attempted to do so by placing a positive obligation on the Irish State to protect the right to life of the unborn fetus. Despite this anti-abortion intention, the wording of the Article is actually framed so as to require a balancing of the equal rights of the fetus and the pregnant woman. This opened the door (perhaps inadvertently) for the development of a category of lawful abortion in Ireland on the grounds of protection of the life of the mother.[9] Such a ground was, however, uncertain as the Irish government failed to take steps to clarify how Article 40.3.3

---

[3] E Wicks, '*A, B and C v Ireland*: Abortion Law under the European Convention on Human Rights' (2011) 11 *Human Rights Law Review* 556, 557.

[4] As will be discussed below, ss 58 and 59 were recently repealed by the s 5 of the Protection of Life During Pregnancy Act 2013. They were replaced by s 22, which makes the destruction of unborn life a crime punishable by a fine and or imprisonment for up to 14 years.

[5] See, eg Health (Family Planning) Act 1979, s 10 which states that nothing in the Act was to be read as authorising the procurement of an abortion. See also the comments (obiter) of Keane J in *Society for the Protection of Unborn Children (Ireland) Ltd (SPUC) v Grogan and others* [1989] IR 753.

[6] Eighth Amendment of the Constitution Act 1932, which inserted the quoted text as sub-section (3) into Article 40.3.

[7] *Roe v Wade* 410 US 113 (1973).

[8] S McGuinness, '*A, B, and C* leads to D (for Delegation)' (2011) 19 *Medical Law Review* 476, 478.

[9] Article 40.3.3 is unusual in the way it approaches abortion, as it accords the unborn fetus a right to life, and then directs that the state defend and vindicate this right as far as practicable, taking account of the mother's right to life. In doing so, it pits one right to life against another, rather than side-stepping the issue of the fetus's right to life to simply provide criteria for when abortion will be legitimate (or prohibiting the practice outright). Barbara Hewson notes that 'the wording could be interpreted restrictively or liberally', particularly as the word 'unborn' is not defined (B Hewson, 'Family: No *Roe v Wade*' (2011) 161 *New Law Journal* 119, 120). However, as the Article enjoins the state to give only 'due regard' to the mother's right, it requires it to 'guarantee' respect for the life of the fetus. This suggests that the balance was meant to be favour of the fetus.

was to be interpreted, and provided no procedures for determining when a woman would be eligible for an abortion under it. This ambiguity left both doctors and women uncertain as to what was permissible, and allowed the gardaí (the Irish police force) to restrain women from travelling to have an abortion elsewhere. This created a situation Fiona de Londras has described as one in which women were 'confined to pregnancy ... by a combination of legal fudge and policed borders'. As she explains:

> From the outset, it seemed clear that some legislative provisions would be required to clarify when and how such clinical interventions might take place without infringement of s 58 of the Offences against the Person Act 1861 ... No such legislation was, however, forthcoming. Indeed, at the time that the 8th Amendment was introduced, not only was there no such legislative clarity, but women were barred from travelling for the purpose of acquiring an abortion (in any circumstances) and there are reports that many women were stopped from trying to leave the country on suspicion that they were travelling for the purposes of a termination.[10]

Judicial confirmation that Article 40.3.3 provided grounds for lawful abortion was not forthcoming until 1992, a watershed year in the history of abortion law in Ireland. That year saw the handing down a crucial decision interpreting how this balancing of rights should be undertaken. *Attorney-General v X* concerned a 14-year-old girl who fallen pregnant as a result of being raped.[11] After notifying the gardaí, the girl and her parents concluded that the best course of action was for them to travel to England so that she could have an abortion. Her parents notified the gardaí of their intentions because they wanted to inquire whether it would be possible use tissue taken from the aborted fetus in the rape investigation. The gardaí responded by seeking advice from the Director of Public Prosecutions, who informed the Attorney-General, who in turn obtained interim injunctions from the High Court prohibiting the defendants from interfering with the right to life of the unborn, restraining all three from leaving the jurisdiction for nine months, and restraining them from procuring or arranging an abortion within or outside the jurisdiction.

The parents and the girl were in England at the time, but cancelled the abortion and returned to Ireland to contest the injunctions. They argued that they had a right to travel from the Ireland to do what was lawful elsewhere, and also that the girl's life was in danger as there was a risk that she would commit suicide if denied an abortion. Their motion initially failed, with Costello J granting the injunctions permanently. He reasoned that Article 40.3.3 required him to act to protect the life of the unborn fetus, and that the risk to the girl's life was of a lesser magnitude than that to the fetus (as the risk to the fetus was certain, whereas that to the girl was not). Therefore,

---

[10] F de Londras, 'Suicide and Abortion: Analysing the Legislative Options in Ireland' (2013) *Medico-Legal Journal of Ireland* 4, 5.
[11] *Attorney-General v X* [1992] 1 IR 1.

it was right to strike a balance in favour of preventing her obtaining an abortion. He accepted that she had a right to travel outside Ireland to obtain medical services, but that the Irish State could restrict that right on public policy grounds (here, the protection of unborn life) and that restraining her from travelling to meet those goals was not disproportionate in this case.[12] The girl and her parents appealed to the Supreme Court.

*X* is a key decision in the history of Irish abortion law because the Supreme Court took the step of explicitly stating that Article 40.3.3 was to be interpreted as permitting abortion where the was a 'real and substantial risk to the life of the mother if such termination were not effected'.[13] Further, it clarified that that risk need not be one of 'immediate or inevitable death of the mother', as such a requirement would 'not sufficiently vindicate the right to life of the mother'.[14] The Supreme Court made clear that a risk that the woman would commit suicide could be sufficient to render an abortion lawful, but that a risk to her mental or physical health would not be enough. The case is crucial also because the Supreme Court held that women seeking abortions were permitted to travel outside Ireland to procure them, and were to be provided with information about the possibility of doing so. It was therefore unlawful to prevent a woman from travelling for this purpose, and to withhold such information from her.[15]

For nearly 10 years following the 1983 amendment, Article 40.3.3 had been open to being interpreted in this way. However, during this period the Irish government failed to pass legislation that would have clarified the effect of the amended Article. Sheelagh McGuinness has rightly characterised the Irish's government's approach in the matter as 'severe inertia'.[16] This failure left those seeking abortions and the doctors who might provide them in a state of confusion. The situation was exacerbated by the availability of criminal sanctions for unlawful provision of abortions which, in the face of the confusion, deterred medical practitioners from making abortion available at all.

Public acceptance of the interpretation of Article 40.3.3 taken by the majority in *X* was tested by a referendum in November 1992, in which the Irish public were asked whether:

(a)   suicide should be removed as a ground for lawful abortion;
(b)   women should be free to travel outside Ireland to procure an abortion; and
(c)   information about abortion services should be freely available in Ireland.

---

[12] ibid [2].
[13] ibid [3].
[14] ibid [3].
[15] ibid [3].
[16] McGuinness, '*A, B, and C*' (2011) n 8 above, 480.

The majority rejected removing suicide as a ground for abortion, and supported the freedom of women to travel and the availability of information.[17] Consequently, the Thirteenth and Fourteenth Amendments to the Irish Constitution were inserted to (supposedly) guarantee women living in Ireland the right to information on the availability of abortions in other countries, and to travel outside Ireland to obtain an abortion.[18] As it had been a controversial inclusion, the suicide ground was the subject of a further referendum in 2002, in which the Irish populace again narrowly voted against removing it as a ground for abortion.[19] The decision in X was confirmed in subsequent cases, including *A and B v Eastern Health Board, District Judge Mary Fahy and C, and the Attorney-General (notice party)* (commonly referred to as the C case) in 1998.[20]

In the same year that X was decided, the ECtHR also held in *Open Door and Dublin Well Woman v Ireland* (*Open Door*) that Ireland had breached its obligation to guarantee freedom of expression under Article 10 of the European Convention on Human Rights (the Convention) in restraining an abortion advisory service from providing information about abortion services available outside Ireland. The Court considered that the restriction created a risk to the health of women seeking abortions, and that this was disproportionate.[21]

Given these events, one might be forgiven for thinking that the clarification of the ambit of Article 40.3.3 provided in X and *Open Door* would have led to a change in practice, providing as it had a clear, accepted ground for procuring an abortion on the basis of risk to the life of the mother, and confirmation that travel was permitted and information could be made available. It did not. As McGuinness has commented, the case law and statutes do not give the full picture of the state of abortion law in Ireland at the time of *A, B and C*: 'it is crucial to consider the severe government inertia on the issue'.[22]

---

[17] See results of referenda on Twelfth, Thirteenth and Fourteenth Amendments respectively: Elections Ireland: electionsireland.org/results/referendum.

[18] Amendments to Article 40.3.3 of the Constitution of Ireland Act 1937 were made on 23 December 1992 by the Thirteenth Amendment of the Constitution Act 1992 and the Fourteenth Amendment of the Constitution Act 1992.

[19] '25th Amendment Protection of Human Life in Pregnancy', *Elections Ireland*: electionsireland. org/results/referendum/refresult.cfm?ref=200225R. 50.42% were in favour of rejection.

[20] *A and B v Eastern Health Board, Judge Mary Fahy and C, and the Attorney-General (notice party)* [1998] 1 IR 464. In that case, a 13-year-old girl became pregnant after she was raped. The High Court accepted that she was at risk of committing suicide, and that she was therefore entitled to an abortion within Ireland.

[21] *Open Door and Dublin Well Woman v Ireland* [1992] ECHR 68. The case was an appeal to the ECtHR following the domestic decision in *SPUC v Open Door Counselling and Dublin Well Woman Centre*. In 1986, the Society for the Protection of Unborn Children (SPUC) had obtained an injunction in the High Court to restrain Open Door Counselling and the Dublin Well Woman Centre from offering women information about obtaining an abortion outside Ireland. The organisations asked the Supreme Court to overturn the injunctions, but it refused and they consequently took the case to the ECtHR.

[22] McGuinness (n 8 above) 480.

Such inertia had already been was noted by one of the judges in *X* in 1992, with McCarthy J stating that the 'failure of the Legislature to enact the appropriate legislation [concerning Article 40.3.3] is no longer just unfortunate; it is inexcusable'.[23] Regardless of these words, as McGuinness notes, this inertia persisted despite the decision in *X* and subsequent cases, and was still persisting by the time *A, B and C* was decided.[24] No implementing legislation to lay down procedures for ensuring women access to the abortions to which they were lawfully entitled was passed, and consequently, both pregnant women and medical practitioners remained in a state of confusion about when an abortion might be lawfully performed. This state of confusion persisted even post-*A, B and C* until legislation was finally passed in 2013, as was evident by the comments of doctors in the wake of Savita Halapanavar's death in 2012.[25] For example, Dr Peter Boylan, of the Irish Institute of Obstetricians and Gynaecologists said: 'The current situation is like a sword of Damocles hanging over us … If we do something with a good intention, but it turns out to be illegal, the consequences are extremely serious for medical practitioners'. Only one minor step was taken in the years between *X* and the post-*A, B and C* period, and this was in many ways a retrograde one at that. In response to the ECtHR's decision in *Open Door*, the Irish government took the minor step of passing the Regulation of Information (Services outside the State for the Termination of Pregnancies) Act in 1995, affirming that doctors and various advisory agencies were permitted to provide information about procuring an abortion outside Ireland. However, despite the holding in the *X* case, the Act limited this provision to the context of one-to-one counselling, and advisory agencies were also not permitted to make appointments for women seeking abortions.[26] No other legislation on abortion in the light of the decision in *X* was forthcoming.

In this context of unclear law there continued to be instances of women being prevented from travelling for the purposes of abortion, such as the 2007 case of Miss D.[27] Miss D was a 17-year-old girl who learned that the fetus she was carrying suffered from anencephaly, a condition incompatible with life outside the womb. Miss D attempted to leave Ireland to have

---

[23] *X* (n 11 above) 147.

[24] As we shall see, even after the ECtHR handed down its decision in *A, B and C*, the Irish government took more than two and half years to take appropriate action.

[25] D Dalby, 'Inquiry Sought in Death in Ireland After Abortion Was Denied', *New York Times* (New York City, 22 November 2012): www.nytimes.com/2012/11/23/world/europe/inquiry-sought-in-death-in-ireland-after-abortion-was-denied.html?_r=0. See also the postscript to this chapter.

[26] Regulation of Information (Services outside the State for the Termination of Pregnancies) Act 1995.

[27] *D (A Minor) v District Judge Brennan*, Unreported, 9 May 2007 (High Court).

an abortion in the UK, but the Health Service Executive tried to prevent her doing so by asking the gardaí to arrest her, and the Passport Office to refuse her a passport. She took her case to the High Court, which confirmed her right to travel. Notably, Miss D refused to take the option of threatening to commit suicide.

McGuinness is right to emphasise the role the Irish government's failure to act on abortion played in effectively maintaining the pre-1983 prohibition on abortion. As we shall see, even post-*A, B and C*, with the ECtHR's direction that Ireland must clarify its laws, the Irish government took two more years to pass legislation that was meant to do so. There is little question that the government of Ireland repeatedly dragged its heels, and so denied many women the chance of a lawful abortion within their own country's borders. In the end, 30 years would pass between the insertion of Article 40.3.3 and the passage of legislation creating procedures to make the right to obtain an abortion where the woman's life was at risk a matter of reality, rather than mere theory. In that time, many thousands of women had little choice but to carry unwanted pregnancies at risk to their own lives because they could not access information, were turned back at the borders, or simply could not afford to travel to England to obtain an abortion to which they were in fact lawfully entitled. Many others were forced to go outside England, and so undertake unnecessary and psychologically burdensome travel when their health was under threat purely because their own government would not facilitate access to abortion on grounds sanctioned by both the Supreme Court and the will of the people.

## III. FACTS AND CLAIMS

The case concerned three women who had travelled to England to procure abortions, referred to in the case as A, B and C. The case was lodged with the ECtHR in August 2005 and heard before the Grand Chamber of 17 judges on 9 December 2009. The Court handed down its verdict in December 2010.

### A. Applicant A

A had fallen pregnant unintentionally in late 2004, having thought her partner to be infertile. Believing she was not entitled to an abortion in Ireland, she borrowed money from a money-lender at high interest and travelled secretly to England when nine-and-a-half weeks pregnant to procure an abortion at a private clinic. She had at this stage delayed seeking the abortion by three weeks.

A's reasons for seeking an abortion were multi-faceted. At the time she became pregnant she was unmarried, unemployed and impoverished.

She already had four young children, all of whom were in foster care due to her problems with alcoholism. The youngest of the children was disabled. She had also had a history of depression during each pregnancy, and was again battling depression when she became pregnant in 2004. Despite her difficulties, she had managed to maintain her sobriety for the year preceding this pregnancy and was working with social workers to regain custody of her children. She worried that a further pregnancy would exacerbate her depression and jeopardise her sobriety. She concealed her actions in seeking an abortion from the social workers and ensured that she did not miss a contact visit with her children, returning home the day after the abortion in time for a contact meeting with her youngest child.

While travelling home on the train to Dublin, A began to experience heavy bleeding and was met at the train station by an ambulance. She was taken to a nearby hospital and a dilation and curettage was performed. Despite experiencing pain, nausea and on-going bleeding in the weeks following, she sought no further medical treatment.

By the time of the application, she had once more become pregnant and had given birth to a fifth child, again suffering depression during the pregnancy. She had regained custody of three of her children, but continued to struggle with depression. According to the case report, she remained of the view that choosing to terminate her pregnancy in 2005 was the right decision.[28]

## B. Applicant B

The facts of B's case are somewhat similar to those of A's, although the background to her reasons differed. B had also become pregnant unintentionally in late 2004 after a failure of the 'morning-after pill'. Like A, she believed that she was not entitled to an abortion in Ireland despite having been warned by two doctors that she was at substantial risk of suffering an ectopic pregnancy.[29] She also wanted to terminate the pregnancy as she

[28] *A, B and C v Ireland* [2010] ECHR 2032, [13]–[17].
[29] Such pregnancies occur when the fertilised egg implants outside the uterus (usually in one of the fallopian tubes). In at least half such pregnancies the egg fails to develop, and the woman suffers a natural miscarriage. However, if it continues to develop, the egg will grow and may rupture the structure in which it has implanted. A rupture of the fallopian tubes, for example, will result in internal bleeding, which can be life-threatening for the pregnant woman and is considered a medical emergency. Consequently, if the ectopic pregnancy is detected early, the usual treatment is to administer methotrexate to halt the development of the egg, which is then absorbed back into the body. If detected later, the egg may be removed via surgery. Both methods effectively terminate the pregnancy: 'Ectopic Pregnancy' NHS Choices www.nhs.uk/conditions/ectopic-pregnancy/Pages/Introduction.aspx.

did not feel able to care for a child on her own. She sought counselling in late 2004, and by early 2005 it was clear that the pregnancy was not in fact ectopic. In mid-January, certain now of her decision but lacking the necessary funds, she borrowed money from a friend to travel to England for an abortion. She stayed two nights in England, one before and one after the procedure. She did not provide any information about her next-of-kin to the clinic, and concealed her Irish address to ensure that her family did not become aware of her abortion.

Like A, she began to experience bleeding during her return journey to Ireland. Two weeks after the abortion she sought follow-up care from a clinic in Dublin that was associated with the clinic she had visited in England.[30]

## C. Applicant C

In some respects, C's case differed considerably from those of A and B, and this was reflected in the different basis of her claim and the outcome. C was a Lithuanian national living in Ireland, who had been receiving treatment for cancer in the three years prior to falling pregnant accidentally. She had discussed the issue of pregnancy with her doctor, and had been told that while it was not clear what effect becoming pregnant would have on her own condition, the chemotherapy she was receiving would be damaging to a fetus during the first trimester. While her cancer was in remission, she unintentionally became pregnant. She sought advice from a number of medical practitioners, including her general practitioner, but (she alleged) she received insufficient information about the implications of the pregnancy for her health. In her view, she also did not receive enough information about the effects of her prior tests for cancer on the fetus she was carrying. She ascribed this lack of information to the 'chilling effect' of the Irish law on abortion.

In March 2005, during her first trimester, she travelled to England for an abortion. Her decision was driven in part by the uncertainty about the risks of continuing with the pregnancy, about which she had learned through research on the internet following her failure to gain what she considered sufficient medical advice from the practitioners she had consulted. She would have preferred a medical abortion, but due to difficulties in finding a clinic in England that would treat a non-resident because of the need for follow-up, she alleged she had needed to wait eight weeks until she could undergo a surgical abortion. Like A and B, she too suffered complications

---

[30] *A, B and C* (n 28 above), [18]–[21].

during her return to Ireland, including bleeding and also infection as a consequence of the incomplete abortion.

## IV. THE ARTICLES 2, 3 AND 14 CLAIMS

A, B and C all claimed that the law regarding abortion in Ireland violated their rights under Articles 3, 8, 13 and 14 of the Convention. C further claimed that the Irish restrictions on access to abortion violated her rights under Article 2.

The Irish government challenged the admissibility of the claims on a range of bases, including that the women had failed to exhaust their domestic remedies in accordance with Article 35(1).[31] A, B and C argued that the Irish State had not provided an adequate domestic remedy, particularly in light of the restrictive interpretation of the existing law that had been taken in practice by the Irish government. They emphasised that for remedies to be effective, they needed to be available in a sufficiently timely manner to resolve the issue early in pregnancy.[32] The Court found that with regard to A and B's claims, there were no remedies to exhaust as they were seeking abortions on grounds that were not within the bounds of the existing law. Had they attempted to claim under the existing law that they were constitutionally entitled to abortions, they would have surely failed, and therefore they were not required to seek remedies in this way. For this reason, their claims were admissible.[33] With regard to C's Article 8 claim, failure to exhaust domestic remedies could not render her claim inadmissible as her claim rested fundamentally on the lack of clarity about how she (and a doctor) could have established whether the risk to her life was sufficient to render an abortion lawful.

### A. The Article 2 Claims

Article 2 of the Convention provides that everyone's right to life shall be protected by law. C claimed that the Irish government's failure to implement Article 40.3.3 meant that an abortion was not actually available even when the pregnant woman's life was under threat. The Court held that this claim was unfounded, as she was not prohibited from seeking an abortion outside Ireland. That she had to undertake such a journey as a result of her fears about her life and health was relevant to her Article 8 claim, but was not sufficient to found an Article 2 claim.[34]

---

[31] ibid [132]–[136].
[32] ibid [137]–[141].
[33] ibid [149].
[34] ibid [158]–[159].

## B. The Article 3 Claims

Article 3 of the Convention prohibits 'inhuman or degrading treatment or punishment'.[35] All three applicants claimed that their rights under Article 3 had been violated, as the criminalisation of abortion 'caused an affront to women's dignity and stigmatised women, increasing feelings of anxiety'.[36] They further argued that the only two options open to them—travelling outside Ireland (which required overcoming social taboos) or continuing the pregnancy—were both degrading and an affront to dignity. The Court found that the claims of all three applicants were manifestly unfounded under Articles 35(2) and (3), as none met the minimum threshold of severity of treatment.[37]

## C. The Article 14 Claims

All three applicants claimed that they had been subject to discrimination, and hence alleged a violation of the rights under Article 14 (Freedom from Discrimination). The Court, however, disagreed and dealt with the relevant matters under Article 8.[38]

## V. THE ARTICLE 8 CLAIMS

A and B claimed that the restrictions on abortion in Ireland, which excluded threats to health and well-being as grounds for lawful termination of pregnancy, interfered with their right to private life. C made a similar but slightly different claim, as she was likely to fall within the grounds for lawful abortion. She claimed that the lack of legislative implementation of Article 40.3.3 of the Constitution interfered with her right to privacy, as it was not sufficiently clear whether she could lawfully obtain an abortion. All three argued that their claims fell within Article 8 due to the intimate and personal nature of pregnancy and abortion.

## A. Operation of Article 8 and the 'Right' to Abortion

As a Contracting Party to the Convention, which it had introduced into Irish law in 2003 with the European Convention on Human Rights Act 2003, the

---

[35] In addition to torture.
[36] ibid [161].
[37] ibid [160]–[165].
[38] ibid [269]–[270].

Irish government is bound by an international obligation to give effect to the rights protected under the Convention.[39] These obligations include the protection of the right to privacy enshrined in Article 8(1) of the Convention, which provides that 'Everyone has the right to respect for his private and family life, his home and his correspondence'.[40]

'Private life' is, as the Court noted, a broad concept within the Convention and it accepted that legislative controls on abortion do interrupt a woman's private life. Issues around abortion therefore fell within Article 8 because, the Court said:

> [L]egislation regulating the interruption of pregnancy touches upon the sphere of private life [which includes] ... the right to personal autonomy, personal development and to establish and develop relationships with other human beings and the outside world ... [and] a person's physical and psychological integrity.[41]

A and B had sought abortions for reasons of health and well-being, and the Court agreed that their claims fell within the Article 8 protection of their right to privacy.[42] As C's claim was based on an inability to establish whether she qualified for a lawful abortion due to the law's chilling effect on information provision, this also triggered the protection of Article 8.

Article 8 places two kinds of obligation on Contracting States to ensure the right to privacy is protected: a *negative* obligation not to interfere with an individual's private life, and a *positive* obligation to ensure that that the right to privacy is given effective respect.[43] This may entail providing a legal framework, resources or directions to public bodies to make sure that this is achieved. A claimant will have to demonstrate that their right to privacy has been interfered with by showing that the State has failed to meet one of these obligations.

However, unlike some other Convention rights, the right to privacy is a qualified right, meaning the State can interfere with it in some circumstances in accordance with Article 8(2):

> There shall be no interference by a public authority with the exercise of this right except such as is in accordance with the law and is necessary in a democratic society in the interests of national security, public safety or the economic well-being of the country, for the prevention of disorder or crime, for the protection of health or morals, or for the protection of the rights and freedoms of others.[44]

[39] European Convention on Human Rights Act 2003, ss 3, 4.
[40] Council of Europe, European Convention for the Protection of Human Rights and Fundamental Freedoms, as amended by Protocols Nos 11 and 14, 4 November 1950, ETS 5, Article 8(1).
[41] *A, B and C* (n 28 above), [106]–[107].
[42] ibid [212]–[214].
[43] See, eg *Marckx v Belgium* (1979–80) 2 EHRR 330, [31].
[44] European Convention for the Protection of Human Rights and Fundamental Freedoms (n 40 above), Article 8(2).

Therefore, to determine whether an interference is justified, the Court will consider whether:

the interference is accordance with the law (that is, it is prescribed by a domestic law or legal provision);

the interference is necessary in a democratic society to pursue a legitimate aim (such aims are outlined in Article 8(2)); and

that the interference is proportionate to the legitimate aim being pursued (sometimes expressed as 'not using a sledgehammer to crack a nut'[45]).

There must be a connection between the interference and the pursuit of the aim. That interference must be necessary to achieve the aim, but should be no more than is needed to do so. In determining whether the interference is necessary to pursue the legitimate aim, the Court is prepared to grant Contracting States a 'margin of appreciation' in how they balance the interests of the person whose right is infringed, and the interest of their society in interfering with that right. The ambit of this margin of appreciation is determined by the nature of the relevant right and the degree of consensus (or lack thereof) amongst Contracting States on how a balance should be struck between protecting the right and other considerations. This margin of appreciation will narrow if consensus develops.

The ECtHR stated unequivocally that Article 8 'cannot ... be interpreted as conferring a right to abortion'.[46] Instead it was necessary to determine whether the interference with that right was justified under Article 8(2). In the Court's view, in the context of abortion, the right to privacy of the woman was to be balanced against other competing rights, and these included those of her unborn child.[47] It was required to consider whether the protection of morals was a legitimate aim in this context, and that the balance struck by the Irish government to protect them in Ireland was necessary in a democratic society and not disproportionate. The key question in the case was how wide a margin of appreciation the Court would afford Ireland. A wide margin would allow it to retain its restrictive laws, a narrow one would cast those laws as out of step with the European consensus on abortion and the Irish laws as an unjustified infringement of the right to privacy of pregnant women.

ECtHR decisions on abortion prior to *A, B and C* had, Elizabeth Wicks suggests, 'shared a common theme: the European Court of Human Rights' reluctance to substitute its own views on abortion for those of the contracting parties'.[48] It had achieved this by declining to take a position on when

---

[45] Ministry of Justice (UK), *Human Rights: Human Lives—A Handbook for Public Authorities* (Ministry of Justice, 2006) 57.

[46] *A, B and C* (n 28 above) [214].

[47] ibid [213].

[48] Wicks, '*A, B and C*' (2011) n 3 above, 556.

life begins and whether pregnancy is a purely private matter, while allowing States a wide margin of appreciation to legislate on such matters.[49] As we will see, part of what makes *A, B and C* an 'anti-landmark' case is that it confirms and continues the status quo on abortion by confirming once more that on abortion (if not other matters of deep moral sensitivity), respondent States were to be granted a wide margin of appreciation. This left Ireland free to maintain its restrictive legal framework, leading commentators such as Adam Wagner to express disappointment that the decision on this front was 'interesting but not groundbreaking'.[50]

## B. A and B's Claims—The Negative Obligation

A and B made a number of arguments in support of their claim that their Article 8 rights had been violated as they were prohibited from obtaining abortions within Ireland sought due to a threat to their health or well-being. They emphasised that pregnancy was an intimate, personal aspect of their private lives. They accepted that the aim of the law was to protect fetal life, but alleged that this aim was not achieved by the law. Irish women were permitted to travel outside the country, and consequently numerous abortions were still performed to end Irish women's pregnancies.[51] The Irish position was, they alleged, no longer reflective of the views of the Irish people, citing evidence that these views had changed substantially since 1983.[52] Effectively, then, they were arguing that the Court should move on from the balance struck in *Open Door* in 1992. This was one of their key arguments, as it entailed that there was no need to protect Irish morals to the degree the law now did. If this were accepted, it would remove the need to protect distinctive Irish morality as a ground in support of the violation of the women's Article 8 rights.

Their other key argument was that the law was a disproportionate means of balancing protection of the unborn fetus with the woman's right to privacy. Accepting the protection of foetal life as a valid goal, they argued that this was only acceptable under Article 8 when 'the health and well-being of the mother [was] given proportionate value'.[53] That had not been achieved, they argued, because women often had to seek later-term, surgical

---

[49] Wicks (n 3 above) 556.

[50] See, eg A Wagner, 'Ireland abortion ruling—the aftermath', *UK Human Rights Blog*, 1 Crown Office Row, 24 December 2010: ukhumanrightsblog.com/2010/12/24/ireland-abortion-ruling-the-aftermath.

[51] According to some estimates, as many as 4,000 Irish women travel outside the country in search of an abortion every year: 'Human rights court to rule on Irish abortion rights', *BBC News*, 16 December 2010: www.bbc.co.uk/news/world-europe-12005803.

[52] *A, B and C* (n 28 above) [170].

[53] ibid [172].

abortions over the safer medical abortions (as clinics in England would not offer medical abortions without follow-up care). Further, women were stigmatised and placed under a psychological burden in having to travel outside Ireland to seek abortions and to do something otherwise illegal at home, while poorer women were discriminated against due to the financial burden of doing so.[54]

The Irish government argued in response that the Irish law was based on 'profound moral values deeply embedded in the fabric of society in Ireland and the legal position was defined through equally intense debate'.[55] As such, for A and B to ask for the law to be changed to align it with other European States was to 'go against the recognised importance and fundamental role of the democratic process in each state and acceptance of diversity of traditions and values in contracting states'.[56]

The government argued that it was not for the Court to scrutinise the moral validity of this view when it was a legitimate goal and supported by the will of the Irish people. On this point, the Irish government emphasised that that will had been tested in numerous referenda and public engagement processes.

On the appropriate margin of appreciation, the Irish government argued that this should be wide given the decision in *Vo v France* and the lack of consensus on when life could be said to begin.[57] It disputed the existence of a consensus on abortion law generally, and stated further that 'There was no discernible argument that the legislation in some states was at some tipping point to be enforced on remaining states'.[58]

The Court was split on its decision on A and B's claims. All agreed there had been an interference, and that this was in accordance with the law and that that law was easily accessible and intelligible.[59] The essential question was whether the prohibition of abortions sought on grounds of a threat to health and well-being was justified. To answer this question, the Court had to determine whether it pursued a legitimate aim, and that the steps taken to do so were proportionate and necessary in a democratic society.

---

[54] ibid [173].

[55] ibid [180].

[56] ibid [180].

[57] The ECtHR has declined to define when life begins, having said in *Vo v France* [2004] ECHR 326 that 'it is neither desirable, nor even possible as matters stand, to answer in the abstract the question of whether the unborn child is a person for the purposes of Article 2': *Vo v France* [85]–[86]. However, Elizabeth Wicks. has argued that despite this statement, the Court did implicitly answer the question in *Vo* when it said that 'the life of the foetus was intimately connected with that of the mother and could be protected through her'. In Wicks's view, this statement suggests that 'there is no doubt, therefore, that the foetus has a "life" in the view of the Court but not one that necessarily ... requires the full protection given the "everyone" under Article 2': E Wicks, 'The Meaning of "Life": Dignity and the Right to Life in International Human Rights Treaties' (2012) 12 *Human Rights Law Review* 199–219, 209.

[58] *A, B and C* (n 28 above) [184]–[186].

[59] ibid [216]–[221].

## (i)  A Legitimate Aim and the Question of Consensus

The Court considered that the Irish law did 'pursue the legitimate aim of protecting morals, of which the protection in Ireland of the right to life of the unborn was one aspect'.[60] It held that it was legitimate for the law of Ireland to reflect the general moral standards of its community, and the Court found that this law did so.[61] As it had in *Open Door*, the Court held that the protection of the right to life of the unborn fetus was one aspect of the protection of Irish moral values.[62] The majority did not agree with submissions that Irish public opinion on abortion had shifted towards greater support for liberalisation.[63] The Court considered that the Irish people's support for inserting an 'anti-abortion' clause into the Maastricht and Lisbon Treaties spoke against suggestions that Irish views on abortion had become more liberal. However, McGuinness argues that this is a simplification of the reasons behind the Irish public's support for those clauses, arguing that:

> These clauses were born of a fear that Europeanization could lead to abortion being forced on the Irish people. How the clauses came about is far from straightforward: in reality, they are not simply the result of a majoritarian attitude on abortion but rather of political horse-trading to appeal to anti-abortion special interest groups in order to gain pro-Treaty majorities.[64]

She provides extensive background to the provisions, suggesting that it is at best 'questionable' whether support for them evidenced majority support for continuing the restrictive approach to abortion in Ireland.[65] Stijn Smet has also criticised what she regards as the majority's failure to give sufficient weight to evidence that suggested that the Irish people's views had changed, or at the very least indicated substantially less agreement on the acceptability of abortion than the majority seemed to think existed in the country.[66]

Regardless, the Court took as a starting point that Irish moral opinion was against broadening the grounds for lawful termination of pregnancy. It was this moral position, and the need to protect it that was the legitimate aim to be balanced against the women's right to privacy. The majority considered that even though the balance had been struck differently in other Contracting States, the balance that Ireland might strike could legitimately differ as the underlying moral position to be balanced was different.

---

[60]  ibid [222].
[61]  ibid [222].
[62]  ibid [222].
[63]  ibid [224]–[227].
[64]  McGuinness (n 8 above) 476, 485.
[65]  McGuinness (n 8 above) 476, 486.
[66]  S Smet, '*A, B and C v Ireland*: Abortion and the Margin of Appreciation', 17 December 2010, *Strasbourg Observers*: strasbourgobservers.com/2010/12/17/a-b-and-c-v-ireland-abortion-and-the-margin-of-appreciation.

This position is one of the crucially important aspects of the majority's reasoning, both in how it led to the final decision, and its implications for future cases on abortion. The majority defined the legitimate aim as, in part, the protection of the unborn life of the fetus, citing *Vo v France* on the impossibility of determining when life begins, and the lack of consensus on that point amongst European Contracting States. In doing so, it shifted the argument in the case away from being about consensus on the grounds for which an abortion may be sought, and contended that the relevant consensus (or lack thereof) to be considered was on the status of the unborn fetus. As we will see in the following sections, this paved the way for it to afford Ireland a wide margin of appreciation on how to regulate abortion.

### (ii)  Was it Necessary in a Democratic Society?

Having decided that the Irish law did pursue a legitimate aim, this left as the crucial question, whether the restriction on their right to private life was 'necessary in a democratic society'. For this to be the case, there needs to be a 'pressing social need' for the restriction, and the restriction must be proportionate.[67] On this point, the Court held that there was a need to balance the right to privacy of A and B with the need to protect the deeply held moral values of the Irish people and consequently the protection of the life of the unborn fetus. The Court was divided on how this was to be struck, with six judges dissenting on the final decision.

The Court has the power to afford Contracting States a 'margin of appreciation' as to how they will strike this balance in part because the State is best placed to know how this balance should be struck within its own society. It is also to allow for difference of opinion between the different State populaces on moral matters, although this is not unrestricted. Where the matter relates to an important aspect of personal identity, as abortion does, the margin should be narrower. However, on sensitive moral issues, it may be wider. The particularly sensitive nature of abortion was hence a prima facie reason to extend a wide margin of appreciation to the Irish State to regulate abortion in keeping with the moral views within its borders.[68]

Another factor in determining the margin is whether a consensus on the matter exists amongst European Contracting States. If there is, this may mean that the margin should be greater. It is this aspect of the Court's decision that has been greatly criticised, and on which the Court itself was divided. In the majority's view, there was considerable consensus between Member States on abortion, with the majority allowing abortion 'on broader grounds than accorded under Irish law'.[69] This should have meant

[67] *A, B and C* (n 28 above) [229].
[68] ibid [232]–[233].
[69] ibid [235].

that the margin of appreciation on the matter was narrow, however the Court avoided this conclusion by finding that the lack of consensus *on the point at which life begins* was the crucial matter. This, the majority considered, was fundamental to the issue of abortion, and meant that the margin of appreciation applied to how the Irish State chose to balance the interests of the unborn fetus against those of the mother. There was, in the majority's view, no consensus on when life begins between Contracting States, nor was any such consensus to be found in the European jurisprudence (citing its earlier decision in *Vo v France*).[70] Science also could not provide a definitive answer to when human life begins; hence there was no consensus on the matter before the Court. Therefore, the majority reasoned that the balance struck in other Contracting States between protection of the rights of the mother and of the fetus could not 'be ... decisive factors in the Court's examination of whether the impugned prohibition ... struck a fair balance'.[71] This lack of consensus justified a wide margin of appreciation on how to balance the rights to life of the mother and fetus, one potentially wide enough to accommodate Ireland's restrictive laws.

The approach of the majority on this aspect of the decision has come under considerable fire, both in the Court itself, and from academic commentators. The dissenting judges considered the majority's approach deeply problematic. It was argued that allowing the moral views within one state to 'override the European consensus, which tends in a completely different direction, is a real and dangerous new departure in the Court's case-law'.[72] The dissenters rightly took issue with the majority's re-conceptualising the issue as one about the point at which life begins (on which there is no European consensus). The issue on which it was necessary to see if consensus existed was not when life began, they argued, but whether abortion should be permitted on broader grounds for A and B's Article 8 right to privacy to have been adequately protected. They stated that the

> issue before the Court was whether, regardless of when life begins—before birth or not—the right to life of the foetus can be balanced against the right to life of the mother, or her right to personal autonomy and development, and possibly found to weigh less than the latter rights or interests. And the answer seems to be clear: there is an undeniably strong consensus among European States ... to the effect that, regardless of the answer to be given to the scientific, religious or philosophical question of the beginning of life, the right to life of the mother, and, in most countries' legislation, her well-being and health, are considered more valuable than the right to life of the foetus.[73]

[70] ibid [235]–[236]. *Vo v France* (above n 57).
[71] ibid [237].
[72] ibid Joint dissent, [9].
[73] ibid Joint dissent, [2].

Elizabeth Wicks points out that the dissenters' criticism of this step is:

> Strengthened by the failure of the majority to explain in sufficiently full terms why the apparent lack of a consensus on when life begins is more relevant to this case than the acknowledged consensus to provide more liberal abortion laws than those existing in Ireland ... To recognise that consensus instead, and then choose to ignore it when determining the width of Ireland's margin of appreciation is indeed an unwelcome new approach that threatens to undermine the evolutive nature of the Convention's obligations. The margin of appreciation is controversial enough already without the Court choosing to depart from its previous practice of restricting the margin on the rare occasions when a moral consensus can be identified.[74]

Paolo Ronchi, too, has pointed out that its use of the principle, 'in no way toed the line of Strasbourg authority on the issue. When a broad consensus exists, Strasbourg has usually narrowed the State's space for manoeuvre decisively'.[75]

Similarly, Wicks has noted how the Court approached the issue of the United Kingdom's law on transsexuals' change of gender, with the United Kingdom originally being afforded a wide margin of appreciation, which was then narrowed when a European consensus on the matter had emerged.[76] She argues that in refusing to 'use [the] emerging consensus [on the grounds for abortion] ... to narrow the width of the margin to be accorded to Ireland', the majority made 'a startling departure from its previous practice'.[77]

This is certainly one aspect of *A, B and C* that makes it a landmark case, as it indicates that the ECtHR is willing to depart from its past jurisprudence to pursue what it considers the right result. This has potentially wide implications for other areas of medical law, as many such areas raise moral concerns similar to those attending abortion—access to reproductive medical services, end of life care, pre-natal genetic diagnosis, and the list goes on. If the Court is prepared to allow Contracting States to walk their own path despite consensus on access to abortion, it is certainly possible that *A, B and C* will be used as support for a State's otherwise unacceptable divergence if similarly sensitive moral reasons can be raised by it in support of its position. This is highly problematic as it goes against the principles underpinning the Convention's protection of all citizens of the EU, and further allows States to take restrictive approaches that undermine the protection of Convention rights on what should be considered unacceptable grounds. In a wider sense, the ruling also does damage to the doctrine of margin of appreciation generally, and so may have more far-reaching implications beyond medical law cases.

---

[74] Wicks (n 3 above) 562.
[75] Ronchi, 'Case Comment' (2011) n 1 above, 369.
[76] Wicks (n 3 above) 561, citing *Goodwin v United Kingdom* (1996) 35 EHRR 447.
[77] Wicks (n 3 above) 561. See also Smet, '*A, B and C*' (2010) n 66 above.

The majority's approach also problematically seemed to suggest that in the absence of consensus on the point at which life begins, the balances struck in those States with wider grounds for abortion could not indicate a consensus on the balance of maternal/fetal rights of the kind needed to narrow the margin of appreciation. But while it is true that when life begins may be relevant to the grounds on which abortion might be permitted, being uncertain about when life begins does not mean it is impossible to come to a position on the ambit of such grounds. For example, Judith Jarvis Thompson has made compelling arguments in favour of permitting abortion even where one accepts that life begins at conception.[78] Part of the reason why we should not (as the dissenters argued) conflate the two questions of when life begins and how the rights of mother and fetus ought to be balanced is that there may be other factors that affect the balance of rights that are not affected by the answer to the question of when life begins. The moral views of the people of the relevant State are one factor (recognised by the Court and the Convention), but concerns about the welfare of the child that might be produced could be another. While it is not clear whether termination on the grounds of fetal abnormality is permissible in Ireland, it might be a legitimate moral concern that affects the balance of rights, where the potential child will be born into significant suffering, or as in *D* have a condition incompatible with life. When life begins is only one aspect of the question of when abortion should be available, and in reducing the issue of consensus to this alone, the majority mischaracterised the relevance of the balances struck in other Contracting States.

Further, the very lack of a consensus about when life begins, and the inability of science to provide one, suggests that this is an issue on which reasonable disagreement might be possible. In the face of this, and given the need for States to allow freedom of religion, and individual views on moral issues, it can be argued that broad grounds for allowing abortion should be favoured. This is best achieved via a permissive regime that still takes some account of the value of fetal life, but allows those who consider abortion acceptable to follow their beliefs, while permitting those who disagree the option of not choosing to terminate unwanted pregnancies of their own.

Of course, for those who consider abortion the murder of an innocent human being, such a permissive approach will always be wrong, but this is the very nub of the argument around the lack of consensus about when life begins—if this is what we disagree on, then it cannot be the basis for choosing one view (that of those who believe life begins at conception) over the views of others to determine what the law shall be. Therefore, in finding that there was no consensus on this matter, the majority's reasoning that the margin of appreciation should be wide (permitting Ireland to continue

---

[78] JJ Thompson, 'A Defense of Abortion' (1971) 1 *Philosophy and Public Affairs* 1.

restricting abortions) actually had the problematic impact of meaning that those who did not share the view that supported the Irish governments laws were bound by those views regardless. This 'pro-majoritarian' argument will be revisited later. What can be said here is that while there is no consensus on when life begins amongst European Member States, the laws of those States are strong evidence that this kind of permissive approach is favoured for exactly these reasons. Therefore, despite the majority's view, there was a relevant consensus that should have narrowed the margin of appreciation.

The dissenters argued that the decision was:

> the first time that the Court has disregarded the existence of a European consensus on the basis of 'profound moral views'. Even assuming that these profound moral views are still well embedded in the conscience of the majority of Irish people, to consider that this can override the European consensus, which tends in a completely different direction, is a real and dangerous new departure in the Court's case-law. A case-law which to date has not distinguished between moral and other beliefs when determining the margin of appreciation which can be afforded to States in situations where a European consensus is at hand.[79]

Despite these concerns, having afforded Ireland a wide margin of appreciation, the Court therefore had to determine whether the balance struck was a fair and necessary one. Given that wide margin, and the profound views to be protected, the majority considered that because Ireland now permitted women to travel outside its borders to obtain abortions, allowed the provision of information about such services, and permitted abortion where the mother's life was in danger, the balance struck was acceptable. A and B's claims were therefore dismissed.

The effect, as Ronchi aptly puts it, was to give the majority of the Court's 'imprimatur to the Irish "anywhere but here" policy'.[80] This 'anywhere but here' policy was, the majority felt, a reasonable way to balance these women's right to make private decisions about their bodies with the need to protect Irish morals, but many have disagreed, as we will discuss below.

## C. C's Claim—The Positive Obligation

In addition to the arguments made by A and B, C argued that there was a lack of legislation implementing the constitutional right to an abortion. She contended that the meaning of a 'real and substantial risk' to the life of the mother was not clear, and that it was not possible to obtain clarification. A law that prescribes an interference with the right to privacy under Article 8 must be publicly accessible, and sufficiently clarify the circumstances in

---

[79] *A, B and C* (n 28 above) Joint dissent, [9].
[80] Ronchi (n 1 above) 367.

which that interference is justified.[81] Those conditions subject to which an interference will be lawful must be available in enough detail to enable a potentially affected person to understand when their rights may be affected.[82] Therefore, to decide on C's claim, the Court had to determine whether the Irish government was under a positive obligation to provide clear, effective, and accessible procedures for determining whether she had the right to an abortion on the basis of risk to her life. Ireland argued that it had provided such procedures. She could first, it argued, consult her doctor, who would be able to evaluate the risk to her life. Alternatively, she could have brought a constitutional action to have the court determine whether she was eligible. The ECtHR rejected both arguments.

In contrast to its stance on A and B's claims, the Court was unanimous in its verdict with regards to C's claim. The Court took the view that the Irish State was required to take positive steps to ensure C's Article 8 right was protected. It was critical of the State's failure to implement Article 40.3.3 via legislation, which was exacerbated by the State's leaving the Offences Against the Person Act 1861 in force without amendment, and the failure to provide clear guidelines for medical practitioners on what would constitute a 'real and serious risk' to the life of the mother. The criteria a woman would have to meet to qualify for an abortion lacked precision, and the combination of these factors 'contributed to the lack of certainty for a woman seeking a lawful abortion in Ireland'.[83] The Court was clear that any rights afforded via the Constitution must be more than theoretical; they must by force of law be given practical effect:

> There is no framework whereby any difference of opinion between the woman and her doctor or between different doctors consulted, or whereby an understandable hesitancy on the part of the woman or doctor, could be examined and resolved through a decision which would establish as a matter of law whether a particular case presented a qualifying risk to a woman's life such that a lawful abortion might be performed.[84]

This uncertainty, and consequent failure to adequately protect her right, derived from the absence of any legislative clarification of the operation of Article 40.3.3, and particularly the lack of any mechanism for determining when a risk would fall within the Article's ambit.

The Court was not swayed by the Irish government's arguments, and following its earlier decision in *Tysiac v Poland*, it held that where abortion is permitted, the state must make the grounds on which it is available clear and have a procedure in place for determining when these grounds will be

---

[81] See, eg, *Liberty v United Kingdom* (2009) 48 EHRR 1.
[82] See, eg, *Kruslin v France* (1990) 12 EHRR 547.
[83] *A, B and C* (n 28 above) [253].
[84] ibid [253].

met. It held that the law was sufficiently uncertain that a medical practitioner would not be able to accurately evaluate whether the risk to her life was sufficient to bring her situation within Article 40.3.3. Submissions to this effect were made by a range of interest groups, including joint submission from the British Pregnancy Advisory Service (BPAS) and Doctors for Choice (Ireland), to the effect that the medical profession were also in a state of confusion about the ambit of Article 40.3.3. They pointed out that they 'faced criminal charges, on the one hand, and an absence of clear legal, ethical or medical guidelines, on the other'.[85] As Wicks has pointed out, this suggests that 'even the life of the mother exception to the prohibition on abortion in Ireland [was] largely illusory' and given that BPAS and Doctors for Choice (Ireland) were unaware of any cases of abortion to save a life in Ireland 'it appears that in reality [at the time] lawful abortions [were] non-existent in Ireland'.[86]

The Court agreed, stating that:

> against this background of substantial uncertainty, the Court considers it evident that the criminal provisions of the 1861 Act would constitute a significant chilling factor for both women and doctors in the medical consultation process, regardless of whether or not prosecutions have in fact been pursued under that Act. Both the third applicant and any doctor ran a risk of a serious criminal conviction and imprisonment in the event that a decision taken in medical consultation, that the woman was entitled to an abortion in Ireland given the risk to her life, was later found not to accord with Article 40.3.3 of the Constitution. Doctors also risked professional disciplinary proceedings and serious sanctions.[87]

It therefore considered that the risk of criminal sanctions had had a 'chilling effect' on C's ability to gain sufficient information and guidance to establish whether she qualified for a lawful abortion. The absence of guidance on the ambit and application of Article 40.3.3, and the risks doctors faced should they make an incorrect evaluation meant there was not an effective procedure for determining when the right to privacy would be subject to interference. The Court therefore did not consider the possibility of consulting her doctor as sufficient to protect her right. As McGuinness writes of *A, B and C*, 'The judgement in this case exemplifies the consequences of an approach to abortion regulation where a government "chooses" to facilitate abortion services through "delegation and doubt"'.[88]

The ECtHR also rejected the Irish government's argument that C could have had the matter clarified for her within the courts, and thereby rejected the idea

---

[85] ibid [207].
[86] Wicks (n 3 above) 569.
[87] *A, B and C* (n 28 above) [254].
[88] McGuinness (n 8 above) 476, quoting M Fox and T Murphy, 'Irish Abortion: Seeking Refuge in a Jurisprudence of Doubt and Delegation' (1992) 19 *Journal of Law and Society* 454–66.

that courts should be 'some kind of licensing authority for abortions'.[89] The Court was unconvinced by the efficacy of such a procedure, and considered it inapt, stating that courts were 'not the appropriate fora for the primary determination as to whether a woman qualifies for an abortion'.[90]

The Court condemned the Irish government's failure to implement Article 40.3.3 through effective legislation, which it said had '[r]esulted in a striking discordance between the theoretical right to a lawful abortion in Ireland on grounds of relevant risk to a woman's life and the reality of its practical implementation'.[91] Barbara Hewson has understandably called these conclusions 'damning'.[92]

Article 8 had therefore been violated in the case of C. The Court held that the Irish government was required to compensate her for her non-pecuniary damage and she was awarded €15,000. The Court did not direct the Irish State to take any specific measures to address the violation but commented that other Contracting States had taken legislative steps to define when an abortion would be lawful, and had put in place procedures for evaluating when the criteria for a lawful abortion would be met.

The Court recognised that implementation of its ruling would be a 'sensitive and complex task', but certainly achievable, particularly given that it was directing the Irish government not to change its laws, but simply to clarify the ambit of an already accepted softening of the original prohibition. Consequently, 'implementation could not be considered to involve significant detriment to the Irish public since it would amount to rendering effective a right already accorded, after referendum, by Article 40.3.3 of the Constitution'.[93]

## VI. AFTERMATH

The Irish government was slow to act on the Court's decision, echoing its previous heel-dragging on matters of abortion, with the Committee of Ministers of the Council of Europe expressing concern over this delay in either putting in place interim measures or implementing the decision.[94] It did eventually convene an expert group to advise on how to implement the decision, and this group reported in November 2012. It recommended that legislation was necessary to properly implement the Court's decision, and

---

[89] *A, B and C* (n 28 above) [96], quoting from *A and B v Eastern Health Board, Judge Mary Fahy and C, and the Attorney General (notice party)* [1998] 1 IR 464.

[90] ibid [258].

[91] ibid [264].

[92] B Hewson, 'Family: No *Roe v Wade*' (2011) 161 *New Law Journal* 119, 120.

[93] *A, B and C* (n 28 above) [266].

[94] 'Govt response to ABC case to be examined', *RTE News*, 14 November 2012: www.rte.ie/news/2012/1114/345607-abortion-ireland-law.

anything less would be insufficient. One month later the Irish government announced plans to produce legislation and guidelines that would give effect to the decision and also the Irish Supreme Court's own decision in the *X* case handed down some 20 years earlier. Following consultations with the parliamentary Health Committee over the first half of 2013, the Protection of Life During Pregnancy Act passed into Irish law in July 2013.

The Act repealed sections 58 and 59 of the Offences Against the Person Act 1861, but retained the general prohibition on abortion via section 22 of the new legislation, which prescribes that 'to intentionally destroy unborn human life' is an offence punishable by fine or imprisonment of for up to 14 years. The Act enshrines the holding in *X* that abortion is lawful where there is a real and substantial risk of loss of the woman's life from physical illness that can only be averted by terminating the pregnancy. That risk must be certified by two medical professionals, except in cases of emergency when certification from one will suffice (and the risk must be immediate).[95] Section 9 makes clear that a risk of suicide is also sufficient to render an abortion lawful, as long as three medical professionals certify that the risk is real and substantial and can only be averted by termination of the pregnancy.[96] Section 18 prescribes that nothing in the Act shall limit the freedom to travel outside Ireland (including travel for the purpose of producing an abortion), nor to obtain or make available information about obtaining abortions outside Ireland.

## VII. IMPACT OF *A, B AND C* AND WHY IT DESERVES LANDMARK STATUS

The decision in *A, B and C* has already had an important impact in Ireland, having at last pressed the Irish government into clarifying its laws, but it has wider implications for the future of how abortion, and potentially other sensitive issues in medical law, will be dealt with in Europe. The significance of *A, B and C* is not that it changes the law in Ireland or that of the EU to any great degree—it does not. The ECtHR did not require the Irish government to liberalise its laws on abortion, only to clarify when the exceptions to the ban on abortion already in place would apply. However, given the impact of the lack of clarity prior to the decision, the post-*A, B and C* amendments in Ireland mean that clear laws should make it easier for women to obtain abortions when their lives are in danger. If other Contracting States attempt to take the approach Ireland took prior to *A, B and C*, it is evident that any challenge on the basis of lack of clarity should succeed. Arguably, this should apply broadly to other areas of medical practice where States might

---

[95] Protection of Life During Pregnancy Act 2013 (Ireland) ss 7, 8.
[96] ibid s 9.

use a lack of clarity to prevent access to services, such as euthanasia or pre-natal genetic testing.

At the Irish level, and also specifically in the context of abortion, the decision effectively deems it reasonable to leave women who want or need abortions to travel a long way from their homes and away from the support of families to obtain them unless they are likely to otherwise die. As McGuinness has commented:

> The Court, through its questionable use of the margin of appreciation and by focusing on narrow examples of the views of the Irish population, has endorsed a system where those like A and B are forced to continue to travel in their thousands each year, under shrouds of secrecy and shame, to Britain and elsewhere to access safe and legal abortion. And of course such a system relies on the mobility of those women and presumes a cosmopolitanism that is undermined by the existence of ash clouds and national borders.[97]

Many women in Ireland will not be able to take advantage of the freedom to travel, and hence their right to privacy has not been fully protected. Numerous commentators have pointed out that for many Irish women the right to travel outside Ireland for an abortion is illusory as a protection of their Article 8 rights. Quite apart from issues around the psychological, physical and financial burdens of such travel, and whether women should have to shoulder these burdens to obtain an abortion, to be an effective protection, all women would need to be able to travel, and it is clear that many cannot. Lisa Smyth puts it well when she writes: 'The existence of a right to travel to obtain an abortion abroad can be small comfort to those finding themselves pregnant without the health or economic resources to have any real choice about their situation'.[98]

So while the Court did require that laws were to be clear, as in cases like that of C, and so has ensured women in her position will have their right to privacy protected, those like A and B will have their rights protected only if they have the resources to do so. For some, even that will be insufficient as numerous women living in Ireland will require visas to move between countries, even temporarily, and may require a visa to return to Ireland after the abortion.[99]

The wider significance of this aspect of the decision is that it goes against what Mary Gilmartin has described as being 'at the heart of the EU project': mobility—'EU citizens should, in theory, be free to move around the EU, and live, work or use services, such as health case, in whichever state they

---

[97] McGuinness (n 8 above) 476, 490.

[98] L Smyth, 'Guest Post: Smyth on *A, B and C*' Human Rights in Ireland, 23 December 2010: humanrights.ie/civil-liberties/guest-post-smyth-on-ab-and-c/.

[99] M Gilmartin, 'Abortion and the Politics of Mobility: Gilmartin on *A, B and C*' *Human Rights in Ireland*, 23 December 2010: humanrights.ie/international-lawinternational-human-rights/abortion-and-the-politics-of-mobility-gilmartin-on-a-b-and-c.

choose'.[100] She makes the point that in resolving the issue of abortion by simply allowing women to have one elsewhere, the Irish government had not, she argues, addressed the real issue, and this was something the dissenters recognised.[101] The impact of consensus on the margin of appreciation is tied up with pursuing the goal of mobility. Not permitting states to stray too far from that consensus, when one exists, is a way of ensuring that EU citizens can move between states without having to sacrifice the protection of their Convention rights. This is partly what is so worrying about the way the decision in *A, B and C* takes a step away from the general trend towards respecting consensus through the margin of appreciation doctrine.

Wicks makes a similar point:

> While the hypocrisy [of allowing women to travel for abortions] might be an understandable compromise for Ireland, it should not have been so keenly approved by a Court whose task is to uphold human rights across a region in which it recognised a consensus to prioritise the rights of pregnant women over those of the foetus. Having already recognised the 'significant psychological burden' faced by the applicants in being required to leave their home country to seek medical treatment prohibited there, the Court should have been more reluctant to present that psychological burden as the very guarantee of respect for the women's private life.[102]

Relatedly, the decision effectively holds that a state is not required to protect its citizens' rights within its own borders if other states have taken steps that will afford them protection. One of the key criticisms of the Irish approach to abortion even in the wake of *A, B and C* is that it relies on other countries, particularly the United Kingdom, to provide abortion services for Irish women who want or need them. As Labour politician Roger Dowds said following the death of Savita Halappanavar in 2012, Ireland has been dodging the issue of abortion for many years: 'The reality is that if Britain wasn't on our doorstep, we would have had to introduce abortion legislation years ago to avoid women dying in back-street abortions'.[103]

As an approach to dealing with such difficult matters, this must be seen to be unsatisfactory. This aspect of the decision has potential implications for areas such as IVF services, euthanasia and pre-natal genetic testing, as it paves the way for the Court to sanction a similar approach to these issues even if a consensus about how the balance of rights should be struck has developed. It suggests that if one state is prepared to offer euthanasia, and others refuse, as long as travel is possible, that this will be reasonable despite the burdens on citizens. It supports the current approach taken by the United Kingdom to such matters, regardless of the obvious problem of

---

[100] ibid.
[101] ibid.
[102] Wicks (n 3 above) 563.
[103] Dalby, 'Inquiry Sought' (2012) n 25 above.

leaving the terminally ill in the position where they must board an airplane to find an end to their suffering.

More broadly, in affording Ireland a wide margin of appreciation to maintain its restrictive laws, the ECtHR has taken a clear stance that on morally sensitive matters it will be less inclined to intervene to prevent interferences with qualified rights. Smet makes the valid point (following Ronald Dworkin and George Letsas) that in being swayed by what it perceived as a consensus within Ireland about abortion, and so permitting a balancing of rights under Article 8 that supported only highly restricted access to abortion, the majority's approach reflected a 'pro-majoritarian bias, leading to a lesser protection of the rights of minorities (in the wide sense)'.[104] In Smet's view, this is a 'strong reason *not* to use the margin of appreciation doctrine in weighing different interests when public morals are involved at one end of the scales, irrespective of the existence of a European consensus'.[105]

She is right, for in doing so the Court's decision has the effect that in areas where a state takes a restrictive approach, as Ireland has, on the basis of that populace's moral views, this will condemn those in the moral minority to be bound to these restrictions, leaving their right to privacy merely illusory.

For those who favour a broadening of the grounds for access to abortion in states such as Ireland, *A, B and C* may not be the landmark, line in the sand, against *Roe v Wade* it appears to be. It could be said that the decision, coupled with *Vo*, actually evidences a reluctance on the part of the ECtHR to go the extra step towards recognising a right to life for the fetus. They could have done so, yet did not. In fact, in supporting the Irish State's position and giving its approval to its permitting women to go elsewhere for abortions, the Court actually did not support Ireland's rather weak commitment to protecting unborn life. Weak, because Ireland is now prepared to let women terminate their pregnancies as long as they do it elsewhere. This inconsistency is exacerbated by the provision of information, which effectively means the Irish government will even help women to find out how to terminate their pregnancies, but only if it involves helping them find someone outside Ireland to do the dirty work. Wicks makes this point forcefully when she writes:

> If the views of the Irish people, and the Irish state, are so profound and fundamental to the continuation of its democratic society, how can the right to travel abroad for an abortion be tolerated? If a foetal life is to be regarded as one worthy of the full protection of the right to life, why are Irish women entitled, by a constitutional provision, to take a short journey across the Irish Sea to terminate their pregnancies? ... [T]he blatant hypocrisy of the Irish solution cannot be a viable or ethically sound way forward.[106]

[104] Smet (n 66 above).
[105] Smet (n 66 above).
[106] Wicks (n 3 above) 563.

It is this very problem at the heart of the Irish solution, which the majority found so compelling, that suggests that if a challenge is brought in one of the other states with similarly restrictive laws, or laws that are being applied in a restrictive manner, they will at least be expected to allow women to travel for terminations. This is one bright spot in an otherwise deeply disappointing decision for those who support a woman's right to choose.

It also suggests that this crucial aspect of the majority's position is open to significant challenge, and so may not hold sway in future cases. Indeed, some of the judges in *A, B and C* pointed to some potential future problems of this kind. Judges Guerra and Casadevall considered that the majority's affording such a wide margin of appreciation to Ireland, enabling it to restrict rights on 'a particularly important facet of individual existence' was wrong. They pointed out that usually in such cases, which would include women seeking abortions on the basis of threat to their health or well-being, the margin should be narrow. They were especially critical of what they saw as the majority's failure to 'make reference to the degree of gravity of the real or perceived dangers to the applicants' health or wellbeing in their individual cases, and in their particular and specific circumstances'.[107]

While they felt that the threat to A and B would fall within such a narrow margin, other cases of greater threat (but less than risk to life), might not, and this issue should have received greater attention. In their view, therefore:

> It cannot be excluded that in other cases, in which there are grave dangers to the health or the well-being of the woman wishing to have an abortion, the state's prohibition of abortion could be considered disproportionate and beyond its margin of appreciation.[108]

It may be that on different facts, the Court might narrow the margin, or at least regard the kind of balance struck in Ireland as insufficient. Similarly, it may be the case that if consensus continues to build, and the Irish people's views shift, the margin of appreciation given to Ireland will not be sustainable. As Jonathan Herring comments, the very reliance placed by the Court on the views of the Irish people as being in support of abortion means that if those views shift, it will become more difficult for the Irish government to justify its strict laws.[109]

## VIII. CONCLUSION

The decision in *A, B and C* was conservative in two senses. It both left the Irish position on abortion essentially unchanged, and also made no great

---

[107] *A, B and C* (n 28 above), Concurring Opinion of Judge López Guerra and Judge Casadevall [3]–[5].
[108] ibid [3]–[5].
[109] J Herring, *Medical Law and Ethics*, 3rd edn (Oxford, Oxford University Press, 2010) 308.

changes to the European jurisprudence.[110] Hewson puts it more bluntly: 'this is no *Roe v Wade*'.[111] However, while many saw *A, B and C* as a blow in the fight for broadening women's right to abortion in countries with restrictive laws, some, such as Wagner, have argued that in recognising that abortion falls squarely within the Article 8 privacy right might 'lead in future to more wide-ranging judgments, along the lines of *Roe v Wade*'.[112] *A, B and C* does not draw a line under the abortion debate, and it is, as Herring has pointed out, certainly still possible for a right to abortion to be recognised in the future.[113] In fact, Herring argues that in one sense the case *did* recognise a right to abortion (via Article 8 rights), but that this was a qualified right, which in the Irish context could be outweighed by concerns about public morality and the like.

Others, such as Wicks point out that the Court's recognition of the consensus on broad grounds for access to abortion amongst Contracting States

> hints at a more interventionist Court in future abortion cases. Despite the Court's willingness in this case to permit Ireland a broad discretion to depart from the consensus on abortion, due to Ireland's uniquely strong stance on the moral status of the foetus, the explicit recognition of an emerging consensus has, in other contexts, been an early sign that the Court's toleration of a state out of step with the consensus may soon draw to an end. The UK's experience in respect of legal recognition of a transsexual's change in gender is a good example of this. Perhaps the days of states being completely free to resolve the maternal-foetal conflict in any way of their choosing are numbered. As long as the Court continues to refuse to grant a foetus an explicit, complete right to life, the door remains open for a prioritisation of the woman's rights. For now, however, the most that the Court has been prepared to do in *A, B and C v Ireland* is to ensure that a pregnant woman is able to access an abortion in circumstances where the state has already conceded its legality. This is an important practical protection for Irish women's rights and life, but it sidesteps the core of the enduring moral and legal conflict on abortion, and one wonders for how much longer the Court will be able, or choose, to do so.[114]

Whatever the future for broader grounds for abortion, one indisputable impact of the decision is that it makes clear that where abortion is permitted, there must be clear guidance on when this will be so. Vague and confusing criteria will not suffice; the relevant legislature must lay down explicit directions on when abortion will, and will not, be lawful.[115] Preventing access

---

[110] See, eg Wagner, 'Ireland abortion ruling' (2010) n 50 above.

[111] Hewson, 'Family' (2011) n 9 above, 119.

[112] A Wagner, 'Ireland must make access to abortion easier in life threatening situations', *UK Human Rights Blog*, 1 Crown Office Row, 16 December 2010: ukhumanrightsblog.com/2010/12/16/ireland-must-change-law-to-make-abortion-easier-in-life-threatening-situations.

[113] Herring, *Medical Law and Ethics* (2010) n 109 above, 308.

[114] Wicks (n 3 above) 565–66.

[115] Herring (n 109 above) 308.

to life-saving abortions through obfuscation, doubt and delegation will no longer be tolerated.

## IX. POSTSCRIPT

In the week before the submission of this chapter, a story emerged in the press of a case that suggests that the new Irish legislation is being interpreted in an arguably restrictive manner. The facts remain somewhat uncertain, and there has been only limited response from the Irish government as yet, so the case must be approached with circumspection. In August 2014, the *Irish Independent* reported that a young woman living in Dublin, known as Ms Y, had sought an abortion under section 9 of the Protection of Life in Pregnancy Act 2013. She was eight weeks pregnant at the time, and the pregnancy was the result of rape. She was a foreign national, and it seems she was therefore unable to travel freely outside of Ireland.[116]

She stated that she was suicidal, a view she has since confirmed to the press.[117] By her account, after her first pregnancy test, she was referred to the Irish Family Planning Association (IFPA) and told that abortion was not legal in Ireland, but that she could travel to England for the procedure. She was informed that it would be six weeks before she could do so as paperwork had to be organised.[118] According to the woman, she then had a number of meetings at IFPA and believed the process for transport to England was underway. She was eventually informed that the cost of the travel and procedure could be more than €1500, which it seems she could not afford to pay. By this time, she was 16 weeks pregnant and had resolved to end her life.[119] She made her first attempt on her life at this time, but was interrupted. She eventually sought out a GP, who referred her to a hospital where she was evaluated by a psychiatrist. By this time she was around 24 weeks pregnant. She was initially told that an abortion would be performed, but a few days later was informed that this was no longer the case and that instead her only option was to undergo a Caesarean section.[120]

---

[116] M Enright, 'Suicide and the Protection of Life in Pregnancy Act 2013', *Human Rights in Ireland*, 16 August 2014: humanrights.ie/constitution-of-ireland/suicide-and-the-protection-of-life-in-pregnancy-act-2013 (accessed 1 September 2014).

[117] K Holland, 'They said they could not do an abortion. I said, "You can leave me now to die. I don't want to live in this world anymore"', *Irish Times*, 19 August 2014: www.irishtimes.com/news/health/they-said-they-could-not-do-an-abortion-i-said-you-can-leave-me-now-to-die-i-don-t-want-to-live-in-this-world-anymore-1.1901258 (accessed 1 September 2014); 'Rape victim forced to have a Caesarean in Ireland speaks out', *Channel 4 News*, 19 August 2014: www.channel4.com/news/abortion-suicide-rape-choice-ireland-victim-speaks (accessed 1 September 2014).

[118] Holland, 'They said' (2014) n 117 above.

[119] ibid.

[120] ibid.

Prior to the procedure being performed, she was shown a document signed by two psychiatrists and a gynaecologist. It appears that her request for an abortion had been denied (despite the three medical practitioners agreeing that abortion was justified by the suicide risk) and a Caesarean regarded as the best option to balance the fetus's right to life with that of the mother.[121]

In the woman's view, by this stage 'I didn't have a choice', although she did in the end consent to the section (after initially protesting via hunger strike).[122] The procedure was performed and the baby, delivered at around 25 weeks' gestation, was still in hospital at the time of reporting. It appears to have been placed under a care order. The Irish Health Services Executive (HSE) has responded to the situation by pointing out that Caesarean section is a lawful means of acceding to a request for termination on grounds of suicide risk.[123]

What should we make of this application of the Act? The case is being called the first real test of the new legislation, with some critics pointing out that the law means that many women may not be able to access a termination, even on the grounds provided by the Act.[124] Doctors for Choice have argued that this case demonstrates the Act is inherently flawed precisely because it requires a balance to be struck between the rights of the mother and the fetus; 'If a young rape victim, certified as requiring an abortion due to the risk of suicide, cannot access abortion services, then the legislation and its implementation are clearly fatally flawed'.[125]

The group has called for the Eighth Amendment to be appealed. Máiréad Enright has rightly questioned whether this case demonstrates an attempt to bring a 'viability threshold' into the Act by the 'back door', opening the way for other women wanting an abortion who present close to the 24 week mark to be treated similarly.[126] Time will tell if Enright is correct, but this case does suggest that in leaving open the option of Caesarean, the Act has created an incentive to delay abortion until viability is reached. It effectively creates a means to continue to deny women the option that the legislation was supposed to ensure could be obtained as their constitutional right.

Whether, in fact, such an incentive affected the actions taken with regard to Ms Y's situation cannot be evaluated without all the facts, but her case certainly provides an example of a context in which such an incentive could operate and how the health and legal systems will respond. If, as it seems, there was a significant and unjustified delay in determining whether an

---

[121] Enright, 'Suicide' (2014) n 116 above.

[122] Holland (n 117 above).

[123] ibid.

[124] H McDonald, 'Woman denied abortion in Ireland "became pregnant after rape"', *The Guardian*, 18 August 2014: www.theguardian.com/world/2014/aug/18/ireland-woman-forced-caesarean-pregnant-rape-friend (accessed 1 September 2014).

[125] ibid.

[126] Enright (n 116 above).

abortion could be performed (leaving that decision until it was too late), then we are, as Enright has suggested, 'firmly back in the territory of the ECHR judgment in *A, B and C v Ireland*—inordinate delay and ineffective procedures rendering the constitutional right to an abortion ineffective and inaccessible'.[127] Had she been offered an abortion early on, a Caesarean would not have been available as a means to balance her rights against those of the fetus. An abortion would have been the only means to protect her right to life in the face of her suicidal state (as required by the legislation). It may be that heels were dragged to open Caesarean section as the only option. Or, it might be that the delay arose for other reasons, perhaps related to establishing whether she was suicidal or as part of determining whether she could travel. Without more information, it is unreasonable to speculate on why the delay occurred.

What we can know, however, is that undertaking a Caesarean section at 25 weeks gestation is a course of action that will be regarded as an acceptable option under the new legislation. We can also question to what extent this can really be said to be the *best* course of action, given the low survival rates and high risk of physical and mental problems associated with such early delivery. Only six or seven in ten babies born at 25 weeks survive, of whom four in ten will have severe disabilities (including profound deafness and blindness, difficult walking and cerebral palsy). Less than a quarter of babies born at this time will survive and suffer no disabilities.[128] For some, even a disabled life is better than no life, and certainly that position has merit. But to deliberately create a situation in which a baby that was otherwise healthy will be born at risk of death or serious disability is deeply problematic. If one really takes the position that the unborn fetus has a right to life that is at least equal to that of the mother, would it not be more coherent to simply refuse abortions beyond the point of viability? There is not scope here for a discussion of this point, but this case and what it has demonstrated about the operation of the Act in practice raises serious ethical questions about what constitutes the best course of action in such situations.

The case also raises the question of the mother's welfare in such situations. Ms Y was raped, yet this is not a ground for termination under the Irish law. Women like her who cannot travel continue to be left to deal as best they can with the potentially life-long result of such assaults. Because that assault left her suicidal, the law should have afforded her the abortion she desired, yet it did not. In her words: 'When I came to this country

---

[127] ibid.
[128] Southampton University Hospital NHS Trust, 'Having an Extremely Premature Baby (Patient Information Factsheet)': www.uhs.nhs.uk/Media/Controlleddocuments/Patientinformation/Pregnancyandbirth/Havinganextremelyprematurebaby-patientinformation.pdf (accessed 1 September 2014).

I thought I could forget suffering ... The scar [from the C-section] will never go away. It will always be a reminder. I still suffer'.[129]

Her baby has been taken into care. Her mental state appears fragile. This was a woman who had been so traumatised that she attempted to end her own life. Yet the best outcome was considered to be pressuring her into a Caesarean that would lead to the birth of an extremely premature baby, and which merely traumatised an already damaged woman further. We should question whether the best way to treat a woman who had been violated once was to violate her all over again. Concern for her welfare was seemingly absent in the decisions taken in this case, as in many ways was concern for the long-term outcome for the baby involved. Interpreted as it was in this case, the new legislation might potentially have created more problems than it solved.

[129] K Holland and R Mac Cormaic, 'Woman in Abortion Case Tells of Suicide Attempt', *Irish Times*, 19 August 2014: www.irishtimes.com/news/health/woman-in-abortion-case-tells-of-suicide-attempt-1.1901256 (accessed 1 September 2014).

# Index

Lightning Source UK Ltd.
Milton Keynes UK
UKHW020213250621
386127UK00003B/32